In Good Company

In Good Company

An Anatomy of Corporate Social Responsibility

Dinah Rajak

Stanford University Press
Stanford, California

Stanford University Press
Stanford, California

Printed in the United States of America on acid-free, archival-quality paper

Library of Congress Cataloging-in-Publication Data
Rajak, Dinah, author.
   In good company : an anatomy of corporate social responsibility / Dinah Rajak.
      pages cm
   Includes bibliographical references and index.
   ISBN 978-0-8047-7609-7 (cloth : alk. paper)—ISBN 978-0-8047-7610-3 (pbk. : alk. paper)
      1. Social responsibility of business—South Africa—Case studies. 2. Mining corporations—South Africa—Case studies. 3. International business enterprises—South Africa—Case studies. 4. Anglo American (Firm) I. Title.
   HD60.5.S7R35 2011
   658.4'080968—dc22
                                                                    2011004849

Typeset by Thompson Type in 10/14 Minion

For Harry, Tessa and Sam

Contents

List of Figures

List of Abbreviations

AGM   Annual General Meeting

ANC   African National Congress

ARV   Anti-Retroviral

ART   Anti-Retroviral Therapy

BEE   Black Economic Empowerment

BITC   Business in the Community

BPD(M)   Bojanala Platinum District (Municipality)

CBOs   Community-Based Organisations

CEO   Chief Executive Officer

COSATU   Congress of South African Trade Unions

CPPP   Community-Public-Private Partnership

CRC   Conflict Resolution Consortium

CSI   Corporate Social Investment

CSR   Corporate Social Responsibility

DANIDA   Danish International Development Agency

DFID   Department for International Development, UK

DME   Department of Minerals and Energy, South Africa

EIR   Extractive Industries Review

EITI   Extractive Industries Transparency Initiative

FDI	Foreign Direct Investment
FTSE	Financial Times Stock Exchange
GBC	Global Business Coalition on HIV/AIDS Tuberculosis & Malaria
GDP	Gross Domestic Product
GEAR	Growth, Employment and Redistribution
GMI	Global Mining Initiative
GRI	Global Reporting Initiative
GTZ	Gesellschaft für Technische Zusammenarbeit (Germany)
HDSA	Historically Disadvantaged South Africans
HR	Human Resources
IBLF	International Business Leaders Forum
ICMM	International Council for Mining and Metals
IDP	Integrated Development Plan
IFC	International Finance Corporation
ILO	International Labour Organisation
ISO	International Standardisation Organisation
JCI	Johannesburg Consolidated Investments
JSE	Johannesburg Stock Exchange
LSE	London Stock Exchange
MDPs	Monthly- and Daily-Paid workers
MMSD	Mining, Minerals and Sustainable Development
MNC	Multinational Corporation
MOU	Memorandum of Understanding
MPRDA	Minerals and Petroleum Resources Development Act
NGO	Non-Governmental Organisation
NUM	National Union of Mineworkers
OECD	Organisation for Economic Co-operation and Development
PPP	Public-Private Partnership
RBA	Royal Bafokeng Administration

RBN	Royal Bafokeng Nation
RDP	Reconstruction and Development Programme
RLM	Rustenburg Local Municipality
SABC	South African Broadcasting Corporation
SEAT	Socio-Economic Assessment Toolbox
SED	Socio-Economic Development
SHEC-List	Safety, Health, Environment and Community List
SME	Small and Medium-Sized Enterprise
STD	Sexually-Transmitted Disease
STI	Sexually-Transmitted Infection
TNC	Transnational Corporation
TRC	Truth and Reconciliation Commission
UCT	University of Cape Town
UMOs	Union Men Officials
UNDP	United Nations Development Programme
USAID	United States Agency for International Development
VCT	Voluntary Counselling and Testing
WBCSD	World Business Council for Sustainable Development
WWF	World Wide Fund for Nature
WSSD	World Summit on Sustainable Development

Preface and Acknowledgements

THE PHENOMENAL GROWTH of the corporate social responsibility movement over the past decade has made it both ubiquitous and curiously hard to pin down. This raises various questions in attempting to capture the practice of corporate responsibility (and approach the multi-layered, multi-limbed 'corporate citizen') ethnographically. In turning the anthropological lens towards transnational processes of corporate capitalism, we are faced with new challenges of conducting ethnography on such a scale; and new problems in attempting to explore the corridors of corporate power–diffuse, embedded and pervasive as they are. At the same time, the scope of anthropology cannot be confined to only those arenas in which traditional anthropological methods of localised participant observation are possible. The multi-sited approach that underpinned my research aimed to connect the seemingly disparate geographies, both inside and outside the company, in which corporate social responsibility (CSR) is performed, enacted and dispensed: an international CSR convention in a London hotel, a corporate head office in Johannesburg or a mineworkers' hostel on South Africa's platinum belt.

The research on which this book is based was conducted primarily over a fourteen month period in London, Johannesburg and Rustenburg between October 2004 and December 2005, after which time I continued to engage with CSR industry events, never really leaving 'the field'. I began and ended the research in London (October to December 2004; September to November 2005). Here, I worked as a part-time volunteer at Business in the Community (BITC), a leading UK-based NGO in the field of CSR which counts Anglo

American among its many corporate partners/members. Throughout this period I participated in CSR conventions, conferences, master classes, award ceremonies, policy discussion forums and other similar events, in many cases offering my services as a volunteer due to the prohibitively high entrance fees (see Chapter 1). During this time I interviewed senior personnel at Anglo American's London offices (particularly those responsible for CSR, external affairs, health, safety and environmental issues), along with their counterparts at other major extractive companies that occupy a prominent position in the CSR arena (including BP, Shell and Rio Tinto). I also conducted numerous interviews with informants at the company's partner non-governmental organisations (NGOs), with CSR consultants and other industry insiders.

From January to August 2005, I lived in Rustenburg, unofficial 'capital' of the platinum mining belt in South Africa's North West Province. Rustenburg's proximity to Johannesburg (approximately 112km North West) allowed me to move easily between the mining operations and the head offices of Anglo American, its subsidiaries and various partners. I travelled to Johannesburg (and less frequently to Pretoria) every couple of weeks to conduct interviews with corporate personnel, national NGO partners, CSR consultants, and government officials, and to attend industry events such as the *Mail and Guardian's* 'Greening the Future Awards' and the Bi-Annual Convention on Corporate Citizenship.

In Rustenburg, where the physical, economic and social landscape is overshadowed by the mines, and most inhabitants are directly or indirectly connected to them, the fieldwork experience was quite different. Even for those who do not work in, on or next to the mines, this is very much a mining town. Conversations in bars or hair salons often turned to matters relating to the mine: the booming profits of one company or another, rumours of layoffs or expansion, the problems of the informal settlements, the appointment of a new mine manager, a platinum jewelry exhibition or charity marathon held by one of the mining houses, and so on. This contrasted with the experience of conducting fieldwork in London, and to a slightly lesser extent Johannesburg, where the daily lives of most company executives and the offices in which they worked were distanced from the practical realities of the mining process and its social world. In many ways the different ethnographic methods that I adopted in Rustenburg reflected the dual reality of the mining business: an operations-corporate, or boot-wearing-suit-wearing, polarity which figured strongly in the narratives of company personnel at both the head office and the 'coalface'.

This multi-sited ethnographic journey is reflected in the structure of the book as it moves across multiple sites and scales[1], from the global in Chapter 1, to the national in Chapters 2–4, to the local in Chapters 5–7. This shift in scales also comes through in the different kinds of materials that provide the substance of chapters. The ethnographic material in Chapter 1 for instance, comes primarily from participant observation in global CSR conferences, policy workshops, annual general shareholder meetings and other similar occasions. Chapters 2, 3 and 4 are more interview-based ('ethnography by appointment'[2] so to speak), and focus more on the accounts of corporate executives and public discourse communicated in official texts such as corporate reports, policy documents, media articles and so on. The later chapters are based on more classic ethnographic fieldwork, rooted in the town of Rustenburg, the mines, mineworker hostels, community projects and everyday social spaces that make up the civic life of the town. Broadly speaking, the first half of the book focuses on public corporate discourse analysed through elite actor narratives; while the second half explores how these discourses are materialised in practice.

I use pseudonyms throughout the book for all those I interviewed and spoke to during the course of my research. Wherever possible the names of the organisations, programmes and projects with which they were associated have also been changed. The exceptions are Anglo American and its subsidiaries, along with other well-known corporations and NGOs (such as Business in the Community and The World Wide Fund for Nature) which would have been impossible to anonymise.

Many debts have been incurred during this project. The research on which this book is based was funded by a grant from the Economics and Social Research Council, UK. I am grateful for their support throughout the project, along with that of the University of Sussex, and in particular the Department of Anthropology for hosting the research. In London and South Africa, I am indebted to all my interviewees and informants who generously shared their knowledge and experiences during my fieldwork, and whose company made it a privilege. I am particularly grateful to the many people at Anglo American and its subsidiaries who gave up their time to talk to me and share their experience and expertise in corporate social responsibility; their openness and insight has been invaluable. I am extremely grateful to Business in the Community for the opportunity to engage firsthand with their activities, providing me with an ideal starting point for my research.

In Rustenburg, I would like to thank Rebecca, Ellen, Evelyn, Xola, Ruth, Brenda and many others I cannot mention here by name. I am grateful also to Mac Kabene at the National Union of Mineworkers; Dan Sonnenburg and Markus Reichardt at SR&I; Michelle Boehme at the University of Potchefstroom; and Sue Cook at Pretoria University, all of whom were generous not only with their time but with their advice. I wish to thank the African Institute of Corporate Citizenship. Ralph Hamann, Paul Kapelus and Nkosi Ndlovu generously offered both practical support and professional expertise on CSR. To Chris, Lore and John Watterson, Tessa Rayner, Bakang Enele, Christine and Karlien Delport, and Guy Havercroft, I am grateful for their hospitality and friendship during my fieldwork in Johannesburg and Rustenburg. The many hours I spent with Ike and Fay Rosmarin, listening to them talk about their life in Rustenburg and much more beyond, are some of my warmest memories of fieldwork. I thank them both for sharing with me their stories and for giving me a view onto Rustenburg that I could never have understood without them. I hope Ike would have enjoyed this book and seen his influence on it, if I had finished it in time.

I owe much to my colleagues and friends at the University of Sussex. In particular, I wish to thank Elizabeth Harrison, James Fairhead, Geert De Neve, Rebecca Prentice, and Catherine Dolan at Oxford University, whose advice and support have been invaluable through various stages of this project. They have been an on-going source of intellectual inspiration and critical engagement. I have been fortunate to benefit from discussions with a number of other colleagues, to whom I am very grateful: Jock Stirrat, Filippo Osella, Jon Mitchell, Deborah James, Pauline von Hellermann and Simon Coleman. I would like to thank Merle Lipton, Saul Dubow, Martin Chanock and Adam Kuper who read earlier versions of work that went into this book and generously shared their insight into South Africa in general, and Anglo American in particular.

At Stanford University Press (SUP), I wish to thank Joa Suorez for her enthusiastic support and expert guidance in the development of this manuscript. I am also most grateful to the anonymous reviewers for SUP for their comments on the manuscript which were particularly insightful. My thanks go to Margaret Pinette and Adam Fishwick for their help in preparing the manuscript.

Chapters 4 and 5 are an expanded and revised version of an article written for the *Journal of the Royal Anthropological Institute* (Rajak 2010). I thank the journal for permission to use this material. I am grateful to *Re-*

search in Economic Anthropology for permission to use selective material from an article (Rajak 2008) in part of Chapters 6 and 7, and to Berghahn Publishers for permission to use material from an article in *Focaal* in Chapter 1 (Rajak 2011). Other parts of Chapter 6 appeared in different forms in chapters written for *Corporate Citizenship in Africa: Lessons from the Past; Paths to the Future* (Rajak 2006) and *Economics and Morality: Anthropological Approaches* (Rajak 2009). I thank Greenleaf Publishing and AltaMira Press for permission to use them. I am also grateful to Zaprock Productions and Jonathan Shapiro for permission to reprint the cartoon 'A Gift from the Corporate World!' by Zapiro in the Introduction to this book.

Finally, I thank my friends and family who have been a source of support during the writing of this book, and whenever necessary, given me an escape from it. Saul, Juliette, Eve and Florence have been a constant presence (even when far away) throughout this project and long before. This book is dedicated to my parents Harry and Tessa Rajak, and to my partner Samuel Knafo. Without them, it could never have been written.

In Good Company

Introduction
Towards an Ethnography of Corporate Social Responsibility

The duties of a manufacturer are far larger and wider that those merely of an employer of labour; we have a wide commercial character to maintain, which makes us into the great pioneers of civilisation

(Mr Thornton in *North and South*,
Elizabeth Gaskell 1854–1855).

IN AUGUST 2002, when Johannesburg was playing host to the World Summit on Sustainable Development, a cartoon by the renowned South African satirist, Zapiro, appeared in the *Mail and Guardian*. The cartoon, entitled 'A Gift from the Corporate World!', shows the doors of the summit opened wide to embrace a Trojan Horse. On the outside of the horse the inscription, 'sustainable development' is written. On the inside, Zapiro shows us cigar-smoking corporate fat cats holding a banner of 'profit, self-regulation and unfair trade' (Zapiro 2002, see Figure 1.4). Zapiro warns us that, like the Trojans[1], in receiving gifts we can unwittingly be embracing our own enslavement. The veiled power of the gift to empower the donor while oppressing the recipient was summed up most poignantly in the words spoken to me by a community worker from South Africa's platinum mines: 'As long as we're dependant on handouts from the mining companies, we'll be their slaves'.

In the past decade transnational corporations (TNCs) have become increasingly important players on the landscape of international development, under the banner of corporate social responsibility (CSR)—a movement promising to harness the *global* reach and resources of transnational corporations in the service of *local* development and social improvement. As big business is brought more closely into the development process—not only as agent of empowerment, but as its architect—novel regimes of local, national and global responsibility are emerging in which corporations are elevated as guardians of the social order and purveyors of a new global moral authority. TNCs have 'cleaned up their act', it seems; they have become responsible, even caring,

1

their power valorised by their status as champions of sustainable development. Disenchantment with the rampant free market fetishism and hard-line neoliberalism of the 1980s has given way to the (re)birth of an era of compassionate capitalism with corporate citizens as its midwives, offering, it appears, moral, and perhaps even spiritual, revitalisation of the 'Market'. It has become commonplace to hear the language of commerce and that of community, of enterprise and 'the social' coupled together where once they were seen as antithetical; as instruments of capital become agents of social improvement, merging bottom line economics with a new register of corporate responsibility. The CSR movement thus claims the happy confluence of economic value and ethical values packaged together in the new human (or humane) face of capitalism. Yet nothing is straight forward about this apparently win-win formula.

As the phenomenon of CSR asserts a symbiosis of 'enlightened self-interest' and social improvement, this book sets out to explore what lies behind this marriage of moral imperative and market discipline. In bringing anthropological approaches to bear on corporate capitalism, my aim is to reveal *how* power is accumulated and exercised through the practice of CSR; to shed light on the new regimes of authority enacted through the (re)emergence of a moral economy of responsibility at the heart of the market economy.

Conventional models of modern capitalist economics claim the independence of 'the market' from the realms of political and social life[2] and from the concerns of morality. Yet even *The Economist* tells us, 'Greed is out. Corporate virtue . . . is in' (The Economist 2004). The image of 'corporate virtue'—which conjures visions of Victorian industrial philanthropists, of Cadbury, Carnegie and Rockefeller—is juxtaposed with that of 'corporate greed', recalling the unbridled corporate greed embodied in Wall Street's Gordon Gekko (Stone 1987) or Tom Wolfe's *Bonfire of the Vanities* (Wolfe 1990). CSR is widely held up as the triumph of corporate good over the selfish pursuit of profit. And the widely used phrase 'compassionate capitalism'[3] even seems suggestive of a merciful and beneficent ruler. How do we make sense of this reconnection of morality to, as Marcel Mauss put it, the 'cold reasoning of businessman, banker and capitalist' (1967: 73)? And, more importantly, what are its effects?

This book then, is about the performance of corporate virtue—at times ritualised and theatrical, at others routine and quotidian—and its place within late capitalism. It is about a new global orthodoxy which claims to unite the exigencies of social well-being with the dictates of profit maximisation in the emancipatory promise of the market. And it is about how CSR

becomes a crucial mechanism by which corporate structures reinvent, reproduce and extend their authority, not only over the economic order, but over
the social (and indeed moral) order, both in the international sphere of global
governance and within the national and local context of post-apartheid South
Africa. Claims to moral purpose, after all, have an enormous power to naturalise economic and political authority.

Through a multi-sited ethnography, I track the trans-local dimensions of
a transnational mining corporation in pursuit of the slippery notion of CSR.
This pursuit took me from the corporate boardrooms of a company's global
headquarters in London and Johannesburg to its mineshafts on South Africa's platinum belt. The company provides a lens through which to reflect on
the wider global CSR movement. As the largest private sector employer, not
only in South Africa but on the whole continent, the company has emerged
as a champion of CSR and leader of the business for sustainable development
agenda, projecting itself as a 'global corporate citizen of tomorrow', and, at the
same time, as deeply rooted in its legacy, as *Proudly South African.*

Not until you are inside 20 Carlton House Terrace, London, will you see
a small sign letting you know that you are inside the London headquarters of
the third largest mining company in the world: Anglo American. The impec-
cably designed lobby is a multi-storey glass atrium decorated with a fountain,
pieces of mineral ores in glass cases, a plaque to Sir Ernest Oppenheimer who
founded the company in 1917, and beaded decorations, sourced and imported
from Kwazulu-Natal. Books of African art sit on the coffee table alongside
copies of the *Financial Times*, and on the reception desk there is a framed
photograph of two small children outside a rural village school in South Africa. Scrawled in children's handwriting at the bottom of the picture, are the
words, 'Thank you Anglo'.

In Johannesburg the Anglo American complex is well known. With its
huge stain-glassed windows and sandstone eagles guarding the front façade,
44 Main Street was built by Ernest Oppenheimer himself. It is said that he
told his architect that he wanted something between a cathedral and a bank
(Johannesburg City Council 1986: 130). A fitting command centre, it would
seem, for a company which the London *Financial Times* described as 'virtually an alternative government . . . until little more than a decade ago, to be
chief executive of Anglo American conferred, at least in South Africa, the status of cabinet minister or top official at the Reserve Bank' (Bream and Russell

Figure I.1. Anglo American headquarters, Johannesburg. Author's photograph.

2007: 9). Around the corner, Anglo American's subsidiary, Anglo Platinum Ltd (the world's biggest platinum producer), is housed in a fifteen storey, 1980's glass office-block—another globalised hi-tech corporate temple.

It is hard not to feel the visceral contrast of moving from these sites to the barren landscape of the Platinum Belt in South Africa's North West Province.

The single lane highway from Pretoria to Rustenburg—"The Bakwena Platinum Highway'—takes you past the Magaliesburg mountains. The clouds of smoke on the horizon and the huge slow trucks signal the platinum mines and refineries which encircle the town of Rustenburg, the urban hub of the Platinum Belt's Western limb. In 2005 the South African Broadcasting Corporation

Figure I.2. Anglo Platinum headquarters, Johannesburg. Author's photograph.

(SABC) news declared Rustenburg the fastest growing city in Africa second only to Cairo[4]. On first entering, the groundswell below the quietened surface becomes evident. Almost as if the mines are physically pushing up through the ground, the pressure from their expansion and the resultant commercial boom is stretching Rustenburg at its seams. In certain places at 5pm every day the ground shakes, accompanied by loud though distant bangs, much like the sound of fireworks far away—the sound of blasting somewhere in the miles of mines underground. Surrounding the mining areas on the outskirts of the city, informal settlements bearing names suggestive of a very different reality— Edenvale, Park Heights and Mayfair[5]—house somewhere between 50,000 and 150,000 people in densely packed rows of semi-permanent homes.

This is a landscape scarred by imposing mine shafts and smoke stacks, smelters, refineries, crushers, barracks style hostels and mountainous slag heaps. It is here that over 40 percent of the world's platinum is produced: blasted from the rock, transported to the surface, crushed, smelted and re-fined by Anglo Platinum's 25,000 employees until it is ready to be flown to the coast. From there it makes its way across the globe to be moulded into auto-catalysts for cars or jewellery for those who can afford it. Rustenburg is the global centre of platinum production, where Anglo Platinum is the dominant player among five multinational mining houses. It is here that I went looking for the tangible products of the phenomenon known as CSR.

Figure I.3. Processing plant, Rustenburg. Author's photograph.

The Rise of CSR

At the World Summit in Johannesburg corporations became firmly established at the vanguard of the global development agenda in an atmosphere of enthusiasm and ebullience (rarely unsettled by warnings such as that of Zapiro's cartoon), heralding a new era of public-private partnership in pursuit of universal goals[6]. Indeed, at the start of the 21st century, few goals have appeared so persuasive in their capacity to recruit support from diverse corners as that of sustainable development. An article covering the event for the *Guardian* newspaper noted that seated next to Tony Blair on his flight to the summit was Sir Robert Wilson, then the Chief Executive Officer (CEO) of the world's largest mining company, Rio Tinto (Vidal and White 2002). Surely this, the article went on, symbolised the extent to which big business has been embraced as both a partner and advisor in international development planning.

In less than a decade since the summit, CSR has been enshrined in a proliferating maze of international codes of conduct, standards, ethical principles and guidelines, management systems, toolkits and toolboxes; all of which serve to delimit an accepted register of values, norms and practices that constitute this new orthodoxy and establish its status as a global regime. The emphasis on the global dimension of corporate citizenship, not only reflects the vast reach of companies and the transnational flow of capital they generate, but claims a capacity for de-contextualisation, abstraction and re-contextualisation in diverse local contexts, enabling TNCs to claim 'the art of being local worldwide' (Nelson 1998: 11). Global values articulated and established in the cosmopolitan realms of CSR in London, New York, Geneva or Beijing and established in international codes and compacts, are seen to give rise to a corresponding set of local practices as they elevate corporations as vehicles of social improvement in localities across the world. Taking on the mantle of global corporate citizenship, TNCs supposedly transcend the parochial politics of national government or the failure of state-led development, promising instead the universal rationality and efficiency of business. It is this marriage of global values and local practice that is held up as the essence of corporate citizenship, promising to incorporate the excluded margins and impoverished people into the webs of social responsibility of TNCs, and the empowering opportunities of the global market.

CSR thus appears as a collaborative venture that subsumes diverse projects and potentially divergent interests (and values)—communal and commercial, ecological and social—within a collective project (Tsing 2000). As it confronts new social and environmental challenges, the CSR movement has demonstrated a powerful capacity to adapt, incorporate and offer itself up as the answer to an apparently limitless range of global concerns within the all-encompassing commitment to sustainable development: from good governance, anti-corruption and responsible payment of revenues to governments, to environmental stewardship, biodiversity and climate change; and from human rights, labour rights and indigenous land claims, to HIV/AIDS, socio-economic development and empowerment. It is the last three on the list which provide the main, though not exclusive focus of this book.

As CSR has gathered momentum over the past decade, and as it recruits support from an extensive and diverse constellation of actors, it has become a platform from which corporations can take an increasingly active role in setting, as well as implementing, the development agenda at a global level. The rise of CSR has established TNCs as more the solution to the challenges of global poverty and under-development, than the cause. Companies themselves have become purveyors of best practice and ethical standard-bearers. The moral high-ground once occupied by NGOs has been usurped, so to speak, by the former targets of their campaigns.

This reminds us that CSR has evolved from a movement amongst campaigners to compel TNCs to 'clean up their act', to a discourse of unity and partnership led by corporations themselves[7]. From behind the barricades at Seattle, Gothenburg and Prague, and in response to consumer vigilantism and non-governmental organisation (NGO) 'brand-jacking', corporations re-emerged extending the hand of CSR to their former combatants; or as one senior executive at Anglo American put it (rather less dramatically), 'we were sick of getting rotten fruit thrown at us on our way in to work, so we decided to engage rather than hide'.

In the vanguard of this movement are those companies which had previously been seen as the very epitome of irresponsible capitalist exploitation—the extractive industries. Once the pariahs of capitalism, those very same companies have emerged today as leaders of the CSR cause. They have done so in the wake of a catalogue of scandals surrounding allegations of the irresponsible exploitation of people and resources through the past century: illegal uranium mining in Namibia (Rio Tinto); exploitation of the black workforce in apartheid South Africa (Anglo American); involvement with paramilitary outfits in Columbia (BP); complicity in the oppression of the Ogoni in Nigeria (Shell); environmental disaster in the Gulf of Mexico (BP again); armed conflict surrounding the Panguna Mine on Bougainville, Papua New Guinea (Rio Tinto again); asbestos poisoning in the Cape (Cape Industries); ChevronTexaco in Angola; Talisman in Sudan; the list goes on. Yet this portfolio of environmental and social irresponsibility has given way to a decade of initiatives[8] aimed at making the mining business, not only socially responsible, but 'sustainable' (perhaps an oxymoronic promise considering the inherently unsustainable nature of extraction[9]). Meanwhile, in the broader arena of CSR, captains of the mining industry have taken up leading or prominent positions on almost all of the central compacts, frameworks or coalitions that have evolved to constitute a 'global' architecture of CSR, such as the UN Global Compact, Business Action for Africa, the Global Business Coalition on HIV/AIDS and the World Business Council for Sustainable Development (WBCSD) (see Chapter 1)[10].

CSR is thus widely seen to be rooted in the age of neoliberalism, arising from increasingly vocal concerns about the overweening power of corporations extending daily into greenfield territories and new areas of economic and social life. Such fears are underpinned by broader discontent about the ravages of the neoliberal economic reforms of the 1980s and structural adjustment imposed as purely technical market mechanisms, without regard for how they might work (or not work) in social terms. CSR is, therefore, emblematic of a post-Washington Consensus era of development which promises to combine a humanised approach to development, with the compassionate face of capitalism, in place of a hard-line devotion to the rigours of free-market liberalisation and a long-awaited trickle down from capitalist growth. But of course CSR has a much longer history, rooted in the twinned legacies of corporate colonialism and industrial philanthropy; a history that has all too often been overlooked in the preoccupation with the apparent novelty of this age of responsible capitalism.

The conventional history of CSR narrated in official reports, the accounts of industry insiders and much of the literature[11], begins, not as one might expect with the renowned philanthropic (and often Quaker) industrialists of Victorian Britain such as Rowntree, Cadbury or Lever, and their self-proclaimed commitment to social improvement (Satre 2005); nor with the philanthropic foundations of their US counterparts, Rockefeller or Carnegie[12]. Nor does it start with the subjugation of large areas of the colonised world by imperialist enterprises such as the British South Africa Company in Rhodesia, or Hudson Bay in Western Canada. Rather, CSR is all too often presented as a distinctly modern phenomenon, the product of millennial concerns about social and ecological sustainability in an era of neoliberal globalisation. Yet, while lauded as a radical re-orientation of business for the 21st century within a new era of responsible capitalism, when we look closer, we find striking continuities with much older forms of corporate philanthropy and the 'empires of profit' (Litvin 2003) it sustained. By re-contextualising the contemporary phenomenon of CSR within these interwoven genealogies of benevolence, power and profit, I hope to draw out the patterns of continuity and change, and in particular, how old regimes of corporate paternalism are reinvented within a modern morality of social responsibility.

By contrast, policy-makers (from governments, multilateral and bilateral development agencies and civil society), corporate leaders and analysts have heralded this movement, as nothing less than the dawn of a *new* era in which CSR, and 'Private Sector Development' (Department for International Development [DFID] 2009) more broadly, aim to bring the great financial resources of corporations and the creative spirit of competition to bear on issues of social development[13]. This notion of 'responsible competitiveness' claims then, that while the laws of the market are irrefutable, our conception of 'value' can be broadened to include sustainability and social welfare, so making social responsibility itself subject to the competitive rigours of the market: 'the challenge is to evolve a responsible basis on which competitiveness is achieved . . . the market will pay a premium for something that meets people's values' (Zadek et al 2005: 4). The result, according to Zadek et al, will be to invert the race to the bottom, and make it a race to the top. Proponents of this vision thus highlight the capacity of CSR to incorporate social goods and attendant values such as community and solidarity (conventionally seen as *opposed* to the cold-blooded rationalism of the market). The assertion is that by providing a template for governance and social responsibility within capitalism itself, produced by the powerful interests which drive it, 'the global market' (if mobilised according to the doctrine of CSR) will incorporate and empower the marginalised and disempowered. This is encapsulated in another of the mantras of the CSR industry—'the triple bottom line'—which urges a new conception of profit that includes, 'sustainable development' and 'environmental quality' alongside 'economic prosperity', claiming an implicit symbiosis of social goods, ethical imperatives and market rationalities, rather than an inherent conflict between them (Elkington 1998: 32). But the notion of responsible competitiveness implies the reverse: social responsibility reshaped by market principles.

CSR thus appears to fill a veritable 'gap in the Market', endowing it with much-needed ethical values and virtues, enabling corporations themselves to address the social and environmental consequences of capitalist development. This view is exemplified by Hopkins who writes, 'it is relatively easy to argue . . . that corporations should stick to making profits and leave development for governments. This, though, is a dance to the death, since the market left purely to profit maximization will not, as things are, fulfil major social roles' (Hopkins 2007: xi). Thus the powerful populism of the 'Make Poverty History' campaign, which captured the imagination of celebrities and school children across the United Kingdom (UK), has been spun to reflect the prominence of business in this mission with the catchy, yet unintentionally ambivalent message: 'Make Poverty Business'[14]. And, according to CK Prahalad's now ubiquitous model (Prahalad 2006), in order to achieve this synergy of corporate profit and poverty alleviation, a company must simply chase the 'fortune at the bottom of the pyramid', incorporating the world's poor as a mass of untapped consumers and grass-roots entrepreneurs waiting to seize the empowering promise of the market.

At the base of this 'business case' for corporate responsibility, we find therefore, a proselytising project that claims to spread market discipline as the source of social mobility. It is here that we hear the battle-cry of a capitalism that presents itself as liberator of the economically disenfranchised; a capitalism which, as Comaroff and Comaroff put it, offers itself up as a 'gospel of salvation' (2000: 292). This celebration of grass-roots capitalism is certainly not new. What is of particular interest and importance is that here it is the goliath of corporate capitalism that, we are told, will deliver on this promise to the Davids of petty enterprise.

For critics, however, CSR represents at best an empty promise or a case of emperor's new clothes; at worst a Trojan Horse cloaking the market in morality, all while companies pursue their own profit-hungry interests and avoid regulation under the guise of benefactors[15]. Thus critics work to expose the gap between the rhetoric of responsible capitalism and the truth about corporate irresponsibility[16]. For others, it is nothing more than a distortion of the pure market and the true purpose of business[17]. In contrast, advocates have elevated big business as the path to development where states, characterised (so we are told) by chronic incapacity or corrupt rapacity, have failed[18].

Figure I.4. 'A Gift from the Corporate World!' *Mail and Guardian* 15 August 2002. © 2010 Zapiro. Reprinted with permission from www.zapiro.com.

Is CSR then, as its champions tell us, the long-awaited magic bullet to poverty, companies stepping into the breach, where the state has failed to deliver social improvement? Or rather, as critics suggest, the usurpation of state authority by transnational corporations? Is CSR simply the smooth surface to corporate power, offering moral purification to the process of accumulation; the most recent, and sophisticated manifestation of a much older legacy of Oppenheimer and Rockefeller, old school philanthropy in new clothes re-branded to respond to the buzzwords and anxieties of the contemporary world, as global corporate responsibility for the 21st century?

The subject of panegyric or polemic but rarely critical analysis, this normative preoccupation with whether CSR is a force for good or a cynical corporate ploy entrenches the ideological faultlines along which the study of CSR has run. But, the danger in reducing CSR to a mere smokescreen that can be blown away to reveal an unchanging capitalist order (as critiques of CSR tend to do[19]) is that we miss the more profound discursive capacity of CSR to transform social relations and projects according to a particular set of corporate interests and values. While this account of the literature on CSR as polarised by the ideological positions of 'advocates' and 'critics' is somewhat crude, it serves to highlight the rather different reading of CSR that I put forward in this book. Neither an ethical counterweight to the pursuit of profit, nor a simple veil to the business of profit-making, CSR, I argue, plays a much more fundamental role in sustaining corporate capitalism. Not because it provides corporations with ethics, but because it provides them with a moral mechanism through which their authority is extended over the social order.

The anthropological approach demands then, that we go beyond the ideological debate, to ask *how* corporate power is exercised through CSR. And more specifically, what it is that CSR enables corporations to do. The ethnographic reading of CSR offered here allows us to trace the ways in which this moral movement creates fresh channels through which the company pursues specific political economic objectives in particular social contexts, at the global, national and local levels. Thus, we begin to see how CSR offers a novel field of corporate practice; crucially one which draws on social, and indeed moral, resources—such as community, mutuality, affection, generosity and care—in pursuit of corporate interests.

The dominant public discourse of CSR extols the corporate contribution of resources (financial, technical and entrepreneurial) to the cause of development. Yet, the ways in which corporations themselves are bolstered and empowered by the social and political resources to which they gain access through their involvement in social projects (healthcare, education, economic empowerment, ecological sustainability and so on) has been overlooked. Here I show how, through the ubiquitous paradigm of bi- and tri-sector partnership (from state-business alliance to NGO collaborations to corporate-community engagement), CSR enables corporations to tap into a wealth of social expertise, political agency and even financial resources, as multilateral development agencies and state governments look to corporations as conduits of development assistance[20]. Not least of these is expertise itself. As corporations enlist the energies of diverse actors with potentially divergent interests to those of business (NGO partners, community leaders, low-wage workers and even anthropological consultants), in the mission of CSR, social problems are re-framed in such a way as to align with the agendas of corporations and make them amenable to the interests of big business.

This is not to say that companies are always successful at achieving these objectives, nor that the agendas themselves go uncontested within and beyond their walls. The ethnography highlights the messiness and ambiguity that is generated through the practice of CSR, and the struggle between different actors, agendas and interests drawn into its intricate workings. Still, this incarnation of corporations as guardians of social responsibility is not simply self-created, the product of a sophisticated corporate public relations machine. It is supported by a coherent framework of practice and knowledge, which produces and sustains the truly discursive power of CSR, in the Foucauldian sense (Foucault 1972); that is, with the capacity to reshape social realities to a certain vision, and crucially, to set the parameters of practice within which these varied actors must operate. The vision championed by this discourse authenticates the role of corporations as architects of social improvement, establishing their influence on development not just as a good thing, but a necessary one.

The ethnography presented here is not an ethnography of the failure of CSR, neither a panacea to poverty nor a fig-leaf to the relentless rigours of neoliberal exploitation. In many cases CSR is effective at achieving particular goals, and it is often more efficient than state service—a comparison which is frequently used as the justification and motivation behind this model of private sector development. If corporate efforts at social improvement were not 'effective', if they had no impact, there would be little more to say other than to consign them to the list of failed development exploits. On the contrary, my interest is in the moral underpinning of CSR and the vision of social improvement it projects; and in the diverse coalition of actors, interests and agendas that are being transformed by the new orthodoxy of corporate-led development. I investigate how CSR creates particular kinds of moral relations within the supposedly amoral realm of corporate capitalism, both at the micro level between employee and company, or community beneficiary and corporate personnel, and at the macro level, between the corporation and the state.

But it would be wrong to say that this is a purely scholarly pursuit. In 2005 when the research for this book was conducted, mining companies were enjoying an unprecedented rise in global metals prices. As a result of this boon, Anglo's earnings rose by 43 percent (1.8 billion dollars) between 2004 and 2005[21]. An article in the *Financial Times* reported: 'Mining companies are generating so much cash at the moment due to high metals prices that it sometimes appears hard for them to know how to spend it' (Bream 2006). At the forefront of this surge was the platinum industry, benefiting from a growing global jewellery market and rapidly expanding chemical, car and electronic industries in China and India[22]. And at the centre of the platinum boom was Rustenburg, exploding on the back of record turnover, the 'second fastest growing city in Africa'. At the same time, the CSR movement was gaining ground daily, building momentum globally and finding particular currency in South Africa as it incorporated the language of Black Economic Empowerment (BEE) promising emancipation and social improvement through business, big and small. In South Africa, multinational corporations, with Anglo at their helm, were lining up (or competing) to commit their resources, their know-how and their creative energies to social goods, from empowerment through enterprise and education, to the provision of anti-retroviral (ARV) drugs free of charge to all HIV-positive employees.

In July 2009, Anglo American announced a 69 percent decline in profits to $1 billion (£608 million) for the first half of the year (Smith 2009). By the end of the year 11 percent of its global workforce would be retrenched in order to make up the $450 million in costs, which the company said must be cut (Sparshott 2009). A large proportion of the 19,000 laid off Anglo employees were at Anglo Platinum which, according to trade unions, was responsible for a fifth of all recession-linked formal sector job losses in South Africa (Smith 2009). This amounts to 10,000 or so former employees at the platinum mines, no longer eligible for company-sponsored anti-retroviral therapy (ART), or other benefits offered as part of the company's CSR to its workforce. The cycle of boom and bust is not new to Rustenburg. It is a cycle known in mining towns the world over[23]. As this book recounts, the dominance of mining companies and their CSR activities in the social life and political economy of Rustenburg, of South Africa and of its other operations across the world is such that the impact of this downturn will be dramatic. This stands as a stark reminder of the vagaries of the global market, and a warning against the exuberant promise of those who saw (and continue to extol the virtues of) the solution to social welfare and development in corporate social responsibility.

In recent months while writing this book, the repercussions of the financial crisis brought home to me more strongly than ever before how precarious are paradigms of development which invoke 'empowerment' in place of entitlement and eschew rights in favour of responsibility, resting on shifting corporate moralities, or as it is commonly called, the *enlightened self-interest* of big business.

Morality and the Market

Anthropologists have shown how grand narratives of market capitalism have relied upon the mystical power of the 'invisible hand' of self-interest, a supposedly natural and innate element of humanity, to provide ideological legitimation to the pursuit of profit (Carrier 1997; Gudeman 2001; Fischer

2009)[24]. Yet this book charts the rise of a new *visible* hand, which appears to conjure morality at the heart of corporate capitalism. Where previously we might have pointed to the great power of free-market ideology to establish self-interest as an infallible value, in order to explain the sustained power of corporations, this is no longer sufficient. Self-interest alone no longer has the currency it once had when free-market triumphalism reigned supreme. And in its place we find new meta-narratives of responsible capitalism and corporate citizenship; a re-moralising of the capitalist market economy, so to speak, which appeals to those very same ties of community, solidarity and even affection, which we were told, were subordinated to the ethic of self-interest and banished from the ideological realm of the 'free market'[25]. TNCs, the champions of 'scientific capitalism' (Ferguson 2006: 79), now display their claims to social responsibility, virtue and even compassion with equal vigour, not as a moral bolt-on, postscript or palliative to the fundamentals of capitalist accumulation, but as integral to the way they do business.

How then do we make sense of the presence of what appear to be distinctly non-market logics—the moral framework of social responsibility and the intricate social relations it generates—within the realm of corporate capitalism and hi-tech extraction? And, more importantly, to what extent does this moral economy of corporate responsibility sustain or transform the architecture of global capitalism?

Over the past couple of years, anthropologists have begun to explore novel forms of ethical economy emerging within the technocracy of contemporary market capitalism in various industries and diverse contexts around the world; from fair-trade flowers in a major supermarket chain (Dolan 2007) and ethical auditing in the garment industry (de Neve 2008), to drug donations in the pharmaceutical industry (Ecks 2008)[26]. They have done so primarily from the perspective of the intended targets, rather than the architects, of these ethical regimes. And in doing so, most have sought to show that, far from offering progressive alternatives to neoliberal capitalism, these new market moralities serve instead to facilitate its expansion (Carrier 2008). Thus, in the oil fields of Ecuador, Suzanna Sawyer suggests that CSR is little more than a series of 'slick corporate manoeuvres' (Sawyer 2004: 7) to better ease the incursion of capital and destroy any collective obstacles to the rapacious drive of neoliberalism. Meanwhile, the imagined intimacy between shoppers in UK supermarkets and coffee, flower or chocolate producers in Costa Rica, Kenya or Ghana work to reinforce rather than challenge neoliberal regimes of production (Berlan 2008; Luetchford 2008; Dolan 2009). For example the fair-trade flower in Dolan's study conveys with it the promise of 'redemption' and 'intimacy' between producer and consumer, but these consumer moralities become new vehicles of control for producers, disciplining workforces in the south (Dolan 2008: 274). In myriad ways then, it seems ethical capitalism has become instrumentalised in pursuit of profit, embedded within surveillance mechanisms and mainstreamed within the marketing schemes of multinationals such as Gap or Coca Cola, reaching out to customers as caring corporate citizens and friends[27]; the humanised antithesis to Joel Bakan's portrait of the psychopathic corporation (Bakan 2004).

For the most part these ethnographic critiques have focused on how such ethical regimes create particular kinds of neoliberal subjectivity. Thus they reveal the agency, or lack thereof, of those who become subject to, contest, resist or re-appropriate the practices of ethical capitalism. But, according to such accounts, the forces with which these actors contend appear simply as the hegemonic (and often monolithic) structures of corporate capitalism. The way in which agency is exercised by powerful groups who create, reshape and reconstitute those structures has thus been obscured.

This book is concerned with precisely this form of agency, that of powerful corporate actors (and their constellation of 'partners'), as it examines how CSR offers a novel framework through which the agency of the company is asserted, by imbuing relations of power with a moral purpose. The primary focus of this ethnography is, therefore, not the targets of the CSR agenda, but its purveyors, and the apparatus[28] through which it is deployed and dispensed in a variety of different, yet connected settings.

The capacity of corporations to colonise greenfield territory, discipline subjects and compel consent in virtually every corner of the world is so often assumed, by simply invoking the insatiable logic of capital to expand and reproduce. The failure to interrogate *how* corporations achieve and sustain their authority becomes, in itself, a tacit declaration of the immutable might of corporate capitalism, unwittingly reproducing the very power it attempts to critique. After all, these structures have not gone unchallenged. In particular, as we have seen, transnational corporations, the mainstays of neoliberal capitalism, have come under significant and sustained attack in the past decade on a number of fronts. In fact, TNCs require constant renewal, need constantly to be remade, seeking not just new sources of legitimacy but new sources of power, new avenues of practice in order to sustain and expand their operations.

Corporate social responsibility represents a new kind of agency for corporations. Not, as its advocates suggest, because it provides ethical norms for markets, nor because it offers 'business as usual, but with a friendlier face' (Maurer 2009: 258). As a fresh discursive innovation, CSR offers corporations a potentially much more powerful field of practice than the classic ideal of a 'free market' detached from the constraints of communal relations, in its capacity to incorporate and colonise, rather than expunge, social and moral life from its project. When it comes to CSR, corporate power works through a moral economy of care and coercion, benevolence and paternalism, rather than through the market discipline of autonomy that it propounds. The reciprocal relations of patronage and clientelism that are created through the corporate 'gift' unsettle the conventional duality of 'the gift' and 'the market' as two distinct spheres: on one side an ideal type of gift exchange which creates and maintains social relations; on the other, an amoral market based on the independence of transactors and the neutrality of financial commerce[29].

Indeed, the (re)emergence of the moral logic of the 'gift' within the context of corporate capitalism disrupts the widespread assumption that the market economy, 'disinfested of intrusive moral imperatives' works through the exclusion of what EP Thompson described as the 'delicate tissue of social norms and reciprocities' (Thompson 1993: 202, 187). Following Thompson, scholars such as James Scott (1985) revealed how the moral economy provides a central frame of resistance against the hegemonic powers of market forces. But, with the rise of CSR, a reversal has been achieved, whereby moral economies of responsibility, generosity and community—and the social bonds of affection and coercion that these create—have become not the weapons of the weak, but the weapons of the powerful. For the moral realm of CSR does not conflict with a bottom line of profit-seeking, two reified ideals—market behaviour and mutuality— locked in a dialectical struggle, according to the classic formulation[30]. On the contrary, I argue, market interests work *through* moral practice. Corporate social responsibility represents a powerful framework through which transnational corporations gain access to new kinds of social and moral resources in pursuit of their economic goals. How this is achieved is the subject of this book.

The Company: Parent and Subsidiary

A handful of multinational corporations continue to dominate the South African economy. They have done so since they emerged in the late 19th and early 20th centuries to provide for the capital requirements of mining the unparalleled mineral reserves on which the country was built (see Fine and Rustomjee 1996; Bell and Farrell 1997; Lester et al 2000: 96). As Greg Lanning wrote in 1979, 'From Cecil Rhodes to Harry Oppenheimer, the mining magnates and their companies have dominated the political economy of Africa' (Lanning and Mueller1979: 19). And, in South Africa, mining became virtually synonymous with one company in particular: the Anglo American Corporation. The company was founded on 25 September 1917, by Ernest Oppenheimer (who later passed on his chairmanship to his son, Harry), with the explicit purpose of tapping English and US, or Anglo-American, capital markets (from which the corporation took its name) for finance to develop the Rand gold mines (Innes 1984: 91)[31].

Here 'continuity and change' seems to be etched not only into the anthropologist's vocabulary but into the very landscape of mineral reefs and mining towns—a place for which the phrase was invented. In South Africa, where the minerals-energy complex provided the basis for the country's industrialisation and economic revolution, and where minerals policy has become an expression of the new authority of the post-apartheid state, Anglo American is territorially embedded in both the historical legacy and the developmental destiny of the nation. This has precluded the kind of supranational enclaving that is seen to characterise oil and mineral extraction in much of Africa today (Ferguson 2005). Anglo's broad social agenda and deep national footprint suggest a much greater continuity with the company towns and industrial complexes of miners, dockers and railway workers documented by ethnographers since the early days of the Rhodes Livingston Institute (see for example Wilson and Wilson 1945; Mitchell 1956; Grillo 1973; and Gordon 1977)[32].

The practice of mining is then, in many ways, deeply territorial, as is the kind of social authority which many mining companies continue to exert in the localities where they operate[33]. This inherent rootedness, combined with Anglo's particular influence in the economic and indeed political life of South Africa (where 35 percent of the company's earnings come from[34]) brings into focus how CSR operates in a complex dialectic between the 'global' and the 'national'. Indeed, as we shall see, the power of CSR lies, to a great extent, in its capacity to claim global applicability (under-written by supposedly universal market values) and at the same time to frame those values in line with particular paradigms of national development.

Since Anglo American moved its primary listing from the Johannesburg to the London Stock Exchange in 1998, and set up its new global headquarters in

London, the company has pursued a programme of global diversification, not only outside South Africa, but outside the continent. The Anglo Group now operates in sixty-five countries across all six continents, and employs 195,000 people worldwide (Anglo American 2006a: 3). Meanwhile, in South Africa, the mining industry has undergone significant diversification, giving rise to a number of smaller producers. This process has accelerated in the past five years as major mining houses such as Anglo have sold off some of their smaller assets to form 'Black Economic Empowerment' enterprises in response to the post-apartheid government's transformation and empowerment legislative agenda.

But, while mining in general, and Anglo American in particular, no longer dominates the South African economy to the great extent it once did, it still accounts for 34.3 percent of total export revenue in the country, and remains the largest private sector employer (Fearnley 2005: 148)[35]. In 2007, 2.7 percent (around half a million people) of the economically active population were directly employed in the mining industry on 691 active mines and quarries and roughly a third of those (175,806 people) worked in the platinum industry (Department of Minerals and Energy 2008: 12). Many times that number work in the vast secondary industrial sector which is dependent on mining. As a result, while gold remains the country's largest industry and employer despite steady decline[36], it has now been surpassed by platinum as South Africa's chief mineral export earner (Makgetla 2004: 272; Dansereau 2005: 54). At the same time, platinum has become, as one executive put it, 'the jewel in the company's crown', of gold, diamonds[37], coal, and base, ferrous and industrial metals; contributing 24 percent of the Anglo Group's total profit in 2006–2007 (Anglo American 2007: 8). As a result, the parent company has steadily increased its stake in its subsidiary Anglo Platinum to a controlling 79.6 percent share[38].

Thus, the platinum deposits of South Africa's Bushveld Igneous Complex have become one of the country's, and the company's, most important economic assets[39]. The Bushveld Complex—a huge single mass of rock which stretches for 66,000km across the North of the country from Limpopo to the North West Province—contains the world's greatest reserves of platinum group metals (Reader 1997: 13). It is a repository of unprecedented mineral and, due to platinum prices, financial wealth.

For seventy years after the first platinum mine opened on the Merensky Reef in 1928, the Rustenburg Platinum Mines, then under the control of Johannesburg Consolidated Investments (JCI), remained a small, and not particularly lucrative operation (Reichardt 2007). In 1994, when the massive

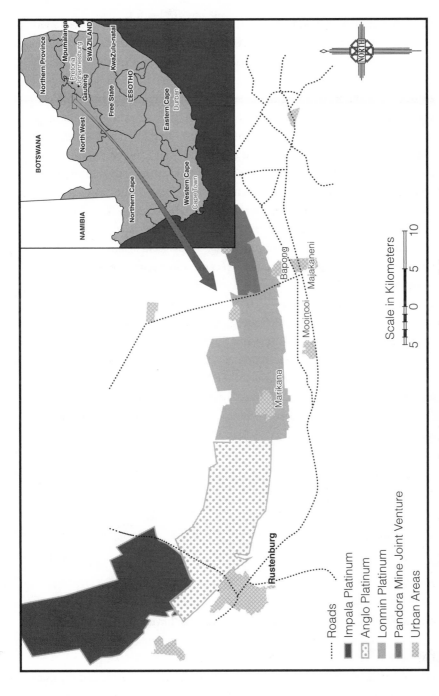

Figure I.5. The Bushveld Complex. Western limb showing approximate location of platinum operations.

conglomerate JCI un-bundled after the transition to democracy, these small platinum operations were sold to Anglo Platinum (known at the time as 'Amplats'). This gave rise to a dramatic programme of expansion in Anglo Platinum since 1999[40], with both the development of new projects and the expansion of the Rustenburg mines, the largest and oldest of the company's operations, and the most productive of all South Africa's platinum mines.

Just as the desolation of recession-hit or post-mining 'ghost towns' are deeply imprinted on South Africa's physical and social geography, so the flip side of this coin—the profits of mineral boom—have equally captivated the social imagination since the days of the great promise of Egoli[41], the city of gold. For platinum, the peaks and troughs have been equally extreme. The atmosphere of profit and prosperity from the platinum boom at the start of the new millennium was personified in the figure of the Amplats chairman himself, Barry Davidson, or 'Mr King Platinum' as he became known in some corners (Nose-week 2004: 9). Stories of Davidson's regime as chairman, when Amplats became a most prized asset of its parent company, were commonplace during my field-work in Rustenburg and Johannesburg. According to Howard Allen, a mine surveyor at the Rustenburg Mines since the 1990s, the terms were clear and the pay-off huge: 'as long as we kept producing, we were allowed to do whatever we liked'. Gary Smithe, manager at one of the Rustenburg processing plants, who had recently returned to the 'coal face' after a decade in 'corporate office', pre-sented a similarly vivid portrait, in which the vast profits of the platinum rush were symbolised by Davidson's own platinum-plated Harley Davidson:

> Anglo Platinum was a major jewel for Anglo American, the money spinner. We were literally printing money so we could do no wrong. Our CEO was driving around on a platinum-plated Harley Davidson. The personality drives the policy and with the last CEO it was, 'we will be the biggest platinum com-pany in the world; we will produce 3.5 million ounces by 2006, *whatever the cost*'. That's when the parent stepped in, bought up all the shares and said, 'we're in control now'.

As he came to the end of his account, Gary Smithe added, 'the cost, by the way, was huge, but living in Rustenburg you must have seen that'.

Platinum City

Over the past decade, the explosion of production on the platinum mines which overshadow Rustenburg has earned the town a new name: Platinum City. Here, the rich mineral deposits of the Bushveld Complex's Western limb are subject to the operations of five major mining corporations: Impala Platinum, Lonmin, Xstrata, Aquarius Platinum and Anglo Platinum, whose operations are the oldest and largest of the five[42]. The division of spoils beneath the ground has translated into an awkward urban geography and social landscape above ground, making the Rustenburg Local Municipality (RLM) a patchwork of industrial zones and urban sprawl which fall under the domain of one or other of the companies that mine the rich seams of the reef below. The visible mark of competing mining houses is not only seen in the towering mine shafts and refineries encircled by high fences and barbed wire. It is displayed on billboards, signposts and newspaper advertisements proclaiming a company's social investment in many of the town's clinics, community organizations and schools—testaments to corporate-community partnership.

Anglo Platinum's operations (known as 'Rustenburg Section') occupy the area to the East of Rustenburg (see Figure I.5), on the outskirts of the city. At the centre of these is the extensive Waterval mining 'village' which houses a vast industrial complex of ten mine shafts, processing plants and tailing dams, together with six single-sex mineworkers hostels housing around 6,000 workers, a small suburb for management level employees, a hospital, post office, convenience stores and two schools. A long central road leads through the complex. The suburban area of neat tree-lined streets and single or double storey houses inhabited by higher-ranking employees sits off the main road, opposite fields of sunflowers. Next to the suburb is the Anglo Platinum sports and recreation club surrounded by well-tended gardens and a bowling lawn. The hostel compounds are further from the central road, adjacent to the various mineshafts that they staff (see Chapter 5). Further along the road, the landscape becomes visibly more industrial, lined with high fences behind which sit the huge, industrial structures of various processing plants (the Precious Metals and Base Metals Refineries, the Waterval smelter and concentrators). Beyond these is the hospital (a second hospital in the town centre services those employees—mainly from the higher ranks—who have subscribed to the company's 'Platinum Health Insurance Scheme').

Further from the city of Rustenburg itself is the Bafokeng Rasimone Mine, a joint venture (50:50) between Anglo Platinum and Royal Bafokeng Holdings established in 1999, which is located to the North of the city within the territory of the Royal Bafokeng Administration (RBA). The current RLM was established in 1999, as part of the local government demarcation process initiated by the post-apartheid transition, which expanded the area of the old Rustenburg Municipality to include the 'tribal areas' of the Royal Bafokeng

Figure I.6. Platinum mine near Rustenburg. Author's photograph.

Nation (RBN)[43] and the Bakwena Tribe. These areas previously fell within Bophuthatswana, the 'tribal homeland' or 'bantustan' carved out by the apartheid government in line with its policy of 'separate development' (see Bozzoli 1991).

The extent to which the area is dependent on mining is clear. According to Rustenburg's Integrated Development Plan (IDP) for 2005–6, mining contributes around 77 percent of the gross geographic product of the RLM and accounts for 50 percent of those formally employed in the greater Rustenburg municipal area (Rustenburg Local Municipality 2005: 23)[44]. In 2005, planned expansions to the mining operations were expected to produce another 10,000 new jobs in the coming years (ibid). The city has grown 'unrecognisably' (according to most long-term inhabitants) as a result of the upsurge in platinum mining over the past three decades, growth that is evident in every dimension of urban life. During the five years of the most intense expansion, in the mid to late 1990s, the population of Rustenburg grew by 33 percent (Hamann 2004b: 208). The population recorded in the last census (2001) was 387,123 (Rustenburg Local Municipality 2005). Today it is estimated to be closer to half a million or more. And, according to the Mayor's 2005 'State of the City' address, 'all indications are that our city may double in size in the next 15 years' (Mabe 2005: 2).

The effects of the platinum boom on Rustenburg were equally manifest in the visible disparity of wealth which defines the city. The expansion of mining has generated a rapid growth in service and consumer industries in the town. The extensive Waterfall Shopping Mall doubled in size while I was living in Rustenburg, filled with shops bearing names such as 'Platinum Interiors', 'Platinum Security' and 'Platinum Reef Hunting'. The streets of Rustenburg city centre are lined with car show rooms selling top-end white BMWs and SUVs. The increasing population of senior and middle-managers employed at the mines, and the success of small enterprises prospering as a result of the rapid growth of Rustenburg's middleclass, has created a severe shortage of housing. Property prices have risen by a few hundred percent over the past five years (Joyce Bekker, Manager of Anglo Group Properties, Rustenburg) and property developers have moved into every available piece of land on which to build new suburbs.

Yet, as the mining boom drew increasing numbers of people to the mines in search of work in the expanding formal and informal economy, the rate of in-migration to the RLM has made it difficult for the local authorities to meet this growth with an adequate provision of housing, services and infrastructure development. According to the Mayor of Rustenburg, 'the infrastructure cannot relax because growth is faster than development'. As a result large areas of informal settlement—Edenvale, Mayfair and Park Heights—have developed on the outskirts of the city. In 2001 a report by a local planning consultancy estimated the rate of growth of informal settlements as 24.2 percent per annum (Plan Associates 2001: 1), and the census carried out in the same year recorded the number of households in the informal settlements as 48,212, out of a total 116,592 recorded in the whole of the Rustenburg Municipality (Rustenburg Local Municipality 2005: 21).

Today, estimates of the population of the settlements range from between 50,000 and 150,000, accounting for somewhere between 15 percent and 30 percent of the total population of the municipality. With the exception of a small corner of Edenvale, the informal settlements have no access to water, nor services for sewage removal or waste collection. There are no schools, few if any roads and only a few settlements are serviced by a single mobile clinic. Rows of semi-permanent homes built from any available material (mostly corrugated iron, cardboard and plastic) are crowded together almost one on top of the next, separated by narrow pathways. Most of the settlements sit directly adjacent to various mining operations. Edenvale, one of the largest of the informal settlements and home to an estimated 20,000–40,000 people, lies next to Anglo Platinum's Rustenburg operations, separated only by the high fence of the hostel compounds and the railroad track which runs through Rustenburg, carrying the products of mining away from the city.

In the context of the global economic downturn, and a drop in the price of platinum from a record US\$2,300 per ounce at the start of 2008 to US\$800 just six months later (Anglo Platinum 2008: 4), the Platinum City bursting at the seams just three years ago looks very different today. Boom-time has given way to recession, and with it, declining demand for metals, waning profits for mining companies and fears of mineshafts closing as operations contract. This time the town earned itself a brief reprieve from the full effects of this economic collapse, its economy buoyed up by World Cup 2010, during which Rustenburg was one of the central hubs. Here, England played the United States in their first match of the tournament, bringing a mass influx of tourists and providing employment for some of the thousands of mineworkers laid off from the platinum industry, for a while[45]. Anglo American backed the bid to host the World Cup in South Africa, and was, according to some, instrumental in its success (Mark 2003). But with the World Cup over, Rustenburg remains subject to the volatile platinum market and diminishing mineral reserves.

The ghost-towns left behind in the wake of industries in temporary or permanent retreat provide an enduring image of the post-closure effects of mining well-known worldwide, a counter-balance to the portrait of CSR in a company at the height of its influence in the febrile growth of a town, as was epitomised by Rustenburg in 2005. Yet even then, despite the seemingly unstoppable momentum of the platinum boom in Rustenburg, the mine closures of 1957 and 1971[46] when platinum prices plummeted and the town went into decline remained strong in the collective memory, warning of the threat to come when the mines eventually close for good.

Outline of the Book

In tracing the routes and routines of the moral movement of corporate responsibility as it connects the financial centres of London and Johannesburg with the everyday lives of mineworkers in Rustenburg, the book moves across multiple sites. The chapters are structured to reflect the construction and performance of CSR, shifting across these different terrains and scales, from the macro politics of negotiating the transition to democracy, to the micro practices of HIV management in a mineworkers hostel, from the global arenas in which corporate virtue is celebrated and valorised, to the routines of management and community outreach at the mines. The chapters correspond to the three primary sites of ethnographic practice: London (home of Anglo American's global headquarters, global financial centre and so-called CSR capital of the world); Johannesburg (the traditional centre of Anglo's power in South Africa); and the Rustenburg platinum mines.

My starting point, in Chapter 1, is London and the cosmopolitan realm of conventions, compacts and policy forums which constitute the 'social life' of CSR. It is here, through the ritualised performance of global corporate citizenship, that companies stake their claim to the moral capital that such a status affords them. And it is here, through the collaborations and coalitions of diverse actors, that the orthodoxy of CSR is forged. These processes serve to project TNCs not only as moral agents, but as vehicles of sustainable development through business and empowerment through 'the market'.

Chapter 2 moves from the wider world of CSR to focus on the particular corporate genealogy in which CSR is embedded. I follow the company back to its Johannesburg headquarters, and those of its subsidiary, Anglo Platinum, and trace the roots of its influence in the political economy and prevailing social imagination of South Africa. Chapter 3 considers how CSR proves a crucial mechanism of mediation between the company and the national imperatives of the post-apartheid state. Here, CSR resonates with the dominant discourse of national transformation and development encapsulated in BEE and 'patriotic capitalism', according to which the company is projected as key collaborator in the delivery of the 'new South African dream'.

The second half of the book looks at how this plays out in the evolution and implementation of three central pillars of the company's CSR strategy: (1) HIV/AIDS management, (2) small enterprise and entrepreneurship development and (3) education. While Chapters 4 and 5 investigate how CSR reconfigures relations between the company and its employees through the practices of HIV prevention, care and treatment, Chapters 6 and 7 examine corporate social investment as it is deployed in the 'community', beyond the 'perimeter fence' of the workplace.

Chapter 4 focuses then on the evolution of corporate strategy and policy on HIV. While CSR claims the confluence of doing good business and doing good, this chapter explores the apparent tension between moral impetus and market interest in which the corporate fight against HIV is framed.

At the point of implementation, this tension translates into a moral economy of treatment which is the subject of Chapter 5. Here, a disjuncture between corporate responsibility and state provision becomes embedded in practices which re-inscribe old boundaries between the workplace and the world beyond its borders, creating a symbolic or moral 'cordon-sanitaire' around the company's zone of interest.

It is not only (nor chiefly) the company that is transformed through the practice of CSR, but the targets of responsibility, for whom the corporation offers the possibility of both moral and material transformation. Thus in Chapter 5, we see how the corporate HIV care programme delivers treatment to its employees, together with the moral values of self-discipline, self-mastery and empowerment. In Chapter 6, the educational benefits of a company bursary, after-school maths programme or small business scheme propound the market virtues of self-empowerment, entrepreneurialism and autonomy, even while they reinvent a moral economy of patronage and dependency, through the intricate bonds of the corporate gift. Thus, as Chapter 7 examines, the practices of 'corporate-community partnership' are uneven, and the inclusive vision of 'empowerment through enterprise' is exclusionary, as they attempt to build commonalities on entrenched inequalities. These chapters bring us back to the central concern of the book, underlining how corporate authority works through the moral framework of social responsibility and the practices it generates, to encompass not only the economic, but the social order.

1 'Let Business Lift Africa Out of Poverty'

Global Corporate Citizenship—
A New Orthodoxy

Who better than Coca Cola, a firm with a better distribution network in sub-Saharan Africa than any aid agency, to get materials out to needy populations? . . . Exhortation not regulation!

(David Cameron, British Prime Minister [then Conservative Party Leader], Annual Business in the Community Conference, 9 May 2006)

IN JULY 2000 KOFI ANNAN (then UN Secretary-General) announced the inauguration of a new Global Compact between business and civil society, symbolically unleashing the vast potential of enterprise in the realm of development:

> Let us choose to unite the power of markets with the authority of universal ideals. Let us choose to reconcile the creative forces of private entrepreneurship with the needs of the disadvantaged (26 July 2000, New York).

In the years preceding and following the launch, the CSR movement gained momentum, recruiting support from seemingly diverse corners and creating coalitions between unexpected partners eager to realise this union of global markets and universal ideals. The primacy of the market as the panacea to poverty has been resoundingly proclaimed not only by leaders of transnational corporations and multilateral development institutions, but increasingly by NGOs held up to represent the 'voice of civil society'. Drawing on idioms of emancipation through the market, CSR has thus demonstrated a great capacity to unite disparate actors (and former combatants) in an apparently mutual enterprise of sustainable development. While Sir Mark Moody-Stuart, former chairman of Anglo American and Shell, commands us to 'let business lift Africa out of poverty'[1], the United Nations Development Programme (UNDP) reminds readers of the *Financial Times* in a half page advertisement that, 'the poor need business to invest in their future. Business needs the poor because they are the future' (UNDP 2005).

This exuberance in the public arena has been matched (and reinforced) by academic tributes from scholars heralding CSR (and its corollary corporate citizenship) as the new hope for development where global corporations transcend the pitfalls of state-led development and the politics of national government[2]:

> Never before has a partnership been created between the highest levels of the UN, business, NGOs and labour representatives. Never before has such a partnership had the open-ended mandate of furthering the core UN conventions and declarations covering labour standards, human rights and the environment . . . The stakes are high . . . the potential gains are immense (Zadek 2001: 102).

One theme emerges most strongly from the literature on CSR, whether from insiders or analysts, advocates or critics: that CSR is a truly *global* phenomenon, exercised through supranational networks of governance and ethical standards[3]. Codes, norms and standards thus appear as components of a new global 'moral order' (Harper 2000). But this preoccupation with the global dimension of CSR—whether as an instrument of social improvement worldwide, or a tool of global governmentality—has resulted in an analysis of CSR disembedded from its social practice. We are left asking, how is this new orthodoxy of 'compassionate capitalism' and corporate responsibility forged? And, what actors and interests work towards sustaining, reinforcing and extending its power?

The main purpose of this chapter is to shed light on these processes, and in particular the ritualised and performative dynamics of CSR, which I argue, are crucial to establishing it as development orthodoxy. I trace the performance of CSR through the circuit of conventions and conferences, policy forums, multi-partner roundtables and award ceremonies that constitute the elite 'global' arena of corporate citizenship, or put another way, the social life of CSR. For it is here that we begin to disentangle the agency of various actors—from captains of industry to representatives of the 'grass roots', from business schools to UN agencies—involved in the production of this powerful discourse; and we begin to see the effects of this apparent shift from agonistic to collaborative, from conflictual to consensual. This alerts us to one of the most striking aspects of the CSR movement: the role of national governments, often described by corporate executives and their NGO counterparts alike as 'missing in action', as they are noticeable as much by their absence as their presence.

Within these arenas corporate executives come together with representatives of global NGOs, and the growing army of CSR consultants or 'professionals', from dozens of small firms or non-profits (the boundary between which is often blurred). Participants extol the virtues of bi-, tri- or multi-sector partnerships, develop international standards and initiatives to improve the global reach of the CSR movement; and present case studies describing 'best-practice' or 'lessons-learnt' from their engagement with 'local communities', the subjects of their ethical endeavours. Such gatherings unfold as highly ritu-alistic theatres of virtue in which awards for the best corporate citizen are presented and inspiring stories of social responsibility are told.

The celebration of corporate virtue, underpinned by a moral register of com-passionate capitalism, seems to clash with the commitment to 'market rational-ity' espoused in the language of 'the business case for CSR', 'enlightened self-interest', and not least, 'the fortune at the bottom of the pyramid'. This reveals what at first appears to be a peculiar contradiction at play in the production of CSR. On the one hand the invocation of markets as the cure for poverty strives to reaffirm the commitment to a supposedly amoral capitalist rationality—the fundamental logic of maximisation. On the other hand, this vision of business-led development underwritten by an ideal of corporate citizenship is anything but amoral. As I argue throughout the book, the confluence of these two apparently discordant discourses—moral mission and market rationalism—is not only central to the performance of corporate social responsibility, but fundamental to the production and expansion of corporate capitalism.

The ethnographic focus of the chapter is London, global financial capi-tal, home to some of the world's largest multinationals and central hub of the booming industry in CSR. As in cities worldwide, one is continuously met with testaments to corporate citizenship. The rhetoric of sustainable develop-ment is emblazoned on bus stops advertising BP (newly incarnated as *'Beyond Petroleum'* rather than 'British Petroleum'). Standard Bank promises to 'bank the unbanked' across Africa. And, even BAE Systems (the world's second big-gest defence contractor) advertises its social responsibility on the London un-derground beneath the slogan 'making the world a safer place'[4]. Thus a senior economist and CSR advisor for the Organisation for Economic Co-operation and Development (OECD) remarked at a 2005 CSR industry event in Lon-don: 'I have always viewed London as being the CSR capital of the world—all the leading CSR organisations are within a five mile radius of where we are now. I think the London CSR community has done a great service to the world, getting governments, business and NGOs to work together'. As a cen-tral site of CSR performance, London thus comes to stand for 'the global', an abstract site de-localized and detached from its UK context, where corporate elites and development policy-makers converge in the service of development; put another way, where 'global-thinking' goes on, and is then crystallized in international codes of conduct, standards, social technologies and reporting schemes. The ethical regimes which emerge from such coalitions are widely seen as new forms of global governance through which accountability, or the appearance of it, is rendered. The corollary to this performance of *global* corporate citizenship, is the 'local', framed around a moral imaginary of 'community' which provides the intended target of these cosmopolitan coalitions. It is here, according to the constant refrain 'think global, act local', that the abstracted ideals of corporate responsibility become tangible as they give rise to empowerment projects, socio-economic development funds, and even the solid concrete bricks of HIV clinics and mine schools: the localised products of 'ethical capitalism'. Thus, the 'global' and the 'local' are seamlessly woven together in a coherent narrative of good corporate citizenship.

The ubiquitous exhortation to 'partnership' is of course nothing new in the development industry. Nor is the power of the partnership paradigm to assert equality and consensus, where in fact inequality and difference reign, as anthropologists of development have shown[5]. In the case of CSR however, the concept of partnership has demonstrated even broader appeal, and greater discursive power, in its capacity to manufacture apparent consensus in a shared enterprise, as all parties proclaim a collaborative venture for a collective goal of sustainable development and elevate 'the global market' as the fundamental mechanism through which this can be achieved. For, as the business-led paradigm of development recruits support from distant corners it asserts a global, national and indeed local alliance between business and society, and thus a congruence of values between the logic of maximisation and the moral imperatives of development.

Theatres of Virtue

In October 2005 senior executives from several of the world's biggest TNCs (including Anglo American, Shell, Vodaphone and Coca Cola) came together with numerous consultants in search of contracts, and NGO representatives (those willing or able to pay the £695 per day fee) at the Regent's Park Marriott Hotel in London, for a convention hosted by *Ethical Corporation* on 'The New Role of Business in Development'. 'The real reason for being in business is to create wealth' the poster announced, 'so is it good business to join the fight against poverty?' As if in response, the conference was opened by the director

of the Shell Foundation, Kurt Hoffman, forcefully asserting the new orthodoxy of a business-led development agenda:

> The challenge in 2005 is not to restate the problems but to apply *business
> thinking* and come up with solutions . . . So Tony Blair's Africa Commission—
> which has placed a welcome emphasis on the role of the private sector—needs
> to push the pro-poor enterprise agenda even further[6].

The underlying theme of Hoffman's speech was the failure of development
led by a reactionary parochial state sector burdened with a moral mission of
upliftment—the modern day legacy of, as he put it, 'the white man's burden'.
The solution, according to Hoffman, is to be found in the world of big business, where technocratic efficiency comes together with competitive creativity. 'Let us choose to unite the power of markets' he announced, quoting Kofi
Annan's battle cry. Yet in spite of the avowed market logic of this corporate
discourse of development, Hoffman went on to invoke Truman's inaugural
address of 1949, harking back to the profoundly *moral* vision of progress and
state-led development that he had just consigned to the failures of the past:

> I believe that we should make available to peace-loving peoples the benefits
> of our store of technical knowledge in order to help them realize their aspira-
> tions for a better life . . . Greater production is the key to prosperity and peace
> and the key to greater production is a wider and more vigorous application of
> modern scientific and technical knowledge (Hoffman 2005, quoting Truman's
> Inaugural Address 1949).

Hoffman's speech thus exemplifies the slippage between seemingly discordant
registers of scientistic rationalism and moral imperative, interweaving contemporary paradigms of sustainable development with anachronistic notions
of corporate virtue to produce a compelling master narrative of corporate
citizenship. Put another way, as the resident anthropologist at one of Anglo
American's 'rival' mining companies remarked: 'we used to say "god bless
you", now we say "let's have sustainable development!" Sometimes, I'm not
entirely sure what the difference is.'

The next speaker on the conference bill, a representative from the World
Business Council for Sustainable Development (WBCSD), echoed the dominant economistic equation: poverty eradication through access to expanding
markets, and profit generation through the vast reserve of untapped customers and aspirant entrepreneurs in developing countries:

> What's the point in expanding markets? The market creates opportunities. *When you're cut out of the market, you're cut out of the social system,* you're not empowered. We don't want to squeeze out development agencies—they can still do development . . . One unique contribution that business provides is enterprise—enterprising ways out of poverty, this isn't about doing good, it's about providing environments for enterprise.

According to this equation the market comes to stand for the social system as a whole. Questions concerning the inequitable distribution of wealth vanish as poverty is recast within this depoliticised framework, due simply to a lack of market opportunities.

Implicit within this vision of empowerment is an ideal (entrepreneurial) actor who can respond to the moral exhortation to embrace the opportunities provided by expanding business, and uplift him- or herself out of poverty as they are brought into the global market[7]. However the mission of CSR goes far beyond the apparent benefits of foreign direct investment and market growth. It offers instead a vision of caring corporations that is a far cry from hard-line neoliberalism. As David Cameron's statement quoted above exemplifies, TNCs are now urged to engage whole-heartedly with the developmental needs and goals of the countries and communities in which they operate, helping to build stable affluent societies with the aim of establishing the conditions for further investment. As such, CSR has figured prominently in recent white papers and policy reports of bilateral and multilateral development agencies. In their 2003 report on *DFID and Corporate Social Responsibility,* the UK's Department for International Development (DFID) went so far as to discourage any move towards 'internationally legally binding frameworks for multinational companies', arguing that a mandatory approach of this kind 'may divert attention and energy away from encouraging corporate social responsibility and towards legal process' (DFID 2003: 9). This highlights the dominant commitment to voluntarism as a mechanism for harnessing the innate competitive ingenuity of business, and the rejection of regulation which have become the mainstay of CSR discourse, propounded by both corporations and many of their partners in development.

Speaker after speaker repeated the refrain of doing good business to do good, attended by compelling promises of 'collective responsibility', 'common goals' and 'win-win solutions' or as the representative from the OECD proposed: 'get business to do what they do best . . . making profits and protecting our people and planet!'[8]. Positioned at the centre of the global economy with their extensive resources and drive for efficiency, TNCs are seen to be perfectly placed not only to implement this agenda but to lead it. Cameron's exhortation—'who better than Coca Cola . . . to get materials out to needy populations' could be heard in various forms from executives and NGOs alike at the conference. Thus the director of the International Business Leaders Forum's (IBLF) Partnering Initiative and author of numerous manuals and 'how-to' books on business-NGO partnerships explained: 'Business knows how to operate in certain parts of the world better than development agencies because of their reach—*we should follow them* into Africa . . . There's so much room for business to teach NGOs how to bring business into development'. We were left in no doubt of this when a representative from the UK-based NGO Business in the Community told the speaker from Anglo American: 'we would love to have a lesson from the university of Anglo American in community social empowerment, let us learn from you'.

This conference on the 'New Role of Business in Development' was only one in the annual cycle of conferences hosted by *Ethical Corporation*, such as 'Climate Change: How to Get your Message Across to Consumers' (March 2007); or 'How to Make Ethical Branding Work' (November 2006). But *Ethical Corporation* is not the only organisation in the CSR event business. Each year scores of events, from large-scale conferences to one-day training and discussion workshops are hosted by the likes of Business in the Community, Chatham House, and the IBLF. These gatherings usually take place in top London hotels at which participants are treated to 'business-leaders' breakfasts', fine lunches and leatherbound conference packs. Common are joint panel presentations by the CSR executive of a TNC, coupled with the representative from a partner NGO offering 'best-practice' case studies and 'lessons-learnt' from their shared experience.

One of the most commonly discussed questions at CSR events was 'how do we get sustainable development into the DNA of business and change its genetic code?' At the same time, the shift towards a corporate model of development has reversed the question to ask: 'how do we get business DNA into development and NGOs?' (chairman, *Ethical Corporation* Conference 'The New Role of Business in Development, 18–19 October 2005). Picking up the anthropomorphism inherent in the notion of corporate citizenship, humanising metaphors which present companies as sentient beings rather than impersonal machines are ubiquitous in the discourse of CSR. Crucially, the concept of corporate citizenship claims on behalf of the company a moral self. Companies thus emerge as 'citizens', complete with conscience, culture, DNA and even heart, through which their moral agency is apparently exercised[9]. One NGO partner of Anglo American, for example, said of the company: 'as a corporate they do have a heart!'[10]. Similarly, the CEO of Anglo American herself states in the company's 2008 *Report to Society*: 'for Anglo American, there is simply no choice or trade-off . . . It is part of our DNA, embedded in our culture, and is fundamental to the way we do business' (Anglo American 2008: 7).

Such events commonly include practical learning and training forums on ethical and social technologies such as 'stakeholder engagement', 'scenario planning' or 'social impact assessment' that contribute to an ethos of technocratic rationalism. These are combined with 'celebrity speeches' by the CEOs of global corporations, government ministers or aspiring future leaders hoping to attach their name to the bold promise of CSR. The Convention launching the 2006 Business in the Community (BITC) Index was opened with David Cameron promising a Conservative rule that offered a 'lighter regulatory touch' to companies that demonstrated social responsibility; a bid, in his words, 'to reclaim corporate responsibility for the political centre-right'. Meanwhile the UK government-funded 'Beyond CSR?' event held at the National Liberal Club was kicked off with a debate between Labour member of parliament and former head of DFID Clare Short and Conservative member of parliament and former cabinet minister John Redwood (22 May 2006). But what had been billed as a political debate, turned quickly into vocal affirmations of mutual agreement, exemplifying the apparent ability of CSR to replace political partisanship with a competition for who can proclaim collective responsibility and societal unity the loudest.

Certain events in the CSR calendar are devoted to generating particular CSR products such as codes of conduct, accountability frameworks, indices and standards. A high point in the CSR year is the launch of BITC's annual Corporate Responsibility Index, 'the UK's leading benchmark of responsible business' (BITC 2006: 4) on which companies vie for top spot as the best corporate citizen. Participating companies submit detailed reports on their CSR activities in four categories: workplace, marketplace, community and environment. These are then ranked by the BITC team according to a set of complicated metrics. Each year, with its 750 members, BITC packs the plush surroundings of the Millennium Hotel in Knightsbridge with over 400 CEOs and CSR executives of some of the world's largest TNCs for the launch of its Index. Yet here the managerial model offered by the Index, as a tool for measuring corporate responsibility, is underpinned by an ethos of zealous moral endeavour. The event unfolds as a highly orchestrated theatre of virtue, with all the ritualised trappings of a speech piped in on video link by the Prince of Wales and awards presented to the companies ranking top of the Index backed by a soundtrack of uplifting music. The presentation of awards is followed by lofty speeches promising to achieve even greater heights of corporate responsibility and thanking 'the public' for such recognition. Within these arenas performers take on the role of what Steven Sampson, writing on the global anti-corruption movement, has termed 'integrity warriors', demonstrating their commitment to 'funding virtue' for the collective good (Sampson 2005: 114).

A few weeks after the launch, more awards are presented in an even more conspicuous celebration of corporate virtue: BITC's annual 'Awards for Excellence' ceremony, a grand event held in the Royal Albert Hall at which around 2,000 CEOs, corporate executives and assorted other 'friends of BITC' are entertained by acts such as Cirque du Soleil, and awards are presented by the Prince of Wales (this time in person) to CEOs for all manner of CSR achievements. In 2006 BITC heralded a new dawn of business in the 'global community' with their 'Year of Africa'. This was celebrated with an 'Africa-themed' award ceremony in order to, as the director of BITC put it, 'remind us where the real challenges in the world are'. At the event, which was combined with the G8 Business Action for Africa Summit Dinner, inspiring stories of business-led development were told, music was provided by the Soweto Children's Choir, and Anglo American won the International Award for greatest contribution to achieving the Millennium Development Goals.

As companies strive for recognition as the best corporate citizens, awards become a marker of success in this competitive market of corporate virtue and social responsibility. While executives take pains to stress that 'CSR is not about winning awards', the symbolic value of such prizes is significant. Presented by organisations that are seen to represent common societal values or the 'voice of community', and at the same time the result of supposedly rigorous metrics, awards act as symbolic proof authenticating the company's moral claims, and more broadly validating the role of business as agents of social improvement. Thus, while CSR may not simply be about 'winning awards' (as executives are eager to emphasise), companies are equally keen to direct attention to those they have won, listing them in annual CSR reports, putting them on their website and referring to them during presentations at other conferences: 'the Global Alliance last year gave us an award for our HIV/AIDS work . . . we also won another 4 awards, but I won't go into those now', the Anglo American executive dropped into his address at the *Ethical Corporation* Convention (18–19 October 2005).

Awards come to symbolise an abstracted form of reciprocal gratitude in return for the benefits provided through the company's moral endeavours, so evoking the kind of social relations associated with the gift. This again unsettles the economistic register of 'social investment' and 'enlightened self-interest'. The formalistic context of award ceremonies contributes further to the ethos of gift-giving. Presentations usually begin with emotive accounts of the social upliftment rendered by the winning company's CSR initiatives. Often these are accompanied by videos of the recipients enjoying the benefits provided by the company: executives reading to underprivileged children in a London school as part of an employee volunteering scheme, a CEO visiting a health clinic in Peru or a large-scale project to provide electricity to rural South Africans. The leadership and commitment of high profile CSR champions is extolled. In response, award-winners thank 'the public' for such recognition, underscoring how awards confer upon the company a kind of moral validation and verification, in place of real accountability to the recipients of the company's CSR. Implicit within this process is an invitation to 'trust', in return for corporate responsibility, as was exemplified in the thank-you speech made by the chairman of a multinational retail company:

> Receiving the award from BITC for 'company of the year' last year was a great morale boost. It's about returning to the company's values as laid down in the 1950s . . . Trust is indispensable and we believe that winning the award shows that we have not sacrificed trust for short-term expediency . . . we operate in a tough marketplace where trust is at a premium.

Here, the personalised vision of reciprocal relations of trust and giving between the company and society is seamlessly interwoven with the discourse of competitive market interests. As I will go on to explore in Chapter 6, despite claims of a shift away from philanthropy towards the language of social investment, and 'responsible competitiveness', the practice of CSR is profoundly bound up with the politics of the gift.

The power of such awards to authenticate the moral claims of TNCs is clear. This is epitomised in BITC's PerCent Club. Now in its twentieth year, membership of the PerCent Club is awarded to companies which devote 1 percent or more of their pre-tax profits to some form of CSR activity. Anglo American, for example, recorded their total 'social investment spend' in 2008 as 1.1 percent of pre-tax profits, \$76.2 million (Anglo American 2008: 38). In recognition for achieving the PerCent Standard, companies receive a big pink tick (check mark)—a logo with which they can emblazon company brochures, websites and other paraphernalia. In 2004 there were '435 big-ticked companies, the mark which recognizes commitment to the community' (Promotional Video shown at BITC Annual General Meeting, London, 1 December 2004). In this way, with their big pink tick, BITC, which describes itself as part community organisation, part charity and part business association, provides companies with a visible stamp of moral legitimacy and community authentication. Similar 'moral capital' can be earned through the leading indices of corporate responsibility (the New York Stock Exchange's Dow Jones Sustainability Index, the London Stock Exchange's FTSE4Good or BITC's Corporate Responsibility Index). Thus during a 'partnership meeting' when a representative from BITC asked their Anglo counterpart what it was that they could offer Anglo American in terms of community activities and strategy, the response was: 'we pay our dues because you're a good organisation and we don't expect anything else out of you. Although, we are intensely competitive with the "Rios" and "BHPs"[11] and we compare our scores vis-à-vis them, very closely', he added, jokingly, 'so we will of course cut our membership if we don't move up the index next time'. Despite the humorous tone, the force of the remark was not lost. It points to the symbolic capital that partnership with BITC offers transnational corporations, as they attempt to leverage a 'competitive moral edge' (Browne 2009: 27) through their position in the annual Index. Return for the gift or donation comes, not from the variety of CSR activities and products that the NGO offers (from employee volunteering schemes, to participation in International Tree Week), but in the less tangible form of moral authenticity accrued to the company through their association with an organisation that claims to give voice to the needs of 'the community'.

Yet of course such events are not only highly ritualised, they are extremely exclusive. While the rhetoric is one of societal consensus and inclusion, the reality is that only those who are invited by the organisers or those who can afford the prohibitively high admission fees can attend. As Sampson writes of the Tenth International Anti-Corruption Conference in Prague: 'underlining the importance of this event were the access conditions: the participation fee for the three days was no less than US\$890 . . . So much for the grassroots element' (Sampson 2005: 114). Likewise the CSR conferences where you would expect to pay a minimum of £895 or as much as £2000 for a two-day function, such as the 'Gold Package' at Chatham's House 2005 conference 'Developing

Local Content in Oil and Gas' which included two master classes on stakeholder consultation and social and environmental impact assessment.

In this way the CSR industry excludes from its discussions all but representatives from very well-resourced corporations or international bodies. The appearance of consensus between speakers and participants, and the unanimous allegiance to the shared goals of development through business is ensured by the exclusion of critical voices and groups with alternative visions, conflicting agendas or simply, smaller budgets. Those with fewer resources, who tell a different story to that of societal consensus and common interests that the CSR movement strives to project, are thus marginalised from this hegemonic mainstream. This was starkly demonstrated at the 2004 Business and Human Rights event entitled 'Spheres of Influence: Understanding Human Rights in Business' (London, 9 December 2004). Tickets for the one day conference chaired by Mary Robinson cost £400 + vat (value added tax). The conference programme promised a presentation by the deputy chairman of Barclays Bank. His speech stressed the need for global financial institutions to safeguard the human rights of their 'stakeholders' through rigorous 'engagement' in order to ensure the 'free, prior and informed consent' of the 'local communities' before financing large-scale projects such as dams and pipelines, in developing countries. Indeed the canonical notions of 'local community' and 'local voices' were prominent throughout the speech.

However the event did not run as smoothly as usual. Outside the conference representatives from the 'local communities' in Thailand and India who had been adversely affected by the Trans-Thai-Malaysia Pipeline and a number of big dams—projects financed by Barclays Bank—had flown to London and demanded entry to the conference and a platform from which to put 'their side of the story' to the audience[12]. While conference security personnel kept the 'gate-crashers' in the lobby (for they had no tickets), suited executives of transnational extractive and retail giants, as well as speakers from Amnesty International, the World Bank and the UN Global Compact passed by and took their places on the podium. Finally, after much delay, a message came from Mary Robinson that the unexpected guests should be invited into the auditorium and given an opportunity to speak. There was a palpable sense of surprise amongst the whispering audience as the representatives from Thailand explained that the claims to 'free, prior and informed consent' were fraudulent, and that they were being forcibly removed from their land by government security forces to make way for the pipeline. A representative from Business in the Community turned to me and remarked:

Wow, I go to these functions all the time, and I've never seen anything like this! I'm amazed they were given a platform to speak. I wonder what the man from Barclays is going to say now.

Few questions followed the accounts of houses bulldozed and villages relocated, and after this unscheduled interruption, the rest of the conference got underway according to the programme as if little had happened. Indeed the conference report contains only a very short paragraph in its introduction briefly mentioning that 'representatives on behalf of communities adversely affected by the activities of companies were also given the opportunity to address delegates'. The report makes no mention that this was an unscheduled and uninvited addition to the conference. On the contrary, it is recorded as if it had been a planned part of the programme. Rather than disrupting the positive ethos of corporate responsibility that the function generated, it thus serves to create the illusion of an arena characterised by openness, transparency and pluralism.

CSR conventions, workshops and award ceremonies thus represent an exclusionary space in which the intangible ideal of global corporate citizenship is enacted by an elite community of ethical experts. This is then, at an ideological level, a world of apparently 'cosmopolitan' values, where universal rationality rather than particularistic cultural assumptions and principles are deemed all important. Within this arena, CSR professionals take on the mantle of purveyors of this global social responsibility, sharing a common set of technical tools and a collective vision of development at the base of which the market principle is held up to embody a natural, and universally valid truth about human and social nature. Within these domains the concept of 'global' itself becomes the subject of competition as companies, their NGO allies and CSR consultants alike strive to demonstrate the coherence, integrity and global reach of CSR, encapsulated in the slogan frequently heard within such arenas: 'make ethical and global rhyme'.

'Make Ethical and Global Rhyme'

In a statement at the 2004 European Conference on Corporate Social Responsibility in Maastricht, the trade union and NGO delegations urged the CSR industry to 'demonstrate its credibility globally, particularly in the developing country context'[13]. As if in anticipation of the demands to prove its 'global' relevance, the CSR movement has given rise to its own expansive international bureaucracy of 'soft regulation' with striking speed. Foremost among the myriad CSR standards, codes and normative frameworks emerging from this international arena is the UN Global Compact to which companies voluntarily sign up. The Compact's ten principles are illustrative of the so-called 'core values' that such initiatives attempt to enshrine as universal public goods. These include commitments to uphold and protect human rights; to eliminate child and forced labour; to encourage the diffusion of environmentally-friendly technologies; and to work against all forms of corruption. While they do not include an injunction to actively participate in sustainable development, as many other frameworks do, taken together the principles constitute a broad entreaty for companies to adopt a position of guardianship over the social welfare of the societies in which they operate.

The compact carries with it the moral authority of the UN. Again, international voluntary codes and conventions such as the Global Compact hold out the persuasive promise of a collective societal responsibility shared between all sectors of society and governed by global regimes of accountability and responsibility, thus removing the need for mandatory regulation. The magic bullet is therefore, according to CSR advocates, to be found not in corporations alone, but in a business-society alliance enacted through a network of multi-stakeholder partnerships and coalitions between companies and civil society[14]. What is striking about discussions surrounding the UN Global Compact (in both the public and academic arenas) is, once again, the absence of the state as a key player in this partnership process—an absence which marks much of the public discourse and academic literature on CSR and to which I will return.

The on-going series of meetings surrounding the production of an International Standardisation Organisation (ISO) standard for CSR (ISO 26,000) represents just such an attempt to enshrine the values of corporate responsibility in a voluntary global framework of technical rationalism. This 'multi-stakeholder' project (participation in which was by invitation only) involved the application of the technical metrics which the ISO uses for every imaginable product from seatbelts to general purpose sacks, to the rather less tangible subject of corporate ethics and responsibility, or as one CSR consultant involved in the process put it:

> It's a bit of a strange thing we're doing. ISO make standards for paper size and paper clips and we're all sitting there, business, unions, NGOs—not a lot of people from the South I'll admit—trying to come up with an 'appropriate size' for CSR, a checklist so we can raise the bar for responsibility globally.

As Dunn has shown in her study of the meat-packing industry in East Central Europe, voluntary standards and compacts such as the ISO series hold out the expectation of global accountability and responsibility through a combination of self-discipline and collaborative voluntarism (self-)disciplining companies 'from the inside out' (Dunn 2005: 176).

Such standards have the effect of transforming the moral discourse of responsibility, and corporate 'self-discipline', into a technocratic framework of supposedly objective 'universal' values and global norms which link disparate localities together in an ethical regime conceived by a select group of elite actors. At the same time, ethical standards are widely seen as the products of collaborative processes and societal consensus on social values, so obscuring the influence of dominant interests involved in the process. The codes and compacts which make up the hard currency of voluntary 'soft' regulation on CSR (if such an oxymoron might be permitted) operate much like the awards and indices discussed above. While they are produced by elite collaborations between multinational companies and multilateral institutions they are generally seen to embody 'the voice of civil society' (Garsten and Jacobsson 2007: 145). Ethical standard-making is thus framed in terms of an objectively identifiable societal or collective need, masking the specific interests behind an apparently universal goal or global social good. This claim was forcefully asserted by the keynote speaker at BITC's 2004 Index launch, one of many UK captains of industry who have put their name behind BITC:

> CSR becomes about understanding the societal consensus on convictions and responding to that consensus . . . business is made up of people from top to bottom and fortunately that reflects societal consensus to a large extent.

Voluntary frameworks thus appear collectively as an almost universal oracle, imposing the illusion of uniformity, coherence and, crucially, *consensus*. In this way, the mechanical tools of codes and standards are used to mask essentially political processes under a veil of neutrality and societal consensus. As Foucault warns, the effectiveness of power rests precisely on this ability to 'hide its own mechanisms' (Foucault 1990: 86). For, just like policy, codes and standards are seen to be the product of supposedly non-moral institutions, which lends them both legitimacy and universal relevance. The mechanics of reporting and accountability systems have great symbolic significance in reinforcing such an illusion. By apparently revealing the internal systems through which the organisation works the implication is, firstly, that companies are essentially rational technocratic machines. And secondly, that self-imposed transparency allows outsiders to see through an organisation to the ways in which authority is exercised at its centre. This fundamentally misdirects attention. Power does not (only) operate through the tangible hard core at the centre of an organisation, but through diffuse, diverse and often very subtle means that are not displayed in the technical manipulations of reporting and monitoring (Sanders and West 2003). The 'rituals of verification' (Power 1997) which attend these voluntary compacts and standards demand that responsibility is demonstrated at the 'global' level through the apparatus of self-monitoring and reporting (chief among these being the Global Reporting Initiative[15]).

These days, almost all large firms produce separate corporate reports on their social and environmental performance annually. Much like the presentations at conferences and award ceremonies, these heavy tomes couple convincing statistical charts with compelling case stories of children in rural South Africa 'uplifted' from poverty or employees empowered through the corporate fraternity. Thus, Anglo's 2004 Report to Society, *Creating Enduring Value*, describes a revolution in corporate responsibility and employee empowerment at the South African coal mines:

> Yebo Siyaphambili, a five-year initiative, will entrench a new set of values identified through a recent survey. The message was clear. Employees want to work in an environment that fosters empowerment, communication, innovation, motivation and productivity. They want to deliver performance excellence—through people. Their vision is that Anglo Coal in 2008 will be an organisation driven by fun and passion, which achieves profit through performance, demonstrates leadership and has the courage to innovate. Employees want to work for an organisation that draws strength from its diversity, expresses care and inspires trust, empowers its people, communicates and is a magnet for talent. Simply put, it needs to be a company with a single, shared vision. Yebo Siyaohambili means 'Yes, we are moving forward together (Anglo American 2004a: 29).

The emphasis on demonstrating social and environmental accountability within these 'global' frameworks requires that diverse social contexts are profiled and distilled into measurable and comparable units, ready for submission to the Global Compact or a similar portal. The 'local' and the 'social' are condensed into best- (and occasionally worst-) practice case studies to provide 'proof' of a company's social responsibility, and more broadly, demonstrate the success of this new global movement. For it is through these mechanisms that a corporation's claims to CSR are verified[16]. This results in a demand for neat packages of knowledge that are measurable, comparable and have a persuasive capacity to demonstrate accountability. These are animated by appealing photographs that fill reports and show suited executives from the company's global headquarters visiting a rural school or HIV clinic, awkwardly observing, and at times even participating in social improvement in action. Next to pictures of smiling beneficiaries, Anglo American's 2008 *Report to Society: Making a Difference* tells of Kumba Iron Ore in South Africa 'helping women . . . to play a meaningful role in uplifting their communities', while employees from Anglo's corporate head office help Dipo Otejo and his fellow pupils at a London Primary School to read (Anglo American 2008: 44, 47). Such images act as visual testaments of global corporate citizenship in practice, of 'global thinking—local acting'.

The message is that the *universal* values of corporate responsibility come from the cosmopolitan world inhabited by corporate executives in London and must be communicated down through the corporate structure from boardrooms to mineshafts, corporate to operations; as one Anglo executive put it:

> If you look at the EU directives on corruption—for the newly acceded countries these weren't part of their values and moral fibre system as they were in UK, France, Germany etc. We need systems to do the same for CSR—to drive it down and embed it in local contexts.

This is reinforced by the practice of 'ethical training' which most TNCs have now instituted for the lower ranks of the company stationed at the operational end of the business. Implicit within these practices is the assumption that corporate ethics are generated at the top, in the global head office and must then be translated down through the company from top to bottom. An Anglo American executive explained:

> At the Ex-Co[17] level, it sounds arrogant, but it's true, they are startlingly bright and they may have been accountants or engineers but they've had to move away from their training because they're exposed to the values of the global political economy . . . At the level where you get the sort of person whose whole world is 'does this piece of equipment work', then for those guys, change is slower. Their attitude is what you can't measure you can't manage because they see it graphed and in numbers . . . Crudely, it's a *softening up* . . . We require every employee to do training and awareness on our business principles—even those on the shop floor and in the mines. It's one way of drip feeding these expectations to employees.

Thus the London office has come to represent the cosmopolitan centre of the company's global corporate citizenship agenda, supported by its proximity to the London Stock Exchange and the international arenas of CSR. Andy Walken, Sustainable Development Manager for an Anglo subsidiary in Johannesburg explained this hierarchy of ethical knowledge:

> It's top-down on the international side. The parent company sits on the international stuff . . . we don't want to do that so we let the parent company fulfil that role and disseminate the knowledge to us in South Africa.

Similarly, Walken's counterpart in the London office of the parent company spoke of sustainable development as an area of expertise that evolved from the amorphous global arena to be implemented in grounded local operations:

> Sustainable Development has come down from something discussed at the World Summit and has got down below policymakers to operators . . . But it takes time—it still sits with people who are beating the drum in head office.

Plugged into the 'global' arena of CSR and sustainable development, a small cadre of London-based Anglo executives do the rounds on the cycle of CSR conventions, and foster an expanding list of 'global partnerships' with high profile NGOs such as World Wide Fund for Nature (WWF), Business in the Community, Engineers Without Borders and Care International. At the same time they work with large consultancies such as Environmental Resources Management to produce in-house CSR principles and strategies (in areas such as health and safety, biodiversity, environmental stewardship, socio-economic development and HIV). These are accompanied by state-of-the-art tools for implementing and monitoring them such as Anglo American's award-winning 'Socio-Economic Assessment Toolbox' (SEAT), released in 2005. The aim of such social technologies is to overcome the 'ethical gap' between corporate and operations, to translate CSR doctrine into local action. Within the competitive market for corporate citizenship, in which companies are ranked on indices and publicly rewarded for their contributions, CSR 'products' such as SEAT (just like technical innovations) are a resource, to be displayed, but not necessarily shared.

The commodification of 'local community', packaged and marketed as the visible product of good corporate citizenship, is integral to the performance of CSR, and of particular importance within the extractive industries. In many ways it reflects the kind of production-orientated logic of the mining business. Industry initiatives such as the Mining Minerals and Sustainable Development project (MMSD 2002) and the Extractive Industries Review (World Bank 2004), promote a normative ideal of 'communities' as the counterpart to companies in their commitment to sustainable development. Activists have similarly mobilised around an idealised notion of community in their campaigns against mining companies (see for example Mines and Communities 2001). The 'community' has thus emerged as a distinct narrative in the discourse of CSR, particularly within the extractive industries (Kapelus 2002; see also Sillitoe and Wilson 2003, and Jenkins 2004). This is not of course a new phenomenon. As Kapelus argues:

> The identification . . . of 'the community' has been undertaken since western capitalism spread through the 'frontier' zones. Requesting permission to mine from 'the chief' or other traditional authority has always been the first step in identifying 'the community' (Kapelus 2002: 280).

The identification and discursive construction of 'community' performs a vital role in pursuit of the so-called 'moral' or 'social' licence to mine; providing companies with a constituency of at least tacit support. Thus Sir Mark Moody-Stuart[18], a former chairman of Anglo American, wrote recently:

> Any major company will seek to command the consent of the people who live in the vicinity of a new mine since the price to pay reputationally and through delays and disruption, for riding rough shod over local opinion is a high one (Moody-Stuart 2006: 24).

Put another way, as Sir Mark stated in his speech to the 'Leadership Conference on Global Corporate Citizenship' in New York in 2009: 'good community relations are good for business'. But, we shall soon discover that nothing is obvious about that apparently simple statement. As I explore in later chapters the identification and demarcation of a target community is instrumental in providing moral legitimacy to corporate authority, while delimiting responsibility. For, elite groups (whether governments or transnational corporations) need a public to underwrite their position of power, an 'imagined community' which they themselves help to construct (Shore 2002: 9).

Tools such as the SEAT, the Safety, Health, Environment and Community List (SHEC-List) or the ICMM's rival version, the 'Community Development Toolkit' are designed to deliver this 'consent of the people'. The SHEC-List, for example, is an operational tool for, as one CSR executive put it, 'technical minds'. The idea is that, armed with the SHEC-List a geologist or surveyor can fly into any locality across the globe and 'remote-sense' the community for potential social or political barriers to accessing the minerals, just as they do the ground for mineral deposits. The great value of such mechanisms is that, like other market-based systems, they convert complex issues of social and environmental control and responsibility into non-political problems that merely require efficient technical solutions—something which mining companies are of course ideally placed to deliver. This normative vision of 'local community' therefore comes into being through the apparatus of 'corporate-community engagement' that the company deploys, the panoply of ethical training techniques and social investment mechanisms that emanate from the company's 'global HQ' in London.

Yet the commitment to this technocratic model of responsibility and accountability is unsettled by its very purveyors. In interviews and at conferences, senior corporate and NGO personnel constantly appealed to the notion of *trust* between the public and private sector, between companies and consumers, between civil society, business and government, so introducing an element of faith, human sensibility and above all, moral relations to the supposed technocratic market rationalism of the corporate arena. Addressing a Parliamentary Group Meeting on CSR, the chairman of Anglo invoked this reciprocal interplay of corporate virtue and voluntarism, and societal trust: 'there are a lot of issues—climate, HIV, etcetera—that are best addressed by coalitions across society—but for these to work you need *trust* . . . So you need to increase trust and trust relies on openness' (Parliamentary Group Meeting on CSR, Portcullis House, 16 December 2004). Armed with their new status as corporate citizens, big business have emerged as the standard-bearers of this moral mission to reinvigorate trust between business and society. Picking up the baton, Anglo's recently appointed CEO, Cynthia Carroll, instructed London's Chatham House, 'public and private must be aligned, *trusting* each other in collaboration' ('Corporate Leaders' Lecture Series, 'Companies, Development and Accountability', 18 June 2008). The constant invocation and reiteration of 'trust' reinforces the morally compelling vision of a collective endeavour, driven by creative voluntarism and governed by virtuous self-regulation. The invocation of trust thus works at an ideological level, whereby its power lies as much in its capacity to 'make friends' as to conceal power relations (Harriss 2003), as it recruits support to corporations, even, as we shall see, from those one might have expected would be least willing to give it.

At the same time, the reliance on a moral discourse of 'trust' runs counter to the very claim that responsibility and accountability (and transparency) can be rendered through impersonal and unassailable facts and figures, dispensing with the very need for trust. For, as Harriss points out 'a basic understanding of the idea is that to trust is to believe despite uncertainty concerning another's actions' (ibid: 757). Despite the economistic rationalism of 'the business case for CSR' and the language of universal ethical standards, appeals to *trust* and the moral authentication it embodies, become the crucial currency in the production of global corporate citizenship, and for this, alliances with NGOs and charities such as Business in the Community are vital. This highlights a broader issue: while accountability has been twinned with responsibility as the cornerstone of corporate citizenship, it is not clear to whom companies should be held accountable. Within these processes of validation and authentication, the parts played by both the recipients of this new regime of responsibility (the smiling subjects of case studies and best-practice models) and state governments are minimal. At best, accountability—or the appearance of it—is seen to be rendered to a diffuse coalition of elite NGO and private sector actors circulating in some amorphous global space which has come to represent 'international civil society'. What is missing from this picture—in which all actors are equally reduced to the status of 'stakeholder' and each appears simply as another node or hub in a global network of multi-stakeholder governance—are the relations of power and politics which define such collaborations.

From Combat to Collaboration

Corporate social responsibility, it's the badge of honour these days . . . nobody sensible would say it was a bad thing, how could it be a bad thing? (James Naughtie, Radio 4 The Today Programme, 15 January 2007).

The title of the XIXth World Trader's Tacitus Lecture delivered in February 2006 by Mark Moody-Stuart was 'Business and NGOs in Sustainable Development—*Common Cause or Endless Wars?*' In this speech he asked: 'can the two work together to *solve* major sustainable development issues such as climate change' (Moody-Stuart 2006: 23). It appears that *common cause* is winning out over *endless wars*. CSR might initially have arisen from a concern in the public domain about the overweening power of TNCs as epitomised in films such as *The Corporation* (Achbar and Abbott 2003) or books such as Klein's *No Logo* (2000); an attempt to rein in that power, born out of a call for TNCs to become more accountable for their activities. But now a shift has taken place. The CSR movement has been so fully embraced by the big multinationals that it has effected an unquestioned transition from calls to 'do no harm' to an expression of companies as active agents of global improvement, bringing in its wake not only rapprochement between NGOs and TNCs, but a whole-hearted marriage under the banner of 'partnership'. This political shift has been viewed by many as rooted in a widespread disillusionment with the failure or reluctance of governments to regulate corporate behaviour, as a result of which NGOs saw a greater possibility for change by going directly to the source, or, as Doane puts it 'by partnering with the enemy' (Doane 2005: 24). Thus an increasing number of NGOs (including Oxfam, WWF and Care) have begun partnering with or advising companies on best practice models, codes of conduct, and principles of good corporate citizenship in relation to particular ventures.

The capacity of CSR to turn former combatants into collaborators was evident at the 2002 World Summit on Sustainable Development (WSSD) in Johannesburg. 'One might have expected the mining industry to be the *whipping boy* of the summit', Anglo's Vice-President of External Affairs told me, 'but instead, we actually got a special plug for addressing these issues', as they were congratulated for their leadership on global issues such as HIV, climate change and poverty. The 2002 WSSD should in fact be seen as the culmination of a process which, Dorsey argues, began at the Rio Earth Summit, ten years earlier:

> Since the Rio Earth Summit and the Johannesburg World Summit on Sustainable Development championed public and private partnerships . . . international conservation groups opened their doors to transnational corporate leaders (Dorsey 2005: 46).

During the past two decades, when NGOs have been seen to champion pro-poor participation, sustainable livelihoods and grass-roots change as the cornerstones of development, one might have expected them, along with institutions such as the UNDP, to be somewhat more reserved in supporting the vision of development through business which CSR promotes. So what accounts for this apparent shift?

The answer lies, to some extent, in the persuasive power of the very concept of collective responsibility for a common cause. Phrases such as 'common good', 'shared values' and 'societal consensus' are key components in the public lexicon of CSR, constantly repeated by speakers from both business and civil society at CSR events and development forums, and reinforced in the multitude of reports produced on the subject. Just as Moody-Stuart argued in his speech that global problems can only be addressed by collective action, so a recent paper produced by a trio of leading NGOs (Oxfam, Civicus and the Global Action Network) stresses that 'to have global influence . . . requires a collective effort' (Waddell 2004: ii). The creative alliance between business and civil society—from the one side resources and competitiveness, from the other proximity to and knowledge of 'the people'—is offered as a far more favourable option than responsibility imposed through 'the dead hand of state regulation', as proponents of voluntary CSR often put it.

Underlying this declaration of collaborative action is a claim of common interests and ethics. This was exemplified by the Director of the Partnering Initiative, in her address to the *Ethical Corporation* conference: 'if you look at what motivates partners, we all have the same interests basically: stable societies, income generation, healthy and educated populations and strengthening the capacity of local entrepreneurs'. As the values which are seen to lie at the heart of this collaborative mission—those of enterprise, entrepreneurship and sustainability—are enshrined in global covenants, compacts and codes, they are projected as universal moral goods so further reinforcing the faith in a collective conscience. During interviews, corporate executives commonly stressed that, both as individuals and as part of a corporate body, they shared the same values as the rest of society; values which were reflected in the company's business principles: 'if you take a poll of the 100,000 employees of the company around the world—you'd come up with the average number of people who have membership of Amnesty International etc—we care about sustainability and human rights and we care about the environment so it's just a question of how we mobilize that spirit' (Executive, Anglo American).

The common target of these novel coalitions is governments in the global South, who are *talked about* at such gatherings yet are rarely present. At the *Ethical Corporation* event for example, although the conference brochure had promised to reveal 'how to avoid becoming a de facto government', representatives from Southern governments were strikingly absent from the list of participants. The lone exception was the ex-deputy finance minister of Afghanistan, now in exile in London. In contrast, as is common at such events, experts and policy-makers from Northern bilateral aid agencies including United States Agency for International Development (USAID), DFID, Gesellschaft für Technische Zusammenarbeit (GTZ) and the Danish International Development Agency (DANIDA),were all present and prominently positioned on the programme. A movement which, led by NGOs, begun with the aim of exposing, and demanding an end to, corporate social *ir*responsibility, has shifted its focus to corruption and mismanagement of resources and revenues by Southern governments at the expense of their people. This allows for campaigns against corporate misconduct to be dismissed as opportunistic activism seeking an easy target, while the focus is deflected to irresponsible governments. As the Anglo delegate at the *Ethical Corporation* conference put it:

> If you want to get at the soft under-belly of a government—why not run a media campaign against a company that operates there with the hope that they'll put pressure on the government to change. After all, it's in our interests because business prospers where there is competent and *honest* government.

Anglo's chairman hammered this point home in the company's 2005 *Report to Society*: 'people ask questions of these companies when the proceeds of industry, particularly the extractive industry, have been misspent over long periods by governments'. The blame is laid squarely with government, while the moral high ground is claimed by the company: 'It may not be our responsibility' he concluded, 'but it becomes our problem' (Anglo American 2005a: 12–13). CSR thus represents a vital resource for companies with which to engage, absorb and contain sources of resistance, reframing social and environmental challenges as part of their own corporate narrative. This was manifest at Anglo American's 2006 Annual General Meeting (AGM).

Anglo American, AGM, 25 April 2006,
Institute of Electrical Engineers, London
After a brief introduction covering the company's growth over the previous year (including a 39 percent increase in earnings due to the recent boom in commodity prices on the world market), the chairman set out the company's CSR agenda. An agenda which, according to his narrative, stemmed to a large extent from the incapacity of the governments in many of the countries in which Anglo operates: 'Some 70 percent of our operations are in developing countries, in many of them government capacities are limited or lacking, institutions are often weak and poverty is a major challenge'. In the hour or so of questions that followed the speech, seven out of the nine related directly to the company's CSR performance at various operations. These were predominantly concerned with human rights abuses resulting from the construction of mining operations in which Anglo has a significant share. They included reports of 'massive health problems' caused by

the Paso Diablo mine in Venezuela; fraudulent claims to 'free, prior and informed consent' obtained from communities in the Cordillera region of the Philippines; and the diversion of water sources in the rivers around the Cerrejon mine in Colombia. Rather than demonstrating the growing concern among investors in the 'social performance of the company' these questions were asked by individuals standing proxy for groups who had purchased a share in the company in order to gain access to Anglo's directors under the spotlight of journalists covering the AGM. While such actions have long been a tactic of activists attempting to gain the attention of large global companies, what is striking now is how companies deal with such challenges given the increasing emphasis placed on CSR.

In this case, Anglo's CSR policies and business principles (*Good Citizenship—Our Business Principles*) were deployed, asserting a common cause with those who accuse them of social irresponsibility. Activists are thanked for bringing bad practices to light which might have slipped under the company's radar and can now be addressed through their sophisticated CSR process. In most cases the chairman demonstrated, by referring to the company's business principles, that whatever misdeed has taken place explicitly contravenes their corporate values, shifting blame from the company itself to the host government or state-owned mining enterprise which manages the operation. For, in most of the cases raised by representatives at the AGM, Anglo American owned a smaller share (mostly around 25 percent) and did not to have a controlling stake in the companies which manage the mines, (many of which are state-owned mining enterprises). For example, a member of the audience asked about the repressive measures used by government security services in response to resistance among the indigenous people of Zulia, Venezuela at the Sucoy mine in which Anglo had a 24 percent share. The chairman replied that: 'Anglo American's share in Carbones de Guasare is relatively small and the company, to my knowledge, is completely controlled by the Venezuelan government. There are things which we have been, on occasion, distressed with, but we are not in a position of control . . . this is a question that you should raise with the Venezuelan government . . . it is certainly not in line with our principles, but the active party is the government of Venezuela. Thank you'.

Thus, while business is placed at the centre of the development agenda, this should not, according to this dominant narrative, be seen as a usurpation of state powers, but a rather virtuous act stepping into the vacuum left by a government's moral abdication of responsibility. Thus the chairman stated at Anglo's AGM: 'extractive revenues have sometimes been subject to whole-sale embezzlement by government . . . Whilst we cannot and should not take on responsibilities that are properly those of governments, *we cannot stand aloof from major governance and social issues in the countries where we oper-ate*'. This discourse underscores much of what is said at such conferences by executives and their NGO partners, and was the constant refrain repeated to me in interviews with Anglo personnel and reiterated in radio interviews, newspaper columns and shareholders meetings. A representative from Care International, for example, commended corporate executives at the *Ethical Corporations conference* for bringing 'best practice' and good governance to the developing countries in which they work

> In a country like Cambodia where there is so much corruption they need people like you, companies like you, to keep coming with your standards and principles. If you can make them understand at the local level, then you can raise the standards of the country through your investments.

The logic behind this project is presented as rational and wholly market-oriented, rather than political. 'The message from the business sector is blunt' explains Fred Phaswana, a non-executive director of Anglo American, 'we want to do business with you, but in various ways you make it very difficult. Let us help you do away with those difficulties' (Phaswana 2006: 62). The prob-lems, we are told, are the problems of poor governance and infrastructure, corruption and bad regulation created by weak African states. The solution is a helping hand from big business in partnership with the development in-dustry, through initiatives such as the Investment Climate Facility or the Ex-tractive Industries Transparency Initiative (EITI). The aim is to create stable, democratic and market-friendly conditions in which business can flourish, encouraging not simply foreign direct investment and the classic neoliberal 'trickle down', but a culture of market-oriented entrepreneurialism, from cor-porate giants, to street vendors. Thus Phaswana asks:

> Can business help African countries achieve a democratic, stable and *clean sys-tem of government*? . . . Business can . . . help African governments understand how to transform their countries, particularly when it comes to *rooting out corrupt practices*, the costs of which inhibit business creation and operation. Those governments must, of course, *be willing listeners* (Phaswana 2006: 65).

Here business is represented as a neutral standard-bearer, purveyors of best ethical practice guiding African governments on this road to prosperity and betterment.

By shifting scrutiny on to governments, the CSR movement enlists support from both NGOs, and bilateral development agencies such as USAID or DFID where good-governance has become the current creed[19]. The result is an elite coalition of 'global' actors, drawn from TNCs, NGOs and assorted other development institutions, who claim to subscribe to common, indeed universal, values such as democracy, freedom, enterprise and efficiency. And, in so doing, they extend a kind of collective moral guardianship over people in areas of the world where, we are told, 'governments are either incapable or unwilling to carry out this role, or worse still, steal the means by which they are supposed to carry out the task?' (Moody-Stuart 2006: 28).

Thus moral authority is not simply claimed by multinational corporations (MNCs) themselves, rather it is endowed upon them, along with the responsibility to ensure that the revenues they pay are put to good developmental purpose rather than into the pockets of corrupt leaders. As all parties appear to unite behind this hegemonic duty of care, the role of TNCs as champions of good-governance is formally authenticated through multi-stakeholder partnerships such as the EITI[20]. This is ensured in no small part, by the support of non-corporate actors who provide a legitimising voice of consent and consensus, highlighting the power of this constant appeal to a shared vision and collective societal responsibility. This is not to say that CSR has effectively stamped out opposition, criticism or anti-corporate activism, nor that international NGOs operate in a homogenous realm of 'global civil society'. As the campaigners outside the Human Rights and Business Conference described above (and similar delegations at shareholder meetings) demonstrate, people continue to challenge motives and expose fraudulent claims to responsibility. Rather, what this suggests is that as corporations are established as instruments of social improvement, rather than exploitation and profit, opposition to this orthodoxy, and other alternatives, becomes further marginalised from the development mainstream of policy-making and power.

Compelling visions of global partnership in the service of local development have proved a particularly powerful tool for recruiting support from non-corporate actors, while marginalising dissenters from the arenas in which these cosmopolitan alliances are forged. Particular NGOs thus emerge as 'partners of choice', or as Patrick Leighton one of Anglo's top CSR executives put it:

I would draw the line between the big and small single-issue NGOs. For example, groups like Earthworks, Care, WWF,—with whom our subsidiary Mondi has a very successful partnership—we can have a rational discussion with. But at the same time, other branches continue to insist on critiquing companies like us whatever we do. Still, it's far from the battleground of the 1990s.

Meanwhile WWF asserts a vision of common values and solutions with companies that once might have been the target of their 'clean-up' campaigns:

> conservation Partners are multinational companies that contribute substantial funding to WWF's global conservation work. WWF understand that corporations have their share of things to answer for but the solutions to key conservation problems will either be *common solutions* or they won't be solutions at all[21].

NGOs who do not embrace this new process are accused of being partisan, 'incidental' or 'purely opportunistic' (Waddell 2004: i). This was manifest at Chatham House's 2006 CSR conference on 'Emerging Rules and Evolving Responsibilities' (London 13–14 March 2006[22]). The atmosphere at the event was triumphant, expressed in soundbites such as 'the most effective agent of change is enterprise!' and 'we believe the only way to achieve change is to trust each other and to dehorn the devil' from TNC, NGO and even union personnel present. Up-beat speeches championing the role of business in sustainable development were given by Malcolm Wicks (Minister for Energy and CSR at the time), the Executive Head of the UN Global Compact, an Associate Director of BITC, the Director of the International Labour Organization (ILO), as well as senior executives from a variety of TNCs such as Total and SAB-Miller. Amongst these, a presentation was given by Bill Eckhart, the Director of Communications of the world's largest advertising conglomerate.

Eckhart's presentation focused on a selection of advertisements which the firm had produced for Coca Cola, BP and Chevron Texaco. With glossy visuals he explained how this form of advertising was a crucial vehicle by which responsible TNCs could 'educate customers and communities' on responsible living in areas such as the environment and health. A flow diagram with companies and government at the top, media in the middle and 'communities' on the bottom illustrated the flow of ethical expertise and knowledge. The presentation was followed by a number of comments from the audience in support of this form of 'ethical education' through publicity and consumption.

No critical questions or comments were made. As a participant at the conference, I asked (a little hesitantly) whether TNCs such as BP, Coca Cola and Chevron Texaco—all companies who had recently been accused of serious environmental and social misconduct—were in a position to provide 'ethical education' to customers and communities. The response was curt, though perhaps not wholly surprising:

> These companies are actually trying to *do something*, unlike the reckless NGOs who destroy brand and reputation with unfounded accusations.

Much more surprising was that during the next coffee break I was approached by two representatives from WWF London, one of whom said:

> We were so pleased when you asked your question. We were hopping in our seats. It's so difficult when you come from an NGO, because you can't say these things because they just dismiss it as, 'oh you're the reckless NGO' and then the audience think it too. So you have to sit quietly or you risk the credibility of your organisation.

Norms of appropriate behaviour within such collaborations are firmly established, and collaborators (particularly those with the most to lose) are understandably reluctant to transgress them. The performance of consensus is all important, and equally ritualised. Thus the expected product of these engagements is, at the very least, demonstrable collaboration, but preferably a clear consensus. Clearly, what appears as a process of mutual collaboration, is dependent on the capacity of such forums to impose consensus through silencing dissent. Those who challenge the orthodoxy of collective goals, risk being labelled as more interested in 'throwing stones' than 'making progress'. Thus a recent article by a leading CSR commentator in the *Ethical Corporation* magazine stated, 'for every constructive builder of change, there are more throwing stones from the sidelines' (Baker 2007). Many TNCs, such as Anglo American, have so fully embraced CSR that critique against them appears like a denial of the collective responsibility and shared vision for which the companies themselves are striving, rising above the fray, putting aside partisanship. Who wants to be seen to undermine that?

Furthermore the speed with which contemporary transnational business operates, demands that solutions to social and environmental challenges are developed with similar momentum and efficiency. But the demand for active 'win-win solutions' tends to shut out debate and critique as cynical, ideological or just a waste of precious time, as opposed to constructive, engaged and practical. This was made clear at BITC's 2004 Annual General Meeting in the resounding tones of Nigel Griffith, another former UK Labour government minister for CSR:

> I want to combat cynicism! I want to make sure that great companies, especially great British companies, are not knocked off their pedestal by some cheap journalism or political activism . . . I want to make sure that our NGOs are working with business on a common agenda so that British companies retain their competitive and ethical edge.

Similarly, at the *Ethical Corporation* conference, a delegate from the WBCSD celebrated the 'bravery' of six UK-based NGOs who had publicly transformed from 'campaigners', to launch a sustainability strategy in partnership with the former target of their campaigns (a leading mining company): 'they have gone from critic to partner with business and they've launched it publicly showing you how much more you can achieve by working together'[23].

The spheres of legitimate action (partnership with business for the common cause) and illegitimate action (misguided anti-corporate campaigning) are clearly delineated, one as ethical, the other as unethical:

> Greenpeace, for instance, has an extremely effective and thoughtful policy group on climate. This is far removed from its dinghy and abseiling image, but if Greenpeace does not have some action involving dinghies and banners from buildings every year or so, much of their membership gets restless and thinks its gone *soft* . . . Just as in the commercial world, competition for customers and funds, or just over-enthusiasm for a particular cause can lead to behaviour which *I consider to be unethical* (Moody-Stuart 2006: 31).

Here Moody-Stuart suggests that the competitive market is created not through the scramble for funding from corporate donors (which in turn affects a process of political co-option through patronage) but through restless members demanding anti-corporate stunts. The strongly instrumentalist focus on 'problem-solving' further narrows the space for critique. Where criticism is voiced, it tends to challenge the sincerity of a claim to corporate responsibility, rather than the parameters of the debate, or the underlying principles[24]. Anglo American and Survival International, for example, can be seen to draw on a shared register and a collective pool of metaphors, references and concepts in the struggle over responsibility, even if they are on opposite sides of an issue.

Thus the power of CSR lies not simply in its capacity to sideline critical voices, but to *colonise* the discourse and, in some sense, the identities of critics. The capacity of CSR to re-appropriate the language and symbols of its critics as a corporate resource draws some of even the most vocal campaigners of corporate irresponsibility into its project. Henrietta Moore notes that:

> The very same language, concepts, and images that are used by activists to try and preserve the ozone layer and prevent environmental catastrophe are employed by multinational corporations to promote images of global responsibility (Moore 2004: 82).

This is reinforced by the language of global values enshrined in international codes and conventions, such as the UN Global Compact, which establish an official canon of concepts, terms and ideas to be reproduced in the policy goals and action plans of corporations, NGOs and consulting firms lending them further authority in a process of mutual, if unintentional, legitimisation.

Differences between parties or barriers to collaboration are framed as variations in register, organisational 'culture' or ethos rather than in value orientations, interests or ideology. Thus the emphasis is on 'getting the language right' (Senior Executive, Anglo American, 13 October 2004), while the common cause is assumed. Similarly the mass of guides, toolkits, 'how-to' manuals and even postgraduate degrees[25], devoted to cross-sector collaboration, focus on overcoming 'cultural differences' which obstruct successful partnering: 'negotiation in the corporate world is seen as hardball, as winning and losing . . . whereas with partnerships, it's about coming to an agreement' (Tennyson 2005).

And yet, in order to compete in this elite market of social virtue for both 'moral' and economic capital, actors must take on many of the forms and practices of commercial markets upon which the industry for corporate responsibility is, ultimately, contingent (Dezalay and Garth 1996). On one side, TNCs compete for index rankings, awards and high profile partnerships, in pursuit of the rather more intangible resource of 'moral' capital. On the other, as corporations have become an increasingly important source of donor funding, NGOs are in competition for a more obvious resource—money. Moody-Stuart described one half of this competitive market for humanitarianism as an effective mechanism for imposing rigour and professionalism on NGOs: 'they compete for funding every bit as aggressively as commercial businesses compete for customers, for their jobs depend on it' (Moody-Stuart 2006: 31). The logic of 'the market' is seen as an unambiguously positive influence, so we are told, on the undisciplined world of humanitarianism and aid[26]. The director of the Partnering Initiative spoke of the need to focus on applying business drivers to 'aid agencies in this competitive marketplace of creative chaos' (Ethical Corporation Conference 18–19 October 2005).

Thus the CSR arena is characterised as much by intense competition as collaboration. Groups strive be selected as the donor's chosen collaborator and win hard-fought funding. In order to do so, NGOs must compete to be seen as the embodiment of ecological virtue, sustainable development or human rights by maintaining a high profile through participation in international conferences, publications such as practical manuals or position papers, and crucially, through the visibility of their personnel within these corporate domains. The symbolic capital they earn through this recognition is translated into financial capital through donor funding. But the relationship between the commercial markets and the market for humanitarianism is not simply a dualistic matter of conversion. The picture becomes complicated when we look at the other side of this process of exchange and conversion—the donors who are in this case, TNCs.

The market model of competitive responsibility attempts to banish conventional ideas of philanthropy from the picture. Just as the director of BITC remarked, 'we are a customer-driven organisation' (the 'customers' being their corporate partners/clients), so Sir Mark Moody-Stuart while delivering the Tacitus Lecture described NGOs as 'enterprises' that *'provide services to their donors* and supporters, whether in effective delivery of development funding or in carrying out a mission on behalf of their members' (Moody-Stuart 2006: 31). Just as the language of partnership obscures the workings of patronage, so the representation of NGOs as enterprises competing in a market for corporate customers denies the relations of power, dependence and frequently deference which are generated by these corporate-charity alliances in the service of CSR. Both the partnership paradigm and the market model attempt to claim CSR as a radical break from the legacy of corporate philanthropy, the former evoking an ideal of collaboration for common cause, the latter appealing to the economistic discourse of the 'business case for CSR'. Both attempt to recast donor and recipient as partners or as customer and vendor.

Yet as is hinted at by Moody-Stuart's slippage into the terminology of 'donor', the dynamics of benefactor and beneficiary prevail: 'without business, there is no development aid, and no money generated to *donate* to NGOs. NGOs did not thrive under communism' (ibid: 30). Thus he seems, perhaps unintentionally, to have slipped from an economistic model of partnership within a competitive market for sustainable development, to an implicit affirmation of the power relations which define what Stirrat and Henkel have termed 'the development gift' (Stirrat and Henkel 1997). The implication is that in order to receive much needed donor funding from TNCs—'*donations*' as Moody-Stuart puts it—NGOs must strive to endorse the centrality of business. In return, this 'alliance' provides TNCs with symbolic capital, which endows their influence with a moral authority. After all, the great value of partnership is that it affords donors a degree of authenticity, a sense that 'we are of and for the people' (ibid: 75).

When it comes to transnational corporations, claims to being 'for the people' (if perhaps not 'of the people') are projected and renewed through the performative practices of CSR, rituals of corporate virtue which, as I have shown here, obscure the relations of power and maintain the illusion of mutual independence that sustain the myth of partnership. The process of co-option, achieved both through the persuasive moral discourse of partnership and the coercive power of giving and withholding funding where the donor sees fit, facilitates the wider expansion and uptake of the kind of business-driven approach to development that CSR advocates. Other alternatives, which once might have been the domain of development NGOs, now disappear from the picture as does the fact that, in many situations, the demands of social and environmental justice require the development movement to challenge rather than endorse the interests of big capital.

'What's Good for Business, Is Good for Development!'

Kofi Annan's assertion of the primacy of markets as the solution to poverty provides a dominant vision of development and empowerment through access to markets—a vision which fully accords with the directives and interests of the neo-liberal political economy. By claiming the happy coincidence of doing good business and doing good—'what's good for business is good for development!'[27]—commitment to the market logic of maximisation is not only maintained, but is endowed with a moral legitimacy and celebrated as the 'win-win solution' for which the development industry has been searching.

At the same time, the landscape of CSR appears to be made up of transparent arenas of competition, diversity and political pluralism in which corporate executives 'confess' past misconduct or errors in judgement, and explain the best practice regimes which they have since developed in partnership with one NGO or another. Indeed the apparent plurality, inclusiveness and collaborative ethos of such arenas serves to create a sense of shared responsibility at work. However, the appearance of negotiation and discussion surrounding how companies should engage the poor has the effect of removing core market values (such as the sanctity of shareholder value) from the table and rendering them immutable and incontestable. Thus Blowfield argues that while CSR may affect corporate behaviour, it leaves untouched these 'non-negotiables', the 'fundamental values of the contemporary capitalist enterprise' (Blowfield 2005: 520, 522). I would go further. Far from CSR leaving intact the unchanging workings of the neoliberal market, it plays a vital role in offering a replenished source of strength to corporate capitalism, by endowing it not only with an ethical countenance, but with a moral purpose. As TNCs incorporate sustainable development within their projects, they gain access to a powerful social resource: partnership. CSR thus provides them with a platform to forge alliances with diverse actors in the development arena (including many who previously would have possessed divergent agendas and conflicting ideologies), enabling them to incorporate social challenges and counter-hegemonic voices, and pave the way for development to be reframed according to their interests (see Shamir 2004).

I have argued here, that the performative and even ritualistic dimensions of CSR practice serve not only to authenticate and celebrate TNCs as agents of social improvement, but also to establish the rules of participation in this realm of global governance. Claims to social responsibility have become shibbolithic, a declaration of common purpose and global citizenship, with which corporations win a seat at (the head of) the table of international development policy and planning. Contrary to mainstream critics of CSR, who see such performance merely as an exercise in corporate branding or reputation management, these theatres of virtue (and the codes standards and initiatives that emanate from them) manufacture a form of consensus which tends to marginalise alternative visions of development through the mechanisms of creative collaboration. As later chapters explore, this discourse of collective responsibility and the practices of partnership it generates proves an equally important resource for furthering corporate interests within the context of national politics and local development planning.

This chapter has shown how the marriage of 'global' values and 'local' practice is constantly performed as a key component of corporate citizenship. In turn, claims to global interconnectivity under-written by shared values are mobilised to assert the universal applicability of particular corporate practices, and the authority they bear, in diverse localities. The formula, 'think global, act local', serves to decontextualise and depoliticise corporate responsibility, producing a vision of corporate citizenship based on a reified notion of 'the global' (as a set of disembedded supranational networks through which CSR is executed) and an idealised portrait of 'the local' (where it is put into practice). Yet, as we move in closer in the following chapters to look at CSR in the context of a particular corporate genealogy and all its historical specificities, it becomes clear that the practice of CSR is deeply embedded in the national politics of South Africa, to where I turn now. The power of CSR lies not simply in claims to a generalised global corporate citizenship, but in its malleability as a discourse that can respond to, reshape and incorporate the political-economic and social dynamics of national transformation. Thus the state—so conspicuously absent from both the cosmopolitan arenas in which corporate citizenship is forged and the scholarly analysis of it—is crucial to understanding how CSR fits into a broader project of renegotiating and re-inscribing the company's economic, social and political position within the context of South Africa. Here, CSR takes on a distinctly national outlook and patriotic flavour, providing the company with a new discourse through which to reinvent the legacy of its past and reposition its present, as it strives to assert its status as both global corporate citizen, and 'Proudly South African'.

2 'Mines Are for Men, Not for Money'

A History of Giving

And they take heart too, for Sir Ernest
Oppenheimer, one of the great men of the mines, has
also said that it need not be so . . . They want to hear
your voice again, Sir Ernest Oppenheimer. Some of
them applaud you, and some of them say thank God
for you, in their hearts, even at their bedsides. For
mines are for men, not for money
(Cry, the Beloved Country, Alan Paton, 1948).

IN HIS OFFICE AT 44 MAIN STREET, Johannesburg, Henry Hammond declared, 'at the end of the day, it's about being the company that we are and being the company that we want to be and we are proud to be. We have a long history of CSR in South Africa and we're proud of that'. This sense of pride in Anglo American's role in South Africa, past and present, resounded equally from most of the executives, who like Hammond, have worked in the company's Johannesburg command centre for over a decade. Central to this is the construction of a collective corporate memory of dynastic philanthropic tradition; of Rhodes scholars-turned-Anglo executives, committed in equal measure to the company, to public service and to South Africa; and of corporate anti-apartheid activism through 'doing good by stealth'. At the foundation of this historical representation, the personal and corporate philanthropy of the Oppenheimer family, and their status as pioneers of progress and industry place them in the role of a South African Rockefeller or Carnegie[1]. Anglo appears, as one ex-Anglo employee put it, 'part American corporate giant, part Oxbridge senior common room'; the legendary marriage of 'US money and British style, they were somehow above the fray'.

Such mythologising—which at first seems strikingly antithetical to the harsh realities of the mining business—equips the 'corporate citizen' with a fitting history and moral self. Narratives of individual responsibility driven by *personal* morality, underpin (and at times clash with) the contemporary expression of a *collective* corporate responsibility: the modern anthropomorphic construction of the company as 'good corporate citizen', animated by the myths of magnanimous individuals who, we are told, once inhabited it. Corporate responsibility is at times represented as old as the company itself, inseparable from its past, as executives recounted a version of Anglo history which claims the status of corporate citizen long before the term was even coined.

This chapter is concerned with the production of a corporate vision of social responsibility and the way in which the company strives to assert its identity and position within South Africa through such a vision. Through the course of my fieldwork, it became clear that the constant narration of what the Anglo name 'means' and 'stands for' was more than mere corporate rhetoric or nostalgic myth-making. It was a discursive component in the broader project of re-positioning the company in the national arena of contemporary South Africa: a project for which CSR provides a crucial platform.

In the accounts of Henry Hammond and his colleagues there was an affectionate yet anachronistic portrait of a company which recalls the model prescribed by Theodore Houser, then President of Sears-Roebuck, in his 1957 book *Big Business and Human Values*. Here, corporations are far more than vehicles of financial gain, and their leaders appear as statesmen and scholars more than managers: 'those endowed with the ability to lead these great organizations should begin to conceive of their remuneration partly in terms of the satisfaction of making a real contribution to national progress' (Houser 1957: 28)[2]. This seems strikingly at odds with the now commonplace notion that the modern corporation hardly resembles a coherent institutional entity at all, but rather, is an amorphous set of financial relationships, barely more than the sum of its shareholders. 'How did we get to this point' asks Karen Ho in her ethnography of Wall Street, 'where corporations have shifted from complex, bureaucratic, social firms into liquid networks of shareholders?' (Ho 2009: 125). These liquid corporate entities are represented as historically, as well as socially, disembedded. In the world of neoliberal corporate capitalism, we are told, novelty and 'forward-thinking' reign, sweeping away history as dead weight in the drive to ever-increasing efficiencies (see for example Cefkin 2009; Ho 2009).

But all companies have a history; a history not just of making money, but one which is defined by and embedded in a particular corporate genealogy and set of national and social relations. In both formal and informal encounters, the narratives of Anglo corporate employees were shaped by recurring motifs, tropes and key narratives; a dominant vocabulary through which the company, its values and its actions, are represented to the world outside its walls. Such accounts involved various, and at times seemingly contradictory portraits of the company. Anglo appears, on the one hand, as a central part of the South African establishment, more like the Church or perhaps the Bank of England, than a mining business[3]. According to this construction the company projects itself as the intellectual and cultural pinnacle of South Africa, beneficent pioneers of change committed to the welfare of their workers and the communities in which the company operates. On the other hand, the company is represented as a tough and technocratic extractive enterprise. The tension between the anglo-colonial vision of the company, and the image of hard, technical men at the coal face—between, as one executive put it 'silver spoon and street-fighter'—continues to be monumentalized in the public discourse of its executives and mid-level managers both in the boardrooms of its headquarters and at the mineshafts of its operations. There is, of course, a power in this tension. Viewed from a more instrumental perspective, one can see the discursive construction of the company as janus-faced: on one side an 'Oxbridge senior common room' looking towards social responsibility and national development; on the other a ruthlessly efficient agent of mineral extraction. The moral authority accrued from the former proves as crucial to the success, survival and reproduction of corporate power, as the economic might achieved from the latter.

Foundational myths are important then, not only in the construction of corporate identity, but in naturalising the company's position in the broader historical landscape of industrial capitalism in South Africa. Here philanthropy plays a key role, neither as the antithesis to the logic of capitalism, nor as the company's conscience, but as the warm-blooded twin to the cold business of mineral extraction and the mechanism through which Anglo's economic and political hegemony in South Africa for much of the 20th century is authenticated. As the founding entrepreneur is cast as champion philanthropist, the constant evocation of the company's history of giving provides a crucial moralising discourse. Jesse Palsetia similarly notes the importance of philanthropy to 19th century Parsi Indian merchants striving to establish their positions within the colonial economy: 'philanthropy becomes one of a set of political semiotics and attributes alongside loyalty, gallantry, honesty, and trustworthiness' (Palsetia 2005: 198). The centrality of moral relations in the establishment, expansion and legitimation of corporate capitalism, challenges the economic orthodoxy that the evolution of the modern market economy involved severing the realm of business from that of moral values and social relations.

Thus, the power and authority of the company in South Africa derives not only from its economic strength, but from the way it is constructed ideologically through the narratives of executives and official company declarations of business principles, mission statements and 'core values'. Such narratives present the company as an engine of growth and industry, an agent of empowerment, and midwife of democracy: the legacy upon which its modern-day CSR is, we are told, built. CSR past and present is thus mobilised to create a history which purifies the past and reinvents the company. Monumentalising the past is of course a central strategy by which elite groups naturalise their position in the present (Herzfeld 2000). While this is often observed in respect to political leaders, historical narrative, tradition and not least nostalgia are resources we scarcely expect to find in giant mining companies. Here, the 'monumentalising' is done, not only through the grand edifices of 44 and 45 Main Street, the Ernest Oppenheimer tower in Soweto, or the mine hospital in Welkom, but through the history they tell of themselves and the company as a 'force for progress' and social improvement. Yet, at other times CSR is employed precisely in order to disassociate Anglo American from the brutal paternalism of apartheid-era labour regimes and divest the company of the legacy of its hotly debated role in the apartheid economy of exploitation and racial oppression. This is achieved, I suggest, not so much through a deliberate corporate 'amnesia', as David Fig suggests (2005), but through the re-telling of a history of philanthropy, morality and social responsibility. The past, it turns out, is a vital and rich asset for corporations.

Dynastic Traditions

During the course of my discussions with Anglo executives in South Africa, I was struck by how frequently they drew on a nostalgic image of the company's golden age spanning the four decades from the 1950s to the 1980s. It was not a *new* era of global corporate responsibility and ethical capitalism of which they spoke, but rather a collective memory of beneficence, virtue and progressive mine management. A time when, according to the narratives of corporate executives, honour and philanthropy flowed freely and the company was staffed at its senior levels by upstanding Rhodes scholars, under the direction of the revered Oppenheimers—Ernest and his son Harry[4]—or one of their successors, most notably, Gavin Relly. Yet this golden age coincided with a time when the brutalities of apartheid South Africa, and its labour repressive economy, would surely make the social responsibility and benevolence of which they spoke impossible.

This romance, albeit a brutal one, is part of a broader national history-telling around mining. At the centre of this fascination with gold and diamond mining stands Ernest Oppenheimer, who appears as founder of modern industrial South Africa, benefactor, philanthropist, civiliser and politician[5]; as 'emperor of metals' or 'king of diamonds' (Gregory 1962: ix). This myth has been told and retold so effectively that it has firmly established the status of the Oppenheimers as makers of South African history. Swept away by this romantic myth-making, Bill Jamieson, in his history of Anglo American, describes the Oppenheimers as the 'nearest the Republic has to a royal family', and Anglo American as the Oppenheimer's own 'patriarchal, precious metals empire' (Jamieson 1990: 3, 5). Reinforcing the mystique he adds, 'if the Oppenheimers hadn't existed they'd have had to have been invented' (ibid: 6).

The 'culture' of the company was a recurring theme in the accounts of long-term present and former executives of its Johannesburg offices, who conjured an image of an organisation populated and powered by senior staffers who devoted their own personal time or money to philanthropic gestures. Thus they assert a historical marriage of big business and morality, claiming an old moral code underpinning and shaping all Anglo action and all Anglo's people. This was manifest in the account of Nicholas Summerson, an Anglo Director of twenty years:

> (Harry) Oppenheimer encouraged all his senior executives to give time to politics, communities, schools—it was expected that they would engage. And I think that was very much the culture imbued by the Oppenheimers and especially Harry Oppenheimer who I think was a great man, or Gavin Relly— the chairman when I joined. I think he was a great South African because he was rooted in the country, he was interested in conservation, he was, of course, a vice chairman, or vice-president of the World Wildlife Fund so he used to see the Duke of Edinburgh and Prince Bernard of Holland but he was a great giver in the *South African sense* . . . The culture was very strong . . . it was imbued in the leadership . . . I'm very grateful to Anglo because I think the first thing one has to say is the quality of thought is really quite extraordinary there—you've got people who are of a very high intellectual calibre and so the culture which was very informal, very understated, there were elements still of the Oxbridge tradition there.

And yet nearing the end of our conversation, almost as a disclaimer unsettling the pride and loyalty he had voiced earlier, Summerson warned: 'one must beware of the mythologizing—sometime, for PR, and in positioning Anglo in market systems—I have utilized that'.

The motif of the company as a family club recurred in the accounts of my informants in Anglo, an expression of a corporate paternalism and patronage which seemed simultaneously anachronistic in the world of modern business and central to its internal, and as we shall see in later chapters external, workings. Indeed, the ethos and practice, of familial, or in this case, family-like relations, are instrumental, rather than antithetical to the workings of corporate capitalism[6]. In the case of Anglo, while the actual kinship of the Oppenheimer family looms large as the company's foundation myth (and Harry Oppenheimer's grandsons continue to embody the dynastic legacy, albeit in a less directly influential manner as non-executive directors[7]), the familial paternalism that continues to be evoked is a virtual kinship knitting the company together through the common experience of Anglo's illustrious graduate trainee programme. Karen Ho similarly emphasises the importance of social relations which connect Wall Street with a network of Ivy League Alumnae (Ho 2009: 13), and we might well expect to find corresponding kinds of virtual corporate kinship through what is euphemistically called the 'Milk Round' of job recruitment from Oxbridge for elite positions in the City of London. However, as we see in the next chapter, this nostalgic vision of the company prevalent among Anglo's seasoned top-level executives in Johannesburg has been challenged, to some extent, by the directives of the Black Economic Empowerment (BEE) scorecard and the national imperatives of 'transformation' in the ranks of corporate management.

Still, the prevailing discourse of corporate responsibility in the corridors of Anglo Johannesburg, and to a lesser extent London, emphasised personal loyalty, generosity and familial bonds over and above the technocratic bureaucracy and new managerial instruments of ethical business (reporting mechanisms, socio-economic toolkits, policy frameworks and so on). Sebastian Hansen, a former executive at Anglo Johannesburg who had been through the company's graduate training scheme in the mid 1980s and stayed with them for twenty years, also alluded to 'the family club' commenting, 'that is why, we were all very *fond* of the company, because behind the meaningless numbers there was this human element'.

Like Summerson, Ingrid Hamilton, another long-term executive at Anglo Johannesburg, spoke of her days as a Rhodes scholar at Oxford. Torn between academic life and Anglo, she explained, she picked Anglo: 'History was my great passion, but Anglo was really a centre of thought and progress in South Africa'. Central to this construction of Anglo as a bastion of intellectualism was *Optima*. This journal, which has been produced by Anglo American and the De Beers group of companies since 1951, appears as a testament to the corporation's aspirations beyond extraction; its desire to be known not simply as a mining company. The interests of the journal are wide. Topics ranged from articles on South African history and art by well-known public intellectuals, to social and political commentary. The language—and politics—of these articles and opinion-pieces change over the course of the journal's fifty years from, for example, 'The Racial Gulf in South Africa' (Lovett 1955) and 'Raising the Standard of South Africa's Urban Natives' (Carr 1959); to 'South Africa's Troubled Townships' (Motau 1985) and 'Building a Strong and Prosperous Africa—the Role of Business' (Wickstead 2005). These articles are intermixed with highly technical articles on mining. The image of the company's cosmopolitan intellectualism, stretching beyond the borders of South Africa, is conveyed through articles by in-house Anglo executives such as 'The Achievements of Japan' by Michael O'Dowd (1970). Under the title is written, 'a manager of Anglo American Corporation . . . (O'Dowd's) special interest in economic history lead him recently to make an extended study tour of Japan' (O'Dowd 1970: 142).

At the very top sat Harry Oppenheimer, his status as patron of South African academy and arts publicly demonstrated by his chancellorship of the University of Cape Town along with the development of his own personal library—the Brenthurst Collection (Brenthurst being the Johannesburg estate of the Oppenheimer family), for which he purchased the only complete record of Mandela's Rivonia Trial from its lead prosecutor, Percy Yutar (Frankel 1999: 305). Elevated to a position far beyond that of philanthropist, much of the historical literature has placed Harry Oppenheimer in a direct line of ascendancy from Cecil Rhodes as African imperialist and ruler. In his biography *Oppenheimer and Son* (which was commissioned by Harry himself), Anthony Hocking describes King Moshoeshoe II of Lesotho conferring an honorary degree on Harry at the University of Botswana, Lesotho and Swaziland:

> The occasion was significant in that Harry was being honoured not for the sake of the corporations he headed, but for what he was as a man . . . You had the feeling as you watched Harry being capped and rising to accept the congratulations of King Moshoeshoe and the applause of the other crowned heads, that history was in the making. In the footsteps of Cecil John Rhodes, Mlamlakanzi of the Matabele, Harry Frederik Oppenheimer was in his rightful place among the all-powerful Kings of Africa (Hocking 1973: 489).

Philanthropy thus becomes twin to the violence of corporate imperialism and re-source extraction, the two glossed into a sanitized portrait of colonial capitalism.

However, at the heart of this reverential myth-making is the company's founding father, Sir Ernest Oppenheimer himself. In another equally adula-tory biography of Oppenheimer (though not, in this case, commissioned by its own subject), Theodore Gregory wrote: 'no more magnificent memorial to his memory can be imagined than the great hospital at Welkom' (Gregory 1962: 581). Addressing the crowd as he laid the hospital's foundation stone on 18 December 1950, Ernest Oppenheimer staked his claim as pioneer of socially responsible mine management and mineworker health: 'only by giv-ing natives the best hospitalisation, the best accommodation generally, and the best of food nourishment can we make them contented citizens who will contribute towards making this a very happy country' (quoted in Hocking 1973: 322). He returned to this theme in his speech to Anglo shareholders at the annual general meeting the following year:

> Both from the humanitarian viewpoint and from the standpoint of the practi-cal interests of the industry; it is important that the closest attention be given to the health and well-being of our native employees (Ernest Oppenheimer, 22 June 1951, quoted in Gregory 1962: 581).

In his history of the Ernest Oppenheimer hospital, the hospital's first chief Di-rector, Dr JHG van Blommestein tells of the dignitaries and journalists who visited from abroad to see this pioneering example of modern working condi-tions in the mining industry:

> After the completion of the Ernest Oppenheimer Hospital at a time when South Africa was not in particularly good odour with the rest of the world an effort was being made to promote trade relations with overseas countries and publicize the many advantages we had to offer. As a result a constant stream of important people and representatives of various institutions were being in-vited to come and see for themselves. By this time, the Hospital had become a showpiece of the Southern Hemisphere, not only in its design and size but because it was devoted solely to the health and welfare of the Bantu mine-workers and the families of such Bantu as hold higher positions on the mines (van Blommestein 1971: 105).

But, this picture of enlightened industrial philanthropy and humanitarian man-agement was disrupted, and another side of the mining business revealed. Van

Blommestein goes on: 'during a visit of representatives of the world press imagine my feelings when I heard one of our well-known engineers airily remarking in the mortuary: "one of our operating theatres"' (van Blommestein 1971: 105).

The doctor's account serves once again to highlight the dualistic representation of the identity of the mining company—on the one hand a pioneering institution led by visionary philanthropists bringing progress and 'upliftment' to its workers. On the other hand, a harsh and technical world of mining dominated by engineers and technical men focused solely on extraction at any cost:

> First and foremost we're here to dig stuff out of the ground, get the valuable metal out of it and sell it. We're not educators, we're not trainers, but we've had to become so (Senior Executive, Anglo American, London).

The image of Anglo as a tough, and technocratic mining company seems at odds with the stories of the intellectualism, culture and philanthropy of the senior executives who appear distanced from or untainted by the harsh realities of the mining business. This polarised representation of the company provides a framework through which company executives and managers narrated their own position and identity within the company. The so-called 'coal-face', the industrial domain of mine management, was held up as the foil to the cosmopolitan, 'socially-enlightened' world of the corporate offices, and vice versa.

These two apparently contradictory representations of the company should, rather, be viewed as complementary, each the perfect counter-balance to the other. The philanthropic aspirations of the company as patron of arts, people and society in general provide a form of cleansing for the company and its directors from the gritty and ruthless business of extraction. Indeed, these older forms of corporate philanthropy could be equated with the kind of moral purification of which anthropologists concerned with the penetration of capitalist economics into 'other' forms of exchange have long been interested (see for example Bloch and Parry 1989; Toren 1989; Hutchinson 1992). They not only offer a form of moral cleansing to the giver, but form the basis of a relationship between benefactor and beneficiary. I will return to this theme and its connections to the practice of contemporary CSR in Chapter 6. At the same time, the ability to 'give' is dependent on the ability to make profits. In order to do so and maintain the confidence of shareholders the company must project an image of single-minded focus on profit-maximisation. Crucially, this duality reveals the mutual interdependence of moral practice and market interests. Through these seemingly antithetical representations, the company simultaneously reaffirms its status as world leader in extraction, and projects itself as committed to the society in which it operates, authenticating its influence in the social and political sphere.

In CSR, it would seem, the company has found the perfect contemporary register with which to reformulate those older claims to responsibility, now cleansed of its former colonial and paternalistic resonances. Yet the concept of CSR marks a significant shift from the philanthropic endeavours of individual patrons to a collective, or corporate responsibility. The narratives of a 'golden age' of Anglo are inhabited by grand individuals: the Harry Oppenheimers or Gavin Rellys who were seen to inspire others with their own personal sense of philanthropy, or as Gavin Relly had put it, to urge their managers and executives to 'get their hands dirty':

> Employees particularly should be discouraged from the comfortable assumption that, because they work for a company which has a good social profile it somehow excuses them from getting their own hands dirty. They can learn much from involvement in *good works* (Relly 1982: iii).

In contrast to this, at the centre of the contemporary discourse of CSR lies the notion of 'the good company' as an entity of its own, independent of the people who inhabit it, a moral being in its own right: 'a corporate citizen'. In a recent in-house report on Anglo American's Social Investment Fund in South Africa it is 'the Fund that cares' rather than the people who run it: 'Anglo American hears you; Anglo American cares' the report tells us (Robbins 2001: 23). This compels us to ask what kind of a 'person' the company is rather than, what kind of people make up the company. With the shift towards 'global integration' under the banner of 'global corporate citizenship' has come the evolution of a new technocratic framework through which the company's CSR or more broadly sustainable development mission is articulated. While the vision of the company inhabited by the ghosts of 'great men of business' and their personal epic endeavours, persists in the corridors of Main Street[8], this new managerial discourse recasts CSR in the economistic register of 'responsible competitiveness', and 'shareholder value', in an attempt to reaffirm market rationalism—rather than moral sensibility—as the bottom line to CSR.

Indeed, Summerson spoke with nostalgia about the end to individual creativity and beneficence wrought by the new age of an internationalised CSR movement:

I think paradoxically—elements of that culture have been lost—while we may be more systems orientated now. You get professional CSR people—but much of their life is taken up with evaluation, monitoring, reporting and I've always been a bit of a critic of the dangers of taking form over substance. I think maybe it's been lost a little bit, that creativity, because as we globalise as we become more like other international companies, the particularities of Anglo in a South African sense have been lost a little bit, and I do regret that, and maybe it's just inevitable with the pressures of global business but I think that culture was very strong of giving back and being involved, you were expected to be involved.

Like Summerson, Ruth Steele expressed a cynicism towards international codes and standards, to which the company has, voluntarily, signed up. According to Steele, the proliferation of codes and monitoring frameworks threaten to crush the 'creative, home-grown CSR' characterised by spontaneity and individual moral drive that, she said, used to be Anglo's hallmark:

> The GRI [Global Reporting Initiative], I think, is in danger of going down a long list of indicators and reporting in terms of indicators without any analysis . . . and destroying the creative CSR that companies have undertaken—work on education, health which aren't even on the global radar yet. In this country we have developed a robustness in terms of local engagement. We are in some senses unique and ahead of the world.

The emphasis in both cases is placed firmly on the distinctly South African nature of this social expertise and innovation.

As emerged from the accounts of executives at Anglo Johannesburg, the imposition of a technocratic framework for CSR was received as the assertion of authority over Anglo South Africa, by the company's new power base in London. During an interview with the London *Financial Times*, the then CEO, Tony Trahar stated that: 'I think the executive management is probably still too South African-centric' (Lamont and Morrison 2004: 10). The impersonal bureaucracy of codes, standards and reporting mechanisms are represented as external to the company's South African context, in an implicit rejection of both the *global* ethical regime of corporate responsibility and the company's new command centre in London. The CSR performance systems—and the imperative to 'report' on them to a seemingly invisible audience whether through the GRI or the London Stock Exchange's [LSE] FTSE4Good Index—were seen as a new form of authority emanating from the company's headquarters in London and penetrating the walls of Anglo's Johannesburg headquarters, so giving new force to Steele's statement that: 'now it's policy that holds sway':

> Anglo South Africa staff were very proud of it being a South African company that had grown so large and so diverse and when they got to London they had to re-brand it . . . nobody told Rio or BHP that they couldn't be Australian . . . I do have concerns about it being a bit ivory tower . . . and I think to some extent the posh English accents don't help and this emphasis on things like Tony Blair's Commission for Africa.

Steele and her colleagues expressed a reluctance to lose the 'South African identity' of the company, while describing London as abstracted from the real world of mining, too 'ivory tower' as Steele put it. Yet, ironically, as we have seen, the image of the 'true Anglo' as depicted by many of the senior executives in Anglo Johannesburg resounds with a kind of reverence towards England. That is, of course, an imagined England of colonial 'English' South Africa, in which the corporate command centre at 44 and 45 Main Street appears as an Oxbridge college staffed by Rhodes scholars—a portrait that, ironically, could not be either more 'ivory tower' or further from the dirt of the 'coalface'. Much like Rosaldo's 'imperial nostalgia' where, 'people mourn the passing of what they themselves have transformed' (Rosaldo 1989), such constructions of the essentially South African nature of the company, in which the CSR of today is a pale shadow of the philanthropy of the past, appear as 'nostalgic creations of imagined past parochialisms' (Stirrat and Rajak 2007: 8). In this way they express an implicit denial not only of the cosmopolitan identity of the company, but crucially, of its new centre of power in London (something I will return to in the next chapter).

'A Force for Progress'?

> You would be wise to resist the notion fashionable among many good people in the world today that business, in order to expunge the *sins of capitalism* in the past, has a moral duty to pay high rates of taxation and assume a high level of social responsibility in financial terms (Gavin Relly, deputy chairman Anglo American, Relly 1982: 1, emphasis added).

In his address to the Financial Mail Conference in 1980, Nicholas Oppenheimer, grandson of Ernest and a director of both Anglo American and De Beers, told of a once 'cordial relationship between business and government' which characterised much of period from the unification of South Africa in 1910 up to 1948. In 1948, according to Oppenheimer, this changed:

> When the National Party came to power . . . there was, so to speak, a divorce between government and business . . . looking back on it, this was understandable. The business world came largely from the English-speaking 'tribe' which had made little or no effort to understand the past frustrations of future ambitions of the Afrikaner tribe. On the other hand Afrikaners thought, with considerable justification, that they had been exploited and looked down upon, and so they were bound to be suspicious of any proposals for the future which came from the business world (Nicholas Oppenheimer 1980: 3).

In the speech, Nicholas Oppenheimer asserts the moral probity of the company by claiming a divorce from government with the advent of apartheid. Suggesting, perhaps, that this giant of a company, which, at the time of his speech, controlled in the region of 50 percent of the South African economy (Lester et al 2000: 188) and was the largest private sector employer in the country, continued to operate for the following forty years as an island, independent of the racial oppression and labour exploitation of the apartheid economy. Oppenheimer concluded: 'although to most intents and purposes government remained firmly committed to capitalist ideals, which permitted business to get on with its prime task of making money' (Nicholas Oppenheimer 1980: 3). It is hard to ignore the (perhaps deliberate) naivety of such an account of South Africa's largest company operating (and prospering) for decades in apparent isolation from the Nationalist Party regime. A leader in the Johannesburg *Sunday Times* in 1962 put the case more strongly: 'It is Mr Oppenheimer and men like him who make the wheels go round in South Africa, who provide it with the sinews of war and enable it to withstand the assaults of the world. Basically, it is they who keep the Government in power' (Johannesburg *Sunday Times* quoted in Hocking 1973: 370). And, in spite of increasingly hostile rhetoric between Anglo and the government[9], there was a mutual dependence, as was manifest in Harry Oppenheimer's speech to parliament in 1955:

> I think everyone in this House is agreed that it is most undesirable to put political power into the hands of uncivilised, uneducated people, as far as we can help it. I think too . . . that the whole population of South Africa is agreed that Native labour has got to continue to be available, to the mines, to our industry, on our farms and in our houses (Harry Oppenheimer, Speech to Parliament 1955, quoted in Hocking 1973: 308).

By the mid 1970s, the outlook was quite different. Companies such as Anglo were beginning to recognise the need for political change (Torchia 1988).
This time however, the company's position was framed not in terms of political imperative, as in Oppenheimer's 1955 speech to parliament, but in terms
of the exigencies of economic growth. Thus Harry Oppenheimer told shareholders at the company's annual general meeting in 1973:

> Until recently, economic growth was achieved by a process of sucking unem-
> ployed or underemployed black peasants into the cash economy. Though their
> productivity and their wages were pitifully low they still were higher than the
> rural areas from where they came. But the possibilities of sustained and rapid
> growth along these lines have virtually come to an end. The modern sophis-
> ticated economy which has been built up cannot grow on the basis of more
> and more units of untrained, undifferentiated migrant labour, and the acute
> shortage of skilled men has made itself felt together with a worrying amount
> of unemployment among the unskilled . . . These are our basic economic prob-
> lems (Harry Oppenheimer 1973).

The extent to which corporations profited from or were harmed by apartheid continues to be hotly debated by scholars (see Lipton 2007); as does the
relationship between Anglo American and the apartheid government. On the
one side, Neo-Marxist historians argue that capitalism and apartheid were
intimately bound up together[10], emphasising that not only were segregation
controls instrumental to the interests of capital in enabling the exploitation
and disciplining of labour, but that industrial capital was instrumental in determining the nature of segregation (see for example Wolpe 1972; Magubane
1979; Marks and Trapido 1987; Bundy 1988; O'Meara 1996). Stressing the
mutual dependence of the politics of apartheid and the process of capitalist accumulation, Packard, for example argues that the interests of the state,
and those of big business 'seldom conflicted to a degree that undermined the
ability of capital to acquire labour or to make profits' (Packard 1989a: 14; see
also Saunders 1988). On the other side, the 'liberals' contend that apartheid
was politically driven and economically irrational, compromising the long-
term profitability of corporate South Africa (see Lipton 1985; Moll 1991). Not
surprisingly, this position was strongly supported by Anglo directors who
actively engaged in the debate in print as well as public discourse, presenting themselves, through their role within Anglo, as both architects of and
commentators on the transformation of South Africa. Thus Michael O'Dowd,

former Anglo director, argued that the values of business, have in the past, and continue to drive the movement towards, rather than against, democracy (Bernstein and Berger 2000)[11].

It is not my intention to re-hash the well-known debates about the relationship between capitalism and apartheid which raged (and continue to do so) in both the academic and public arenas for four decades. What is of interest here is the rather Darwinian capacity of corporate giants such as Anglo American (despite the size of their bureaucracies) to re-invent and re-position the company *in relation to* the politics of the past and the new dynamics of national transformation, rather than be *independent from* them.

In the wake of apartheid, the Truth and Reconciliation Commission (TRC) held a series of hearings on the moral complicity of business in apartheid, '[probing] the extent to which (predominantly white) firms were advantaged or disadvantaged by the system and [asking] whether business had done enough to end apartheid' (Nattrass 1999: 374). The TRC indentified three orders of business responsibility in relation to apartheid. First order involvement was defined as active collaboration in the architecture of apartheid. The second order involved supplying the means (for example the security apparatus) for state repression. And the third was more broadly categorized as profiting from the apartheid economy (ibid). Unsurprisingly, the focus of the argument from the business submissions was that apartheid damaged rather than profited business[12]. In their submission to the TRC, Anglo wrote that they were disadvantaged by the animosity of the National Party and its apartheid policies (Anglo American 1997: 13). Their submission does however contain an apology, if a fairly limited one. Having protested the government restriction on family housing at the mines to no more than 3 percent of the black workforce, the company failed to provide married quarters to even this tiny fraction (ibid: 4[13]). For this they apologised, referring to it as a 'missed opportunity to 'oppose apartheid and hasten its demise' (ibid: 12). Yet, as Fassin points out, in the decade following the end of apartheid, progress on the transformation to family housing has remained extremely slow (Fassin 2007: 186) (see Chapter 5).

Within the broad category of 'business', which the TRC approached as a single group rather than on a firm-by-firm basis, the mining industry received particular attention:

> Business was central to the economy that sustained the South African state during the apartheid years. Certain businesses, especially the mining industry,

were involved in helping to design and implement apartheid policies (Truth and Reconciliation Commission of South Africa 1998: 58, paragraph 161)

Indeed its final report published in March 2003 explicitly states that: 'the blueprint for 'grand apartheid' was provided by the mines and was not an Afrikaner state innovation' (TRC 2003: 150). The TRC criticises the mining industry, specifically naming the Chamber of Mines and Anglo American, for failing to acknowledge at the hearing, their repression of black trade unions, the lack of regard for worker health and safety, and above all their 'moral responsibility for the migrant labour system and its associated hardships' (TRC 1998: 33, paragraph 63). Still, as Nattrass argues, by representing any profitable activity as profiting from apartheid, the TRC effectively placed 'corner-cafe owners in the same camp as Anglo American Corporation and Armscor' (Nattrass 1999: 390).

In her submission to the TRC as director of South Africa's Centre for Development and Enterprise (a pro-business think-tank heavily funded by Anglo American, from which the organisation draws a number of board members), Ann Bernstein argued:

> Corporations are not institutions established for moral purposes. They are functional institutions created to perform an economic task . . . They are not institutions designed to promote some or other form of morality in the world . . . This does not of course absolve individuals within companies from moral choices, but this is a different matter (Bernstein 1999: 9).

Following Milton Friedman (1970), Bernstein dispenses with the notion of moral responsibility altogether, contending that the sole responsibility of business is to do business, and thereby create economic growth and employment. According to this position, business was a natural catalyst in the demise of apartheid and the drive to democracy. A year later, she reinforced this position, in a report co-authored with the chairman of AngloGold arguing that 'simply by doing what it knows how to do—generating profits for itself and its shareholders (business) will unleash processes favouring modernisation and development, and indirectly facilitate moves toward democracy' (Bernstein and Berger 2000: 24). This leads to her conclusion—a self-conscious echo of Adam Smith—that, 'morally laudatory consequences can follow from morally neutral actions' (ibid). As we shall she in the next chapter, Bernstein's argument foreshadows the apparently progressive discourse of empowerment through enterprise and emancipation through the market that has gained such currency in post-apartheid South Africa, bolstered considerably by the CSR movement.

However, Bernstein's neat separation of the morally neutral act of doing business from the 'different matter', as she put it, of individual moral choice within the company is at odds with Anglo's own representation of itself as very much the sum of its people. It jars with the constant emphasis, by its executives, on the individual sense of responsibility and philanthropy of those people. Bernstein's unconvincing appeal rests on the separation of personal morality from a depersonalised notion of corporate responsibility; which, according to Bernstein, is solely the responsibility to do business and make profits. The false dichotomy between corporate and individual has the benefit of claiming business (and market behavior more broadly) as amoral, while simultaneously displacing the individual moral responsibility of powerful actors within the company, who, according to this logic, are simply following the central rule of business: to make profits.

According to Nattrass, executives and business organisations avoided Bernstein's extreme free market advocacy for the amorality of business. Instead, most big businesses invoked CSR as a central pillar of their defence (and continue to do so), highlighting their acts of social investment and upliftment as a form of quiet activism if not direct political challenge to the apartheid regime. Anglo American, for example, in its submission highlighted the work of the Chairman's Fund (established in 1974 to administer grants to various good social causes) and its increasing focus on black education and urban conditions through its support of the Urban Foundation. In the wake of the 1976 Soweto uprising, a group of companies led by Harry Oppenheimer and Anton Rupert (chairman of the Alcohol and Tobacco firm, Rembrandt) established the Urban Foundation with the aim of returning stability to the townships through private sector-led development with a focus on black education (Mann 1992: 250). While today the Foundation is remembered by Anglo executives such as Summerson, Steele and Hamilton, as progressive and radical, at the time, it was lauded by conservative elements in society for 'preserving an economy endangered by African revolt against conditions in the townships' (*Financial Mail* quoted in Pallister et al 1987: 142).

Indeed, accounts of the Anglo Chairman's Fund, evoke more the classic portraits of the dynastic corporate philanthropy of the Oppenheimer's, than a progressive (if silent) stand against apartheid. Initially a greater share of the fund's resources had gone towards supporting the research of white academics, for example subvention of the Harry Oppenheimer Institute in the Centre for African Studies at the University of Cape Town (UCT) (which continues to award scholarships today). But, the shift towards more 'hands-on' involvement in black education initiatives in the late 1970s and 1980s was, according to Ingrid Hamilton, a testament to the company's early commitment to 'black empowerment' and quiet resistance to apartheid. Still, Anglo's own journal *Optima* captured the prevailing ethos of philanthropic largesse, reporting on the Fund's endowment of the first agricultural school for black children in South Africa in 1977: the school was named 'Phandulwazi' meaning 'the seeker after knowledge' after its benefactor: 'a praise name conferred by the people of Ciskei on Mr Oppenheimer' (*Optima* 1978: 124). Today, the Chairman's Fund continues to make grants for 'worthy causes' the greatest proportion of which go to education development initiatives, from 'grass roots' education to endowments of some of the country's leading higher educational and cultural institutions. And while the language has changed to reflect the contemporary discourse of corporate social responsibility and investment (the fund is now managed through 'Tshikulu Social Investments'), it continues to project the company's image as a chief national patron of the arts and education[14].

Throughout the 1980s the Fund maintained the policy stated in *Optima* in 1978:

> The Fund is not concerned either to promote or to oppose the South African government's homeland policy and projects within these areas are not evaluated in terms of that policy. (*Optima* 1978: 120)

According to Ingrid Hamilton, the Fund adopted an official policy of apolitical development merely to safeguard its survival in a political environment hostile to its work. This 'quieter form of resistance' provided education for black children and adults where the regime denied it and empowerment where the regime attempted to oppress, she explained. What Hamilton and her colleagues referred to as 'doing good by stealth', critical outsiders described as a moral gloss to the company's role in sustaining the apartheid economy; or as Max Harper (former advisor to the African National Congress [ANC] on minerals policy) described it, 'a very colonial kind of liberalism!':

> The big mining companies saw themselves as against apartheid. A very colonial kind of liberalism! . . . These companies had financed apartheid and profited from it. Johannesburg Consolidated Investments (who owned the Rustenburg Platinum Mines at that time) were making armored cars for the regime, even while they were giving money to their 'causes'.

Nevertheless, executives both in London and Johannesburg consistently narrated the company's contemporary role as corporate citizens as the latest incarnation of their role as 'agents of progress', in keeping with a grand legacy of corporate social activism. As evidence, they cited Harry Oppenheimer's financial support for the Progressive Party; along with the work of the Urban Foundation and Anglo Chairman's Fund. They emphasised the engagement of top Anglo executives such as Michael O'Dowd and Bobby Godsell with the academic critique of the role of business (see Godsell and Berger 1988, and O'Dowd 1991). And they highlighted the company's support for the legal recognition of black trade union rights, and the consequent rise of the Congress of South African Trade Unions (COSATU) in 1985, as the deteriorating political situation in the 1980s gave rise to an increasingly reformist spirit within business (Crush et al 1991: 184)[15]. Thus Chris Carrick an executive at Anglo London remarked:

> Yes, it's not something new for extractive industries which have always played an active societal role albeit on a rather paternalistic model . . . the concept of CSR is not entirely new to us. Back in 1955 before it was fashionable to have a mission statement Ernest Oppenheimer said *"the aim of this Group is, and will remain, to earn profits for our shareholders, but to do so in such a way as to make a real and lasting contribution to the communities in which we operate"*. . . Of course people say, yes but you were operating in South Africa, engaging with the political regime, because of course we were a South African company then. But undoubtedly the company was a force for progress within that political context.

Time and again executives invoked Oppenheimer's words as the fundamental doctrine of the company's CSR today: a surprising strategy considering the context in which they were first spoken over half a century ago in the early years of apartheid[16]. In an interview with *The Guardian* newspaper in July 2005, Nicholas Oppenheimer also summoned the legacy of the founding father: 'my grandfather was determined the company would make a real and sustained long-term commitment to the peoples in the country' (Macalister 2005). In the same interview he stated, 'I am an African', evoking the spirit of 'African Renaissance' ushered in by Thabo Mbeki[17], while simultaneously recalling his words to the Financial Mail Conference in Johannesburg over two decades earlier, when he quoted Thomas Browne: 'we carry within us the wonders we seek without us—there is all Africa and her prodigies within us'

(Nicholas Oppenheimer 1980: 10–12). But, as the account of Chris Carrick quoted above showed, narratives of CSR—and of corporate identity in general—draw on the twin motifs of both continuity and change. Carrick asserts a break from the company's paternalistic past and simultaneously appeals to that past as the basis for Anglo's modern-day corporate citizenship; so creating a corporate biography which effectively re-makes the past to confront the political and social challenges of the dynamic present.

However, only when considered in the context of the vast economic power that Anglo had accumulated by the 1980s, can we see how such narratives of good corporate citizenship are instrumentalised, exposing the interplay of economic ideology and pragmatism which shape this process of corporate reinvention. Not only is CSR deployed to authenticate (or perhaps cleanse) a legacy of exploitation. It becomes crucial in shaping the future, in negotiating the political transition and seeking new channels through which to sustain the economic hegemony and political influence of corporate giants such as Anglo through the upheavals of national transformation. Importantly, we begin to see how the current orthodoxies of 'empowerment through enterprise', 'patriotic capitalism' and 'corporate citizenship' that have come to define the development discourse of post-Apartheid South Africa (rather than, say, redistributive social justice and reparation) are rooted in the reformism of the 1980s, and a 'market-driven' model of development which Anglo had a hand in shaping well before 1994.

'Revelation, Not Revolution'

The 'official' company history of CSR, published in a pamphlet produced by the company entitled *Anglo American's Corporate Social Investment in South Africa* describes in exuberant tones the company's history of giving, their role in the demise of apartheid and as midwives of the new South Africa; a history echoed by long-standing Anglo executives in both London and Johannesburg. According to the pamphlet,

> In August 1985, a group of South African business men broke every rule in the apartheid book by travelling to Lusaka to speak with top leaders of the ANC in exile. The Lusaka delegation was headed by Anglo American chairman, Gavin Relly (Robbins 2001: 1).

It was in the mid-1980s, according to collective corporate memory, that the company abandoned its 'doing good by stealth' policy and directly challenged the regime by meeting with the ANC in exile. In fact, the delegation to Lusaka was not only led by Gavin Relly, but, according to Nicholas Summerson, most of the delegates were 'Anglo people'. Summerson, who had accompanied Relly on the Lusaka mission, explained that a lot of other delegates, lacking Relly's 'courage and foresight' had dropped out 'under bullying from President Botha'.

During our discussion, Summerson spoke of being attracted to Anglo by 'all the exciting scenario work' they were doing in the mid 1980s:

> At a dinner, I had sat next to someone in the very early days of the scenario-forecasting process. Anglo was the first I think in developing forecast scenarios and that's how I got into it.

Indeed, the company's scenario-forecasting, we are told by the CSI pamphlet, had great influence beyond the company and has entered into not only the official company record, but the history of a country in transition:

> So we've always been driven by this idea of socio-economic development that is sustainable and political configurations that are stable. That is what Relly was doing in Lusaka, and that is certainly why Anglo American, also in the mid-1980s, put many millions of Rands into . . . futures research and scenario planning (Michael Spicer, former Executive Vice-Preseident of Anglo Corporate Affairs Division, quoted in Robbins 2001: 5).

The result of this 'futures research' was the best-selling book, *The World and South Africa in the 1990s* by another well-known Anglo executive, Clem Sunter, published in 1987. It contains two alternative paths to the end of apartheid—'the low road' of violent struggle and 'the high road' of liberal reform. Following the mineworkers struggle of 1987 (a critical event in the struggle against apartheid) Anglo American commissioned a confidential internal report. The report bears the sub-heading 'the Lure of the Low Road', describing the confrontational approach taken by the strikers as the path of the 'low road' (Oke 1987: 11). According to company history, 'before long, tens of thousands of key South Africans were familiar with the low and high road possibilities' (Robbins 2001: 5). Again the bond between Anglo and the ANC is invoked: 'after Nelson Mandela was moved from Robben Island to Pollsmoor Prison on the Mainland, he asked to see Sunter, having read (his) book' (ibid). The concord between the ANC and the company is further asserted as the pamphlet states 'after Mandela's release the first businessman he asked to see was Gavin Relly' (Robbins 2001: 1). But the influence of Sunter's 'scenarios' transcended political boundaries, we are told, appealing in equal measure to Mandela and to the Nationalists in government, as the 'high road' and 'low road' were adopted into the political lexicon:

> Then FW de Klerk, South Africa's new president, started using the terms, high road and low road, as the only realistic options facing the country—and by then most reasonably informed South African's knew exactly what he was talking about (ibid).

The conventional history, told by Anglo executives (both in London and Johannesburg) and documented in reports, thus reinforces time and again Anglo's influence and position at the centre of the politics of transition. Later on, the official account presented in Robbins' pamphlet tells of how, when the country was on the path to 'outright chaos' after the assassination of Chris Hani, it was Anglo American executive Bobby Godsell, together with other business leaders, and the churches, who brokered a peace (Robbins 2001: 7). And when in 1994, an international mission led by Henry Kissinger and Lord Carrington failed to persuade Mangosuthu Buthelezi to join the election process, it was a group of corporate executives from Anglo American-related companies who stepped in and brokered a deal 'behind the scenes'. What is more, we are told, it was in an Anglo American plane fuelled and funded by the company that the central figures were flown between KwaZulu-Natal, Johannesburg and Cape Town (ibid).

What this account does not include is the shift in the early 1980s whereby the company switched its support from a 'Buthelezi solution', quietly funding the Buthelezi commission and endorsing Chief Buthelezi as the future leader of a post-apartheid South Africa, to courting the ANC whose socialist politics Anglo directors had, until this point, opposed. This shift was crucial, not only as evidence of the company's profound pragmatism as critics have generally seen it, but as it gained the company access to the arenas in which the prospective political economy of the post-apartheid state was being discussed and planned[18].

The relationship between Anglo and the ANC, we are told, was further sealed with the establishment of the Brenthurst Group of top South African businessmen which, according to Robbins, 'was formed as a sounding board which the government could use when necessary' (Robbins 2001: 7). Against accusations that the group was an attempt to manipulate the new government, the Robbins report states 'it was in fact, President Mandela himself who asked for this kind of assistance' (ibid). This rose-tinted picture of the relationship between the ANC government and Anglo American smoothes over the struggles that ensued as the new regime attempted to assert sovereignty over the nation's mineral wealth. But still, Max Harper, former ANC adviser, described that powerful corporate influence at work during the 'Brenthurst Proceedings' when he was coordinating the ANCs new minerals policy between 1993–1995, or as he put it 'Anglo and their friends, they thought they could teach us 'terrorists' how to run the economy':

> Look, what Madiba[19] did—which I disagreed with at the time—he created the Brenthurst meetings—a dialogue. OK, dialogue is good, but business thought they could always short circuit us. That's why they were so arrogant—they were allowed to be. The key to the whole thing was that under colonial Roman Dutch law, the ownership of the surface rights was linked to the sub-surface rights . . . Settler farmers sold the rights to the mining houses, who pursued policies of consolidation . . . So all the mineral rights were privately held when we took power in 1994—the only state ones were on state land. In 1994, the statement the ANC put together was that the mineral rights are the property of the people. Which is how it works in the UK or the US and Europe—it's part of your national patrimony . . . After 1994 they (the companies) thought they could get on with business—and in many ways they did.

The proud (or perhaps even brazen?) representation of the company's intimacy with the ANC before and after their election to government and their influence on national politics is striking. Of particular interest is the way in which company discourse casts political involvement and influence as corporate social responsibility. Often they seem even to draw an implicit and at times explicit divide between what they refer to as 'the practical side' of CSR pursued through the Chairman's fund, and the less tangible side of their corporate citizenship which derives from their 'impressive network of influences and endeavours at the top level of national life' (Robbins 2001: 18). According to this vision, corporate citizenship means direct involvement in the politics of government and the affairs of state.

By fostering links with the future government from the mid-1980s the company ensured not only its invitation to the table at which the 'new South Africa' was being designed, but held on to its central position in the South African economy post 1994. By the mid 1980s Anglo had accumulated vast economic power, expanding into every corner of the South African economy. Describing this unprecedented monopoly capitalism, Duncan Innes wrote:

> Like a colossus, strode Anglo American, concentrating ever greater areas of production and ever larger resources of capital under its single control (Innes 1984: 207).

Domestic exchange controls (introduced in the early 1960s to stem the flight of capital overseas), and additional restrictions from international financial sanctions—albeit 'incremental and limited' sanctions (Lipton 1988: 2)—made it difficult for companies to invest outside the South African economy. As a result, Anglo American diversified beyond mining. Bream and Russell state that, 'in the latter years of apartheid the giant conglomerate had so expanded and diversified from its original core industries of gold and minerals that it dominated just about every sector of the South African economy' (Bream and Russell 2007: 9). By 1976, the Anglo Group controlled top positions in every one of South Africa's economic sectors with the exception of agriculture, and all top five mining companies were under Anglo control (Nattrass 1988; Clark 1993). By 1982 Anglo American controlled 53 percent of listed shares on the Johannesburg Stock Exchange (JSE) (Lester et al 2000: 188) creating a vast interwoven complex of cross-holdings and assets. As a result, and despite global diversification since 1994, Anglo American, along with the five other leading conglomerates, continues to exercise an enormous influence over the South African economy, ensuring that capital is still 'more highly concentrated in South Africa today than in most other developing and industrialized countries' (ibid: 99; Fine and Rustomjee 1996).

Yet this unparalleled dominance over the South African economy, arguably, made the company all the more exposed, their influence all the more precarious, and their control over mineral reserves tenuous, when it came to navigating the politics of transition. Summerson spoke explicitly of Relly's intentions and efforts in Lusaka to redirect the ANC away from their socialist politics: 'he advised them to abandon their socialist economic sentiments and to embrace the globalising free market'. In the same year that he went to meet the ANC in Lusaka, Gavin Relly enjoined the graduating class of UCT to pursue the 'high road' of free enterprise to freedom:

> It is no use trying to deny the link between individual rights and capitalism, it is there for all to see. As a matter of history the concept of human rights grew up in the world along with capitalism and it does not exist in reality outside

the capitalist world. The Soviet Union indeed has an admirable Bill of Rights in its Constitution. I do not know if they learn it in the labour camps but if they do it is probably little consolation to them . . . This is relevant to our situation in South Africa, because one way of characterising our need for change would be to say that we need to move from a capitalist to a free enterprise society (Relly 1985: 5).

Thus Relly offered the free market as the only real alternative by which South Africa would be unshackled from the oppression of apartheid: 'giving free market forces full rein . . . will (release) a powerful impetus for progress, particularly in terms of human initiative' (ibid). Or, as he had put it in his speech to London's South Africa club four years earlier, follow the path of 'revelation, not revolution' (Relly 1981: 8).

A similar future, in which liberation is synonymous with freedom to participate in 'the market', had been mapped out by Nicholas Oppenheimer in his address to the Financial Mail conference in 1980:

We must draw everyone into a truly free enterprise economy . . . it seems clear to me too that the private sector has a responsibility to pay wages in the market economy which allow workers to do more than subsist. There are real benefits to doing this. After all, spending money is fun and we must look to the time when Blacks have discretionary income (Nicholas Oppenheimer 1980: 10–11).

Here the free market comes to represent the ultimate freedom. Liberation from apartheid is understood, almost exclusively, in terms of freedom to make money and freedom to consume. Relly and Oppenheimer's vision of a future South Africa governed by the emancipatory powers of the free market must, of course, be understood within the context of the cold-war politics as they characterised the battle-lines of the struggles in South Africa. Nevertheless, it is hard not to hear the echo of Relly and Oppenheimer's proselytising promise of liberation and progress through free enterprise in the words of Anglo American's chairman, a champion of CSR, over two decades later: 'let business lift Africa out of poverty' (Cronin 2006).

To attribute the reigning neoliberal vision of development in post-apartheid South Africa—according to which opportunity has become synonymous with the market, and enterprise the source of empowerment (see Chapter 3)—to the intervention of Anglo American would seem a melodramatic echo of the company's own rhetoric. But their role in shaping the future government and political economy of the country to their own interests is evident. Looking back at the work of the scenario planners and horizon scanners which Summerson spoke of and which we find summarised in Clem Sunter's famous treatise, *The World and South Africa in the 1990's*, I was struck by the quote:

> What makes South Africa tick? If you know the rules of cricket or football and have studied the strengths and weaknesses of the best players on either side, you can exclude many possibilities. We say exactly the same about the world and South Africa; but understanding the 'rules of the game' and the main actors, you can narrow the range of possibilities (Sunter 1987: 14).

The idiom on which Sunter hangs his predictions—that of 'the rules of the game'—implicitly invokes classical representations of the market model, complete with its own internal logic, rules, winners and losers. The normative effect of these scenarios—not simply predicting the future, but creating it (narrowing the range of possibilities until all alternatives to one hegemonic vision disappear)—is evident in the South Africa of today. Today, CSR seems more powerful in the country than ever before, and arguably more pervasive than in other countries; a testament to the extent to which the country has embraced business, and business embraces everything. The picture of the omnipresent influence of Anglo American working behind the scenes to broker deals and mould South Africa in the image it wants, has passed into public mythology. But, as one young Johannesburger said to me: 'I'm convinced that Anglo actually runs South Africa—who do you think got us the 2010 World Cup?'

The carefully calculated efforts to ensure the company's survival in the dying stages of apartheid, and shape the volatile transition to their advantage, are celebrated today as CSR, part of the company's grand legacy of 'giving back' to the country. As corporate philanthropy is reconstructed as corporate citizenship, Anglo's power and influence—real and mythologised—is naturalised and authenticated. The principal point to be made here is that CSR is neither peripheral to the exploitative workings of corporate capitalism (as critics would have it), nor a neutral mechanism for corporate transformation. Rather, it is much more profoundly bound up with the survival, the reproduction and adaptation of corporate hegemony. CSR has been central to the way in which Anglo confronted the particular political challenges of transition, repositioning itself, while successfully seeing off the fear of nationalisation or redistribution. The status of corporate citizen sustains this political influence, and serves as a mechanism through which the company's relationship with the new government can be recast.

Thus while the discourse of global corporate citizenship seeks to portray companies according to a liberal imaginary of global market rationality which transcends the messy politics of the state and of history, the particularities of Anglo's role in South Africa expose these depoliticising claims to cosmopolitan values. Instead, the power of CSR discourse is shown to rest precisely on its capacity to adapt to the particular historical and national contexts, and to mobilise a nationally-rooted collective corporate memory as part of the process of reinvention. After all, as Nafus and Anderson point out, it is precisely the 'ethos of newness' which appears to rule in the world of modern business, that 'allows people to mine the past with great plasticity', so long of course that it is 'made new again' (Nafus and Anderson 2009: 154).

Despite claims of a shift away from the kind of dynastic paternalism, evoked by Hamilton, Summerson and their colleagues, to a technocratic enterprise, at the heart of the CSR discourse the moral register of trust and benevolence, continues to resound much more strongly than the managerial. This is not only so in the narratives of executives, but, as I explore in Chapter 6, comes to define the practices of CSR in relation to the intended targets of this moral vision of responsibility, obscuring the lines between philanthropy and corporate citizenship, and reviving the paternalism of the gift within the contemporary discourse of empowerment through enterprise. Even the enduring appeal of iconic dynastic founding fathers—simultaneously revered and condemned—has been 'made new again' in the reification of leadership that has become a key component of discussions surrounding CSR. 'Leadership is everything' I was told, time and again: an implicit refutation of the technocracy of ethical codes and bureaucratic management systems that had been put in place within the company and industry-wide in order to 'mainstream' and professionalise CSR. Thus, the corporate champions of CSR are frequently represented as 'visionaries of sustainable development', while the Anglo chairman—described by fellow Anglo executives as 'something of the patron saint of CSR'—was seen to personally embody the company's moral authority. In the idolisation of individuals and the reification of leadership then, we find a deeply humanized portrait of the corporation, and an implicit acknowledgement that the determining reality of big business is not, as economic orthodoxy commands, the supposedly amoral logic of the market.

3 'Proudly South African'
A Division of the Spoils

IN JUNE 2007 THE LONDON *Financial Times* reported changes afoot in Anglo American. The company was, according to the article, embarking on 'a new era' following the appointment of Cynthia Carroll, the company's first female CEO:

> Ms Carroll demonstrated her determination to shake up the old Anglo culture last week by sacking Mr Havenstein as chief of Anglo Platinum one of the group's most prized assets . . . Compounding the impression of a new era at Anglo American, an extraordinary chapter has ended . . . Mr Godsell[1] . . . is one of the last of Anglo managers from the stable of Harry Oppenheimer (Bream and Russell 2007: 9).

Was this then, as the article suggested, the end of an era, a radical new departure? The 'lofty Oxbridge style' and family club, told and retold by a cadre of elite executives, giving way to the new global corporate citizen, as the old 'patrician leaders' of Anglo South Africa 'left the stage' (ibid)? This certainly seemed to accord with a discussion between top executives at Anglo's London head office in 2005:

> Chairman: The idea of having some kind of standard is a good one . . . It isn't a special case for Anglo, although Anglo has a special insight because of its experience. The South African government, on the one hand is concerned by the size and ubiquity of Anglo and on the other will approach Anglo and say, "can you lead this initiative" and "what do you think of this?" This is the consequence of being a very large company—that's not unique to South Africa.

Chris Carrick: The chairman's involved in an initiative looking at what to-morrow's global company looks like—its identity, how it expresses it. Anglo in South Africa uses the slogan *Proudly South African*. It obviously doesn't describe itself as *Proudly South African* in Brazil or in China. But nowhere does it describe itself as *Proudly Brazilian*. *Proudly South African* is a statement of its history and identity in South Africa.

Chairman: The really interesting thing is, how you can take a set of values and apply it *globally* . . . Can you have a *global corporate value*? I think you can, and if you don't have that global corporate value, you're corporation will fall apart.

Thus the chairman ended the discussion (and our interview) with a resounding affirmation of global corporate values that superseded the particular national commitment encapsulated in 'proudly South African'. The portrait of the cosmopolitan corporation transcending the parochial politics of national contexts is commonplace. In the case of Anglo, it is not only the geographical rootedness that such claims to global corporate citizenship attempt to escape, but the parochialism of the past, as corporate discourse strives to project the company as 'Fit for the Future' (Anglo American 2008: 10).

And yet, during my fieldwork in South African, the company's enduring commitment to its 'Proudly South African' roots was communicated not only in the accounts of executives and managers, but in a variety of more public media, affirming the company's commitment to national development, with a resounding message of 'patriotic capitalism'. It was not uncommon to see Anglo American and Anglo Platinum advertisements in South African newspapers and on television, proclaiming the companies as 'Passionate about South Africa' or 'Proudly South African'. One such advertisement exhorted, 'you've got to love this place. We do!' It continues, 'that's why, we've invested about R12 billion in the past 5 years on assisting black business to benefit this country's economy'. Another pledged to empower a 'platinum generation in the waiting' under the bold title, 'Leaders grow Leaders'. The iconography of the advertisement is striking, a mother elephant proudly leading a pack of baby elephants through the bushveld. Here Anglo Platinum, metaphorically takes on the mantel of delivering the new South African dream (and the values of empowerment through enterprise embodied in it) to a generation of aspiring entrepreneurs previously disenfranchised from doing business in a 'free market'; just as America's corporate giants had brought the promise (though not necessarily the fulfilment) of the 'American Dream' of market opportunity and upward mobility to thousands of workers and communities in the post-World War II era (see Ho 2009). As the company seeks to reposition itself in relation to the post-apartheid nation and new economy, 'patriotic capitalism' thus appears as a potent expression of corporate responsibility and cultural authenticity.

How then do we make sense of these two seemingly conflicting constructions of the company, on the one hand 'Proudly South African', on the other 'global company of tomorrow'. How do they play out in the articulation and delivery of corporate social responsibility? And specifically, how do they relate to the political imperatives of national transformation in South Africa and the economic exigencies of the global financial markets? These are the questions with which this chapter is concerned.

The fluidity of global business in the neoliberal economy is so often assumed by scholars and claimed by corporations. But this dominant image of corporate capitalism, characterised by deterritorialised networks of capital, which, as Emily Martin puts it, 'flow unimpeded across all borders' (1997: 243), emphasises change to the neglect of continuity[2]. More specifically, it overlooks the ways in which TNCs are themselves territorialised and localized in various ways. As we have seen, companies are not simply generic models driven by a universal conception of shareholder value and the ineluctable logic of capital. Even within the capital markets of volatile investors, where perception translates into capital, the need to project a corporate image of stability, efficiency and confidence, makes the narrative and performative aspects of corporate practice increasingly important: 'every giant company needs a story of purpose and achievement' (Froud et al 2006: 4). Equally important, I argue, is the projection of a certain future. In Anglo American, the construction of that story has been told through the reinvention of a South African past, as much as the vision of a 'global future'.

On one level this tension can be read within the frame of a classic global-national dialectic: each exerting its pull on the direction of company strategy and corporate behaviour; each demanding a corresponding discourse and set of practices that establish the company's claims to globalism/localism and thus appear to conflict with the other. The former seeks to abstract from the local, reflecting the globally diverse geography of operations, and equally diffuse capital investors. The latter works to sustain and renew the company's economic hegemony and social authority within a country in transition that is, to borrow Burawoy and Verdery's words, neither 'rooted in the past', nor 'tied to an imagined future', but rather, 'suspended between the two' (1998: 14). Thus also at play here are the temporal dynamics of continuity and change that run through the book, raising questions about how a company constructs the story of both its past and its future as vital resources in its survival and success.

In many ways the interplay between the discourse of 'patriotic capitalism' and the model of global corporate citizenship—and the struggles over identity and authority that this chapter explores—point to a kind of persistent rootedness, challenging the conventional representation of global companies as 'supra-national' entities that transcend borders and escape the socio-political contexts in which they operate. Too often the power of global corporations and the resilience of big capital to political upheaval and social change is taken for granted without showing *how* it is achieved, or the struggles, contradictions and internal messiness that emerge in the processes of adaption and renewal. In doing so we fail to see the resources corporate elites draw on (whether economic, social or moral) to negotiate new political orders, legislative imperatives and social challenges, and we miss the new forms of corporate practice that are generated in the process.

CSR represents a central framework for such engagement at different levels and with different groups, not only for forging much needed alliances within the new order, but for accessing the social (and political) capital they bring. Here the CSR movement demonstrates once again, this time on the national stage, its capacity to forge an apparently collaborative and consensual future, conveyed through its vision of 'patriotic capitalism'. CSR is thus mobilised to reflect and re-appropriate the idioms of transformation, BEE and national renewal. Commitment to this mission is, we are told, manifest in 'empowerment transactions' and BEE partnerships between Anglo (and its cohort of corporate citizens), and a new generation of entrepreneurial BEE companies vying for a slice of the market. CSR thus represents an important vehicle for the company's projection of its role as key collaborator in the new South Africa. This alliance between big business and the state is, in turn, seen to be rendered through the commitment of both parties to tri-sector partnership, as a central means to stimulate growth and create development. Thus, the discourse of CSR asserts, as one Anglo executive put it, 'a symbiotic relationship' between government, business and 'the community'. Running through the chapter then, as in previous chapters, are questions of collaboration and partnership.

However, contrary to the lofty portrait of Anglo 'above the fray' conjured by executives in the previous chapter, here we see the company very much *in* 'the fray'. The predictive technologies of the company's celebrated scenario-planning, while a powerful mechanism for influencing the direction of change, could never fully smooth the transition, nor turn uncertain futures into certain outcomes and insulate the company from what investors call 'political risk'. At the same time, the rose-tinted vision of collectivity and collaboration—from the highest levels of corporate leadership and central government to community development—belies the political complexity of the relationship between South Africa's biggest private enterprise and the state.

This directs us to consider to what extent the transition to pre-eminent corporate citizen and standard-bearer of BEE represent 'transformation' (to use the political register of the post-apartheid state[3]), or the revitalisation of long-established corporate hegemony in the new South Africa? For some analysts CSR brings social transformation and economic democratisation, South Africa's corporate giants extending the hand of empowerment and the wealth of market opportunities to communities and individuals (see for example Visser and Sunter 2002; Lynham et al 2006). While for others, the professions of good corporate citizenship are just lip-service paid to the South African government, as the company depatriates its command centre and the logic of shareholder value reigns supreme, undermining the company's social responsibility to South African development. Thus they argue, rather than effecting deep transformation, 'patriotic capitalism' as the expression of a home-grown CSR, merely furnishes the old structures of corporate South Africa and the political elites of the new regime, with the very means, as Max Harper (former ANC policy advisor) put it, '*to divide and defend the spoils*' (see for example Bond 2000; Murray 2000; Carmody 2002).

As this chapter sets out to show, CSR represents neither a teleological process of wholesale corporate transformation in line with the new dictates of the post-apartheid economy, nor merely the gloss to an old order of corporate power and privilege, refurbished, but reproduced. Rather, what I show here is a terrain of mediation, ambiguity and friction as different actors within and beyond the corporate bureaucracy engage with the imperatives of BEE and CSR in different ways and work to carve out their roles, their positions and crucially their authority within the company. As they do so they change the company in important ways, yet at the same time adapt to a persistent older corporate order.

Going Global

As the previous chapter highlighted, from the days of scenario-planning and Anglo's advocacy of the 'high road' of (neo) liberal reform, to the contemporary ideology of 'patriotic capitalism', the role and power of CSR can only be understood in relation to the dynamics of transition and the political-economic transformation of post-apartheid South Africa. The triumph of a neoliberal doctrine for the new South Africa was realised in a dramatically rightward shift in economic policy. The social democratic and redistributive vision of development set out in the government's Reconstruction and Development Programme (RDP) in 1994, gave way to the 'extreme neo-liberalism' of 'GEAR' (Growth, Employment and Redistribution) just two years later (Carmody 2002: 257)[4]. Dubbed 'Greed Entirely Avoids Redistribution' by its critics, GEAR marked a move towards orthodox economic reform (Lester et al 2000: 319)[5]. The part played by South Africa's largest companies in achieving this shift was significant as they lobbied for liberalisation to gain access to larger fields of capital investment abroad, and to create a climate ideal for foreign direct investment (Carmody 2002: 259; Andreasson 2006).

In 1998 Anglo American was the first South African conglomerate to delist from the Johannesburg Stock Exchange and move its primary listing to the London Stock Exchange's FTSE100, accompanied by the establishment of its new global headquarters in London. Within a few years most of South Africa's major companies had followed in its wake, moving to London or New York, seeking new capital markets overseas, among them, Old Mutual, South African Breweries (now SAB Miller) and Billiton (now BHP Billiton, another of the world's largest mining companies). This not only facilitated their rapid global diversification, but allowed them to allay investor fears concerning the 'political risk' of dependence on their South African portfolio of assets in a period of apparent political uncertainty. Anglo American's profits increased by 24 percent the year following their move to London 1999–2000 (Dansereau 2005: 56). According to corporate rhetoric, with this move, the company assumed its 'rightful' position among the world's top corporations (Johnson 1998: 21). The move North, was accompanied by a shift in the balance of both financial and political power within the company. While Anglo's move to London was facilitated by the government's programme of economic liberalisation (GEAR), it was not uncontroversial. Friction surrounding the company's commitment to South Africa played out (in the public eye) through oscillating expressions of harmony and antagonism between Anglo senior management and the South African government. In an interview in 2004 with the London *Financial Times,* Anglo's then CEO, Tony Trahar, remarked, 'I think the South African political-risk issue is starting to diminish, although I am not saying it has gone' (Lamont and Morrison 2004: 10). Some commentators at the time connected this remark directly with prevailing fears concerning the dramatic fall in Anglo's share price after the draft Mining Charter was leaked in 2002 calling for 51 percent of the mining industry to be transferred to BEE ownership (Msomi 2004: 2).

The advent of the Mining Charter in 2002, and the (often fraught) period of negotiation between government and the mining industry preceding it, marked a key shift in business-state relations. Max Harper, one of the government advisors involved in drafting the new minerals policy, highlighted the various interests at play, and crucially, the need for the old mining houses to find ways of forging a relationship with the new government. At the same time, he emphasised the financial imperative for companies 'to show shareholders they were in control', and reduce the appearance that the company was vulnerable to the demands of the new post-apartheid government, by translating government mandates into their own agenda:

> There was a leak from within industry (they deny it of course) that 51 percent of mining companies would have to be owned by blacks, and although it knocked 2 hundred million dollars off the stock exchange over night[6], it turned out to be a good thing . . . When the actual Mining Charter was released 26% seemed reasonable after the claims of 51 percent . . . Now the companies are slowly realizing that the days of the Brenthurst meetings are over and they don't have this hot line to government anymore . . . They realized that they need to take control of this, to say 'we are driving this from the business side'—to show their shareholders they were in control, they have actually claimed a kind of ownership of the charter.

Similarly, Ruth Steele, an executive at Anglo American's Johannesburg office, spoke about the damage to investor confidence abroad caused by the leaked draft Mining Charter:

> When the mining charter was released to the media two years ago it dropped a couple of billion rand[7] off our asset value. It was, as you can imagine, a fairly sore point. We have clawed our way back but it's been hard . . . the company needed to change ownership to 20% BEE ownership over a short period—we have worked to rationalize this to the international investor community.

According to people on both sides of the negotiations (government and business) after much wrangling and bitterness over the Mining Charter, all parties scrambled to claim ownership of the Charter and to assert a unity of purpose between business and government: 'after all the hostilities are over and the Charter has been finalized, everybody claims it as their own' (Harper).

Yet the discourse of 'political risk' has prevailed and proved a potent cata-lyst in friction between the government and TNCs, and Anglo American in particular. In 2004, President Mbeki responded to Trahar's comment to the *Financial Times*, in his weekly on-line newsletter, *ANC Today*. In this piece, the President acknowledges that the company has been an 'important player in the processes that resulted in the level of development we achieved'. He comments that the government readily agreed to Anglo's request to move their primary listing to the London Stock Exchange because 'the South Afri-can capital market would not be big enough to finance the large investments visualised by the company in our country and region' (President Mbeki, quoted in Loxton 2004: 1). However, after this prelude he presents a forceful critique of the company's actions during the apartheid era and the apparent betrayal of their debt to South Africa:

> The poor and despised who worked for Anglo American . . . during the years of white minority rule, paid a pittance for their labour, are today's voters. For 10 years they have made the point clearly and firmly that they care too deeply about the future of their children to allow their own painful past and the instincts it invokes to determine that future . . . Throughout the colonial and apartheid years Anglo American did not seek a London listing and did nothing that would generate speculation about the future of its Johannesburg head office. It is *now* saying that democratic South Africa presents the busi-ness world and our country with higher risk than did apartheid South Africa (President Mbeki 2004: 12)[8].

The conflict between Anglo and the government—cast in terms of a per-sonal contest between Tony Trahar and President Mbeki—was the focus of intense media attention for over a month (see for example Loxton 2004; Msomi 2004; Munusamy 2004; Nkala 2004). Throughout, the company's po-sition as pre-eminent South African company (whether in terms of practical economic power or a status derived from its iconic position in South African history) seemed to be both contested and, at the same time reaffirmed. Recall-ing Anglo's famous scenario forecasting in the latter years of apartheid (see Chapter 2), Mbeki asks, 'what information does it have or projections into the future, that say that there is a persisting political risk in our country?' (Mbeki 2004: 12). In explaining, Anglo's position in relation to these national political dynamics, executives often appealed to the apparently irrefutable imperatives of the global market, and the incontestable discourse of 'shareholder value'. Ruth Steele contrasted the company's economic dominance and market rationalism, with what she portrayed as 'petty' political 'sensitivity':

> Yes, there was a lot of sensitivity from Mbeki when we moved to England, but a lot of companies were moving then . . . and were getting a lot of abuse for it, it was petty . . . But you know under the last government, the economy was moribund . . . Anglo basically ran the economy. Afterwards we had to quickly build up our operations outside South Africa—now we have operations in South America, Australia, China. Ultimately it's our shareholders that we have to answer to, or we wouldn't be the third biggest miner in the world.

Similarly, another Anglo executive remarked, 'it's hard to see the bigger picture, the global picture I suppose if you're caught up in politics in Pretoria, or wherever'.

The appeal to 'shareholder value' is persuasive. Ralph Hamann has argued that the authority of mining companies in South Africa, is indeed only 'proximate'; that the real power lies outside the company itself, 'with investors, who are prone to divesting from companies perceived to be exposed to uncertainties and risks'[9] (Hamann 2004b: 192). According to this argument, the real constraint to a wholesale corporate embrace of national economic transformation and BEE, are the exigencies of the global share market and its investors, portrayed as a globalised elite with the power to 'destroy R25bn within a day' (ibid). This reified notion of 'shareholder value' is held up as the determining logic of business superseding the national political-economic imperatives in which the company operates.

But 'shareholder value' is a particularly malleable and forceful idiom which can be employed to pursue all manner of diverse interests. It is forceful, because by appealing to the huge financial might investors wield, 'shareholder value' stands as a metonym for the supposedly incontrovertible logic of the market: the imperative to maximise investor returns. But it is also malleable in that it can be mobilised to validate what appear to be antithetical elements of corporate strategy. The 'black box' of shareholder value, as Karen Ho describes it (2009: 123), is thus instrumentalised to legitimate seemingly contradictory interests: invoked both in defence of bottom line principles, and in advocacy of the lofty ideals of corporate responsibility[10]. Thus Bafana Hendricks, housing chairman at the National Union of Mineworkers (NUM) head office in Johannesburg, challenged the patriotic claims of companies such as Anglo American, and their status as 'Proudly South African', suggesting that global diversification has shifted the balance of power, and interests, away from South Africa, towards 'globetrotting' executives and globally dispersed shareholders:

> I must say, I see a lot of zeal and zest in the companies, but there is an English saying that a leopard does not change its spots—the companies will never change unless there is an instrument of legislation forcing them to do it—they wouldn't do it willy-nilly because they want to. These people are globe-trotting with interests as far afield as Finland and Russia, they have many other interests . . . and of course, as they always say, there are the shareholders in England or America.

In the end, he stressed, the interests of investors in Finland, England or America, can always be invoked as a trump card in any negotiation, so abstracting corporate strategy from the national political-economic framework, and apparently superseding the social responsibilities of employee housing reform, layoffs or the rise of sub-contracting: 'so they tell us, "we must answer to our shareholders, without shareholders, there are no jobs"' (Hendricks). So where does this leave the commitment to 'patriotic capitalism' and empowerment through enterprise?

In parallel with its global diversification, Anglo American unbundled and streamlined its South African operations to concentrate on seven core mining interests. These are: coal, base metals, ferrous metals, industrial minerals, gold, diamonds (through a 45 percent share in De Beers, a private company which remains under the control of the Oppenheimer family), and platinum. Those assets not considered to be 'core', along with more marginal mining ventures, have been sold off as part of 'Empowerment Deals', in response to the government's directives for redistribution of market share to new black-owned and -managed companies. This enabled the company to win political capital at home, while at the same time, freeing up financial capital for investment abroad. The sale of assets to BEE companies has, in turn, been projected as a significant element of Anglo's CSR work and their commitment to the twin legislative imperatives of 'empowerment' and 'transformation'. Meanwhile however, as Carmody reminds us, between 1994 and 1999 a far greater level of capital ($1.6 billion more) was invested abroad by South African companies, than entered the economy through foreign direct investment (FDI) (2002: 264).

Patriotic Capitalism and the New South African Dream

The government's need to perform a balancing act between wealth redistribution and economic growth (and between the demands of 'capital' and those of 'labour') complicates the picture of 'hyper liberalisation'[11]. James Ferguson describes President Mbeki's propensity to 'talk left' but 'act right' (Ferguson 2006: 117). However, this was much more than rhetorical sleight of hand. It alerts us to the political imperative of embedding economic reform within a framework of moral legitimacy—one which I argue here is achieved by the appeal to 'patriotic capitalism'.

Embraced by politicians and business leaders alike, the concept of 'patriotic capitalism' advances an ideological vision of new entrepreneurs empowered to help themselves to a piece of the market with a helping hand from the country's proud corporate citizens. In making business itself the foundation of the 'new South Africa', the concept gained increasing momentum throughout the late 1990s and 2000s (Comaroff and Comaroff 2000)[12]. This particularly South African rendering of corporate citizenship coupled with a celebration of 'grass-roots' capitalism refocuses the pro-business agenda as a patriotic project that promises to embrace the whole population, from street hawkers to BEE mining ventures, from micro-finance schemes to social enterprise, within an ideal of entrepreneurialism.

The government's reform and 'redistribution' agenda has thus been re-framed in terms of *economic* empowerment. The term 'black economic empowerment' originated in a demand for economic redress for the exploitation and dispossession of the black population under apartheid (Innes 1992: 125). Since then it has been 'mainstreamed' within a market-orientated model of development that reflects the orthodoxy of private sector development discussed in Chapter 1, according to which economic freedom and entry into the market economy have become synonymous with liberation from poverty and oppression. The state's development agenda is thus increasingly dependent on and directed towards the expansion of business (both large and small) as a means to achieve broad-based black economic (and social) empowerment. Entrepreneurial training schemes and small enterprise creation dominate development planning, both in the public and private sector, so affirming the implicit message that 'everyone can be a businessman in the new South Africa'.

The commitment to 'patriotic capitalism' has been encapsulated in the ubiquitous 'Proudly South African' brand, widely adopted by South African businesses of all types and emblazoned on cereal boxes, billboards for South African Airways and brochures for Anglo American. The role of South Africa's corporate giants as key collaborators in this project of market expansion and empowerment through enterprise was reaffirmed by Jonathan Oppenheimer, in a speech at London's Chatham House:

We need to build a sense of national identity and we have to achieve this in the economy . . . it must be leveraged into increased employment, increased economic growth and not be seen simply as a transfer of ownership because then it will not happen. It must be translated into the expectation of our common citizen that tomorrow will be better than today . . . Anglo American, De Beers and our family stand ready to put our shoulders to that wheel (9 June 2004).

The project of forging a new identity through the economy—and the vision of national renewal and transformation that Oppenheimer proffered—was not, he stressed, to be realised through a simple redistribution of assets and ownership, but through the limitless potential of economic opportunity. Interestingly, as he rhetorically placed the full weight of Anglo American, De Beers and the dynastic legacy of the Oppenheimer's behind the promise that tomorrow would be a better day for South Africa's 'common citizen', Jonathan Oppenheimer invoked the past, reciting those well-worn words of his great-grandfather from over half a century earlier: 'the aim of this Group is, and will remain, to earn profits for our shareholders, but to do so in such a way as to make a real and lasting contribution to the communities in which we operate'. A hint perhaps of the strong currents of continuity with the past that accompany even seemingly dramatic political and economic change.

On the stage sitting next to Oppenheimer was the chairman of the South African Communist Party, Blade Nzimande, who similarly emphasised the need to work together in the mutual business of building the 'new South Africa'. Indeed the language of collective endeavour, of nation-building through patriotic capitalism, has demonstrated a strong discursive capacity to recruit even groups whose interests and principles often conflict with those of big business. Thus Webster and Buhlungu argue that the union movement, previously so instrumental in the anti-apartheid struggle, has been neutralised by the imperative to '[sacrifice] their "narrow" interests to the overall demands of national development' (Webster and Buhlungu 2004: 243). Above all, business-state alliance and public private partnership are emphasised not only as the foundation of good corporate citizenship, but as the basis for development more broadly, drawing together the business of statecraft with the interests of big business in mutual legitimation. Affirmations of collective purpose have come from both sides. This was manifest in a discussion with a high-ranking Cabinet Minister, during which he told me:

There is no hostility between government and the corporate world. We work well together. Their job is to make profits for their shareholders and our job is to govern for the broad masses of the country . . . in the end we all want a strong, affluent society . . . that then opens up the opportunity for all sorts of black entrepreneurs into business.

Yet this collaborative ideal of business interests and government policy allied for the benefit of society was unsettled as the Cabinet Minister added: 'they make the decisions how to spend their money . . . how do I go and tell Anglo American how to use their money, it's their money'.

The ethos of patriotic capitalism was equally evident at the 2004 Bi-annual Corporate Citizenship Convention, 'Driving Responsible Growth and Competitiveness in Africa', a grand event in the opulent surroundings of Johannesburg's Sandton City attended by senior delegates from all of South Africa's major companies and banks. The convention was opened with a rousing call to arms by the CEO of First National Bank:

It's not about doing something in a philanthropic way . . . It's actually about generating growth . . . you have to get the hearts and minds . . . The key for us is building on this being South African because there is such a strong national pride and patriotism that it's a much stronger rallying cry because we all want the same thing for South Africa no matter what colour, creed—we all want the same thing (Johannesburg 21–22 September, 2004).

Within this collaborative ideal of development, CSR has gained great currency projecting a business-state alliance in pursuit of the shared goal of empowerment, whereby big business unleashes the entrepreneurial spirit and potential in all society, or as the advertisement declares, 'leaders grow leaders':

In a developing country with an unusually substantial private business sector a key challenge is to free the entrepreneurial capacity of large and small players in our industry in order to increase the rate at which they mobilise investment and occupy their rightful place (Chamber of Mines 2003: 35).

The beneficiaries of this movement, we are told, are those who, assisted by various schemes of corporate social investment, can grasp the opportunities of the market and empower themselves through enterprise. 'We're looking for winners' Clem Sunter, chairman of the Anglo Chairman's Fund, states, explaining in a company brochure how the Fund selects its targets and 'partners'. Yet it is not only entrepreneurs in the making who are expected to possess such market virtues: 'we're also backing some of the more entrepreneurial NGOs . . . most importantly' he reiterates, 'we're looking for winners' (Sunter quoted in, Robbins 2001: 34). Re-invoking the principles of 'the High Road' for the new South Africa, this time it seems 'winners' come in the shape of enterprising NGOs that can play by the 'rules of the game' and compete in the marketplace of development.

Corporate citizenship is thus cast as an expression of allegiance to both the goals of the post-apartheid development agenda, and the primacy of the market as the mechanism through which they are to be achieved:

> We support free enterprise as the system best able to contribute to the eco-nomic welfare of society as well as to promote individual liberty. Without profits and a strong financial foundation it would not be possible to fulfill our responsibilities to shareholders, employees, society and to those with whom we do business (Anglo American 2002: 3).

For the major mining houses such as Anglo the discourse of patriotic capital-ism has particular significance. In a country in which mining has retained such economic and political centrality, the establishment of a new mineral pol-icy stood as an important symbol of state sovereignty over the country's min-eral wealth, and an expression of the government's authority over its exploi-tation (Dale 1997; Fedderke and Pirouz 2002; Dansereau 2005). The mineral policy, many years in the making, is articulated in the Mineral and Petroleum Resources Development Act (the MPRDA or Minerals Act) which was finally signed into law in June 2002 (Chamber of Mines 2003: 22). The act requires companies to convert their 'old order' mining rights into 'new order rights'. In order to do so, and in competing with other companies for new exploration rights, they must meet a number of social and labour targets (Hamann 2004a: 280). These include employee training and literacy education, housing, em-ployment equity, procurement of goods, services and capital equipment from black-owned and managed companies and affirmative action to increase the recruitment of 'HDSAs'—Historically Disadvantaged South Africans (both in relation to race and gender)—in management and technical positions[13]. The targets are codified in an 'empowerment charter' for the industry (the Min-ing Charter). Its mission is to create 'economic democratization' both within old mining houses and across the industry; as the Charter states, 'to create an industry that will proudly reflect the promise of a non-racial South Africa' (Department of Minerals and Energy [DME] 2004a). The contribution of min-ing companies towards this goal is to be measured according to a 'scorecard' which provides a checklist of commitments to 'broad-based socio-economic empowerment'. Thus, while the Charter itself is voluntary, its attachment to the MPRDA gives it 'teeth', making the allocation or conversion of mining rights (in theory) contingent on fulfilling the BEE targets.

The corporate commitment to 'patriotic capitalism', has thus translated into a range of initiatives covering the full spectrum of large and small business. At one end large-scale high profile 'Empowerment Transactions' between the old guard of mining houses and new start-up ventures, whereby old established mining companies sell (or in some cases give away) a share of the industry to make way for new entrants. At the other, small enterprise development schemes and BEE procurement systems aim to deliver both the intangible value of inspirational corporate leadership and the tangible benefits of practical assistance. The main organ through which Anglo American provides support for aspiring entrepreneurs is Anglo Zimele (meaning 'to stand on your own two feet'). Established nearly twenty years ago Anglo Zimele epitomizes the model of social enterprise, a commercial firm with a 'social purpose': 'to empower black entrepreneurs' through the provision of a supply chain fund, business start-up loans and equity, and advice on a variety of aspects of business practice from corporate governance and accounting to health, safety and environmental responsibility (Anglo American 2008: 23). Anglo Zimele was commonly invoked as testament to the company's commitment to addressing 'the legacies of the apartheid era', as Tony Trahar, the former CEO told shareholders at the 2006 Annual General Meeting:

> This is particularly relevant for Anglo American in South Africa where a great deal still needs to be done to address the legacies of the apartheid era. Anglo American has been at the forefront of business attempts to spread opportunities to new black entrepreneurs . . . Last year we had the honour of hosting President Mbeki at an exhibition that he asked us to stage about the work of Anglo Zimele, our business development incubator. At any one time this is invested in some 25 to 30 companies supporting over 2,000 jobs (25 April, Institute of Electrical Engineers, Savoy Place, London).

Indeed, corporate reports, along with the accounts of executives, were filled with details of capital invested in new BEE ventures, held up as evidence of Anglo American's pledge to good corporate citizenship:

> Anglo American South Africa Ltd, its business units and independently managed subsidiaries have demonstrated their continued commitment to South Africa's economy by spending R8.9 billion on direct procurement transactions

and business development initiatives with black-owned and managed small and medium enterprises during 2005 (Anglo American 2006b: 1).

Case studies are presented of success stories, such as that of Extreem Kwizeen, contracted to cater for functions at Vergelegen, Anglo's famous wine estate (ibid). Meanwhile, Anglo Platinum has won recognition for its expenditure on BEE procurement ventures (the second highest in the group), recording a spend of R1.98 billion for 2005.

However it is, arguably, the Mining Charter's stipulations on ownership that have, since its inception, been the most controversial. Article Two of the Charter commits extractive companies 'to [achieving] 26% HDSA ownership of the mining industry assets in 10 years by each mining company' (DME 2004a: 4.7). According to the Charter 'ownership of a business entity' can be achieved in a number of ways: a majority shareholding position, (50 percent equity plus one share); joint ventures or partnerships (25 percent plus one share); or, broad based ownership, such as employee share ownership schemes (DME 2004a: Article 2). In the Anglo Group, 'major empowerment transactions' have included, for example, the 'disposal' of the company's interest in AngloVaal Mining in 2003 for US$231 million to a consortium comprising two of the most well-known BEE mining companies. Thus Anglo's CEO stated that, 'Anglo American has been the catalyst on the formation of today's leading BEE mining houses with an estimated market capitalisation of R40bn' (Trahar 2006: 8). Anglo Platinum was again noted for its role in a number of such 'empowerment transactions' including the sale of its 17.5 percent interest in Northam Platinum to Mvelaphanda Platinum in 2000 and the 50-50 venture in the Bafokeng Rasimone Mine (Anglo American 2005c: 2). Represented as manifestations of 'partnership' and corporate citizenship, such deals are listed in Anglo Platinum's annual report under the heading 'empowering our partners' (Anglo Platinum 2008: 82).

However, Anglo American's 2008 annual report notes that, due to the global economic downturn, 'many BEE companies which acquired equity within Group assets during the commodity boom, are likely to experience considerable financing difficulties' (Anglo American 2008: 23). Even before the current recession, when global metal prices were surging, the value of such transactions was questioned by some. On occasion, the old mining houses even bought back assets they had sold as part of their asset redistribution programme, at a profit after they had failed to yield any returns for their new BEE 'partners', as in the case of Johannesburg Consolidated Investments, sold by Anglo for R54 a share, they bought back its two most profitable gold mines when they were trading at R21 a share (*The Economist* 1998, cited in Carmody 2002: 265). Ambivalence about the nature of BEE deals as instruments for reforming the industry emerged during my conversation with the Cabinet Minister. After reinforcing the pervasive message of state-corporate collaboration in the shared goal of economic transformation, his tone became less enthusiastic:

> There have been some shifts and changes, they're not seismic, but they have enabled some new entrants to come in. Sometimes these deals haven't been so hot—it's not easy to *take over loss-making mines and turn them around.*

The implicit suggestion was that the apparently generous transferral of certain assets to BEE enterprises served a dual purpose: simultaneously 'disposing' of assets which were no longer proving profitable to the established mining companies, while fulfilling the BEE demands of the Mining Charter. Such BEE deals enabled companies to avoid transferring or extending ownership in the company itself, while magnanimously releasing large chunks of their assets to BEE enterprises. Indeed, Ruth Steele commented that hostility towards the Charter among senior executives was mainly focused on the 'ownership' stipulations that made 'some people in the company worry 'are we giving away the family jewels?'[14].

Like the Cabinet Minister, Elias Makoe, a recently appointed CSR manager for an Anglo subsidiary, questioned the company's apparent zeal in responding to the Charter, with their array of empowerment and transformation efforts, stating that, 'ownership is where the power is, *not* management'. Makoe stressed that neither BEE procurement and transactions nor employment equity dealt with the question of ownership. While the former involved releasing a share of the industry (but not necessarily the company) through the sale of assets to black-owned companies, the latter focused on internal diversification of management within the ranks of the corporate hierarchy (equally required by the BEE scorecard). It is to the latter that I turn now.

Transforming the Company

In the years following the Mining Charter's release (2002), Anglo American and its subsidiaries put in place a number of initiatives to meet the HDSA recruitment targets for 2009 set out in the Charter's BEE scorecard. From maths and sciences programmes for children in mining areas, to university bursaries, the aim of these has been to create a pool of technically trained, management-level recruits[15] (see Chapter 6). The success of these initiatives is recorded in Anglo American's 2008 'Report to Society', which announces that the company has more than fulfilled the targets of the Mining Charter:

> The Group has achieved 27% representation at top management level, while at senior management, middle management and supervisory levels it achieved 29%, 46% and 64% respectively. The Group achieved 44% representation at a management level against the mining charter target of 40% which comes into effect in 2009. At the end of 2008, 10% of our employees were women, meeting the mining charter requirement of 10% by year 2009 (Anglo American 2008, 89–90).

Yet, Elias Makoe had explicitly questioned whether appointments such as his own, could alone challenge the hegemonic structures of corporate power both inside and outside the company. 'Management', as he put it, was not where the 'power' lies; even when it involves those at the very top of the company. Similarly, the Cabinet Minister qualified his initial praise for the appointment of Lazarus Zim in 2003, the first black CEO of the Anglo American Corporation of South Africa, by implicitly casting doubt on the level of actual transformation *within* the company:

> BEE is not just about equity . . . it's not an instrument that you wield to get compliance, but to open up the economy and allow more people to enter the market . . . But, who makes the decisions? It's a very important question. Fortunately Lazarus has been appointed CEO of Anglo South Africa. But if they're not empowered to make decisions—who makes strategy? Who decides the directions? Those are important questions for BEE. I'm sure Anglo will comply with the mining charter. They will have such and such percentage of black engineers, etc. but the question is—who is making the decisions?

Xola Sejake, a senior official in the Department of Minerals and Energy, echoed some of the Minister's concerns about the pace of transformation *within* the major mining houses. He argued that 'empowerment deals', which appeared as generous and 'patriotic gifts', widening access to the market for a new cadre of black businessmen, failed to change the internal workings of the company, or diversify their senior management and board of directors[16]. Indeed Sejake was explicit in his critique of the pace of transformation in the major mining houses. When I entered his office he was reading the 2005 CSR Report of one of South Africa's mining multinationals, he commented:

The Employment Equity Act was a requirement long before the MPRDA came into force and look at the statistic which this company brags about in their report. Level A, the lowest level, is 99 percent black, then level E, the highest, is only eight percent, in a country that is majoritively black, where whites are a minority and the equity act came in four years ago. How long does it take? Anglo Platinum recently had an opportunity to change the *complexion* of the board when they had to vote for the continuation of board members and they chose not to . . . If they're giving all these scholarships—then where are all these black managers and engineers? The company management must reflect the demographics of the country . . . That is what we are trying to do. You would not expect anything different in the US or UK or Japan . . . So we are pushing them by law.

As if defending his position from the attack common among corporate leaders that government interference in the efficient workings of the free market was driven by political interests and ideology, rather than economic rationality, he added:

It is not irrational behaviour by the government. And investors like the rule of law. Now they have the Mining Charter and they must change. It's not just a bunch of politicians saying this. It is a constitutional imperative and it is also an economic imperative.

Thus he highlighted the recurrent stereotypes which prevail in the mutual imaging between government and business, unsettling the discourse of common interest and accord. For Sejake, unconvinced by the CSR reports, the rhetoric of 'transformation', and the language of partnership between big business and government (despite his own high-ranking position in the DME), a tension between the regulatory role of government and behaviour of big mining companies was inevitable. State regulation was paramount, he stressed, 'if we want to make these companies responsible . . . we must force them, they will not do it of their own will'.

This found echoes within the company. Dominant corporate narratives strove to present the company as a progressive force within South Africa, downplaying the importance of national regulation (and in particular, the Mining Charter), and representing CSR as the product of home-grown voluntarism and an ethos of social responsibility deeply embedded in the company. But, this representation was contested from within, by a number of black senior managers who described the company as conservative and slow to transform both the internal hierarchy and the way they do business with the world outside its walls. Like Sejake, they emphasised the importance of mandatory state legislation, representing CSR as a 'forced change' driven by government legislation and state imperatives. These two positions are exemplified in the contrasting statements of Ruth Steele and Elias Makoe, who joined the Anglo Group as a senior manager in 2003. Steele suggested that the Charter merely reflected the company's on-going CSR work of many decades:

> It is tackling aspects that were already being tackled—it is pushing it, possibly, faster and further than it is—but it was already happening. The same with housing and nutrition . . . we were already doing it, and in many ways we go beyond and above the Charter, look at HIV for example.

Like many veteran Anglo executives, Steele rejected the notion that CSR within the company was the product of new national government legislation, asserting that corporate self-regulation and responsibility superseded state regulation.

In contrast, Makoe argued that the current transformation and improved CSR agenda of Anglo American and Anglo Platinum was the result of a 'forced change', brought about not by the personal morality and collective humanity of the Anglo establishment, but by the post-apartheid government:

> With the advent of the Mining Charter, everyone woke up and you can see a movement of managers wanting to lead this mandate. It's a change, but I must add that it has been a *forced* change—by legislation, something that the company can't afford to ignore, because to have mineral rights you have to do these things . . . Here there was a rush to pick up the pieces because the Mining Charter was demanding they set up a socio-economic plan and good policy foundation and submit a document to government. Because . . . policy has been very much cooked from inside without consultation with labour unions, without consultation with communities.

Long-term white Anglo executives, such as Summerson and Steele, extolled the company's 'old-style' CSR practices as the creative spirit of personal engagement and generosity repressed by the rigidity of a new national and international CSR technocracy (see Chapter 2). In stark contrast, Makoe described such traditional philanthropic endeavours as discretionary, at times arbitrary and 'cooked from inside' of the organisation with little regard for the intended recipients of this largesse. Nox Ndovulu, a regional SED manager for Anglo

Platinum, supported Makoe's account, questioning the impact of the kind of ad hoc giving that had constituted CSR in the company: 'the Charter has meant that they have had to change from a lot of ad hoc donations which were perceived to have little impact'.

Thus it was as agents of transformation and translation, between the legislative imperatives of the 'new South Africa' and the company, that many relatively recent black recruits to the ranks of middle and senior management described their roles within Anglo American and various of its subsidiaries. This role of mediator was exemplified by Ceasar Matsela, who was working on employee housing strategy at the corporate office in Johannesburg:

> Look, when I started this hostel thing, I was a clear engineer—this line must be this long etc . . . But because of my background as a black South African, I've been exposed to these things. For me it's an easy learning curve—not as steep as for *another type of South African* . . . I must take whatever I get from labour and soften it—to communicate it to my team in such a way that they understand.

With these few sentences Matsela expressed the interaction of competing, conflicting and overlapping factors—race, background and technical discipline—that define attitudes, and to some extent role, within the company. Both Matsela and Makoe represented themselves as formal and informal intermediaries translating, in some cases reluctantly, 'external' demands into norms and registers acceptable within the company. For Ceasar Matsela this involved negotiating and translating the demands of labour (the unions) and 'softening' or mitigating them to make them understandable (or acceptable) to those of his colleagues, who he euphemistically referred as 'another type of South African'. Echoing this, Dr Florence Ngubane, a socio-economic consultant with the company remarked: 'change is very difficult in those mines, to fit into the new South Africa . . . so you're looking for the right people, the right point to push a little from this side, or this side, inch by inch . . . you understand?'.

These acts of 'translation' are central to the broader process of transition in contexts where all actors are working to transform their status both individually and collectively. However, while managers recounted their role and experience as one of 'mediation'—between state imperatives and corporate interests, between the demands of labour and those of management, or between the very language of bureaucratic 'transformation' and corporate culture—at times it was they who were expected to adapt, rather than the company. In this sense, their narratives spoke of the continuity of old power structures within the company, as well as change.

This was exemplified in Leonard Xixo's account. An ex-ANC activist and officer in the post-apartheid government, Leonard Xixo was recruited into one of Anglo American's subsidiary companies to fulfill the newly formalized function of liaison with government. Xixo began by referring to himself as an 'old leftie':

> Mining companies in the past never had to deal with this—in the past they enjoyed a very cosy relationship with government . . .You know the business leader of the company in London—he went to school with Tony Blair, they watched rugby together . . . Mbeki—he's on his own. He didn't share a school with Ralph Havenstein[17]. How do they align? Our development is held back to a large extent because of *distrust* between government and business.

Xixo highlighted the role of personal relations ('the family club' recounted by veteran Anglo staffers) in securing and maintaining corporate power. Counter to the dominant discourse of corporate citizenship in which a depoliticised conception of trust is invoked as the basis of business-society collaboration (see Chapter 1), Xixo presented an explicitly politicised rendering of 'trust' (or the lack of it) contingent on exclusive social networks and shared 'habitus'. When he spoke of such networks between senior Anglo executives in London and the political arena in which they operate (hinting at old-boys networks between the business leaders and politicians), he juxtaposed these links (perceived or real), with the 'distrust' between the old elites of corporate South Africa and the political leadership of the new regime, contesting the claims to collaboration in a collective vision.

In contrast to the fond evocations of a 'family club' or 'Oxbridge senior common room', many black executives in the company exemplified by Xixo, Makoe and Ceasar Matsela, described a hegemonic corporate ethos (or as Xixo put it 'a colonization of culture') with a strict if unwritten code of behaviour to which senior staff must adapt or become marginalised[18]. According to Xixo:

> Anglo has its own ideology, its own culture, its own rules and regulations for promotion. You have this *colonization of culture*—its more 'English' than 'English' and it helps to be more 'English' . . . I have worked here for four years and it's the first time I can say, I can dress the way I dress today. That's a culture and if you want to change it—you cannot march in. If you want to carry people along with you, you have to march at their pace or they'll tell you 'piss off, you're a screw-head'.

The particular symbols of power within the company which Xixo, Makoe and their colleagues emphasised, echoed almost word for word the criticisms of 'corporate Anglo', as 'more English than English', expressed by operational managers at the mines. They conformed to another recurring trope in the narration of the company by its employees: the duality of strategy and operations, head office and coalface, suit-wearing and boot-wearing.

Makoe echoed Xixo's account, commenting that his personal unwillingness 'to talk the talk' or adopt the dominant norms of communication has meant his further marginalisation and thus weakened his position in decision-making and policy processes:

> In certain instances you get colleagues who can communicate things well to the leadership above and those like me who don't because I will call a spade a spade and that is an impediment because it won't go down with certain leadership.

Makoe drew a direct connection between issues of 'transformation' internal to the company and relations with the world outside through the company's external corporate social investment programmes. Again the underlying question of authority, and decision-making power within the corporate structure came up, as Makoe played on a dual interpretation of the term 'relevant':

> When it comes to development, one of the concerns I have is that we should look at it with different eyes because largely it's about how much we spend and not really about empowerment. This activity must be seen to be run by a *relevant* person in terms of race—a black person.

In one respect, he describes his role, and value, within the company, in terms of bringing fresh 'eyes' to the policy process and mediating between the company and the so-called 'community'. But, at the same time, he suggested that part of his value to the company was seen to lie in being able to present a *relevant* face in a prominent and visible position of engagement with actors outside the company (whether government officials, union representatives or community organisations): 'a lot of the perceptions are that Elias will sort it out because he knows the community better', he added.

The proportionately small number of black executives, and the prominent position of those few in CSR or public affairs departments, threatens to give the impression, as Xixo put it, of 'putting a black face on it to smooth things over'. This has given rise to widespread criticism of 'transformation' within companies as 'tokenism' or 'blackwash' (see for example Murray 2000; Bond 2000). However, the accounts of Matsela, Xixo, Makoe and their colleagues confounded this kind of one-dimensional analysis, suggesting a rather more complex interplay of authority, expertise and role, at play. They draw attention to the ambiguities and tensions surrounding the position of 'transformation agents' within the company.

The Cabinet Minister had said, 'I'm sure Anglo will comply with the mining charter . . . but the question is who is making the decisions'. Florence Ngubane's account of working as a CSR consultant with the company seemed, at first, to offer a straightforward answer to that question:

> We try to work with the companies, but often the transformation manager . . . he's not empowered to do anything—they don't prepare the very manager who is supposed to transform the company, so how can they do it. The mines have a good way of doing it. These guys who are appointed transformation managers, they get a good package . . . but they have no real authority.

Yet when she turned to talk about her advisory work on the 'frontline' as she put it, the picture changed significantly:

> Of course when you get down to the frontline, which is where I like to be it's a different story. Yes you might have a struggle on your hands with this mine manager or this one here, but you become tough you know. And then . . . they begin to realise, in fact we really need her . . . even if they don't like it.

Far from simple 'blackwash' or 'greenwash', Dr Ngubane's final comments highlight that CSR plays a much more vital role in the company's operations, and crucially its performance. From internal transformation, to external empowerment transactions and broad-based black economic empowerment through business (small and large), patriotic capitalism has emerged as a powerful narrative through which the company articulates its claims to corporate citizenship in the new South Africa. The bold promise of this *new* South African Dream envisions a generation of aspirant entrepreneurs in the making, galvanised by the country's corporate giants to realise the apparently limitless opportunities of empowerment through enterprise. The discourse of CSR serves on the one hand to project the company's status as a global corporate citizen, and on the other, as a vehicle through which the company reinvents itself, and its moral authority, as collaborator in the development of the new South Africa. Yet the power of CSR lies not simply in the public discourse which this chapter has focused on, and the forceful advocacy of a market-oriented vision of development that coincides with the interests of big business. It is materialised in the practices and projects—from HIV management at the mines to entrepreneurship training in the 'community'—that CSR generates, and which provide the focus of the chapters to follow. As I go on to explore in the next chapter, within the broad moral framework of CSR, Anglo's moral authority in South Africa (and beyond) has been renewed significantly by the way in which the company has positioned itself at the forefront of the fight against one of the most urgent and contentious challenges facing the post-apartheid state: HIV/AIDS.

4 'HIV/AIDS Is *Our* Business'

Market Logics and Moral Imperatives

*I always remember in my time in Shell . . . there
was a case when an individual in the Netherlands
died and the pension was to be paid to his wife,
but it turned out he had another wife . . . Shell had
one wife—the official wife—on its books and then
this other wife fronted up and said where's my
pension and the pension fund managers said 'who
you?' and sat there scratching their heads. Much
to my pleasure and amusement they said we'll pay
both of them because he had been running two
whole households. If that was a government—you
see it time and time again—governments waiving
responsibilities. There's an underlying morality, a
duty to your staff—but that has to be tempered of
course. You don't want it to get out or everyone will
be coming forward saying I have two wives*
(**former chairman of Anglo American, London**).

In July 2002, at the XIVth International AIDS Conference in Barcelona, pro-
testors targeted two transnational corporations in particular as they marched
to the chant:

Coke and Anglo you can't hide,
We charge you with genocide.

Today, as indicated by its slogan, 'HIV/AIDS is *our* business—caring together', Anglo Platinum places HIV management not only at the centre of
its CSR strategy, but at the heart of its business. On August 6th 2002, its parent company, Anglo American, became the first major company to offer anti-
retroviral therapy (ART) 'free of charge' to its Southern African workforce of
over 100,000 employees[1]. Since then it has been widely recognised as a pioneer
among business and champion within the extractive industries in the fight
against HIV, earning the company a prominent place in the evolving global
architecture of HIV management. Indeed, Anglo American's HIV agenda
represents the cornerstone of the company's CSR practices and the basis of
their reputation as global corporate citizens, by which they distinguish them-

selves from other leading extractive companies in the competitive global market for corporate responsibility.

The elevation of Anglo and its cohort of socially responsible corporations should be viewed within the broader development orthodoxy discussed in Chapter 1, which promises to harness the reach and resources of multinational enterprise in the service of global health crises and supersede the economic, political or bureaucratic impotence of state healthcare systems. Underlying this is the promise of a confluence of efficient business and caring corporation that combines benevolent intent with economic self-interest. The discourse of CSR thus offers an apparently unassailable rationale for intervention: HIV poses one of the most significant threats to human capital for labour-intensive businesses operating in Southern Africa.

Anglo's status as leaders in the Global HIV arena has been both reflected in and reinforced by the awards and prizes they have amassed celebrating their work in this area. In 2004 Anglo American were granted the 'Award for Leadership' by the Global Business Coalition on HIV/AIDS (GBC). Two years later they were once again honoured 'for their efforts to use their resources or core competencies to fight AIDS' at the GBC's fifth annual dinner attended by Tony Blair, Graça Machel, and Elton John (Holbrooke and Moody-Stuart 2006). This line-up of international figures, together with the international activism exhibited at the Barcelona AIDS conference, directs attention to the *global* dimensions of social responsibility as the driving force behind the engagement of business in the fight against HIV. Yet this movement, led by Anglo American and a handful of other multinationals (such as Old Mutual and SABMiller) that walk the line between their former South African identities and their transnationalism, speaks as much to *national* imperatives as to *global* citizenship.

The previous chapters have shown how the discursive power of CSR rests, to a large extent, on its malleability—its capacity for both abstraction and re-contextualisation within particular political and social frameworks. On the one hand, as was discussed in Chapter 1, CSR promises a *global* vision of sustainable development through 'the market', underpinned by an appeal to universalist ethical norms. On the other, Chapter 3 examined the way in which Anglo American mobilises CSR in order to negotiate and incorporate the *national* discourse of economic empowerment and transformation, so authenticating the company's position within post-apartheid South Africa.

However, while the ideal of corporate citizenship has demonstrated a great ability to co-opt support and manufacture consensus around a promise of

shared responsibility, this chapter explores the way in which HIV management represents more a site of struggle than a force for unity. As such, I focus
here on HIV management as a lens through which to explore the friction between corporate citizenship and state welfare provision which is glossed over
by the appeal to collective responsibility. Within the HIV arena, the company
and the state assert competing claims to moral authority. The authority exercised by the company through its HIV interventions—both in and beyond the
workplace—is established as distinct and indeed outside that of the state, demonstrating how CSR serves as a mechanism through which the company consolidates its power over a particular field of society, in this case, its workforce.

As Brooke Schoepf has underlined, practices of HIV management often
serve as elements in a hegemonic process 'that helps dominant groups to maintain, reinforce, re-construct, and obscure the workings of the established social
order' (Schoepf 2001: 338). Schoepf's insight has particular significance when it
comes to analysing corporate social responsibility programmes, where care is
mediated through the company-worker dialectic. Social relations between employer and employee are being transformed as a result of these new corporate
healthcare regimes, creating connections between the most personal realm of
sexual conduct and family life, and the political economy of global corporate
capitalism. Recently, anthropologists have become increasingly interested in
neoliberal regimes of care and novel forms of pharmaceutical governance (see
for example Nguyen 2005; Petryna et al 2006; Reynolds et al 2006; Ecks 2008).
However, research has focused on the subjects of such regimes and the new kinds
of 'therapeutic citizenship' they create (Biehl 2007: 73), neglecting the actual apparatus of corporate care programmes on which this chapter concentrates.

By tracking Anglo's HIV intervention—from the evolution of policy to
the practices it generates, from the corporate boardrooms in this chapter, to
the mineshafts and hostels in the next—I explore the interplay of global agendas, national politics and local practices that constitute CSR. Across Anglo
American's operations, the world's largest workplace roll-out of anti-retroviral
therapy (ART) is now in operation, making Anglo the 'largest single business
customer for AIDS drugs in the world' (Knight 2005: 22). In South Africa, the
state roll-out of ART has been blocked, delayed and patchy, placing pressure
on the private sector to fill the vacuum. Robert Thornton tells us, when the
state roll-out eventually came in 2003, it was 'unconscionably slow . . . it was
not until the end of 2005 that all fifty-three districts were served by at least one
hospital. Still, it was not enough. Approximately 85,000 people were receiving
treatment by the end of 2005, out of the 5.2 million who were infected' (Thorn-

ton 2008: 186). By September 2007, UNAIDS estimated that 371,731 people were receiving ART from the state service out of an estimated 1.7 million who were in need of treatment. A further 100,000 were being serviced by the private sector, bringing the total ART coverage to 28 percent (UNAIDS 2008: 11)[2].

Within the mining industry, where HIV prevalence is higher than the national average (estimates of HIV prevalence within the industry range from 20–25 percent of the total workforce[3]), the pressure to respond to the HIV crisis has been further compounded by debates surrounding the migrant labour system; debates which have been ongoing for over half a century[4]. For, while migrant labour is a feature of most urban economies across the world, the scale (both in terms of numbers and length of time) and the human cost of labour migration in South Africa has been unparalleled (Fassin 2007). As Campbell's study of HIV transmission at the gold mines makes clear, 'the life situation of migrant workers . . . renders them particularly vulnerable to HIV' (Campbell 1997: 273; see also Elder 2003). Thus the epidemiology of the pandemic has been determined, in part, by the political economy of migrancy upon which the mining industry continues to depend. While TNCs are emerging as key actors in the landscape of HIV management in sub-Saharan Africa, the new regimes of corporate care they produce can only be understood within much older regimes of migrant labour[5].

However research on this new role for corporate Southern Africa—presented as simultaneously moral and market-orientated—has tended to fall within one of two camps, both of which are burdened by a normative preoccupation with whether CSR represents a great leap forward, or merely the empty rhetorics of compassion. Mainstream literature, predominantly from the field of business and management, is dominated by an instrumental approach, replicating the managerial discourse of corporations in pursuit of economistic support backing the 'business case' for a corporate ART roll-out[6]. This is provided through actuarial projections of the impact of HIV on business efficiency. George, for example, urges companies to pursue the financial benefit of 'offsetting employee morbidity and mortality' through the provision of a workplace treatment programme (George 2006: 179). Rosen and Vincent estimate that a one-year extension of 'an infected employee's life expectancy' through ART reduces the company's net costs by 8 percent (Rosen and Vincent 2004: 320); and Fearnley's case study of HIV at Anglo Platinum's Rustenburg plant seeks to prove that 'ignoring the epidemic' would reduce the value of production by around 23 percent, while a corporate ART roll-out will reduce the value of production by only 10 percent, thereby saving the company money (2005: 146)[7].

Meanwhile, the critical literature is concerned with exposing corporate care programmes as a mask veiling the exploitative practices of the past or the hypocrisies of the present[8]. Marks, for example, warns that claims to corporate benevolence have an enormous power to neutralise the past, for which the cost of the corporate care programmes is a small price to pay (Marks 2006: 571)[9]. 'One can set up care programmes', Didier Fassin agrees, 'provided one does not bring up the past' (Fassin 2007: 189). However, while this alerts us to the dehistoricising tendencies of CSR discourse, particularly in the context of the South African mining industry, in reducing CSR to mere mystification—or a corporate attempt to 'buy their good name' (ibid: 184)—we run the risk of overlooking the actual outcomes (intended and otherwise) produced by this marriage of moral imperative to market interests, and its ability to reshape social relations to a particular set of corporate values. The 'business case' for CSR obscures the boundaries between the exigencies of capital and human care, tying the sexual health and moral lives of workers to the financial health of the company. Here, once again, we find both continuity (with the regimes of apartheid-era mining and the paternalism of Victorian industrialists) and change; a corporate intervention that combines the cold, hard economics of labour productivity with the moral discourse of responsibility.

In taking on this duty of care, the company's interest in the beneficiaries or targets of its mission—those who constitute a vanguard of ART recipients within the context of patchy and slow public sector delivery—differs from the interests of the state. The disjuncture between corporate responsibility and state provision translates into an awkward topography of authority, and fragmented and uneven service provision, at the national and (as we shall see in the next chapter) local level in Rustenburg. Thus, I argue, one of the unintended outcomes of the extension of CSR into the realm of HIV management, is to have accentuated socio-economic inequalities long in the making that persist in contemporary South Africa. This forces us to question the claim to collective goals upon which the discourse of CSR is based, or put another way, that 'what's good for Anglo American, is good for South Africa'.

Global Partnership

Anglo American has emerged as something of a standard-bearer for the role of TNCs in the evolving global landscape of HIV governance, placing them alongside the Gates Foundation and other such corporate, philanthropic vehicles[10]. Thus, although Anglo's HIV work focused predominantly (until very recently) on their business units in Southern, and particularly, South Africa (operations which account for around 36 percent of the company's total earnings[11]), HIV represents the centrepiece of the company's claims to *global* responsibility. During the course of my fieldwork, in virtually every interview, workshop or convention, Anglo personnel, whether in London or Johannesburg, emphasised the company's HIV work as the defining element of their identity as global corporate citizens.

The collective voice of this movement can be found in the Global Business Coalition on HIV[12], an organisation that was chaired by former Anglo American chairman, Sir Mark Moody-Stuart. But the company's influence extends beyond business coalitions, as embodied in the recent appointment of Moody-Stuart to the advisory board of the UN's Global Fund to Fight HIV, Tuberculosis and Malaria. His appointment has been seen as indicative of eagerness within the bi- and multi-lateral development agencies to mobilise TNCs in the fight against AIDS, alerting us to the increasing influence of big business in shaping a global public health agenda for HIV. But, Biehl warns, the new wave of corporate philanthropic benevolence should be treated with caution, signalling a Trojan Horse within the arenas of global health governance from which pharmaceutical TNCs can 'defend [their] vision and interests' (Biehl 2007: 82). In contrast, Bendell suggests that the Global Fund appointed Moody-Stuart in order to avoid showing partisanship to any particular country or pharmaceutical company (2003: 4), highlighting the extent to which Anglo American is seen to transcend both the potential parochialism of national agendas, and the conflicting interests of market competition and public health within the pharmaceutical industry. Anglo is thus taken to represent a neutral authority within the volatile politics of global HIV governance, setting a standard in the pursuit of tri-sector collaboration for the provision of treatment (Chirambo and Caesar 2003: 9).

The company's status as champions in the global fight against HIV is reinforced and authenticated as Anglo executives do the rounds of the CSR circuit in London, presenting case studies and statistics, testaments to the success of their treatment programmes at operations such as the Goedehoop Colliery, the exemplary model of the company's HIV work, and talk about the company's R30 million partnership with the South African sexual health NGO, *LoveLife*. In so doing, corporate executives assert commitment to the orthodoxy of 'multi-sectoral partnership', which is elevated as the foundation for 'mainstreaming' HIV management into every aspect of social, economic and political life. As the company's HIV policy puts it, 'Anglo American strives to form alliances and build partnerships in order to develop a common vision and shared strategy with all stakeholders' (Anglo American 2004b: 3). Multi-sector partnership (at all levels—global, regional, national and local) was very much the focus of the keynote address on corporate responses to HIV given by Chris Carrick, an Anglo executive, at the *Ethical Corporation* conference on the 'New Role of Business in Development Countries' (London, 18–19 October 2005). For, according to Carrick, it is only through partnership that 'we can share knowledge and experience across global geographies and can achieve a *seamlessness* between company activity and public provision'.

Indeed the partnership between Anglo (through its Chairman's Fund) and the NGO *LoveLife* (one of the most recognised South African brands working in the field of youth sexual health and HIV-awareness) has been held up as an exemplar of corporate-NGO collaboration of the kind discussed in Chapter 1, described by the Executive Director of the UN Global Fund:

> An exciting example of how the Global Fund's investments can help leverage in-country partnerships and resources. This initiative will provide a strong model in Africa of nationwide effort to establish comprehensive HIV and AIDS services, including prevention, treatment and care in public clinics (Richard Feacham quoted in Knight 2005: 27).

Thus, we are told, the state sector can learn from the private, governments from corporations (and their collaboration with NGOs). According to this formula, global ethical agendas and national socio-political imperatives are perfectly in step, a smooth synergy to produce tangible results in diverse local settings across the continent.

This elevation of public-private partnership, as the solution to healthcare provision in developing countries, has been the subject of a proliferation of reports and working papers (see for example Nelson 2006, and International Finance Corporation 2004) in which international bodies such as the ILO, UN-AIDS and the Clinton Global Initiative advocate a multi-sectoral approach that enlists the service of business and civil society. Strikingly less prominent in this picture of global synergy is the state, which is prescribed the role (if any) of 'coordinators' and the job of 'harmonizing' this collaborative mission (Chirambo and Caesar 2003: 31; Beckmann et al 2005: 3). As Biehl notes, the discourse of global public health portrays national governments as 'a kind of middleman mediating the work of science-minded international organizations and the interests of local communities' (Biehl 2007: 96). The involvement of business as partners in healthcare provision is roundly (and perhaps naively) welcomed as the latest orthodoxy of the development industry. Concerns about the success of this multi-sector partnership paradigm, or 'hybrid approach' as it is sometimes called, are framed in terms of the efficiency and capacity of the state, rather than relations of power and authority between business and the state. This is exemplified in the recent ILO report on 'HIV/ AIDS Workplace Programmes and Public-Private Partnership (PPP) through Co-Investment'. The report raises concerns about the potential failure of states to fulfil their end of the bargain, so creating a discrepancy between benefits provided by business and public healthcare provision (Beckmann et al 2005: 3). Thus corporate responsibility is juxtaposed with state incapacity. Some practitioners and researchers such as Rosen et al (2003) have even gone so far as to refer to an unofficial 'AIDS tax' on business estimated at between 1 and 12 percent of the wage bill depending on country and sector, so framing HIV as an externality imposed on business by the state.

The vision of multi-sector collaboration working to create 'seamless synergy' in HIV management, rests on an ideal of public-private partnership which belies the complexity of power relations between the state, business and NGOs (as well as between corporations and their employees). The Global Business Coalition opens its statement on HIV/AIDS Workplace Protocols, with a question which hints at this complexity, a question which it does not, however, claim to answer: 'any effort to advance the establishment of comprehensive HIV workplace programmes by business has to be underpinned by . . . one key question: *where do a business's responsibilities start and end?*' (Mistry and Plumely 2002: 6). The question is brought into sharp focus as we consider this global ethical agenda and the exhortation to business-society collaboration in relation to the national politics of HIV and specific business-state dialectic in South Africa. For, as HIV management becomes a canvas onto which individual and collective claims to moral authority are projected, the tension between CSR and the state becomes apparent.

National Crisis

In January 2005, at the Balalaika Hotel in Johannesburg's Northern Suburbs, a three-day workshop was held entitled 'Practical Strategies to Manage the Impact of HIV/AIDS on Your Business'. The workshop was run by one of Anglo's best known directors, Clem Sunter, who, according to the brochure,

'[was] back by popular demand' to tackle the issue of HIV. The workshop followed the principles laid down by Sunter and his team of scenario planners in
the late 1980s as they surveyed the post-apartheid future on the horizon and
urged the country to pursue the 'High Road' of liberal reform, rather than
the 'Low Road' of revolution (Sunter 1987)[13]. According to these principles,
business, indeed all of life, is best strategised as a game—much like the classic
model of market rationality—complete with rules, players, winners and one
imagines (though he did not explicitly say this) losers. The biggest *game* being played in South Africa today, according to Sunter, is HIV. Yet, he went on,
what is at stake in this 'catastrophic game', is particularly complex because it
combines 'human tragedy with cold economics' (Balalaika Hotel, Johannesburg 27 January 2005)[14].

In Sunter's 1987 forecasting, HIV had been identified as merely a 'wild
card' in the broader game of socio-economic transition (ibid); enough none-
theless for him to be dubbed 'business' own Aids "prophet"' (Dickinson 2004:
630). His prediction was underwritten by a survey of 60,000 mineworkers conducted by the Chamber of Mines between 1986–1987. The survey showed 0.3
percent HIV prevalence among South African miners (Packard and Coetzee
1995: 112). The highest prevalence was among Malawian mineworkers—3.76
percent according to Jochelson et al (1991)—one of the countries from which
the South African mining industry imported a significant portion of its workforce. The findings of the survey, according to Dr Toby Zwick, medical advisor to the Chamber of Mines, sparked 'a raging discussion' in parliament.
In the end, the response was simple, parliament and the Chamber of Mines
came out in favour of mandatory pre-emptive HIV testing for all foreign
mineworkers, and 'repatriation' of sick mine workers in order to select and
maintain a 'healthy' workforce. An article appeared in the *Journal of the Mine
Medical Officers' Association* setting out the industry's position: 'no known
carriers will be engaged [and] all recruits from *high risk areas* will be tested
at source' (Brink and Clausen 1987: 15, emphasis added). Such a response effectively externalised HIV as an extraneous social risk or 'hazard' encroach-
ing on the borders of the workplace. Mining companies thus attempted to
insulate themselves against this 'threat' to productivity, and ultimately profit,
by cutting off the supply of labour, and supposedly the infection, '*at source*'.

The genealogy of this discourse can be traced back to apartheid efforts to
externalise so-called 'social problems' at the mines. Colonial discourse from
the 1930s and 1940s, perpetuated by much of the mine medical establishment

as well as the apartheid government, located the source of tuberculosis epidemics at the mines in the physical and moral failure of workers to make the transition from rural life in the 'homelands' to industrial civilisation at the mines, or as Packard put it, from 'healthy reserve' to 'dressed native' (Packard 1989b: 686). This was evident in the 1932 Tuberculosis Research Committee which stated that, 'this want of resistance to tuberculosis is . . . a biological character of the African Native' (quoted in Packard 1989a: 206). Such pseudo-scientific discourse provided support for the policy of 'separate development' between the 'homelands' and the apartheid state, according to which the temporary tenure of black mineworkers within the boundaries of the workplace was determined by their objectification as a productive resource[15]. Mamdani writes: 'this meant, on the one hand the forced removal of those marked unproductive so they may be pushed out of white areas back into native homelands and, on the other, the forced straddling of those deemed productive between workplace and homeland through an ongoing cycle of annual migrations' (Mamdani 1996: 7).

The separation of workplace from home life came to be seen as an essential element in the political economy of the mining industry, shifting the cost of the reproduction of labour, and the care of sick or injured workers, from employers to employees. In effect, rural households subsidised the social and medical costs of the industry (Trapido et al 1998). The realities of impoverishment in the 'homelands', of households fragmented through the migrant labour system, and of the poor conditions of work and life at the mines, were glossed into an idealised myth of the 'healthy reserve' to where mineworkers were expected to return when their contracts ended. Such narratives served to externalise responsibility. They attributed the source of 'infection' to mineworkers themselves, and social conditions *outside* the mines, rather than the political economy of labour exploitation in which they were embedded; or as Didier Fassin puts it, to the 'susceptibility' of the 'African body' rather than the 'working conditions that are wearing it away' (Fassin 2007: 139).

The industry's initial response after the 1986–1987 HIV survey followed this same logic. This was manifested in the prevailing practice of 'repatriation', an important mechanism within the broader displacement of social responsibility and healthcare costs from mining houses to mineworkers themselves. Just as mine medical officers in the 1940s had pursued a policy of swift 'repatriation' of tuberculosis infected mineworkers once they became 'unable to function' (Packard 1989b: 692), so in 1987, the Chamber of Mines moved to institute a similar policy for HIV-positive miners. In the years following the 1987 survey and the decision to begin pre-emptive HIV testing of workers from 'high risk areas', the National Union of Mineworkers (NUM) protested against this blanket discrimination of HIV-positive workers. Added to this were protests from the Malawian government against the expulsion of foreign workers. In 1991 the Chamber signed an agreement with the NUM that allowed mining companies to retain the right to pre-emptive testing[16] (as a result of which the number of Malawians employed at the mines was substantially reduced), but conceded that HIV-positive workers who were deemed 'fit for work' by the mine medical establishment would be permitted to work. When they became too sick to work, they would be 'repatriated' (Brink and Clausen 1987).

However, during a second survey which tracked the HIV status of 2,292 gold miners (the Carltonville Cohort) annually between 1990 and 1998, prevalence increased from 1 percent in 1990 to 26 percent in 1998 (Randera 2003: 2)[17]. A year later the Minister of Mines and Industry, Susan Shabangu, publically (and controversially) stated that 'indications show that forty-five percent of South African mine workers are HIV positive' (quoted in Fassin 2007: 181). While most people agreed that prevalence was less than 45 percent, Shabangu's statement had a powerful political impact. In the wake of these results, Anglo American rapidly scaled up its HIV prevention efforts. Timing played a crucial role in another aspect, as Toby Zwick at the Chamber of Mines explained to me:

> By this time, 10 percent or thereabouts of the HIV population at the mines were entering or in the AIDS phase of this destructive virus and the industry was beginning to see the impact of this disease in terms of absenteeism, sick leave, people going back to communities to attend funerals, needing to support HIV-positive relatives, increased TB prevalence and increased resistance to TB which really scares them[18].

The shift towards a more proactive intervention, which focused on prevention strategies at the mines, certainly marked a change in response from Anglo as the industry leader, to that of a decade before. However the focus on containment of the epidemic through prevention—centred around the ABC mantra of HIV management ('Abstain, Be Faithful and Condomize'[19])—placed the burden of HIV management on a nascent CSR function within human resources and was seen to be outside the domain of the core medical services provided by the mine to its employees. The ABC message, relayed through conventional mechanisms of peer-education and AIDS awareness campaigns, thus maintained a tendency to frame HIV as a 'risk' or 'threat' to production and labour efficiency from which the 'healthy workforce' must be protected. No direct support was offered to HIV-positive workers who were able to continue working only until they were too sick to do so, at which point their contract was severed. As one Anglo Platinum doctor put it, 'before the advent of the ART roll-out . . . they were only interested in the *negative ones* and how to keep them negative and if you were positive you were stuffed'.

'Taking a Stand': Moral Imperatives

In 2002 this changed. HIV topped the bill at the 2002 World Summit on Sustainable Development in Johannesburg. The same year the company were met by activists at the Barcelona conference. 'At that point', an Anglo executive recounted, 'we said, *we have to take a stand* and we just decided to hold our nose and jump'. In addition to the growth of international AIDS activism targeted at business, and in some cases, specifically the company, a number of other factors culminated in Anglo's decision to begin a corporate roll-out. These included a personal campaign waged by the company's senior vice-president for health; the continuing refusal of the South African government to provide ART through the state health service; and, most significantly, the dramatic drop in the cost of ART provision (due to consistent campaigning led by the Treatment Action Campaign for cheap, generic drugs). As a result, the cost of treatment dropped from roughly R48,000 per person per year in 1998 to R10,000[20] a year in 2004 (McDonald 2004). According to Matthew Waywell, senior medical advisor in the company:

> Something just sort of snapped within Anglo. One day the CEO called me in and said, 'about this treatment thing—let's do it'. I was shocked—it was a 180 turn. I was very despondent at the time because I had been led to believe all along that we were going to provide treatment and I had presented this proposal and they had sent it back to me and when that happened I thought, to hell with this crap. Even by the CEO's own admission he made a 180 turn.

As the largest private sector employer not only in South Africa, but on the continent, Anglo's decision to extend its HIV intervention from prevention to treatment had significant political ramifications. It was not until over a year later (November 2003) that the government committed the state to a nationwide roll-out of ART drugs. In the years leading up to this, the government's ambivalent position towards ART was top of the public and political agenda in South Africa[21]. As part of the government's national strategic plan for HIV/AIDS released in June 2002, President Mbeki established a panel of scientists to discuss various responses to the pandemic, a number of whom rejected the link between HIV and AIDS altogether (van Rijn 2006). Meanwhile, the Minister of Health, Dr Manto Tshabalala-Msimang, earned herself the nickname Dr No among campaigners and the media, on account of her anti-ART stance, as she publicly emphasised the importance of nutrition over and above the use of ARV treatment. The Minister openly challenged the efficacy and safety of ARV drugs, suggesting that they would cause more harm than good to those who use them (Cullinan 2005). The effect of the government's hostile position on ARV has been to mystify the therapy, enshrouding it in rumours of toxicity and miasma[22]. As a result, the right to ARV treatment became the most powerful rallying point for civil society struggle in the post-apartheid era.

Informants disagreed over the extent to which Anglo's decision directly catalysed the national roll-out. But few disagreed over the tension this caused between Anglo and the government. Chris Carrick, a senior Anglo executive in London, described the government's response to Anglo's decision as 'kafkaesque': 'to announce a big health programme to support our workers and to be attacked by the government!' Yet his further comments suggested that this response was not wholly unexpected:

> Government were heavily critical and said that we should have done it in consultation with the Ministry of Health . . . but when we called to consult with the health secretary a week prior to the announcement, she was 'unavailable'—which I suppose we weren't entirely unhappy about as we knew what her comment would have been.

According to Matthew Waywell, a senior medical advisor in the company, despite being unable to contact the Minister and 'warn' her of the impending announcement, the CEO, together with Waywell and a handful of other senior executives decided to 'go public anyway': 'we said, let's just do it!'. Like Carrick, Waywell described the Minister's response to the announcement as less than positive: 'ooh she was pissed off! She called me up and said: "what are you doing? You're really squeezing me here"'.

This was echoed by Ruth Steele in the Johannesburg office, who explicitly pointed out that the company's 'stand' on HIV was independent of state legislation and went far beyond the social responsibilities laid down by the

Mining Charter. On the contrary, she implied that in taking the initiative the company was met with criticism, rather than support, from the government:

> The charter does not directly address HIV/AIDS but we *took a stand* two years ago and made a commitment to provide ART treatment. We were roundly lauded by some and criticised by others . . . and it's not hard to guess by whom . . . we wanted to create enough pressure to make the government get its act together.

By narrating the decision in these terms, Anglo personnel cast their intervention not simply as corporate strategy, but as a moral mission claiming both an underlying political motivation and social impact that reached beyond the company itself; or, as it was so often retold to me by executives, as the company 'taking a stand' against the ineptitude of government. Giles Babish at Anglo London pressed the point home:

> Now HIV is not an issue that stops at the factory gate or the perimeter fence. It is transmitted through sex and that's primarily happening in the community and not in the workplace. If you're looking at the lives of your workforce, if family structures are falling apart, if you have large numbers of orphans, if there are constant funerals, even if they aren't your workers' funerals, if society is falling apart then you cannot stand by.

According to this narrative, corporate South Africa led by Anglo American stepped into the breach, taking the moral high-ground in an effort to lead government to it. Waywell stated, 'we were, and are, unapologetic . . . when the biggest company in South Africa takes the decision it does create serious pressure. I know it irritated the hell out of them and the health minister still moans today, "you created a problem for us"'. The claim to moral authority was unambiguous as he added, 'well, I think we provided a solution'.

The extension of corporate responsibility over the terrain of HIV management challenges—rather than accords with—the moral authority of the state. This picture of friction between the state and corporate responsibility disturbs the idealised vision of multi-sector partnership and a 'seamlessness' between state provision and CSR that is propounded as a central doctrine of global corporate citizenship. Yet, with the South African government 'missing in action' from the fight against HIV, as corporate executives often put it, it is another form of partnership that has served to authenticate the company's claims to moral leadership, in this case between Anglo and one of the coun-

Figure 4.1. The LoveLife brand. Author's photograph.

try's best known NGOs, *LoveLife*, as the mutual critique of government thus brought business into close alliance with national (and international) NGOs. *LoveLife* focuses on youth sexual health, through public awareness campaigns and the establishment of national adolescent-friendly clinics. According to Anglo executives, *LoveLife*'s 'very trendy, national, high profile brand name' (Ingrid Hamilton) inspired Anglo to develop the partnership, despite the more conservative attitudes of some of their colleagues:

> Some of our senior people were a bit sniffy about getting into bed with *LoveLife*. As an organisation they . . . produce some fairly sexually explicit material, including even very graphic, detailed information on masturbation techniques. But it wasn't up to them. (Chris Carrick).

Anglo executives invoked a forceful patriotism underlying the company's commitment to fighting the HIV pandemic, as leading corporate citizen of the new South Africa:

> We need to build on the sense of patriotism amongst young South Africans saying 'your parents' generation and their parents fought against apartheid—are you going to let them down by devaluing yourselves and sleeping around' . . . and this is what our partnership with *LoveLife* is all about—that is the vision we share (Chris Carrick).

Through this partnership (and 'shared vision') with the popular *LoveLife* brand, Anglo has been projected as standard-bearers of the new South Africa, delivering on the promises of empowerment for which the previous generation 'fought' and which, in the case of HIV, the post-apartheid government failed to deliver. A front page article in *Business Day* reported: 'it is increasingly clear that corporate South Africa is beginning to take the initiative in getting to grips with the disease . . . stepping into the breach where government has so obviously, and tragically failed' (*Business Day* 2002: 2). In somewhat more muted tones, the London *Financial Times* published an article entitled 'Making up for Perverse Policies', applauding business for simultaneously serving the needs of the country and the interests of shareholders:

> In a country with more than 5 million HIV-positive people, businesses are supporting HIV/AIDS prevention and treatment programmes. This helps to compensate for the government's poor record to date on addressing the disease, while helping to ensure a productive workforce and the wellbeing of communities where companies operate (Reed 2005: 12)[23].

Corporate South Africa thus appears as the paragon of social responsibility with Anglo at their helm; their moral leadership in 'taking a stand', juxtaposed with the failure of the post-apartheid government to confront the HIV crisis. Just as the claims to corporate citizenship, discussed in the previous chapter, project the company as icons of South African industry and architects of national development, so their HIV intervention is cast as reaching far beyond the narrow financial interests of the company itself.

'Just Good Business': Market Logic

However, reluctant to dispense with an underlying 'market logic', executives seamlessly interwove expressions of moral urgency and corporate virtue with the cold calculations of the cost of HIV in terms of human capital, in an effort to reaffirm the primacy of 'shareholder value'. The corporate discourse of HIV management, thus slipped seamlessly from the moral to the managerial:

> The decision was taken partly because this was simply the right thing to do— people were dying—morally you had to do something . . . There's an underlying morality . . . but that has to be tempered of course . . . this is, of course, not just a humanitarian mission; it's just good business practice . . . There's a clear obligation to shareholders not to blow their money (former chairman, Anglo American).

On another occasion, this coupling of moral activism and corporate pragmatism was expressed as Carrick described his confrontation with shareholders:

I remember doing a presentation to the shareholders and saying 'look we don't know the net cost of this yet. We have a health economist on this, we know the benefits such as reduced absenteeism, loss of skills, improved morale' . . . And this rather feisty woman said—'supposing the health economist tells you the net cost of this is really rather large, will you still do it?' I said 'yes—we are the largest private sector employer in South Africa and we've *taken a stand on this*. Partly for our own *self-interest* and partly in an attempt to persuade the government to take a sensible line on this' . . . If we don't do something we're looking at perhaps virtual societal collapse.

The logic of 'enlightened self-interest' focuses on countering loss to profit wrought by HIV, costed in terms of increased levels of absenteeism, loss of manpower and increased accidents due to impaired physical or cognitive function. 'We have a commercial justification for taking a moral stance, you see', an Anglo manager explained. Five-year projections of these costs are mapped onto graphs for each business unit and provide an economic risk assessment model for the company's investment in an HIV wellness programme (Anglo Platinum 2003d). Thus the company's 2008 annual *Report to Society* sets out the bottom line calculations of the HIV intervention:

The total monthly savings at an individual level were . . . calculated to be $219 . . . the cost of providing treatment was $126, giving a net saving of $93 per month at an individual level . . . The overall impact of HIV/AIDS on the Group, including the cost of the ART programme, was calculated at 3.4% of payroll (Anglo American 2008: 34).

These actuarial logics sustain a broader narrative of 'shareholder value' which reinstates—and apparently provides proof of—a bottom line to moral probity. Thus one Anglo executive explained: 'look the bottom line is that . . . it's just good business sense. If you spend thousands of dollars training someone to drive a truck and they then die of AIDS, you have to train someone else'. The simplicity of this equation, and the language of market efficiency in which it is cast, belies the relations of power in which corporate care programmes are embedded. By casting social responsibility as a facet of shareholder value, HIV management can be distilled into productive outputs to provide apparently irrefutable evidence of efficiency.

This was born out in my discussion with Dr Matthew Waywell, a senior Anglo executive, during which he presented the contrasting cases of the Goedehoop colliery (which aptly means 'good hope') and the Rustenburg platinum mines, and the respective success and failure of the Voluntary Counselling and Testing (VCT) and wellness programmes at each:

> Goedehoop and Rustenburg—it's like chalk and cheese. The manager at Goedehoop moved there about 18 months ago and said, 'how's the AIDS programme going?' They said, '5 percent have been tested'. He said 'this is pathetic' . . . He got everyone involved . . . They went from 5 percent to 92 percent uptake of VCT in 2004. They have a workforce of 1177. 90 percent of these were tested that's 1059 employees and 22 others. Of these 191 are HIV positive (that's 18 percent). Of the 191, 176 have enrolled in the wellness programme and the other 15 are thinking about it. Of those, 65 are on ART, and of those 63 are at work. That was 2004, now it's 2005 and he's reset the clock: 'now we start again with VCT'. Last time I saw him he said 'Doc, we're up to 100 VCT uptake' . . . Anglo Coal puts VCT targets into managers' performance ratings. They measure their VCT uptake day by day. I can call him—I'll call him now and say 'what is your VCT uptake for today?'

At this point during our discussion, Dr Waywell got up from the table, went to the phone on his desk and asked his secretary to connect him to the Manager's office at Goedehoop. The mine manager was out. Waywell then turned to Rustenburg, his tone less up-beat:

> My assessment to the response in Rustenburg is that it's pathetic—out there they have missed the boat completely and something must be done . . . What you see there is a lack of commitment, lack of leadership . . . At Anglo Platinum they claim that HIV is 25 percent in their report, it should be 35 percent. Why don't they know? Those section managers in Anglo Platinum need to be held accountable. Someone should put a rocket up their arse.

Waywell's recitation of the numbers tripped off his tongue, well-rehearsed after constant interviews and public engagements. The same numbers were recited to me in interviews with executives in London and were presented at CSR conferences and conventions. Indeed where Goedehoop had become something of a flagship case for workplace HIV management, Rustenburg was seen as the opposite, and, as such, received rather less attention in the narratives of executives[24]. Numbers are powerful in their ability to demonstrate 'proven' success (Porter 1995), and, as such, apply an actuarial mechanism for measuring the success of their HIV interventions in terms of a quantifiable 'output'. But such metrics of efficiency (the numbers of workers in VCT, on ART and 'back at work') impose a 'bottom line' of profit and loss, which objectifies the targets of this intervention as 'human capital', isolated from the host of social interactions and processes outside the work space in which they are embedded.

This approach, reflective of the broader discourse of 'enlightened self-interest', did not go uncontested within the company. For those such as Bridget Kessler and Elias Makoe, who worked on the 'social' as opposed to the 'medical' side of HIV planning within Anglo subsidiaries, the preoccupation with 'numbers', as Kessler put it, was indicative both of the technocratic and production-focused culture of mining companies, and the dominance of a traditionally bio-medical approach to worker health:

> So what are you telling me? That you would do anything different if it's 20–25 percent prevalence, rather than 25–30 percent? . . . The whole HIV issue has been melted down to two figures—how many workers have had VCT and how many are on ART. We have meetings with our counterparts in London, and that's what we discuss—the numbers! How many people are infected, how many are in VCT, how many are on ART (Bridget Kessler).

Yet the friction surrounding this preoccupation with 'figures' for VCT and ART was revealing of a deeper tension in the formulation of corporate responsibility: the tension between the narrow focus on protecting the company's human capital, and the broader moral mission of 'taking a stand' on HIV. 'Does anyone care about anything other than that?' Kessler asked, 'and when I say "anyone", I mean the decision makers'. The demand for numbers then, comes to symbolise the authority of the Group head office over the subsidiary as it demands empirical proof of the efficiency of its HIV intervention which, like production rates and profits, is measured in standardised, quantifiable units. Indeed, this demand for 'numbers' as the visible output of the programme is operationalised in much the same way as production targets (though without the same incentives and penalties, if an operational manager fails to meet a 'target'):

> It's the process of internal competition—beating up the laggards. If, as a business unit, you read in the annual report that 90 percent of the company is successful at this—it could be production, it could be getting workers into VCT—and you're in the 10 percent, you feel bad . . . you feel the peer pressure that you're ruining the picture. People in business are essentially competitive—nobody wants to be the dragging tail (former Anglo chairman).

Thus the idea that business has taken the reins, where the government has failed to act, goes beyond the elevation of Anglo and its cohort of socially responsible corporations as moral agents. It advocates the extension of market principles—encapsulated in the notion of 'responsible competitiveness'—as a superior system, not only for the organisation of economic capital, but for the efficient distribution of social goods. The catchy concept of 'responsible competitiveness' might more aptly be termed 'competitive responsibility', as it attempts to introduce market-based incentives and inject the competitive spirit of business into the processes of HIV management.

Yet the modern, technocratic discourse of 'the business case' for HIV management—which instrumentalises CSR as a mechanism to safeguard 'human capital'—recalls a much older logic. As Shula Marks reminds us, 'benevolent concern for the lives and limbs of its workers' is not new in the mining industry (Marks 2006: 570). South African mining companies have long been concerned with maintaining the basic health of their employees in order to sustain productivity. Health management in the workplace traditionally combined a paternalistic ethos with a Taylorist order which attempted to maintain living labour capacity by eliminating threats to low output such as absenteeism, and other manifestations of employee autonomy (Crisp 1983). This logic found concrete expression in the establishment of the Ernest Oppenheimer hospital at the Welkom gold mines in the 1950s; a model of both modern medicine and progressive mine management, according to its first director, Dr JHG van Blommestein:

> This was an era in which there still survived an *idée fixe* . . . that workers were just hands . . . that expenditure not directly relevant to profit must be kept at a minimum. However, the winds of change blew . . . directors and managers began to realize that every day lost by a sick or injured man adds to the cost of production (van Blommestein 1971: 100).

Over three decades later Dr Guy McAllister at the Anglo Platinum hospital in Rustenburg described a similar shift from 'labour battery'[25] to responsible corporation with the advent of the HIV wellness programme:

> Occupational health used to be just about being 'fit for work'—a rubber stamp, a certificate to work . . . If someone couldn't work, you got rid of them and got another . . . fatalities were budgeted for: 'we'll budget for fifteen fatalities this year etcetera'. They don't do that anymore.

McAllister stressed that the new socially responsible company no longer 'budgets for fatalities'. Yet, as discussed above, the contemporary model of 'the business case' for a workplace ART programme relies on just such a set of (albeit more sophisticated and compassionate) actuarial calculations, now cast in the language of 'shareholder value'. Thus, with a simplicity that seemed both irrefutable and reminiscent of van Blommestein's colonial discourse, the chairman of Anglo American proclaimed the synergy of responsibility and productivity, in his address to the Leadership Conference on Global Corporate Citizenship in New York, 29 January 2009, stating simply, 'healthy workers are more productive'

This discourse of 'enlightened self-interest' asserts harmony between the market logic of the 'business case' for CSR and the moral imperative to 'take a stand' on HIV where the government has failed. Yet, such a neat formulation glosses a central tension between the two. For, while projecting themselves as leaders in the fight against HIV, the corporate intervention in HIV management demonstrates the interplay of competing rather than complementary interests that are conflated under the all-encompassing concept of corporate responsibility. The moral discourse frames the company's HIV intervention in terms of a broad social project. But the 'business case' narrows the field of CSR, presenting responsibility and risk as two sides of the same coin. More specifically, this alerts us to a subtle yet important reconfiguration of the notion of 'high-risk behaviour' which has long been central to models of HIV management. As such, employee sexual health—and consequently welfare— become a function of corporate risk management, recasting risk to the employee, as risk to the company[26]. The effect is to externalise HIV as a 'social risk' or threat to productivity and profit from which business must insulate itself. As the chairman explained to me:

> There are also things in the country happening which have an impact on the operations, such as education, crime, HIV . . . conflict—things which are not caused by the company—but impinge on it—you could say. *This is not our fault, but we're getting zapped by it.* But if you're thoughtful you say 'these things are external, but it is affecting the operations and that's a risk we have to deal with'.

During our conversation, the chairman drew a parallel between the threat of HIV, and physical attacks on the workforce from beyond the borders of their operations, against which the company must protect itself:

> When the marauding gangs of paramilitary people came swooping down out of the hinterland and attacked your operation—what the role of the company in removing those people is—is tricky. There might be a national involvement—but you'd certainly strengthen your defences.

He evoked a vision of the company, isolated and under siege from the world outside its territory. Like the marauding gangs 'swooping down out of the hinterland', the chairman represented the greatest threat facing business in South Africa (that of HIV) as an externality, against which, in the absence of 'national involvement', the company should 'strengthen [its] defences'. Thus, the chairman, along with many of his colleagues, stressed that while the company offered a solution to the crisis in the areas in which they operate, the source of the problem lay outside the domain of the company, extraneous to the business of mining. Yet, the imperative to externalise the 'threat' and insulate the workforce from it, runs counter to the extension of corporate social responsibility into the realm of social 'upliftment' and community development beyond the company's 'perimeter fence' (Anglo American 2005a: 16).

'Knights in Shining Armour'

The tension between social responsibility and externalisation—and between the productive efficiency of the workplace and the broader socio-political context in which it is embedded—has played out in the evolution of HIV policy within the company. Crucially, it has resulted in a division between prevention activities and treatment, as the company has shifted its focus (and resources) from the former to the latter. In our discussion Dr Waywell had remarked that, 'for us, all treatment was part of a comprehensive response so there was no divide between prevention and treatment'. But the decision to begin an in-house ART roll-out shifted the terrain of HIV management within the company, from the domain of socio-economic development (SED), to that of core medical services. And with this transfer in management (from CSR personnel to mine medical personnel) came a shift in focus, from prevention to treatment. Just as McAllister had commented that before the ART roll-out 'they were only interested in the *negative ones* and how to keep them negative', so he went on: 'then "health" came along and they had ART, they were the *shining stars* and the *knights in shining armour* and they were only interested in the *positive ones*'.

McAllister's comment reveals more than the struggle over HIV management between a bio-medical paradigm and a social-scientific approach of which several anthropologists have written (most notably Seidel and Vidal 1997 and Farmer 1997). What became clear in the accounts of HIV policymakers and planners within the company is that the faultlines along which the HIV agenda is riven were not purely epistemological, but represented a deeper cleavage between treatment and prevention. Responsibility for the wellness programme comes under the mine's medical services and personnel, who are formally embedded within the traditional structures of company management. Since Dr van Blommestein's day and before, medical services have been a core part of the mine operations, financed by the core operational budget. In contrast, the SED unit (relatively new as it is) under whose responsibility 'prevention' falls, sits outside the central hierarchy of mine management and core operational functions, and is financed by the 'community budget'. Informants (whether core mine management or CSR personnel) were almost unanimous in pointing out that this translated into a striking imbalance, both in terms of budget and managerial authority; though they disagreed as to whether this was deservedly so. Anglo Platinum's 'community-based' intervention plan instructs that the 'community budget' can amount to the equivalent of 35–50 percent of the workplace HIV budget. At the same time, the 'community budget' was vulnerable, it seemed, to the fluctuating profit margins of the company, to a greater degree than the medical budget, as outlined in the strategic plan for Anglo Platinum's Community HIV Programme, Circle of Hope:

> Change in the financial strength of the company or internal policies of Anglo Platinum may mean that in the future peer education programmes will have to prove their worth to secure continued funding (Anglo Platinum 2003a: 67)[27].

The division between 'prevention' and 'treatment', was equally evident in the accounts of Anglo Platinum managers involved in the strategic planning and delivery of both the wellness programme in the workplace, and the prevention and support programme for the wider 'community'. Sister[28] Martha Lesego, coordinator of the wellness programme in Rustenburg commented, 'with the HIV programme we have two sides—the prevention side and the treatment side . . . The two sides are supposed to work together. We try, but . . .', at this point she shrugged her shoulders and tailed off. Elias Makoe, an Anglo SED coordinator was clear in his assessment of this division: 'with HIV there is a separate budget: ART's in health—the clinical side. We don't have much to do with them, we only deal with the prevention strategy . . . of course their budget is a lot bigger'. On one level, this separation signifies the territorial competition within the company as various actors stake out moral and managerial claims to ownership of the HIV agenda. The policy field of HIV management thus provided a canvas onto which actors projected individual and collective moral claims to champion the needs of the poor, the 'at risk', and the 'infected'[29]:

> HIV is fascinating to me—on an individual level everyone refuses to take ownership but on a professional level everyone gets very territorial, everyone wants a piece of it and it's very nasty (Bridget Kessler).

This terriorialism was equally emphasised by medical personnel, as exemplified by Dr van Zyl an Anglo Platinum mine doctor:

> It's very fragmented. HR were looking after it and I think they were very attached to it. Oh there's a lovely territorialism to it and suddenly the doctors now want it, and the people who had been punting the ABC (and we all know how successful that is) had been indoctrinated by the whole 'ART is toxic'[30] thing pedalled by the government. So there was a lot of resistance when 'Health came' onto the scene offering treatment.

Yet, the struggle for moral capital in the competitive field of HIV management, should not be seen simply as the inner wrangling of a corporate bureaucracy. These bureaucratic and budgetary details are significant as they both reflected and reinforced the discursive construction of two distinct communities: the workforce for whom the company claimed direct responsibility, and the 'broader community' to whom the company's prevention efforts, but not its care programmes, are extended. The cleavage between 'prevention' and 'wellness' (as the treatment programme is called) thus marks a spatial division between the workplace and the world outside its borders. This reinforces the sense of defensive containment and insulation from 'social risks' or 'threats' which are externalised—both spatially and politically—as outside the company's domain. Thus, paradoxically, the practice of CSR serves as mechanism for delimiting responsibility, rather than incorporating it.

This emerged clearly from the account of Anthony Roth, a project manager at TEBA (Formerly, The Employment Bureau of Africa, an organisation established in the 1920s to recruit labour for the mines), who spoke of the difficulties he faced in attempting to work with the company on a home-based care initiative for HIV-positive workers returning 'home' after they had left the company:

> For Amplats it's still all about treatment. There's very little prevention work— nothing really done to address the migrant labour situation which creates the conditions. Rustenburg is a perfect example—a highly mobile population, no proper, stable family life, squatter camps—and the company's only interested in treatment.

The separation of treatment from HIV prevention and support work beyond the immediate territory of the mine was, according to Roth, revealing of a myopic corporate view of HIV management, narrowly trained on the workplace, and abstracted from the political economy of labour migrancy and the social lives of mineworkers. As I will go on to discuss in the following chapter, this not only sets the workplace apart from society, but separates workers from their own households and dependants to whom the company had yet to extend these benefits.

This division is reified in formal company policy and the managerial tools with which CSR is operationalised, which attempt to neatly circumscribe the company's social responsibility. Thus Anglo's Socio-Economic Assessment Toolbox (SEAT) asks users (the company's managers charged with its implementation at each operation): 'do you understand the relationship between on-site activities and community impacts?' (Anglo American 2003b: 5). A clear distinction is drawn between 'impacts' caused by the operation and 'issues of concern' for the operation. A list of potential issues for concern includes: 'increased incidence of STDs [sexually-transmitted diseases] and HIV/AIDS due to influx of jobseekers and creation of market for prostitution'; and 'increased crime and disorder . . . brought about by a breakdown of traditional values and lack of respect for authority' (Anglo American 2003b: 55). This classification was similarly reinforced in the dominant register of executives, who repeatedly invoked the 'avocado' metaphor for corporate responsibility: 'CSR is like an avocado, with a solid hard core of operational *responsibilities*, outside of this is a softer layer of community *issues*, surrounded by an outer skin of host country and global *issues*' (Chris Carrick).

The spatial division between 'on-site activities' and 'community impacts' was formalised in the HIV intervention programme developed by Anglo Platinum in 2002 under the title Circle of Hope, which described its strategic approach as one underpinned by a combination of 'economic impact containment' and 'compassion' (Anglo Platinum 2003c: 4). The duality between 'on-site' and 'community' was captured visually in the Circle of Hope intervention model, which maps the target zones of the programme's activities and their interaction with the mine's operations. The map is simple—on the left hand side is 'HIV/AIDS community intervention'; on the right is 'HIV/AIDS workplace intervention' (Anglo Platinum 2003a: 22). The two are drawn as distinct and separate areas. A second diagram shows a different configuration of this relationship, one which places the workplace at the centre from which interventions radiate outwards echoing Carrick's 'avocado model' (Anglo Platinum

2003a: 34). But both models represent the workplace as clearly bounded and spatially separate from (rather than rooted in) the outer layer of 'community'.

The company appears caught between projecting itself as global corporate citizen confronting the HIV crisis in the absence of government action, thus extending its reach beyond the accepted zone under its control; and, at the same time, attempting to delimit its responsibility by externalising HIV as an extraneous threat to production against which it must, as the chairman put it, 'raise its defences' or get 'zapped'. The company's HIV intervention is thus simultaneously represented as a virtuous act (stepping into the vacuum left by the government), and a defensive action (protecting themselves from an outside threat imposed on their business and beyond their control). On the one hand, the corporate 'stand' on HIV appears as a radical manifestation of corporate moral responsibility. On the other, the logic of 'enlightened self-interest' casts labour as a facet of production—as 'human capital'—divorcing the workforce and workplace from society, and conflating development and social responsibility with the desire to maintain productive efficiency. The company's pioneering systems of HIV management attempt to make worker sexual health amenable to the kind of predictive logics which turn uncertainties into certain outcomes in order to insulate the company from the volatile fears of investors. The fickle vacillations of capital markets are then, intimately connected to corporate regimes of responsibility (explored in the next chapter) which attempt to manage a very different set of uncertainties at the mines.

In the following chapter I examine how this tension between externalisation and responsibility plays out in the routines of care at the mines. And how it is spatialised in the demarcation of 'moral space' around the mines, delimiting the boundaries of corporate responsibility (while consolidating the company's authority) within the company's particular zone and target of interest: the workplace and its workforce. Thus we find a disjuncture between the encompassing vision of the company's 'stand' on HIV, projected at the global and national level, and the exclusionary practices of HIV management at the mines which serve to recreate a separation between the dominion of the company and the world outside its borders. I now turn therefore, to Rustenburg, to the Waterval mining complex and the so-called 'community' beyond the workplace, and to the informal settlements which occupy a liminal position between the two. For it is through the re-inscription of borders that separate the workplace from society—and the spatial artefacts they create—that the tension between responsibility and profitability, between the discourse of moral imperative and that of market rationality, are brought to light.

5 The Moral Economy of Treatment

Corporate Responsibility in the Workplace

'I AM A PIONEER, WE ARE PIONEERS' said Sister Martha Lesego. At the time, I was interviewing her in her small office in the back corridors of the mine hospital from where she coordinated the HIV wellness programme at the Rustenburg platinum mines. She described her work in terms that mirrored the grand narrative of the company's intervention as a moral 'stand': 'what we are doing here, it hasn't and isn't being done by anyone else—not the government, no one. And without it, the workforce will be destroyed'.

In this chapter, I pick up the analysis of the company's HIV/AIDS intervention where the previous one left off, to examine the micro-practices of HIV management at Anglo Platinum's Rustenburg operation. Here HIV prevalence in the 27,900 strong workforce was estimated to be 28 percent (95 percent Confidence Interval: 0.235–0.328), the highest of all the Group's operations (Anglo Platinum 2003d: 21), 3 to 4 percent higher than the estimated average prevalence across the whole company (Stevens et al 2006: 138) [1].

I turn then, to the mines, the mine hospital, the hostels and the SED office, the central hubs of the company's HIV prevention and care programme. Therapeutic intervention programmes inevitably involve a pastoral ethic alongside the clinical dimension, which brings a moral dimension (alongside the managerial) to the business of HIV management. But what happens when this ethic of care operates within the context of corporate capitalism and the political economy of labour productivity? From nutrition, condom distribution and therapeutic care, to empowerment, self-discipline and compliance, the company's holistic approach to HIV encompasses all aspects of life. An approach which, according to a Chamber of Mines medical representative, is not driven by the oppressive dogma of public health, but by a 'primary commit-ment to the liberty of individuals' (Le Grange, quoted in Campbell 2003: 24). Yet, despite this progressive vision of autonomy and empowerment, I argue that the corporate intervention in HIV management creates a moral economy of treatment, trust, compliance and control, which extends the oversight of the company into the domestic—and moral—lives of its employees.

I explore here how the practices of HIV management serve to insert the company's authority into the intimate realm of family life and sexual conduct. Through the new technologies of HIV management old boundaries demar-cating the company's zone of responsibility are re-inscribed, erecting a meta-physical 'cordon-sanitaire' between the workplace and, what is described in official corporate discourse as, the 'world beyond our perimeter fence' (Anglo American 2005a: 16). In some ways this spatialization of the workplace re-invents an older legacy of paternalistic concern with the physical and moral integrity of the mining compound—a concern which was motivated more by the need to maintain living labour capacity, than to ensure the well-being of workers[2] and which, at the same time recalls the ambitious social schemes of 19th and early 20th century philanthropic industrialists, of Cadbury's Bourn-ville or Carnegie's steel town.

Through the daily routines of HIV management, the company attempts to 'make legible its subjects' (Scott 1998: 2) and protect the social fabric of its work-force—its human capital—from the physical infection, 'moral contagion', and ultimately, threat to productivity, brought by 'outsiders'. Both Lisa Rofel (1999) and Jonathan Crush (1992) have described hi-tech modes of panoptical surveil-lance in the management of industrial spaces and the kinds of worker subjectiv-ities they engender (in China and South Africa respectively). Here however, I ex-plore how CSR provides an unexpected platform for the extension of corporate authority which simultaneously 'sees' beyond the confines of the mine and de-limits a zone of social responsibility within its borders. Unlike Scott's imagined state, the ethnography presented here reveals the limits of the (corporate) 'pan-opticon'. Relations between mineworkers and those outside the workplace con-found legibility, and the attempt to neatly circumscribe and spatialise corporate responsibility. Despite the extension of CSR into the moral sphere of the family, the subjects of this corporate gaze remain, in part, beyond corporate control.

Instead, this territorialisation of corporate responsibility creates liminal spaces between the company and the world beyond its domain. As increas-ing numbers of workers are opting to live outside the hostels, mostly in the informal settlements that sit cheek-by-jowl to the mining compounds rubbing up against their eight foot fences, the distinction between workplace and society is increasingly anachronistic. Crush et al note that, since the demise of apartheid, 'the spatial perimeter of hostels has become much more permeable than formerly, facilitating higher levels of social contact between migrant miners and people living near the mines' (2005: 297). Yet, I argue, it is the very permeability of the physical borders (across which movement was previously more rigidly controlled) that has placed increasing importance on symbolic 'moral' borders that are re-constructed—rather than dissolved—through the corporate practices of HIV management.

Around the mines in Rustenburg billboards proclaim that the company is 'teaming up with' labour unions and 'working together' with community organisations and traditional healers to fight the pandemic. These stand as visual testaments to the company's local commitment to partnership and 'seamless synergy' espoused by the doctrine of corporate citizenship and discussed in previous chapters. Yet as this chapter shows, practices generated by

Figure 5.1. 'That's why we're working together', a billboard at the Anglo Platinum operations, Rustenburg. Author's photograph.

the company's HIV intervention create zones of inclusion and exclusion at the (dis)juncture between corporate responsibility and the social world beyond the platinum mines. In so doing the company rubs up against the state, represented at the local level by the Rustenburg Local Municipality (RLM), resulting in a fragmented patchwork of authority and development. Thus a central purpose of this chapter and those that follow it is to illuminate the potent, if unintended, capacity of CSR to create and entrench disparities between a vanguard of beneficiaries, those who become subject to its social responsibility (or the targets of its empowerment work) and those who are excluded from it.

'Know Your Status!'

In Anglo American's 2004 *Report to Society* there is a picture of the chairman receiving voluntary counselling and testing (VCT) at Goedehoop, one of the company's South African collieries. The caption reads: 'Sir Mark Moody-Stuart being counselled by Sister Evalyn Thwala at Goedehoop Colliery after volunteering to have his HIV status tested. Sir Mark urged as many Anglo American employees as possible to *know their status*' (Anglo American 2004a: 38, emphasis added). In the picture, the chairman and Sister Evalyn sit next to each other, looking intently at the plastic Oraquick stick which shows the results of the new 20-minute HIV tests that the company is using. To demonstrate the efficiency of these quick tests, the company's chief medical advisor, Dr Matthew Waywell, performed an Oraquick test on himself during my interview with him, echoing the chairman as he told me forcefully 'we need to get as many of the workers as possible to *know their status*'. The mission is clear according to Waywell: 'no-one leaves the mine without a test'.

At the heart of Anglo Platinum's HIV intervention message the injunction to 'know your status' resounds. Within the compounds billboards declare 'I know my status . . . do you?' Each month the mine magazine reports the number of employees who have undergone VCT, alongside a message from the company: 'management would like to encourage employees to keep on going for VCT . . . knowing our HIV status is the best thing to do!' (Anglo Platinum 2005c: 14). Articles present case studies of model employees: 'fellow employee . . . recently publicly disclosed that he is HIV positive . . . We applaud you for your brave action and pledge unconditional support' (Anglo Platinum 2005d: 14). In addition, the company gives 'thank you packs' to reward employees who participate in VCT, imbuing relations between employer and employee with an ethos of trust and reciprocal exchange.

Figure 5.2. 'I know my status . . . do you?', a billboard at the Anglo Platinum mines near Rustenburg. Author's photograph.

Peer-educators, recruited predominantly from the mine hostels, are charged with conveying this message. The six single-sex mineworkers' hostels, which housed just under 6,000 employees, roughly 50 percent of the 'MDP workforce' ('monthly or daily-paid'[3]), plus a small number of contractors according to the hostels' coordinator, represent the central axis around which HIV management practices revolve. The expectation, according to the Circle of Hope Business Plan, is that the message will radiate outwards from this core into the community, creating circles of HIV awareness around the hostels[4]. According to the programme's local-level coordinator, 'the hostels are a perfect interface between the company and the community . . . we don't want to restrict the message to the company'. However, the low uptake of VCT at the Rustenburg operations (in comparison to that at the Goedehoop colliery for example) was the subject of concern both at the operational and corporate level. Low uptake was almost invariably explained in terms of the need to foster a greater sense of 'trust' among the workforce: 'we need to get the workforce to trust us and then they will come forward to be tested' (Deryck van Zyl, Rustenburg mine hospital). Similarly, the company's chairman explained that the success of their campaign to manage the epidemic, relies to a great extent on 'trust':

> If you can get to a state in a company where people feel that they are actually looking after each other, trust each other, it's not just a question of health it

affects corporate performance as well, this is something which pays off (Sir Mark Moody-Stuart, Interviewed on Radio Four, *Today Programme*).

Once again we find the recurring theme of 'trust' pervading the discourse both of corporate executives and frontline practitioners at the mines, offering an idealised promise of corporate collectivity that claims the interests of the company and those of its employees as one—a promise that is encapsulated in the image of the company chairman receiving VCT described above. According to this vision, from an underground mineworker in Rustenburg to the chief financial officer in London, everyone is wrapped up together in a collective, transnational movement to combat 'a *common* enemy' (Sunter 2004: x). As a recent Anglo American advertisement in the British newspaper *The Guardian* stated, 'from miner to mineralogist, geologist to environmentalist, everyone at Anglo American has the same unity of purpose' (Anglo American 2010: 17). The exhortation to 'trust' invites an intimacy between mineworker or beneficiary and management which provides this benefit. Thus, within the very modern practice of VCT, a moral economy is constructed according to which treatment is given in return for the employee's trust. As Biehl similarly notes in his ethnography of HIV treatment in Brazil, the bond between care providers and patients is assumed to create and rely upon 'trust' and 'support' (Biehl 2007: 304). But while the idea of trust is commonly seen to invoke a warm and egalitarian ethos of solidarity and communal values, it often obscures relations of power and control, particularly where it is deployed within an existing corporate hierarchy of management and worker.

The notion of 'trust' invoked in the message of corporate responsibility delivered by Dr van Zyl, Sunter or the chairman is stripped of the dynamics of power which defines the relationship between company and mineworker, and the particular legacy of labour exploitation in the South African mines[5]. For Dr Guy McAllister at the mine hospital, the lack of trust was symptomatic of this legacy: 'the company does have good intentions. But one of the big problems is a mistrust among the general workforce of anything corporate, anything Anglo'. McAllister explained that there was an attitude among mineworkers who had seen colleagues being dismissed in the past, that if they came forward for testing and were found to be positive, they too would be dismissed:

What they don't realise is that their peers are dismissed, not because they were HIV-positive, but because they were too sick to work. Even now, the average CD4 Count when they present is 75—so they're almost dead. If they come forward and it's not too late, we can look after them. That's the message we're trying to get across to them. Once they trust us that we're not going to dismiss them if they test positive—then more will come forward.

Peer-education is presented as the key mechanism for engineering this trust between mineworkers and the company. While peer-education almost invariably involves a proselytising project[6], this takes on a particular resonance when mediated through the hierarchical relations between company and employee. This was manifest in the emphasis that peer educators and their trainers placed on overcoming mistrust of the company among the workforce. As one put it: 'my job is to make them see that they don't have to be scared, if they come forward, the company will look after them'. According to this paradigm, the company is delivering not only medical care, but the moral values of self-discipline, empowerment and the duty to participate. The vision propounded by the company's HIV intervention draws on ideas of 'empowerment' which have become a central doctrine, not only of Anglo's CSR mission, but of the new South Africa. The array of 'empowerment' technologies that are employed in HIV awareness workshops among employees (such as self-esteem building exercises, 'trust games' and role-plays) aim, as one trainer put it, 'to create a solidarity and empower people to take control of their destiny'.

However, through the process of VCT and ART, the company strives to produce participants who are not only empowered, but also compliant. The moral exhortation to trust and to empower oneself embodied in the battle-cry 'know your status!' simultaneously represent an implicit extension of corporate authority that asserts itself precisely through the demand for 'self-mastery' and compliance in the beneficiary/employee. Following VCT and a positive test, employees who chose to enrol in the wellness programme undergo two months of preparation before starting the programme. In 2004, Martha Lesego, coordinator of the wellness programme explained, the company shifted from an 'ART programme' to a more comprehensive 'wellness' approach, which she described as a 'holistic supermarket type of service'. The wellness model aims to incorporate every aspect of participants' well-being from the first stage of 'knowing their status' to ensuring a nutritional diet, physical exercise, defence against and treatment for opportunistic infections and, ultimately, adherence to the ART drug regime. When a participant's CD4 Count drops to 250 or below, they begin ART. But the corporate wellness programme is not only concerned with the physical components of care: 'we want to empower people to look after themselves, to eat well, to be disciplined', Lesego stated.

Both corporate executives and frontline health managers consistently underscored the need to create a 'culture of compliance' among recipients referring to those who were not compliant as 'defaulters'. During the two months when employees are required to demonstrate their eligibility for the programme, they must 'prove their ability to adhere'. Medical staff at the mine stressed that this was vital given the epidemiological risks of multi-drug resistance if treatment is repeatedly interrupted and then re-started. Thus Dr van Zyl commented:

> *Compliance* is a huge issue. There is a big fear of resistance, so we must make sure people don't default on their treatment. You need to take 97 percent of your drugs to be compliant and avoid multi-drug resistance . . . If someone comes off their treatment for a month we stop it altogether. So far, about a third of the people we've started on ART have dropped out for different reasons—some have died, a larger group have left the company and about the same number were non-compliant and defaulted on their treatment. The first six months they are *loyal to themselves*. As soon as they start feeling better, they start skipping[7].

Lesego explained: 'one of the key things that participants need to learn in the wellness programme is self-discipline . . . making them stick to the regime . . . especially when they leave the mine to go on leave'. This was echoed by Ruth Steele, an executive at Anglo corporate head office in Johannesburg, who stated that: 'the challenge that remains is *self-discipline*, because it's a lifelong commitment, a challenge getting them to commit to the daily regime and to understand they can't miss even one'.

The imperative for self-discipline and compliance is underscored by a moral discourse which juxtaposes those who come forward to 'know their status' and 'take control of their future', with those who do not; those who demonstrate self-discipline and those who 'default'. The term 'defaulter' attributes responsibility for the failure of treatment to the patient, neglecting the broader social and political factors, and the relationship between patient and provider (in this case between company and employee), that determine the capacity or will to comply (Packard 1989b: 698). The promise of empowerment and self-mastery on the one hand, and the demand for compliance and adherence to the provider (in this case the company) on the other, are contradictory. The concept of compliance, while deriving from medical jargon referring to a patient's physical compliance to a particular drug regime, does not operate in a vacuum. Rather, it is embedded within and contingent upon the relationship between the patient and the healthcare provider. The medical discourse of 'compliance' is problematic in that it potentially clashes with other components of therapeutic care, such as the promotion of empowerment and autonomy. As Sumartojo notes, 'the word compliant has the unfortunate connotation that the patient is docile and subservient to the provider' (Sumartojo 1993, quoted in Farmer 1997: 349). The discourse of compliance takes on a further dimension when deployed within a management-worker dialectic as in the case of Anglo's workplace care programme.

This alerts us to the tensions surrounding the multi-faceted relationship between company and employee, health provider and beneficiary, doctor and patient. As Dr Toby Zwick, Health Advisor at the Chamber of Mines, pointed out:

> Very clearly white workers are offered benefits and the health care is *exogenised* from the main mining business. Whereas, for black workers healthcare is an endogenous system. The doctors are part of management and are employed by the owners and therefore will always side with the owners. But, if one goes back to doctors ethics, the primary *responsibility* is to side with the patient.

The demand for trust from workers in return for treatment from the company, neglects or simplifies the awkward position and conflicting responsibilities of the mine's medical practitioners: committed to their patients, yet embedded within the structures of mine management. For example, Dr McAllister (like many of his colleagues) had been a mine doctor for twenty years since going to medical school on an Anglo scholarship. His integration within the core structure of mine management was evident:

> My job is to represent Anglo in terms of guaranteeing a fit and healthy workforce . . . as long as they are improving, we're happy to keep them on. We have a benchmark, and if you can get over that hurdle, you can work for the mine . . . But an 85 kilogram man who has dropped to 40 kilos is not going to recover all that muscle and I have to tell their supervisor whether they are fit for work.

The coercive bond to which the conflation of these varied kinds of relations could give rise was captured by the National Union of Mineworker's health and safety officer in Rustenburg: 'it's difficult when they do these things; it's good, but we need to find a balance so it is not still that the worker must be over-obedient to the master who gives them these things.'

Repatriation: 'A Hand-Over to Nothing'

> Now the government is giving ART through hospitals but not clinics, which is a big problem and constraint to actually reaching people. The big question now is, what do you do with workers who leave your employment or you have to get rid of for other reasons? (Chris Carrick, Anglo London).

In 2005, the wellness programme was, according to Dr McAllister, 'relatively cheap' at about R300 per person per month. This was in part because two thirds of the medical costs of HIV are incurred in 'the final illness' and, McAllister explained, most will have been 'sent home by then'. The wellness programme was provided to mineworkers for as long as they were employed at the company. If they were laid off, assessed 'unfit for work' due to illness or left, they were given three months of ART and then handed over to the state service. The Anglo American 2006 *Report to Society* states, 'we strive to ensure that individuals leaving our employment continue their treatment through other programmes' (Anglo American 2006a: 27). Thus Zuneid Moosa, a doctor at the Platinum Health Hospital in Rustenburg explained:

> We provide ART for as long as they're improving and are fit for work, and 95 percent of those on ART are healthy and back at work. But once they've plateaued, those who aren't well enough to work get medically boarded,[8] dismissed and passed on to the government health providers.

Anglo Platinum sets out this process as formal protocol, 'Progression towards AIDS: Step 3: creation of an interface between Anglo Platinum and labour sending areas':

> Where employees do not meet the required level of performance or attendance, as determined by the company, and exceed the sick leave allocation, employees will be referred to the company designated medical officer. The medical officer will *confidentially* discuss and determine the contents of the medical examination and the prognosis with the employee. An opinion will be provided to the company as regards to the employees prognosis and ability to fulfil the job requirements. If the employee is declared to be *permanently unfit to work*, with no possibility of rehabilitation, the HR manager will investigate the viability to invoke the procedures and principles of dismissal because of incapacity in terms of the Labour Relations Act 1995, Act 66 of 1955, and applicable codes of good practice. A *medically repatriated* employee will not be able to access the workplace care and support programme. Anglo

Platinum will commit to follow up the cases for a period of six[9] months to ensure that the employee has made a smooth transition into the community care
and support system within the labour sending area (Anglo Platinum 2003c: 9,
emphasis added).

Despite the focus on creating an 'interface' between the 'services offered
in the workplace environment' and 'the community environment' (ibid: 4),
the transition from company employee to 'repatriated employee' represents a
boundary. The consensus among the company's ART providers and coordinators in Rustenburg was that once a mineworker had left the company, hope of
a 'continuum of care' (Anglo Platinum 2003a: 58) was at best highly optimis-
tic. Lesego commented that:

> If a person gets *medically boarded* the company will support them with ART
> for three months and then transfer them to the government stream . . . As you
> are aware the government is not yet very far along with their roll-out.

McAllister was even more explicit about this 'hand-over to nothing':

> When workers leave the employment of the mine we write a very nice letter
> detailing the status of the patient, his CD-4 Count . . . 'this person is on such
> and such a combination' . . . and it goes to a Sister in a little rural clinic in the
> Eastern Cape . . . and then it stops. It's a hand-over to nothing.

With the high turnover of staff in the lower grades of mine employment (one
shaft manager put it close to 100 percent turnover in five years), the hope, according to McAllister, is that sometimes treatment will be picked up by other
work places if they've moved jobs. 'Unless of course they're too sick to work'
he added.

As yet, no studies have traced the trajectories of HIV-positive mineworkers who have left employment at the mines after a course of ART, or recorded
the number of former employees who have been successfully transferred to
other sources of ART provision—namely the state—and how many have not.
But, there is little doubt that in the context of the current economic downturn, on account of which Anglo Platinum has cut a significant portion of its
Rustenburg workforce, that few laid off Anglo employees will be in a position
to find a permanent job at another mining company that offers the benefits of
a workplace HIV wellness programme, making the chance of a 'continuum of
care' slim.

Yet, while most of the mine's medical staff acknowledged the difficulties of ensuring uninterrupted compliance to a drug regime, given the job insecurity of the mining industry, few spoke explicitly about the concerns this raised for multi-drug resistance[10]. Concern was however expressed by Gilbert Mogapi, an Anglo Platinum socio-economic development officer at the Rustenburg mines:

> Once it is rolled out, the service cannot be interrupted. Once you start with ART you can't discontinue it, if you come off it for a month, you cannot go back on because of the danger of multi-drug resistant strains. Even in places where the roll-out is the most advanced, like in Gauteng or the Western Cape, you might wait 6 months on a list. In rural areas in the Eastern Cape, it's virtually non-existent. And if your treatment has been interrupted for a month or so, then it's difficult to start again, unless you're put on a different combination of drugs.

However, such fears were dismissed by Dr van Zyl. It was precisely the expectation that (in spite of the company's efforts) few employees would in fact find treatment elsewhere after leaving the Anglo care programme that allayed concerns about multi-drug resistance:

> If you have a quick, clean cut then it'll be ok. If you completely suppress it, it's fine, and if you don't suppress it at all, it's fine—well not for them—but fine in terms of mutant strands. It's if you partially suppress it, or come off and on sporadically, that you get escaped mutants and that has severe epidemiological consequences. Also remember that, at this point, the number of people in the company on ART is still pretty small because VCT uptake has been slow.

A number of issues emerge in what van Zyl said. He was firm on the company's policy to mitigate the risk of multi-drug resistance by demanding either full compliance or complete termination of treatment because of the 'serious epidemiological consequences' of partial suppression or sporadic treatment. At the same time, he, like McAllister had made it clear that the likelihood that workers who were dismissed would find alternative sources of ART was at best unpredictable, and thus there was no way of knowing what the treatment regimen of former employees would be once they left the Anglo medical system. Van Zyl further suggested that the risk of multi-drug resistance was minimised as the cohort of Anglo workers on ART was 'still pretty small'. However the commitment to increasing participation in VCT and enrolment in the wellness programme demonstrates the hope that this number would grow significantly over the coming years.

As Farmer argues in relation to the epidemiological models of tuberculosis, multi-drug resistance is cast as a problem that is 'ostensibly biological in nature' (Farmer 1997: 348). Where social dimensions are taken into consideration, they are, generally, distilled into a formulaic narrative of 'blame', whereby drug resistance is explained in terms of patients' failure to comply with the drug regime. Rather, multi-drug resistance should be viewed as the product of particular political and social relations. In this case, fears of multi-drug resistance are revealing of the limits of corporate responsibility, and the disjuncture between a corporate HIV intervention and state provision. This challenges the dominant projection of the company's HIV intervention as a moral and political 'stand' against the ineptitude of government. In practice, the corporate care programme reflects the particular interests of the company: to maintain worker health as long as they are within the spatial confines of the workplace, the structural confines of the Anglo system, and, crucially, as long as they are economically productive.

The enduring terminology of mineworker 'repatriation' in both official company HIV policy, and in the everyday discourse of medical personnel and hostel managers, was striking: an artefact of colonial and apartheid labour regimes that has persisted for almost a century. Apartheid-era 'influx controls' on the movement of black labour between the constructed dual worlds of 'homeland' and workplace have long been dismantled. Yet the discursive separation of the mine from broader society remains a significant element in understanding how contemporary discourses of HIV management at the mines serve to re-inscribe spatial, moral and political boundaries between the workplace and society. According to Circle of Hope policy, a line was drawn which represents the limits of corporate responsibility once workers become economically unproductive and subject to 'medical-repatriation'. This boundary undoubtedly reflects the very real practical challenges of 'tracking medically-repatriated employees in labour-sending areas' (Anglo Platinum 2003c: 7). At the same time, it reveals a discursive partition recreated through the mechanisms of HIV management; a border which represents the migrant mineworker's temporary tenure in the workplace and his return to his 'home' outside the corporate domain as two distinct worlds. This boundary is circumscribed through the practices of social responsibility and care in the workplace and hostels. Here, as I will go on to explore in the next section, the authority of the company is consolidated through the daily regimes of the HIV wellness programme, and old forms of corporate paternalism are embedded within a new managerial discourse of CSR.

Health, Hygiene and Morality in the Hostel

During our discussion in his London office, the company chairman stressed that CSR was a radical break from the corporate paternalism of the past. Today, he said, the company was no longer in the business of regulating the social (and moral) lives of their employees; it no longer aimed, as he put it, 'to build a Bourneville and have a social club—but no bar because it's bad for people'. That, he said, would be the company 'stepping too far into people's lives'. In contrast to the chairman's rejection of Victorian corporate paternalism, the drinking habits of mineworkers were top of the agenda at a monthly hostel managers meeting I attended. During the meeting the company nutritionist asked about opening hours: '8am! So they can drink all day if they're not working? Is that good for them? Especially if they are HIV positive.' Steyn, the Hostel Coordinator, responded that it was 'safer for the men to drink in the hostel, than have them go drinking in the shebeens[11] in the squatter camps'.

This contradiction encapsulates a tension at the heart of the company's HIV management practices. The modern technologies of HIV management and containment give new force to old orders which the advent of contemporary CSR had supposedly consigned to the past. From sport and leisure, to health and hygiene, and from safe sex to 'feeding' as a productive system, the moral, and at the same time economistic, discourse of HIV management is embedded within the daily dispensations which attempt to regulate the working and domestic lives of employees.

As Steyn underlined, the Anglo Platinum hostels at Rustenburg Section are much changed from the kind of compound described by Francis Wilson in 1972 as a 'labour battery': 'now the company cares about their health . . . we are more socially responsible' (Steyn). And yet, in spite of these improvements in mineworker accommodation at Anglo and its cohort of socially-responsible companies, Elder describes hostels as 'old apartheid spaces' (Elder 2003: 4) which persist in the post-apartheid political geography of South Africa. Despite the directives of the Mining Charter and pressure from the National Union of Mineworkers (NUM) to 'upgrade' the hostels to apartments with single rooms and family units, progress has been slow. At Rustenburg Section only fifteen individual family units had been built by 2005, which, according to Prosper Masinga (a NUM shop steward at one of the Waterval mineshafts) 'cater only for those with higher positions'. At the monthly hostel managers meeting in May 2005, the housing coordinator explained that progress on this process of upgrading had been 'put off for the moment' in an attempt to 'cut costs' due to the apparent volatility of the economic climate.

In 2008 the company completed its de-densification programme reducing the number of mineworkers per room to two, refurbishing the units and re-branding them 'single accommodation villages', rather than hostels (Anglo Platinum 2008). One of the aims of this was to counter the increasing number of mineworkers moving out of the hostels and into the informal settlements, a cause of serious concern within the company. But, despite the hostel refurbishment, family accommodation is still available to only a handful (fifteen to twenty) of lower-ranking mineworkers. Thus, the prevailing structure of employee accommodation provided by the mine to lower-ranking employees is one in which a resident, whether he is single or not, is as Ramphele writes 'expected to live as a "bachelor"' within the confines of the hostel, until he goes on leave and returns 'home' to visit his family (Ramphele 1993: 20).

Hostel A, one of the six single-sex hostels at Rustenburg Section, housed over 1,000 men in dormitories of around six per room, 70 percent of whom, according to Kobus, the hostel's manager, came from outside the province[12]. The hostel is surrounded by an eight foot fence with a turnstile gate attended by a security guard and close-circuit television. To enter, residents must swipe their 'ID card'. Visitors—whether wife, friend or child—must be met outside the gates by their host and 'signed-in' on the official visitors register. Until 2003, no women were allowed into the compound. Since then, they are allowed for visits, but only during the daytime. Inside, the hostel consists of an extensive area covered in parts by lawns dotted with trees between which clotheslines are hung. The dormitories—single-storey barracks-style buildings are arranged in rows, with communal toilet blocks dispersed between the living units. Mineshafts and slag heaps run along one side of the hostel, separated by the perimeter fence. Inside the fence, another series of single-storey units house the sports shop, nurse's station, and employee bank (into which the wages of mineworkers are paid and which offers advice and small loans). In the centre of the compound there was a newly-installed 'learning centre' filled with orange plastic chairs and tables covered with Circle of Hope pamphlets on HIV-awareness, advice on safe sex and recognising the symptoms of tuberculosis. Next to the meeting room is the hostel's lounge and bar—also filled with orange plastic chairs, two televisions and pool and baby-foot tables.[13] Beyond the bar and lounge is the hostel's extensive canteen and recently-renovated kitchen.

Figure 5.3. Inside the hostel compound. Author's photograph.

Residents of the hostel staff two mineshafts. Despite the close proximity of
the shafts which tower above casting their shadow over the hostel, mineworkers are bussed between the hostel and the shafts in company buses in time for
each shift to ensure maximum efficiency. Kobus, manager of Hostel A for the
past eleven years, told me that, 'the buses will also take the men, for free, to
sports, if they have a contest or training at another hostel because we like to
support their leisure activities as well'. But, if residents want to go 'into town'
they must pay for a seat on one of the 'combies' (minibus taxis) controlled by
private firms, which congregate outside the hostel gates. These run the circuit
between the hostels and the town centre 24 hours a day, because, as Kobus
explained, 'the men work in eight hour shifts every day, so they are coming
off shift all through the night and day'. On the piece of scrubland immediately
outside the hostel there are stalls selling everything from football t-shirts to
hot food, and a few stray goats. According to Kobus, 'we're not allowed to have
this really, but I turn a blind eye, because the men like to be able to go out and
buy a beer or a home-cooked meal'.

Figure 5.4. Outside the hostel fence. Author's photograph.

From the physical space of the hostels in which mineworkers live, to the involvement of the company—through the agency of the hostel manager—in their personal lives, the hostel serves as an encompassing institution in which the interaction between its occupants and those outside is circumscribed by the routines of movement between the workplace and the hostel. The figure of the hostel manager comes to embody this merging of public and private, personal and professional. Kobus, like most of the hostel managers I talked to, spoke about his role in very affectionate terms, a combination of manager of welfare, morale, discipline and finances. He described his commitment to 'protect his men', and his efforts to 'educate those who aren't infected' and 'look after those who are'. And, he recounted the many ways he strives to improve the hostel and the lives of 'his men' who live in it:

> When I first arrived—the hostels were very old, but I've made big changes in the last five years. The hostel isn't overcrowded anymore. Room density has been lowered from twelve to six per room. The rooms can hold ten, but in some, there are only two, because too many men are preferring to move out of the hostel into the squatter camps . . . Now, they can choose to share the room with friends, we don't tribalize anymore. The kitchen has been really upgraded and we have community, social spaces like the 'learning centre' where we do induction sessions on HIV, and also the bar and the lounge for leisure time. They've got a sporting shop here where they can buy sporting goods and not with cash, but it comes straight off their salary.

Kobus added, 'we want to make it clear that we will take care of people and they shouldn't go to the informal settlements—where it's not safe'.

Despite the blurring of the boundaries between private and public within the hostel, Kobus stressed that absenteeism (a particular concern in the context of high HIV prevalence) is not his responsibility: 'if they don't go to work that's not for me to interfere'. But he added, 'if they're sick, that's my concern. It's very different from when I was in human resources that way, you see I'm working for the company, but what I'm doing is for the residents'. Thus he underlined the ambivalent role occupied by hostel managers, often conflicted between their commitment to residents described in terms of personal responsibility, and their status as agents of the company's direct authority over the domestic lives of its employees. The figure of the hostel manager embodied a paternal- ism that had been reinvigorated by the imperatives of responding to the HIV epidemic at the mines, yet clashes with the progressive discourse of empower- ment and self-mastery in which the intervention is cast in corporate policy.

A focal point of the hostel's welfare regime that is driven to a large extent by the company's HIV agenda, is food. This reflects the emphasis placed on nutrition as part of company's holistic approach to wellness. The 'Palladium Public Health Module', a scientific nutrition system targeted at 'maintain- ing and extending the wellness of HIV positive employees', has been adopted within the hostels (Anglo Platinum 2003c: 2). Over lunch in Hostel A's can- teen, Kobus explained the care that was taken to ensure a balanced nutritional meal for mineworkers everyday: 'you see here, today we have fried chicken, rice and butternut squash—they've got their protein, their starch and their vegetable, and you can see it's good.' In addition to the scientifically formu- lated diet, before going on shift each day, residents are given Morvite[14], a vitamin-supplemented porridge. 'This is to keep the men healthy—you know, especially the ones who is HIV positive—this boosts their immune system', explained Kobus; or as Steyn, the hostels coordinator said, 'the theory is they'll be more productive if well-fed'.

This concern with the nutritional sustenance of mineworkers—and its re- lationship to HIV and worker performance—was a central topic of discussion for the monthly hostel managers' meetings. During these meetings discussion focused on what was referred to as 'correct feeding procedures'. At the May meeting, for example, one of the managers commented: 'you know, the other day I was sitting with the unions and they were complaining that the food in the hostels was inadequate for people with HIV . . . but what about the squatter camps? Are they complaining about the food people eat there?' Steyn replied:

'communication needs to go out that the food in the hostels is scientifically formulated for nutritional balance with special concern for HIV. We can track the food groups and check they're eating right in the hostels. If they live in the informal settlements we can't feed them well'. The contrast between the hostels as a 'healthy' environment where employees are looked after and the informal settlements was reinforced further by Bruno, manager of Hostel B, who expressed concern that residents were selling their portions of Morvite: 'I've seen kids running around the squatter camps with packets of Morvite—where else could they be getting them from? This means that I have men in the hostel with HIV that aren't getting their supplements and it's costing us money'.

Steyn put up the most recent cost and nutritional analyses of 'feeding returns' at each hostel, noting that at Hostel C the proteins were lower than at the other hostels: 'you should be giving them 270 and you're only giving them 257. Why is that Jurie?' Jurie, Hostel C's manager, replied that his 'feeding budget' was inadequate to meet the new nutritional requirements of Palladium:

> Palladium says we have to give a protein, a starch and greens with every meal. But I'm giving my men rice or pap every other day, because those are the only starches I can get and still keep in budget and they are complaining . . . Look, they're not going for the maize meal, so I'm giving them more vegetables—it's less protein but more nutrition.

The company nutritionist suggested finding an alternative way to 'get their nutrition up'. But Steyn responded that the budgets were calculated precisely according to the number of hostel residents:

> Each of your *feeding budgets* is done on the number of workers you have in your hostel, so you shouldn't be over-spending—but on the graph I can see that some of you are feeding 100 more people than are living in your hostel.

Bruno explained:

> What is happening is that people are going back to the squatter camps and leaving their swipe card with a friend or someone, so they are coming in to eat the meals and we're feeding more than are living in the hostel.

Steyn asked how this was happening despite security on the entrance turnstiles:

> I don't agree with that, if you have the "Tribal Reps", or guards, or what is it you call them? . . . Prefects . . . yes; if you have the prefects on the turnstiles checking faces on cards it shouldn't happen. The guard should be checking ID

cards with each man coming in. If some of those living in the informal settlements are coming in with someone else's card, then you're over-spending on feeding them, instead of getting the nutrition up for the residents.

The focus on 'feeding' as part of the broader HIV wellness programme encapsulates the synergy of scientific workforce management, 'enlightened self interest' and caring corporation that constitute CSR. Yet at the same time, the legacy of colonial industrial paternalism persisted within this contemporary approach to HIV management, most explicitly in the linking of 'feeding regimes' to productivity. The discussions surrounding the Palladium public health model were reminiscent of the colonial government's interest in nutrition and worker efficiency documented in Fred Cooper's account of labour management on the Mombassa docks in the 1940s:

> The committee looked at how many pounds of maize meal, salt, beans, and meat the Railway and the Public Works Department gave their workers; the Government Biochemist said this was not enough, and the "Biochemist's Diet" entered the lexicon of scientific wage determination (Cooper 1987: 65).

Just as Steyn and his colleagues were concerned that HIV positive workers who live outside the hostels do not 'feed themselves properly', so Cooper cites the 1942 colonial committee into malnutrition and labour inefficiency, reporting that the diets of dock workers 'do not provide the resistance to disease and the essential alertness which Government should expect from its servants' (quoted in Cooper 1987: 60).

The conflation of corporate responsibility for employee health and HIV management, and worker performance and productivity, was equally prevalent among operational managers at the company. A number of times, technical line managers at the smelters, refineries or mine shafts spoke of the benefits provided by hostel living for the nutritional health of mineworkers. 'It's a holistic system' a smelter manager said to me, 'I'm sitting here running the technical plant, but if my men aren't eating right, if they're not healthy, then this is going to affect performance, no? And I must worry about that.' A couple of weeks later I was talking to Geoff (a rock mechanic) and Terence (a mine doctor) at Rustenburg's Keg and Barrel Bar. Both Geoff and Terence were in their early thirties, both had been with Anglo Platinum since company bursaries put them through university. Terence had come through recently on what the company described as an 'HDSA bursary'—a scholarship for 'historically disadvantaged South Africans'[15]. In contrast, Geoff referred to himself as 'third generation Anglo': 'my father was a mine manager with Anglo, my grandfather was a mine manager with Anglo'. He added (laughing) 'I'm technical, he's medical' (referring to Terence), 'he fixes what we break'. Geoff said he had heard rumours that 'apparently they are going to close the hostels?' Terence said that he had not heard this, and thought it unlikely. Geoff replied:

> What I don't get is that HIV is a big problem and malnutrition is a big problem right? But if you close the hostels or privatise them or move them all out to private housing or whatever, then they're not going to be eating right and their immune systems will be weaker, at least in the hostels we can feed them right. So there's going to be a lot more fatalities and possibly a lot more mine accidents if they're all sick—no?

The imperative to encourage workers to stay in the hostels (and out of the informal settlements) where their health can be monitored and maintained, similarly provided the rationale behind the promotion of sports in the hostel. Again, like the vision of Bourneville that had been rejected by the chairman, these discussions recalled the 'philanthropic' ideals of Victorian industrialists, and their preoccupation with the moral upliftment of workers through physical endeavours, underpinned by a vision of muscular Christianity[16].

The extension of paternalistic responsibility over the physical and moral vitality of the hostel was exemplified by Kobus, who described with pride the hostel's sporting achievements as a central aspect of the social life of the compound:

> We play in formal tournaments against other hostels, other companies and outside teams. For the past five years straight we've walked the North West Boxing Championships and won the cup in every weight category. It's really good when you see the residents putting so much energy into staying fit and healthy and promoting the Anglo name as well.

Such concerns reinforced the discursive construction of the hostel as an independent welfare community, in which Welfare Officers were charged with the job of encouraging and organising sports in the hostels. Their role in the health of the hostel residents became the subject of debate at a hostel meeting:

> Bruno: In the new system, the welfare officers have been demoted to level 5— you can't do that to these guys ... They're working really hard to look after the men, they're doing overtime on weekends, they're doing sports training, they're getting people into sports. Otherwise, what are they all going to do? Spend all their time in the squatter camps?

Steyn: Look, 90 percent of the soccer is contractors and I don't see the need for Anglo Platinum to spend the money to do the soccer for contractors that aren't Anglo Platinum. There's no business sense in that.

Jan: *Our objective is to keep people in the hostels and out of the informal settlements.* If we want to do that we can't cut the sports. We need the welfare officers . . . I have one who's our champion boxer . . . But he's being retrenched [laid off], so I've been giving him free meals and letting him stay because he does more than anyone to promote sport in the hostel and it's good for the men. Is it ok Steyn, it I keep him living in the hostel?

Kobus: But hey, I've got plenty of men who are working, but are sick with HIV and their sons are coming to look after them on the weekends. So my guy, who's working, his son only gets two nights in the hostel and Jan's guy whose not even employed by the company anymore gets seven months for free?

Steyn: I don't know Jan. I want to see figures—how much is he costing the hostel? How many hours is he working on welfare and how many men is he recruiting to sports?

As Steyn's final comment highlights, there was a sense in which everything targeted at maintaining the health of workers generally, and managing HIV in particular, was measured and calculated. Inputs (such as 'feeding returns', the number of residents recruited to football or the number of free condoms given out each month) were weighed against outputs, which were measured by the HIV prevalence rate, the numbers of workers in VCT and on ART. Circle of Hope guidelines instructed that 'peer educators must keep good records . . . statistics should include the number of people reached, the number of condoms distributed . . . statistical analysis is important in evaluating the performance of the mine peer educators' (Anglo Platinum 2003a: 39). Benjamin—an underground mineworker, chief peer-educator, and Hostel A's champion long-distance runner, told me: 'I think the message is getting through, last month we gave out 18,000 condoms—free of charge—in the hostel, in just one month'. These measurements, recorded by peer-educators, VCT counsellors and medical staff, and reported to the corporate HIV team, then form part of broader calculations of the cost benefit analysis of HIV management, demonstrating the capital saved in increased productive efficiency. These numbers then are important as much for the actuarial logics that 'prove' the 'business case' for CSR and demonstrate shareholder value, discussed above, as for what they actually signify[17]. But the conflation of HIV care with productive efficiency consolidates the fusion of work life and domestic life under the scrutiny of company management.

As Kobus took me around his hostel, he constantly emphasised the commitment to cleanliness throughout the institution: the bar, the grounds, the water, the kitchen, the dormitories, even residents' own personal fridges. Hygiene was a recurring theme in his accounts of hostel life. In the spotless industrial kitchen, he said: 'we don't have . . . infections here, it's kept very, very clean . . . The hostels are not the way they used to be—squalid . . . bad food. Now it's all sanitary, it's clean . . . it's a healthy place to live'. The concern for cleanliness seemed symbolic of a broader concern for maintaining the purity of the hostel from pollution of all kinds: from the risk of food contamination and infections, to the sense of a deeper threat of contagion from the proximity of the informal settlements to the workforce. Implicit within this concern is an imperative to 'protect' or 'defend' the company's workforce from the potential moral and physical corruption which surrounds the territory of the mine. The extension of responsibility over the physical and social health of the hostel reinforced the discursive construction of a figurative cordon-sanitaire encircling the compound as an independent welfare community.

As I left Hostel A, Kobus pointed over the railway track which ran alongside the North side of the compound. On the far side, the track was lined with a densely packed row of semi-permanent shelters haphazardly built from corrugated metal sheeting—the edge of the Edenvale informal settlement. Kobus instructed me: 'drive straight past the shacks, don't stop there, it's not safe . . . that's why we have these big fences'.

Borders and Boundaries

> Cross the boundary onto mine property . . . it is easier to get in than out if you are a miner; the reverse is true if you are a wife or dependent (Crush and James 1995b: xi).

My aim in the previous section was to show how the boundaries that Crush and James speak of are consolidated, not only through the physical apparatus encircling the mine, but through the less tangible regimes of social welfare and the discursive practices of corporate HIV management. Through these practices the company claims the health of mineworkers as subject to their relationship with the mine. While the extension of corporate responsibility over the domestic realm of its inhabitants blurs the boundaries between public and personal life, the mechanisms of HIV management simultaneously serve to sharpen other social boundaries. By defining the parameters of space, and indeed corporate authority, in this way the company demarcates an exclusionary zone within which social relations with 'outsiders' are legitimised, or de-legitimised. Thus Benjamin explained to me that the gate security measures were:

> To keep illegal people out and keep the people inside safe because there's a lot of risks outside in the squatter camps—there is a lot of HIV. But you can leave when you want.

Martha Lesego outlined the limits of corporate responsibility thus: 'ART is a benefit provided by Anglo to its employees . . . not to dependants or contractors. That is a clear boundary'. Thus mineworkers, who receive treatment, are differentiated from their own families, who in most cases owing to the weakness of state provision, do not. At the time this research was conducted in 2005, only 130 adults were receiving ART through state provision in the North West Province (State of the Province Address by Premier Molewa, NW Provincial Government 10 February 2006)[18]. Since then the roll-out has been scaled up, but HIV prevalence in the province remains at 29 percent, significantly higher than the national average (21 percent) (UNAIDS 2008: 18). Meanwhile access to ART remains severely restricted in the informal settlements which have virtually no medical services.

Employees who voluntarily subscribe to the company's Platinum Health Insurance scheme receive benefits (including ART) for their spouses. Subscribers are treated in the Platinum Health Hospital in central Rustenburg as opposed to the mine hospital in the Waterval mining complex. Dr van Zyl described the difference:

> Those who subscribe to the full-cover Platinum health insurance get treated in the company's Platinum Health Hospital in town—which means you get more first-world surroundings, no waiting rooms filled with hundreds of people or shared wards. It's the same doctors though. This one used to be the "black hospital" and that one, the "white hospital". Still, the MDP's . . . the monthly- and daily-paid workers—the black labour force—they mainly come here.

Only a small proportion of the workforce have subscribed to the Platinum Health Insurance: 'at most 5000, out of 25,000 and that's across the board—so most of those will be in the higher grades' (Dr McAllister). The company's 2006 *Report to Society* stated that, 'the majority of employees *choose* to rely on the national health system for the health care of their families'; but goes on to acknowledge that this source of health care is, in reality, unreliable: 'although

ART is available in this setting, waiting times are long and service provision is patchy' (Anglo American 2006a: 27, emphasis added). Clara Xorile, a health professional at Anglo Platinum Rustenburg, stated that this was not a matter of 'choice'. The health insurance scheme, according to Xorile, is not only too expensive for most workers, but fails to acknowledge the physical distance between migrant mineworkers and their families, who are excluded from the welfare community of the mine. This makes the demarcation of corporate re-sponsibility appear easier: 'for many their wives are in the rural areas so we don't even come into contact with them'. This was echoed by Prosper Masinga, a union shop steward at one of the Rustenburg shafts, illustrating the sense among mineworkers that, irrespective of physical distance, the boundary be-tween mineworkers and their dependants persisted: 'you see, their policy is to encourage us to take out their health insurance for our families, but you know it's not cheap. For the lower grades it's not affordable'.

The partition between the corporate domain of the workplace and 'home', as two distinct spheres, thus prevailed in the discourse of HIV management. The transition from one to the other had been identified as a key point of intervention at which to urge employees to 'get tested'. Thus, Benjamin, the chief peer-educator at Hostel A, said that his guidelines were to target em-ployees for VCT on their return from leave: 'we must approach them when they are coming back onto the mine from home'.

This way of 'seeing' the workforce as bounded within a clearly delimited zone of responsibility which corresponds with the physical space of the work-place has been replicated in the collective response from the unions. As Ram-phele argues, the dominant categorisation of mineworkers as 'migrant labour-ers' has delineated 'legitimate shop-floor issues' from 'non-trade union ones' (Ramphele 1993: 3–4) in such a way as to make it difficult for the unions to formally campaign on issues related to workers' home-life. Billboards around the mines announce that the company is 'teaming up' with labour unions to fight HIV. But from my conversations with NUM representatives and shop stewards at the mines in Rustenburg, it became apparent that 'teamwork' is, for the most part, limited to the national level of negotiations between the NUM and corporate management, which have historically (and continue to be) focused on banning pre-emptive HIV testing and ensuring employee consent for all HIV testing, counselling and prevalence surveys (Campbell 2003: 24)[19]. Thus Homer Bogopane, Health and Safety Officer for the NUM in Rustenburg remarked:

At the national level . . . they make agreements and joint statements. Here we are in charge of the annual bargaining over housing, the living-out-allowance and wages. I try to get all the companies to sign health and safety agreements with the NUM at the local level. But these don't include HIV. We are not so involved in their workplace ART schemes, except to ensure that they are always voluntary.

Bogopane highlighted the on-going struggle to raise the living-out allowance for mineworkers who opt out of hostel living. Yet this battle was once again framed in terms of the threat posed by the informal settlements to mine employees, reinforcing the discursive boundaries erected through CSR: 'every year we are pushing to raise the living-out allowance, and we will continue to fight until it is sufficient for a man to live in a dignified home, so he does not need to rent a shack in the squatter camps surrounded by crime and danger.'

The demarcations between the corporate 'community' of employees (those metaphorically inside the 'perimeter fence') and those outside it are reproduced within the mine's workforce; entrenched through inequalities between sub-contracted employees who work alongside the company's 'permanent' workforce' but are not eligible for the care programme and fall outside the purview of collective bargaining between trade unions and mining companies. The evolution of CSR has correlated with a marked increase in the number of employees working under flexible and temporary contracts who are, to a large extent, excluded from the spheres of responsibility constructed by the company, enabling companies to outsource their responsibilities and externalise the financial and social costs of occupational health and the reproduction of labour (Crush et al 2001)[20].

The exclusionary gaze of the company on its (permanent) workforce, its human capital, thus translated into a division, whereby the dependants of mineworkers were rendered invisible to the company's exercise of responsibility, even where it extends into the intimate realm of personal relations and sexuality. In many cases the separation between mineworkers and their dependants is not marked by geographical distance. Where dependants live in the informal settlements just outside the insular male world of the hostels (described by a union representative as 'still very much a boys choir') they remain beyond the figurative boundary of responsibility that follows the contours of the perimeter fence marking the limit of the company's domain.

Clara Xorile described how her work at the Anglo Platinum mines was equally circumscribed by a figurative boundary of responsibility, whether or

not it was marked by physical distance between mineworkers and their dependants. This boundary separated the workplace, from the informal settlements right outside its fences in which not only the partners and families of
many employers live, but increasing numbers of mineworkers:

> I have one patient now who was in a car accident and he is here in the Plati-
> num Health Hospital for the employees with insurance and his wife is in the
> Paul Kruger Hospital in town with less good facilities. I meet with the men,
> and they are sitting here with me, but they are sleeping in the squatter camp.
> I hear that their wives are sick or depressed or have AIDS but she doesn't have
> medical aid. Here, if they don't appear on the system, they aren't helped. There
> must be a way I can force the company to look after women, because the com-
> pany is looking after men and not women . . . not their families, the com-
> munity, the squatter camps. My boss says, 'I have employed you for the mine
> employees and not the squatter camps outside'. And I said, 'I have to go where
> the problem is'. He said, 'don't do it on my time'.

In 2008 the company announced its intention to extend ART to dependants
(Anglo American 2008: 30). This poses a major practical challenge, specifically
in relation to 'tracking' dependants back to 'remote areas' (ibid), highlighting
the geographical and discursive border between the territory of the company
and the world outside the workplace. It also raises questions about who the
company will categorise as 'dependants', and whether this will incorporate or
further marginalise those who live close by in the informal settlements, but
who subvert the classic portrait of the migrant miner's rural home life.

Despite Sister Lesego's comment that 'we are looking into providing a mobile clinic caravan for the squatter camps', the coordinator of the one and only
health clinic that operated in Edenvale at the time expressed deep frustration:

> We are right here. Right next to their operations, in the informal settlements.
> A lot of their workers are living here and using the clinic, but they do not *see*
> us. Perhaps because we are in the settlements we are not *visible* to them.

Yet the informal settlements are formerly mapped on the spatial diagram of
Circle of Hope's target zone. They are in plain view, marked as 'high risk areas
for transmission for STIs [sexually-transmitted infections]', surrounding the
hostels which sit in a ringed circle at the centre along with the mine hospital and medical stations (Anglo Platinum 2003a: 34). This suggests that it is
not the visibility of the informal settlements that is at stake, but *how* they are

'seen' by the company, and how that relates to the particular interest of the company in this target zone.

Through the mechanisms of HIV management and workplace care programmes, the company attempts to preserve the social and physical integrity of the workplace against the threat of HIV, juxtaposing the moral world of the mines with the informal settlements, cast as immoral, unclean and dangerous. As Schoepf argues, in discourses surrounding the spread and containment of HIV 'a major social fault line is drawn between people of high moral repute and stigmatized "others" . . . represented as bringing sickness— constructed as social pollution' (Schoepf 2001: 344). Schoepf clusters migrants together, as a stigmatised group including 'miners', 'prostitutes' and 'transport workers'. In contrast, the discourse of HIV containment at the mines re-draws these 'social fault lines' in order to protect the moral fabric of the mine and its workforce of miners as 'insiders' with a legitimate position in society, from the 'social pollution' and physical infection brought by 'outsiders'.

This was replicated by union shop stewards and NUM representatives. For example, Prosper Masinga, a shop steward at one of the Rustenburg shafts spoke of the need to protect mineworkers from 'becoming victims of the prostitutes in the squatter camps': 'at the Anglo mines here, people are crowded into rooms of eight people and they don't have their families so they're going into the squatter camps'. While criticising the company's housing policy and the separation of worker from family, union representatives replicated the dominant configuration which locates the source of corruption and infection in the informal settlements. This reinforced rather than contested the discursive boundaries of the mine resurrected through the company's HIV management practices.

In scapegoating particular 'high risk' groups outside the boundaries of the workplace, such moralising discourse not only erects metaphysical boundaries between the two but serves to displace the source, or cause, of HIV as an extraneous threat outside the corporate domain. Thus, the community affairs officer for Anglo Platinum Rustenburg commented:

> You will understand, with the establishment of the mines, there is a great mushrooming of these informal settlements, and it is a great burden to us because they are unsafe places with no sanitation and very high HIV. People who live there are unemployed so there is a lot of drinking and crime.

An article in Anglo American's journal *Optima* similarly speaks of an influx of squatters to mining areas, bringing 'crime, disease and prostitution'

(Russell-Walling 2006: 51). This register was pervasive within the company, and the mining industry more broadly. A British anthropologist who had been a long-term 'social impact' consultant to mining companies working in South Africa recounted his first visit to the Rustenburg mines: 'I went down there to have a look. And I was pretty worried about the labour problem . . . Brothels right outside the compounds. AIDS like you wouldn't believe.' Underlying his description of 'brothels right outside' the hostels was the imperative to insulate the company's workforce from threats surrounding the territory of the mine. Once again, the contemporary corporate model of HIV management is mapped onto much older social faultlines as it recalls colonial attempts to classify, stratify and segregate the 'working population' from the 'non-working population', in order to protect the former group from the social contagion and lawlessness of the latter (Cooper 1987).

Despite the powerful separation of the workplace from the broader social world in which it is embedded, Circle of Hope aimed to extend its reach 'beyond the perimeter fence'. A key component of the company's community outreach and surveillance activities involved 'mapping' the 'community', through a 'sexually transmitted infection (STI) surveillance programme' within a 10km distance from business units. The aim was to create an economic risk profile of the pandemic by targeting 'female commercial sex workers (and) female partners of male attendees' (Anglo Platinum 2003d: 8). Public health centres outside the workplace, such as general practitioners' offices and Department of Health Facilities were used as STI surveillance hubs (ibid: 10). The data collected is compiled to create an STI profile or map of the workplace and mineworkers when they leave the workplace and enter the 'community'. For example, the report states that 'for the month of October, the surveillance programme captured a total of 462 reported sexually transmitted infections (344 male and 118 female)' (ibid: 8); figures which are then broken down by average age, type of infection, job grade of workers and categories of 'sex worker' and 'partners' of male mine workers[21]. The mapping process aimed to identify high-risk areas for transmission for STIs which can then be 'divided into discrete, manageable zones' (Anglo Platinum 2003a: 38). The desire for nice sharp boundaries (arguably a product of the geological and cartographic tendencies of an extractive company) cleanses this map of the intricate social relations which straddle the workplace and the informal settlements.

As Scott points out, the process of demarcation, classification and rationalisation not only enables the state—but in this case the company—to 'get a handle on its subjects' (Scott 1998: 2), but also to 'remake' social realities in its image. It does so by aiming its interventions and social benefits at particular targets and zones; thus making them distinct from those areas and people who are not in its line of vision or interest, and creating a kind of map of 'legibility' which territorialises the company's responsibility. The great advantage of such tunnel vision is that it brings into sharp focus certain limited aspects of an otherwise intricate and messy reality, making it amenable to careful observation, measurement and control, and isolating that particular 'slice of social life' (to the exclusion of others) that is of interest to the observer, in this case, the company (ibid: 11).

And yet, in spite of the mapping, profiling and routine practices of surveillance, the corporate panopticon is limited in its capacity both to 'see' and discipline the workforce, and to insulate it from so-called 'externalities' which remain 'illegible'. Cooper tells us that while the colonial state strove to 'preserve the infant urban working class from the contagions of the idle, the criminal, and the rural' (Cooper 1987: 181), their efforts resulted in a more fragmented workforce, 'but not in a purified city' (ibid). The same could be said of the company's workplace HIV intervention. Between 2004 and 2005 the number of hostel residents across all Anglo Platinum's operations dropped from 15,885 to 14,928 (Anglo Platinum 2005a: 91). As mineworkers opt to live outside the hostels in increasing numbers they move beyond the paternalistic authority of the company's CSR, contesting the boundaries that such endeavours have resurrected. With the cost of housing in Rustenburg prohibitive even for middle-income households, there is only one viable option for mineworkers who choose not to live in the hostels, as Bafana Hendricks, Chairman of Housing for the NUM explained:

> What happened is that when people opted out of hostels, way back after 1990, people were tired of living in the hostels where their lives were being dictated to by the company, so they moved into the squatter camps. If the worker is not living in the hostel, he is entitled to a living-out allowance. Since 1994, the NUM has argued that it's not enough and has proposed 1200 rand across the industry. But in platinum it's between 800–950, in gold around 700. So unless housing is made affordable where else can they live but in the squatter camps.

Prosper Masinga, who himself lived in Edenvale, echoed this:

> If you live outside the hostels you get the living out allowance—this is 811R which means you cannot afford to live anywhere but the informal settlements. But rent for a room in there is only 250Rand.

But for Prosper, the choice was simple, as was clearly the case for an increasing proportion of the workforce: '80 percent[22] I think live outside the hostels and many are in the informal settlements . . . if you live outside the hostels you can sleep with your girlfriend, you can have visitors, you have your space. You have freedom'. Even Steyn, while clearly concerned about the number of employees opting to move out of his hostels, implicitly acknowledged the major attraction of the informal settlements in contrast to the hostels—freedom:

> More and more are moving out of the hostels. It's pretty bad, the hostels are getting emptier . . . With all the informal settlements developing around Rustenburg it's convenient for them to bring their families, their girlfriends, whoever they want.

The compound is, as Elder (2003) writes, 'intimately tied to other spaces'. The connections between the workplace and those who are peripheral to the immediate focus of corporate responsibility (other than as a threat from which the workforce must be protected) confound managerial attempts to make them *legible* through the practice of CSR. This disrupts the company's attempt to spatialize corporate responsibility, and defies any attempt to analyse corporate power either as an all-inclusive, all-seeing social authority in the model of (and in place of[23]) Scott's state, or as a new form of deterritorialised supranational corporate enclaving divorced from any 'broader social project' which Ferguson describes in his critique of Scott's analysis (Ferguson 2005: 370). As an instrument of social control, the practice of CSR incorporates particular aspects and techniques of government to survey, map, know, care for and manage its subjects. But the ethnographic account of CSR presented here reveals a 'topography' of corporate responsibility and authority that neither usurps, nor works together with that of the state, but is far more patchy, disjointed and messy.

'Thinking Beyond Boundaries'

Circle of Hope describes its vision as 'thinking beyond boundaries in the fight against HIV/AIDS by empowering the infected and affected with faith, care and support' (Anglo Platinum 2003b: 2). The moral overtones of this mission connect with the portrayal of the company as a vehicle of broad social improvement and compassionate capitalism. This vision is valorised by a pervasive discourse within global development arenas which elevates corporations as partners in the fight against HIV. At the same time the market logic of 'the business case for CSR' strives to reassert the primacy of 'shareholder value', proclaiming the moral imperative of 'taking a stand' and the bottom line of profit maximisation as harmonious. Thus the logic of CSR presents the interests of the company and those of its employees—and society in general—as one: 'the thing about AIDS is it teaches you the value of humans and human capital. A good response to AIDS is synonymous with good management and good management is good business and good business is one to invest in' (Chief Medical Officer, Anglo American).

But there is a fundamental contradiction between 'valuing humans' and 'valuing human capital'. The logic of 'enlightened self-interest' casts labour as a facet of production (as 'human capital'), conflating development and social responsibility with the desire to maintain productive efficiency and thus glossing the tension between these two imperatives. In this way core business concerns are recast as corporate social responsibility. By framing ART as a *benefit*—provided 'free of charge' by the company to its employees—a perception is generated that, as Toby Zwick of the Chamber of Mines put it, 'I am being looked after and I am *apparently* not paying for it'. But the endurance of the language, and indeed practice, of 'repatriation' brings into sharp focus the limits of CSR.

While workplace treatment programmes have often proved efficient vehicles for an ART roll-out, particularly in relation to the prevailing weakness of state programmes (and arguably take some of the pressure off the demand on public service delivery), this 'privatisation' of care through CSR is problematic. Corporate policy and practice on HIV management—and in particular the division between 'prevention' and 'treatment'—is premised on an imaginary of two distinct and separate communities: 'the working community' and the broader social community. As the practices of HIV management and containment extend the company's authority into the intimate realm of its employees' moral lives, they work to define the territory under its purview while rendering the spaces outside it (the informal settlements) as the locus of contagion, corruption and immorality or as one Anglo executive put it, the place of 'gunfights, prostitution and drinking in the townships'. While corporate executives extol the progressive paradigm of CSR evoking idioms of partnership, solidarity, trust and empowerment as a far cry from labour regimes at the mines in former times, the practices of HIV management establish a hegemonic duty of care over the workforce which is embodied in the affectionate paternalism of the hostel manager. HIV management can thus be seen to reinvent older constructions of the spatial and moral integrity of the mining compound simultaneously proclaiming and delineating the responsibility of the company as a paternalistic institution.

The result is the emergence of a vanguard or island of ART recipients, employees who depend on their corporate employers not only for their livelihood, but for their very survival. They are thus divided from society outside the workplace, and from their own dependants. As responsibility for the informal settlements is displaced between the company and the municipality, their liminality comes to embody the disjuncture between corporate authority and state provision. This tension undermines the visions of public-private partnership in health provision extolled by corporate executives and development professionals at the so-called 'global level' of CSR and development policy-making. Thus, through the progressive mechanisms of CSR, we see a much older process at work: the enduring capacity of capital, as Fred Cooper described it 'to create a stark dichotomy between job and no job' (Cooper 1987:181). Despite the hope of the company's chief medical officer that 'obviously we cannot allow our operations to become islands of privilege' (quoted in Knight 2005: 26), one of the unintended effects of corporate-sponsored HIV treatment has been to reinforce the economic and social inequalities in South Africa according to which the trajectories of the epidemic have been patterned.

The central issues which have emerged in this chapter concern the way in which CSR serves as a mechanism of social management at the mines. In the next chapter, the focus moves beyond the workplace to corporate social investment in the community, and moves from HIV management to the compelling promise of empowerment through enterprise and education.

6

Between the *Market* and the *Gift*

Corporate Responsibility in the Community

All gifts have an inevitable tendency to pauperise the recipients

(Charles Dickens, *Hard Times*[1]).

You must always be ready to concede all that you can. When you want something from a person, think first what you can give him in return. Let him think that it's he who is coming off best. But all the time make sure it is you in the end

(Ernest Oppenheimer to his son Harry, quoted in Hocking 1973[2]).

SITTING IN SANDRINGHAM GARDENS Retirement Village in Johannesburg, Ike Rosmarin spoke about his life in Rustenburg. For forty years, Ike had been manager of the Victoria Trading Store on the Rustenburg Platinum Mine and chairman of the town's Red Cross:

Did Rebecca tell you about the water and the school? . . . Well, when Rebecca, my domestic worker, moved to Bleskop[3] in the 70s there was no water there—not until the Rand Water Company came from Jo'burg and put water there quite recently. So I used to drive out there three times a week to deliver a big water tank to Rebecca and Abe. When her grandson, Nelson, was still just little . . . we arranged a birthday party for him in his classroom at the school, so we bought cake and biscuits and a tank of water for all his class mates to the school and had a party in his class. When we came out of the classroom there was a big crowd of school children with receptacles for water . . . So the next day I went to see Charlie Stott who was the manager of the Rustenburg Platinum Mine and I told him that the school had no water and something must be done. Immediately we got into his Mercedes Benz and drove to the school and he spoke with the principal. You've seen the mine shaft, just opposite Rebecca's house—the Turfontein mine shaft. Well two weeks later Charlie Stott had a pipe built from the mine direct to the school to pipe water.

In this portrait of classic corporate largesse, the iconic figure of the mine manager looms over the town as the paternalistic and all-powerful 'big man'. The grand gestures of corporate beneficence have, we are told, been banished by the advent of the modern discourse of corporate social investment (CSI) and its focus on progressive buzzwords such as sustainability, empowerment and participation aligned with the political agenda of the post-apartheid government. In so doing, mining companies have moved away from the rhetoric of philanthropy towards that of capacity building and social investment programmes allowing them, as Stirrat and Henkel comment with respect to NGOs, 'to avoid the charge that they are patrons' (Stirrat and Henkel 1997: 73). Nox Ndovulu, Regional CSI manager for Anglo Platinum described this shift: 'the company used to have all these ad-hoc projects and donations . . . now we have these structures to align with and to fit what we are doing into the local development plans'.

This chapter examines the ways in which corporate responsibility is practiced, dispensed and deployed in the so called 'wider community' of Rustenburg beyond the immediate territory of the mines. Mine ethnographers have revealed how the paternalism of managers was a crucial vehicle of control over workers[4]. But, the philanthropic endeavours of those such as Charlie Stott toward the so-called 'wider community' were traditionally viewed as peripheral to the core business of mining, operating within the moral world of gifts, distinct from the supposedly amoral realm of 'the market', and the logic of profit-maximisation that drives it. In contrast, as we have seen, contemporary CSR claims a position within core business practice and the capacity to change the way in which business itself is done. In this way CSR claims a radical break with the legacy of corporate philanthropy, charitable giving replaced by the technocratic rationalism of 'responsible competitiveness' and a market-driven paradigm of 'social investment', while corporate-community partnership takes the place of the mine manager's paternalism. Thus Anglo's annual Report to Society tells us: 'from philanthropy to partnership, the nature of Anglo American's relationships with host communities is changing' (Anglo American 2008: 38). This was encapsulated in the remarks of the former chairman of another mining multinational: 'I don't see it as my responsibility to spend shareholder money on grand philanthropic gestures, it's actually how we build security for long-term business investment. It makes the company a much more attractive partner to a host government or host community'. By drawing on a powerful paradigm of 'empowerment' through enterprise and education, the doctrine of CSR asserts that 'the market' itself offers the route to upliftment and emancipation from poverty; that the interests of material accumulation can be pursued alongside those of moral well-being.

The commitment to 'empowerment through enterprise' (Anglo American, 2005a: 14), and the practices through which it is enacted, strive to convert 'beneficiaries' to the values and virtues of market capitalism with an injunction to 'help yourself' to a piece of 'the market' and grab the opportunities and freedoms that it offers: 'to uplift and empower' as the company's frontline CSR officers so often said. However, while the promise of CSR holds out this vision of mutual independence and self-sustainability, I argue that the practice of CSR re-invents older relations of patronage and clientelism which recreate the coercive bonds of 'the gift', inspiring deference and dependence on the part of the recipient, rather than autonomy and empowerment.

In the *The Gift* (1967), Mauss identifies reciprocity as one of the key distinguishing characteristics of the gift economy. The bonds created through the interplay of gift and counter-gift provided Mauss with a model of the social contract: an essential method of creating social cohesion and solidarity, and forging diplomatic alliances between donor and recipient. The power of the gift is thus seen to lie in its ability to 'make friends' (Sahlins 1972: 186[5]). The obligation of reciprocity implicit in a gift is therefore crucial in ensuring the continuation of these ties—providing a mode of socialisation that rests specifically on the imperative for the debt to be repaid with a commensurable return.

But, Mauss' preoccupation with reciprocity seems to have led him to neglect what happens when a gift is not, or cannot be, reciprocated. He hints briefly at it commenting 'the unreciprocated gift debases the recipient' (Mauss 1967: 63), but takes it no further. If the gift carries an inherent expectation of reciprocity, what happens to the unreciprocated or unreciprocable gift? If the reciprocity of gift-giving stands for social cohesion and stability, a denial of reciprocity presumably signals instability, fragility and inequality. As Parry puts it the unreciprocated gift 'denies obligation and replaces the reciprocal interdependence on which society is founded with an asymmetrical dependence' (Parry 1986: 458). The expectation of reciprocity inherent in the gift leaves the receiver in a position of indebtedness and vulnerable to the whims of the donor. As this chapter will explore, the experience of the company's partners and beneficiaries suggests that the 'friendship' inspired by the gift of CSR is characterised not by the Maussian ideal of mutual interdependence, but by deference and dependency in return for the patron's provision. Sahlins reminds us that, a relationship cannot be, in material terms, simultaneously 'reciprocal' and 'generous' (1972: 134), for commensurable reciprocity would cancel out the latter. It is precisely the impossibility of reciprocal return which both demonstrates the company's generosity and ensures the power it achieves over recipients. Herein lies the capacity of CSR to command compliance and co-opt allegiance to the company's authority.

This points to a central paradox that this chapter sets out to unpack. On the one hand the discourse of CSR is framed in terms of commitment to the orthodoxy of 'economic empowerment' (discussed in Chapter 3), and its attendant values of 'self-help' and 'autonomy' which solicit the voluntary participation of people in attempts to re-make themselves into ideal type market actors (Cruikshank 1999: 86). On the other hand the practice of CSR is embedded in the social relations of patronage and clientelism which carry with them the moral bonds and coercive properties of the gift, rendering this quest for 'empowerment' elusive.

'Uplift and Empower'

> I remember when . . . in the old days the concept of CSR was a bunch of thugs in a truck coming in to 'persuade' the community that the operation was a good thing, or there was the time when (the company) literally flew in a plane full of prostitutes to try and convince the community leaders. (Head of CSR at a transnational oil company, over coffee at the Corporate Citizenship Convention, Johannesburg 21–22 September 2004).

In the CSI offices at the Waterval mining village a shiny copy of Anglo American's award-winning Socio-Economic Assessment Toolbox (SEAT) sits on the desk of one of the CSI team, Jerry Mosenyi. This weighty ring-binder—the latest in 'social technology'— provides a step-by-step guide to implementing community development for front-line CSI officers like Jerry, from community profiling to stakeholder consultation, and crucially, techniques for 'building trust' with the community. SEAT instructs users that the business unit should 'lay the foundations for *trust*' and demonstrate their 'commitment to being responsible *neighbours*' through partnership (Anglo American 2003b: 11). In Rustenburg however, the development landscape is defined not so much by this neighbourly ideal of collaboration, as by a fiercely competitive arena of CSI. This is visible on most corners, displayed on numerous billboards which front schools, clinics and community organisations announcing the 'social investment' of one or other of the five multinational mining companies that operate within the Rustenburg Local Municipality (RLM). Others stand alone, merely reminding passers-by of a company's environmental values or commitment to the community. It is equally visible on almost every page of Rustenburg's weekly English and Afrikaans newspaper, *The Herald*. Headline articles celebrate 'One Million Fatality-Free Shifts' at a certain mine (Rustenburg Herald 2005a: 2); announce 'empowerment deals' between one or other of Rustenburg's old mining houses and new BEE companies (Rustenburg Herald 2005b: 7); or recount competitive charitable fund-raising events between two companies (Rustenburg Herald 2005c: 3). Each week the newspaper informs readers of the constant cycle of stakeholder meetings and community consultations held by the various mines. These aim to build such trust and, as Gilbert Mogapi (an Anglo Platinum SED officer) put it, 'make friends' with the community[6].

Thus, from newspaper advertisements promoting Anglo's investment of millions of Rand in the 'community' of South Africa to billboards in Rustenburg, the mining houses strive to claim social development as a commodity and present themselves as the primary local supplier, and as Rustenburg's Mayor said, 'to win the best reputation in the community'. It is not only reputation for which companies compete through their CSI activities, but something more intrinsic to their survival. Quoting the mine manager of Anglo Platinum's Rustenburg Section, Grace, a long-term employee of Anglo's community development office, explained the role of CSR:

> You know we think CSR is just giving out a few things but then you realise how crucial it is. A few years ago CSR was just a 'nice-to-have', but . . . we had a meeting with the mine manager the other day and he said to us that "in a rugby match the guy with the ball is being protected by all the other players from being attacked and he sees CSR as protecting the guy with the ball[7].

CSI in Rustenburg (and indeed nationally) is then a highly competitive affair, as companies work to project themselves as ideal corporate citizens, leaders in the community's development, and empowerers of the next generation of South African leaders in their own image (as the Anglo Platinum advertisement instructed, 'leaders grow leaders'[8]). A Joint Development Forum was set up in 2004 with the aim of bringing the CSR teams of the various companies together in a bi-monthly meeting to discuss their plans, share knowledge, avoid replication and facilitate collaboration. By the time I arrived in January 2005, the Forum existed in name only. The last meeting was held in late 2004 and there seemed little enthusiasm to resurrect it among the various CSI officers I spoke to at Anglo Platinum as well as at their 'rival' companies. The Rustenburg Community Foundation was met with similar failure when trying in 2005 to bring the various companies together at what they called a

'Mining Conversation Desk', in order to work on a collaborative plan for post-mine closure development entitled 'Beyond Platinum':

> We managed to get Xstrata, Impala and Anglo here around the table and once they were here they shared on the surface issues that don't affect them much, but once they walked out of here, that was it. But we need the corporates because we have no idea what they're doing (Adelle Farmer, Director of the Rustenburg Community Foundation).

Mine management personnel such as Marius du Plooy attributed the competitive, as opposed to collaborative, ethos to the exigencies of the national Mining Charter:

> Well, there's always a difference between what we say and what we do—we all say now that this is no longer a competitive issue . . . but to score points on the charter scorecard it still has to be your name on the project.

The claim to ownership attached a corporate branding to 'partner' NGOs or community initiatives, as one local NGO director relayed, describing the difficulty he faced in seeking additional sources of funding: 'Then you think, ok we'll get funding from somewhere else. But, the challenge is that no other company wants to touch you once you're seen as an Anglo Platinum project, or an Impala project'. Underlying this need to 'score points' through social responsibility, there was a broader imperative to claim 'the community' as a constituency, or even a product of the company. Sarah Kwena, a CSR manager at Impala Platinum explained:

> We just get on with running our own Impala projects, in *our* areas and try not to cross the other companies where possible. *We only share one community* with Anglo—and so we share a little bit of information with them . . . but we still do our own projects.

Kwena's comments underscored how the notion of 'community' was mobilised as the subject of this competition over social responsibility. Implicit within the pursuit of 'community partnership' there were barely hidden (and sometimes explicit) claims to ownership. To a certain extent, this was reflected in the formal processes of CSR as stipulated in Anglo's all-encompassing Socio-Economic Toolbox, which demanded of front-line CSR officers, 'do you have a profile of *your* associated communities'. The slippage that ran throughout the manual from a neutral reference to 'the community' to a possessive assertion of '*your* communities' was revealing of this underlying sense of ownership (Anglo American 2003b: 5).

Thus, just as partnership has become a key doctrine of the CSR canon within the 'global' arenas of corporate citizenship in London, so it figures prominently in the company's CSI agenda at the operational level, where the rhetoric of 'societal consensus' is translated into the pursuit of 'community consensus'. Within this competitive marketplace, 'community partnership' has become a most-prized asset for both donors and recipients. For corporate donors, the great benefit of 'community partnership' is that it endows their intervention in local development and governance with a moral authority and legitimacy achieved through the rituals of grass-roots participation. The discursive practices of partnership serve not only to extend the company's influence over the particular targets of its development work, but in so doing, to construct a 'community' of beneficiaries which implicitly authenticates its claims to moral authority as a vehicle of upliftment and empowerment. For recipients meanwhile, corporations represent one of the very few sources of funding, as they compete for subvention from companies for various community initiatives (I will return to this later on).

Corporate rhetoric stresses that CSR and community engagement should not be seen as an isolated function within the company; that social and environmental welfare, with regards to both the workforce *and* the wider community, should inform every aspect of business practice and decision-making, and be 'mainstreamed' into the mindset of every smelter, hostel or health and safety manager, and every rock mechanic, geologist and surveyor. But at Rustenburg Section, as at most operations, CSI—or socio-economic development (SED) as it is called—is a separate unit which occupied offices in a couple of disused dormitories in a former mineworkers hostel in the Waterval Mining Complex. The SED team whose job it is to implement this empowerment agenda was made up of six full-time and two part-time employees. In contrast to the starkly male world of technical extraction, the company's SED unit, often referred to as the 'soft side', has traditionally been inhabited mainly by women (in 2005 the balance shifted with the recruitment of three men to the team). At the same time, until 2005 the team was almost entirely made up of white women, all of whom expressed a deep sense of rootedness in the company, as their commitment to 'community upliftment' merged (and at times conflicted) with an equal or possibly stronger sense of responsibility and loyalty to the company. Gill, who had worked in the SED unit for a number of years and whose husband was a technical manager with the company, told me, 'I have lived *in* Anglo for 30 years', while Elaine another member of the team described herself as 'third generation Anglo'.

In the two years prior to this research (2003–2005), four black members of the team were recruited, and the former white manager of Community Affairs was moved to the corporate office in Johannesburg. This has been accompanied by an increasing drive to professionalise local-level CSR as an area of development expertise, rather than paternalistic and amateur philanthropy (in part through the implementation of SEAT). However the recruitment of black staff within the CSR/SED unit is taken by some, not only outside but inside the company, as a testament to the company's attempt to resist, rather than embrace, transformation. Thus Leonard Xixo, an executive from the Johannesburg office stated:

> Of course they want to fire the whites and hire as many blacks as possible to the sections that deal with the community—because that's how you put a black face on the company—that's the face that outsiders see—and so you can say 'look how we are transforming and empowering'. Tell me, how empowered are these CSR officers in Rustenburg? How much authority do they have?

Gilbert Mogapi, one of those newly appointed to the Rustenburg SED office, echoed Xixo's comments: 'ah yes—you can see we have undergone a face-lift. With our new boss Nox, we now have the right face'[9].

Empowerment Through Enterprise

In Rustenburg, the elevation of community partnership as the central mechanism through which 'empowerment' is achieved is coupled with the imperative to embed 'sustainability' into the town, and guard against the ever-present threat of decline into a 'ghost-town' when the mines close or cease to churn out profit. The SEAT overview for example, instructs frontline CSR operatives to consider whether 'the community is *viable* or *unviable* post-Anglo' (Anglo American 2003b: 116). Central to this agenda is the promotion of small and medium-sized enterprise (SME) and entrepreneurship development through a combined focus on training, business start-up support and preferential procurement tenders for BEE companies through the corporate supply chain. Thus the language of CSR expressed in both official company policy, and by the company's front-line CSR agents in Rustenburg, stressed the rejection of 'a culture of dependency' on hand-outs and gifts, and the creation of a new ethos of 'self-empowerment':

They can ask us for assistance if they need it but we try not to encourage it because we want them to be sustainable. We have a policy that we won't give money to something unless the school or organisation contributes one third as well. Because otherwise they become dependent on us and start thinking they can't do anything themselves (Elaine, Anglo Platinum SED Office, Rustenburg).

Equally, Jerry Mosenyi explained: 'Now we talk about 'empowerment', not charity. With the Mining Charter, it means that the company can't try to be Father Christmas anymore'.

From loans and advice services for small enterprise, to entrepreneurship training programmes such as *The Business*[10] (an intensive six-month training course for aspiring business people run at the Anglo Platinum Mines), the company projects its commitment to teaming up with the community in pursuit of 'empowerment through enterprise', a mission which has infused almost every aspect of its broad CSR agenda[11]. Thus Gilbert Mogapi explained, 'we are trying to bring the idea to the people that even if you are HIV positive, you can still start a business and stand on your own'. Mogapi's remark revealed that intrinsic to this approach is the creation of a new class of empowered, entrepreneurial and self-sufficient citizens who are not only the ideal beneficiaries of CSR but embody the core values of the new South Africa—citizenship, enterprise and transformation—thus claiming the convergence of business values with those of the community, and indeed the nation. Under this new rhetoric, 'donor' and 'recipient' have been re-categorised as 'partners', 'investors' and crucially, 'social entrepreneurs', recalling the remarks of Clem Sunter (chairman of the Anglo American Chairman's Fund) as he explained how the fund selects the targets of its support: 'we're . . . backing some of the more entrepreneurial NGOs . . . most importantly . . . we're looking for winners' (Sunter, quoted in Robbins, 2001: 34). Thus donors assert an affinity with the participant of an entrepreneurship training scheme or education programme, as a partner in this collective enterprise of empowerment.

Often, an explicit sense of moral vocation, or even spiritual duty, attended the narratives of individuals charged with conducting the empowerment work of the company at the 'coalface'. This was exemplified by Betty Fisher, another CSR officer at the Rustenburg mines:

My passion is nutrition. I'm reading up a lot about nutrition and I've become very passionate about feeding and this new hydroponic system . . . I have visions of being a Mother Theresa in khaki pants and white shirt . . . I have visions of going and doing my thing, taking hydroponics up and down Africa and *uplifting* people from poverty.

According to these narratives, the CSR manager appears in the figure of a missionary conducting the 'moral work' of the company, and in so doing bringing the sacred realm of morality into the profane realm of business. As Gill put it, 'I am the conscience of the company'. This was reinforced by the ubiquitous use of the term 'upliftment' by CSR personnel I spoke to in Rustenburg. Conjuring images of progress up the vertical social hierarchy, accompanied by an almost spiritual ascent, the word resonates with colonial missionary ideals, yet seems strikingly dissonant with the economistic model of extending access to market opportunities according to which BEE is conventionally represented.

The zeal of CSR rhetoric thus enhances this sense of a moral mission of economic empowerment infused with a faith in the power of conversion while elevating the company as both architect and agent of that vision. At the centre of this project of social improvement is an ideal entrepreneur who can respond to the moral exhortation to 'help oneself' by embracing the opportunities provided by business, to become, as Gordon puts it, 'an entrepreneur of himself or herself' (Gordon 1991: 44). This was fervently projected in an article in the mine newsletter, advertising *The Business* under the title, 'The Ultimate Entrepreneur':

> Surely we are the generation to bring liberty to our children from the disaster that befell our ancestors . . . I believe that in the next generation in South Africa, we will see the rise of a new breed of entrepreneur, a society not dominated by counterproductive bureaucrats and paper pushers! A society where parents will teach their kids, 'dream yourself a radical new business idea, develop it into a financially successful enterprise and retire before you are 40'.

The article implores readers, 'it is time . . . to develop an *entrepreneurial mindset* and [learn] to become your own boss' (Zwennis 2003: 16). From this standpoint, participation in the market comes to stand for the promise of individual autonomy denied black South Africans under apartheid, while freedom becomes synonymous with freedom to enter the market. According to this logic, individuals are freed from the constraints of the past by liberating the market player that resides within them to pursue the 'new' South African Dream: as one informant explained to me 'in the new south Africa, everyone can be a businessman'.

As an evangelical project, 'empowerment through enterprise' claims to spread market discipline as the source of social mobility. It is here, in this promise to 'uplift and empower' encapsulated in Zwennis' fervour, that we hear the battle-cry of a capitalism that presents itself as liberator and saviour of the oppressed and marginalised; a capitalism which, as Comaroff and Comaroff put it, offers itself up as a 'gospel of salvation' (2000: 292). This celebration of grass-roots capitalism is not new, nor is it unique to South Africa (see for example Smart and Smart 2005; Blim 2005). What is of particular interest and importance is that here it is the goliath of corporate capitalism that, we are told, will deliver the 'South African dream' to the Davids of petty enterprise. The didactic promise of CSR is therefore seen to lie less in the tangible material benefits delivered through the company's programmes, and more in the intangibles of empowerment and infusion of the entrepreneurial spirit.

In order to attain the emancipatory and transformative power of the market, a conversion is thus required. As Bourdieu tells us, 'one must speak not of adaptation but of *conversion*' (Bourdieu 2000: 23). This process of proselytism is necessary, we are told, in order for beneficiaries to acquire the essential values and virtues of maximisation, an individualism required by market enterprise. Anna-Clare Bezuidenhout described the process which those selected for *The Business* must undergo:

> There's so many levels of transformation we're working on. It's a mammoth task—transforming someone into a different animal. We do six months entrepreneurial training and we call it "the army", not training, because it's really toughening up. We call it "self-mastering people"—so that people who go through it can say "I am the master of my own destiny" . . . with the whole apartheid system, and the dependency it has created, unless you *change that mindset*, they'll still fail.

According to the brochure, those selected for *The Business* undergo 'six months of tough entrepreneurial army training', following a model developed by the American Foundation for Teaching Entrepreneurship, and tried and tested on 'youth at risk' in the Bronx (a borough in New York City). This process of individual transformation promises to 'break the poverty culture of unemployed people; extinguish bad traits (those behavioural patterns of South Africans that perpetuate poverty cycles) and foster entrepreneurial qualities' (*The Business* promotional brochure). The discursive practices of CSR thus strive to change 'hearts and minds', and turn 'job-seekers' into 'job-creators':

to create exemplary empowered subjects in the shape of the 'ultimate entrepreneur'. But the 'ultimate entrepreneur' is adept at much more than just business, for entrepreneurialism, we are told, encompasses every aspect of the participant. Thus *The Business* aims to 'awaken champions amongst the previously disadvantaged societies and breed people that have: no time for drugs; less risk of HIV-AIDS; and no time for crime or racist activities'. This language of conversion is captured in the account of 'empowerment' given by Marius du Plooy, a manager at Anglo Platinum, Rustenburg (who had earlier spoken about his vocation to become a church minister):

> With the new transformation and BEE, there's a big social impact internal and external to the company. It's one thing to get a guy empowered—give him training in business or technical management—but this guy now moves from a low income to a high income bracket—which changes his place in the community. That's good but we have to make sure this is in a constructive not destructive way because money can be dangerous in inexperienced hands. Parasites jump on him. So he has to learn the right *mindset* as well.

On first appearances, the goal of 'empowerment through enterprise' demonstrates an impressive power to recruit, or co-opt allegiance to this 'market ideal', not only from aspirant entrepreneurs, but from those outside business. NGOs and community organisations have similarly converged on the language and competitive logic of business as they re-cast themselves as 'social entrepreneurs', while reframing 'sustainability' as 'profit-making'. Thus Anna-Clare Bezuidenhout, Director of *The Business*, spoke of her position as both community development leader and business woman (the former increasingly cast in the mould of the latter):

> Yes I run this NGO, but I am also a business woman. I am a *social entrepreneur*—we are people who are passionately pursuing community development and are passionate about transforming South Africa. And social entrepreneurship is really the future of South Africa . . . it means we are sustainable, we can look after ourselves.

Whether development officer, HIV peer educator or participant, all roles have been remoulded according to this ideal of the charismatic entrepreneur, blurring the boundaries between enterprise and social welfare. Deborah James has written recently of the 'return of the broker' who combines entrepreneurial flair with opportunism to mediate between the state, the market and the community in post-apartheid processes of land reform: 'drawing on notions of consensus they embody "the people", drawing on ideas of free choice and enterprise they embody "the market"' (James 2011: 318). Shifting between the register of 'community' and that of business, Anna-Clare similarly appeared to personify the values of the new South Africa—entrepreneurialism, citizenship and participation. But at the same time, as we shall see, she embodies the contradictions of her position, simultaneously entrepreneurial and disempowered by her position as client to a corporate patron.

The scarcity of funding for community development organisations, intensified by the virtual demise of state-funding (and the short-term nature of most corporate support), makes social entrepreneurship an economic imperative for NGOs, as much as an ideological or spiritual aspiration. This demands financial resourcefulness and opportunism not only for project survival but for the livelihoods of staff. Thus, like Anna-Clare, many of the NGO personnel I spoke to divided their time between their community work and a series of business ventures, while becoming, in effect, service-providers for company CSR departments.

While sustainable enterprise and 'empowerment through business' provide the backbone of the company's CSR policy, the reality is that nearly all of the community organizations officially listed in the RLM were dependent on money from the mines (the secondary source of funding being local churches). For example, an Anglo Platinum report that assessed and ranked home-based care organizations in the RLM for future partnership potential explicitly noted the almost complete lack of alternatives to corporate sources of funding for the NGOs, including 'minimal, if not zero' commitment from government[12]. The report concluded that NGOs and community-based organisations (CBOs) do not partner amongst themselves because of the competition between them for the scarce resources (Anglo Platinum 2003c: 14)[13]. This was reinforced by Clara Xorile a health professional at Anglo Platinum's Rustenburg mines, who previously had spent many years as a 'community social worker':

> I spent 10 years working at a mine, then I left the mine and went into the community to work for an NGO as a community social worker dealing with victims of violence. But I found in the last years that the government does not want to support NGOs. So I moved from one NGO to another, but as a professional you can't work for six months without a salary. So I came back into the mines . . . that's where the money is.

Already a picture starts to emerge in which NGOs and community organizations, desperate for survival, must compete to become the partner of choice for one of the mining companies operating in the area. This has the broader effect of drawing community organizations working further afield in rural North West Province towards the mines in the hope of funding, thus creating a 'hotspot' of NGO activity within the 50km zone of 'responsibility' of the various mines and a dearth beyond its border. The weakness of the NGO sector in the post-apartheid period (see Ramphele's discussion of the demobilisation of civil society [2005] and Habib and Taylor [1999]) has contributed further to the dominance of this privatised, corporate model of company and service provider, as CSR takes the place of, rather than 'thickens', so-called 'grass-roots' civil society[14].

To illustrate this, let me return to Anna-Clare Bezuidenhout and *The Business*, whose experience accorded with those of other NGO 'partners' or 'service providers' working in Rustenburg. Anna-Clare's account disrupted her empowering vision of 'social entrepreneurship' above, as she spoke of the asymmetry of power and the expectation of reciprocity inherent in the relationship between donor and recipient:

> When the mine opened about four years ago there was a lot of demonstrations—a lot of people toyi-toying around looking for work and with expectations of the mine—so we were part of (the company's) attempt to please the community because they couldn't give jobs to everyone—so others could have training.

She went on to explain how the mine gave them a plot of barely usable land on which to set up the project and a minimal budget.

> They make use of us when they have to brag about their CSR when they have important people they bring them to see us . . . whenever the mine wants to bring people there . . . whether it's from Jo'burg or America we must give up whatever we've planned, so they can have their photos taken in front of everything and put it in the magazine. They like to talk about us when they're talking about community development . . . They don't listen to our financial realities . . . We're constantly getting feedback from their top management that our statistics aren't good enough, but their expectations are unrealistic . . . they expect people to be in business the minute they leave our training . . . they don't realise economic empowerment is a process, that transformation is a

process. They just want tangible results. They put in 500,000 rand and want to see a major miracle . . . *But they're giving it to us for free, so what can we do.*

A similar account came from an employee at Peer-2-Peer, a local NGO specialising in training for HIV peer-educators:

> We sign an annual contract with Anglo for R150,000 annually. They renew it each year. So this year a few months back, we went to Johannesburg and signed the contract. Then they call us a couple of weeks later and say "oh we've reworked the contract, come back to Johannesburg and sign it again". So I'm thinking, "ach, piss off", but they act like we should be so goddamn grateful for their R150,000. The message is very much—you provide the trainers, but the who's, the where's, the how's—that's all from Anglo. I've tried to stake out our ground, to have more of a say and control over the design, but they're *giving* us the money, isn't it. It would have been a better project if we'd had a part in the design . . . But they need something in quotes on a billboard (Deborah Naudé, Peer-2-Peer, Rustenburg).

The funding provided by the company is bound by conditionality and brings with it the coercive powers of the gift. The company demands, in return, the implementation of projects that accord with its particular vision of development. This asymmetry of power is not only neglected but veiled by the elevation of the partnership paradigm. In this case, the NGO is trapped between the impossible demands of the company, and the inability to voice their discomfort due to a fear that their funding will be taken away and that, after all, they are indebted to the company for this 'free gift'.

Interestingly, while CSR managers within the company appeared surprisingly candid in their accounts of the difficulties of partnership (the more senior the executive, the greater the level of apparent openness), their NGO counterparts were often reluctant to speak to me without proper authorisation from their corporate partners:

> If you've spoken to Bridget Kessler at Anglo, you've probably heard everything you need to know about the project. If you want to talk to me as well you'll need to get authorisation from Bridget (Abigail, Community Forum, Rustenburg).

In other cases there was a striking disparity between the enthusiastic account of partnership told by NGO personnel, and the account given by their corporate counterpart (initially I had imagined the opposite would be the case).

Leleti Katane, regional director of *Ayeye*, an NGO working on a youth project in partnership with Anglo at the Rustenburg mines, spoke of complete synergy of interests between the two parties:

> We work very well together. It's a question of leadership and in Anglo they really have the *leadership* . . . They really took *ownership* of the project. They wanted to work within a very specific radius of their operation—I would say not more than 50km around the mine—*which made perfect sense not to go beyond 50 or 60km* because very few of their workers lived there. So we focused on those areas close to the mine.

In contrast to this account, Katane's counterpart at corporate headquarters, Johannesburg, Ingrid Hamilton, described the collaboration thus:

> *Ayeye* would have liked us to have just written a cheque and kept out of it. But we said 'no, if we're going to really unlock value and have an impact for us, we need to be involved and *we want to focus on the mining areas*'. At first we encountered a lot of *resistance* within the organisation . . . We said 'look we want to work in the mining areas'—which they didn't like . . . There were definitely *control issues* and you know, there are different operational norms and, well I suppose, 'cultures' in an NGO as opposed to in a corporation where you're used to a fiercely competitive world where efficiency and professionalism are key. That's not necessarily the case for an NGO. They have other qualities.

Where Hamilton remarks that *Ayeye*, 'would have liked us to have just written a cheque', Katane praises Anglo for 'leadership' within the partnership. Hamilton speaks of 'control issues', while Katane described the company 'taking ownership' and championing the project. Hamilton's veiled criticism of the lack of professionalism and competitive efficiency within the partner NGO contrasted with the unambiguous enthusiasm Katane expressed for their corporate partners. Crucially, where Katane commented that 'it made perfect sense' for the company to direct the NGO's work towards the specific 50km zone around the mines, Hamilton suggests that the company had to overcome 'resistance' within the NGO to this demand. The contrasting accounts—the first deferential, the second critical—speak more to the imbalance of power between recipients of the corporate gift and their corporate donors, than to the clash of 'cultures' or perspectives.

The hierarchy of power relations within the partnership was further illuminated by Alice Sibaya, whose organisation was partnered with Anglo Platinum on a large-scale community development project in Rustenburg. While the tone of Sibaya's account echoed Katane's in its enthusiasm and positive overtones, she slipped from referring to her corporate counterpart (Jen) as 'my colleague at Anglo' to 'my boss'. One incident which she described was particularly telling:

> It took us many weeks to come up with this framework. I had been working with Jen intensively—it was a pretty hectic process. I got quite carried away with it, and had this much broader vision of an integrated development system—how we could create something sustainable and replicable for the whole of South Africa—and really . . . develop something much bigger than the company. One night I stayed up all night working on a strategy for this vision and I took it to Jen. I shouldn't have, but I was just so carried away with it, and had this great hope. But Jen is really a great boss, so she just said—put this away and *she didn't fire me*. We joke, Jen and I, that it's because we are two women, I mean there's 20 years between us, but we're totally aligned, I'm very open and she's very open.

Such relationships between corporations and NGOs are at best precarious, at worst they make the pursuit of accountability impossible. For, no matter how fervently the parties assert a collaborative venture for a collective goal, the asymmetry between giver and receiver cannot be completely eliminated. After all, 'he who pays the piper not only calls the tune but attempts to make sure that it is performed' (Stirrat and Henkel 1997: 75–76). Thus Grace, an SED officer at Anglo Platinum in Rustenburg explained:

> The *service providers* don't realise that they need to justify the continuance of the project . . . I was talking to a guy today who was very narked [annoyed] that I was asking things like attendance records and he said he actually found it very hard to have the quality of the project questioned. But I have a right to expect results if I'm *giving* him the money.

Grace recast the so-called 'community partner' as 'service provider' who must deliver a particular service to the company in order to ensure future funding. Thus she shifted the discourse from one of equal collaboration to a commercial transaction between customer and vendor who must guarantee a 'value-for-money' service that will yield the returns the client demands. Yet slippage between the language of service provider, on the one hand, and Grace's embodiment of herself as donor on the other ('*I'm* giving him the money'), blurs the lines between the disinterested market model of client and service provider, and the expectation of reciprocity inherent in gift relations, transforming the company—and in this case Grace herself—from client to patron.

By extending the hand of patronage to civil society organisations—giving and taking away social investment where it sees fit—the practice of CSI further weakens NGOs as it strips them of autonomy under the banner of empowerment. Anna-Clare Bezuidenhout expressed this sense of impotence:

> We had a very negative experience with the previous CSI manager, he gave us nothing. Then the next one liked us and started to take ownership—but then it started again with the struggles within his unit and because of political in-fighting he moved to another department . . . One of the big problems people have with the mines is that if you get to know one person and then they leave . . . you never know whether the next person is going to support your project or whether they'll just cut you off. They throw a bit of money at you but they'll never make a contract over six months.

Anna-Clare's narrative of precarious 'partnership' dependent on the whims and personal discretion of CSR managers unsettles the confidence in the market model of social enterprise and sustainability achieved through responsible competitiveness. Her account was however echoed by those within the company, the front-line CSR agents, who were themselves subject to seemingly arbitrary policy changes and decisions from above:

> 'Special needs' has been stopped. But now Nox has taken over from our last boss and she's very in favour of it, maybe it will come back. That's often what you find—people have their pet projects, or their thing that they'll fight for (Grace).

Indeed the narratives of both the company's SED team, and their NGO partners alike increasingly reinforced an account of CSR exercised through personalised relations of patronage. This disrupts the representation of CSR as a significant departure from philanthropic largesse—a sustainable enterprise implemented through the technocratic tools of needs assessment, stakeholder consultation and evaluation laid down in the Socio-Economic Assessment Toolbox through which accountability is seen to be rendered. It highlights the precarious relations between donor and recipient, and the instability which characterised the practice of CSR, as corporate personnel appeared to give and withdraw benefits/projects where they saw fit.

However, this account of CSR officers taking on the mantel of personal patronage implies a greater level of agency within the corporate hierarchy than their own narratives of uncertainty and bureaucratic opacity suggested. On the one hand, the SED team described their work constrained by a sense of 'unpredictability' and apparently 'discretionary' changes in policy from above. On the other, the actions and outcomes which this situation gave rise to served to increase the company's power over its beneficiaries, in ways unexpected and unintended by those frontline CSI operatives, yet instrumental to the financial and political interests of the corporate agenda. Crucially, the relations of personal patronage, through which CSR was enacted, provided the company with a flexibility to claim responsibility (and the moral authority it afforded them), while simultaneously off-loading it.

Hard Times

Thus there was, it seemed, both freedom and frustration in the webs of patronage generated by the company's CSR activities. Front-line CSR practitioners often saw themselves acting as local patrons and benefactors—a role which at times inspired a sense of individual honour and achievement, at others, discomfort. In this way corporate social responsibility was personalised and shifted from the corporation as a whole to an individual. 'You see this is how we empower the community' Daniel Enele (an SED officer at Anglo Platinum), explained:

> We needed some land clearing—so I got young people from around here who were unemployed to form a company and I contracted them to do the job and then they have something to take home and they were so happy and now in the village they'll shout 'hey Mr Enele'. This is the thing that Daniel has done. This is what motivates me—to see myself doing these things and see them happening—I can feel proud of that.

But, the sense of honour derived from this role of patron was often outweighed by a contrasting sense of failure and impotence as a result of this individualisation of corporate responsibility, as they struggled to maintain relationships with community organisations in a context of shifting company policy and unpredictable resource flows. While on the one hand they had become individual patrons driven by personal commitment, they remained, on the other hand, trapped under the weight of the company's hierarchical bureaucracy and subject to internal corporate decisions over which they had little, if any, control. The sense of alienation from the corporate command centre (referred to simply as 'they') and its bureaucratic machine was similarly evoked by Kobus, manager of Hostel A:

> You have your budget and here I've been planning to build my men a soccer pitch. My hostel has won the soccer tournaments every year for the past five years. So I cut and saved. But then someone puts 100,000 Rand on your budget from somewhere else and they tell you, you must make cuts of 10 percent. I can't build it now. If you don't keep your eye on it, they'll put money on any budget they can to make the cuts.

Jan, the manager of another hostel at the Rustenburg Platinum Mines, echoed this:

> We have no control over our budgets. They're abusing our budgets. I looked at my budget yesterday and I have overspent by 1.2 million! They've written off 1.2 million of labour costs against my budget and I have no idea where it comes from. I have control of only the very basics—of my feeding budget only. My feeding budget is 199,000 and I've spent 103,000. But for everything else— I don't know what they are doing.

Indeed, almost all front-line CSR officers spoke of their budgets being suddenly cut or projects prematurely curtailed, reinforcing this corporate-coalface duality:

> My biggest worry is that with the current climate in the company we're not going to be able to give as many bursaries so I'm not going to be able to select as many kids for the *Platinum Future* programme which is so sad, because it does so much good. But then we really don't know what's going to happen. I come in some mornings and I don't know if our jobs will still be here. Maybe they will have made a change (Grace).

As a result, Grace and her colleagues spoke of having to creatively negotiate ways to fulfil commitments to their beneficiaries and sustain relationships they had personally built up. This reinforced their role as patrons to an array of community 'clients', intensifying the shift from corporate to personal responsibility:

> But you have to be flexible . . . These pipes needed painting so I went to the community organization and found some people to do it, but there was no more money in the CSI budget so I had to get the money from the operating

budget, not my CSI budget—so you have to be clever to find ways to *empower* people through business (Daniel Enele).

Yet, for the recipients of Enele and his colleague's creative empowerment schemes, the ubiquitous rhetoric of 'empowerment' appeared at best an impossible goal, at worst an extension of corporate control. Christa Vos, second in command at *The Business* made clear the difficulties of working as an NGO partner within, what she found to be, an unpredictable and opaque corporate climate. At the same time, she hinted at how this uncertainty and alienation is perhaps deployed strategically by the company:

> The company's CSR guy has the position but not the authority, he's not empowered enough and not skilled enough and so can't implement—just like a pipe that you voice things to and he pipes it up into the ether of the company above him and it disappears. You must still show me a skilled CSR operative who can navigate the company . . . We as outsiders are always having to witness political power-plays and games. Some of them will kill an initiative dead on the ground . . . There's no way you can take them to court. You can't make the company comply to their contractual obligations. So you are 200,000R overdrawn at the bank because they haven't delivered the money yet and now they say 'we have to cut costs, we can't afford it after all'. In the end that kills social entrepreneurs.

While the company pursues empowerment through enterprise, as both the method and the goal of its CSI, Vos made clear that they are left unequivocally in the weakened position of recipient, making it impossible to contest the prescribed positions of donor and recipient, with or without a contract.

The chain of giving, and the relations it creates, continues through the 'partner' NGOs to the very target of empowerment: those who *The Business* promises to transform into 'the ultimate entrepreneur' (Zwennis 2003: 16). Godfrey, an ex-mineworker, was paralysed in a car accident in his forties. No longer able to work in the mines, he applied many times to Anglo Platinum's various entrepreneurial training and support programmes for help starting a small business. Eventually after two years they enrolled him, with forty other people from the Greater Rustenburg area, on *The Business*. When the course finished, according to Godfrey, the company said that they would provide further assistance in the form of business start-up loans and, most importantly, the offer of tenders through the new BEE procurement programme of their supply chain. Since that time Godfrey has heard nothing:

Anglo has been very good to me—they have given me a lot—they really want to help people like me to empower themselves . . . Now I can empower myself. They were very *kind* to me—they used to send a car to come and collect me here, and take me to the training. I learnt a lot and now I want to start a business making toilet paper to supply the mines here . . . But they keep delaying. Every time I phone I speak to a different person who says they don't know what's happening. They're going through this restructuring you know. It's called 'Fit for the Future'. So everyone is in a mess and no one knows what's going on—but I am waiting and waiting. I've spoken to Elias[15] who has been very kind to me, and to the procurement manager at the mine, so I'm hoping that something will come up. But it keeps being delayed . . . They haven't had a good year—so maybe that's it.

In Godfrey's account, the language of self-empowerment was intermingled with that of giving, generosity and personal kindness. He expressed both gratitude for the transformative and empowering training which the company had given him, and disappointment that he had been left hanging by the people who had showed him such 'kindness'. What was particularly striking about Godfrey's account, was that while he was effectively alienated by the layers of opaque (at least to outsiders) bureaucracy which surround the mine, at the same time he spoke knowingly about the current re-structuring of the company: 'Fit for the Future'. He recounted how many times he had phoned the company, each time speaking to a different person. But he could find no one to give him any answers. Godfrey—and the buck—was passed to various people within the company who referred to the restructuring and cost-cutting within the organisation, which was on the lips of many of the CSR officers I spoke to. Despite this, in order to make sense of this institutional maze Godfrey presented a sympathetic understanding of the company and its financial constraints: 'they haven't had a good year'.

Indeed, for both front-line CSR officers and their community 'partners' or clients, a narrative of possible financial crisis, or of cost-cutting regimes and recovery plans initiated to avert such a downturn, loomed as a constant threat to their empowerment work. At the time this research was conducted in 2005, despite surging platinum prices such concerns focused on the damage to platinum profits wrought by an increasingly strong Rand and steadily weakening Dollar:

Look, I wouldn't want to be in Jed Thornton, our mine manager's position with the unions clamoring on your door on one side and the community on the other and having to increase profits. They all have their expectations. But what can he do? Look, I work in SED and I hate to see projects cut, but my husband explained it to me. They're not making enough on production of each unit of platinum. He's got a 500 day recovery plan and if we don't start making more money in that time then they'll have to close a shaft (Gill, SED Office, Rustenburg).

Anglo Platinum has had a bad year, everyone's budget has been cut. You've really come in the middle of this transformation. It's turmoil really and it's given them an opportunity to flush out all the . . . well, thank god we weren't flushed out (Elaine).

This is the fourth year that Anglo Platinum have been involved. They look like they're committed—but you never know, year to year. This is precarious—not just because it comes down to having champions—like Grace in the company who push our cause . . . None of them have signed an agreement saying they'll support us for three to five years. It's very much year to year and so if the company isn't doing well, there's always that threat that they'll cut their investment in the trust . . . Anglo nearly pulled out at the beginning of last year—they were going through pretty tough times and I said, 'come on guys, I know the market is volatile . . . *but what did you do with all the money you made when the price was good?*' (Judy Steinburg, Director of *Platinum Future*).

The prevalence of accounts like those of Gill and Elaine, Judy and Godfrey, from both CSR officers and beneficiaries, reveals more than that the company was not having a good year, and the consequent vulnerability of CSR projects to such fluctuations. When considered against the claims of senior executives that 'we'll be mining platinum in Rustenburg for 100 years to come', the political expediency of these crisis narratives starts to emerge. The experience of Godfrey, Elaine and Grace was one of insecurity, their perception one of instability and short-term planning in which 'no one knows what's going on'.

Yet within the company there are clearly areas in which this 'disorder' and 'uncertainty' are tolerated in contrast to areas of total control and efficiency. While CSR and SED can seem, at the operational level, messy and arbitrary, the production of platinum is as controlled and lean as possible. Every hour worked by every one of the 25,000 employees involved in the production of platinum is planned, organised and monitored. Intense surveillance and hierarchical control surrounds both the actual processes of extraction and the lives of mineworkers who live in hostels next to the shafts in which they work, doing eight- hour shifts, six days a week. The scale and efficiency of the operation is awesome. When it comes to production the company has as near to total control as possible. Indeed the rigours and dangers of mining demand strict supervision and constant, precise monitoring of the myriad technical processes which go on 24 hours a day, 365 days a year at the mines, as does the constant pressure on managers to meet the production targets imposed from the head office in London. At the Precious Metals Refinery, the manager David Iron, told me:

> 450,000 measurements are taken in and scanned every 3 seconds at this plant, I am responsible for every one of them . . . I am responsible for the safety of everyone of the 2,000 people who work in this plant. I am responsible for every unit of production through the plant everyday. I start my day at 6:00am with admin and quiet time. Then 6:30 is the security briefing. 6:45 safety, health and environment will report any incidents or injuries. I then report on this to head office. But right now we're at 161,000 man hours worked injury free [*there is a big sign at the entrance to the refinery displaying this figure*]. The rest of the day is technical things. That's what I like—on a day-to-day basis, superb operational performance, I like the details.

The narratives of confusion and flux from front-line CSR personnel and their local partners and clients, conflict with the picture of 'superb operational performance'. They conflict with the rigour of the '500 day recovery plan' and the new order of economic efficiency and streamlining, under the banner of 'Fit for the Future', designed, as I was informed, by management consultants from London. The crisis narrative of economic down-turn controls the flow of SED and CSR resources (which are seen to be expendable) not only within the organisation, but to Rustenburg as a whole, as the company is the primary supplier of development funding to the town, enabling the company to expand and contract its 'community' presence according to its needs.

Thus, in contrast to the imperative for enforced and absolute rigour in technical performance, responsibility beyond the technical is diffused, frustrated and displaced through the working of the 'mine's bureaucracy'[16]. As was exemplified in Godfrey's story, not only is the pursuit of accountability impossible through this organizational complexity and shifting management structures, but the very concept of accountability becomes void. The company, while being 'responsible' is under obligation to none of the recipients of its empowerment initiatives—the great benefit of gift relations. This highlights a certain continuity with the company's position on corporate giving almost three decades ago:

How much should it cost: how much should you invest? In Anglo American, certainly, we are never sure that we have arrived at the 'right' ratio between profits and corporate giving, and recent experience with the gold price has convinced us that the sum to be given should not be determined too precisely by what the preceding year's profits happened to be. Need tends to increase in times of recession—when a company usually is least able to be more accommodating—and vice versa (Gavin Relly 1982: iv).

While CSR management systems and policy are certainly more sophisticated and far-reaching today than they were when Relly, the then chairman, made his statement, the financial dynamics behind CSR practice remain equally volatile. As the company recasts core business processes and imperatives as CSR, they also become subject to the same unstable and unpredictable flows of resources: supply chain management becomes BEE procurement, employee training becomes social upliftment and, as I will go on to discuss in the next section, recruitment becomes 'empowerment'. In so doing, the company simultaneously demonstrates its status as vehicles of empowerment, while achieving a greater level of flexibility which enables them to expand, contract, cut costs and off-load responsibility, according to their needs, or will.

As Gavin Relly's statement exemplified, the sanctity of market efficiency— in short the bottom line—can always be invoked to almost any end, whether the provision of social benefits or the curtailment of them. In previous chapters I talked about the malleable discourse of shareholder value which once again comes into play here, as it provides an abstract rationale, distant from the realities of the mines, for any manner of corporate behaviour, any seemingly arbitrary policy decision or budget cut, as much for extending the boons of corporate profit through community investment projects, as for cutting them. In the current global recession, this is likely to be accentuated. For even in boom-time, narratives of financial hardship or the need to streamline, to be 'fit for the future', play a crucial role in enabling companies to expand and contract as they see 'fit'. But Timothy Mitchell reminds us that it is rarely (if ever) 'asked at whose cost efficiencies [are] to be made, or in whose hands control [is] to be strengthened' (Mitchell 2002: 230). As she described her frustration, Judy Steinburg, Director of *Platinum Future*, had rhetorically asked the company, 'what did you do with all the money you made when the price was good'? But as Relly (perhaps unintentionally) implied in his use of the term 'accommodating', underlying the notion of 'responsibility' is a sense that, in the end, all is dependent on the will of the company. So-called beneficiaries, such as Godfrey, cannot, therefore, hold the company accountable when the gift of empowerment disappears.

Empowerment Through Education

The targets of corporate empowerment begin much younger than Godfrey. For the model of empowerment through education asserts a long-lasting bond between the company and the targets of its CSR work. This claim was manifest in an Anglo American advertisement entitled 'We Have Come a Long Way', which appeared in the *Mail and Guardian* newspaper during my fieldwork,:

> We made your acquaintance some years ago when you were still a young person with ambitions to arm yourself with higher education in readiness for the challenges of the future. Our relationship grew during your years of university education when we assisted you with a scholarship/bursary, and after graduation you may even have spent some time at one of our subsidiaries.
>
> We are pleased that our paths crossed when they did. We are happy to have known you. We are proud of your achievements and the contribution you are making in our democratic South Africa. We, too, are passionate supporters of our beautiful country, as our active involvement in efforts to secure the 2010 Soccer World Cup[17] for South Africa indicated. Please let us renew our acquaintance and see it blossom into a wonderful friendship (Anglo American 2005d: 11).

The twin targets of education and youth provide a morally compelling narrative not only for Anglo's CSR agenda, but for the relationship between the company and the new South Africa. Education provides a central canvas onto which mining companies can project their moral claims as investors in the future of South Africa. As is epitomised in the advertisement above, Anglo American claims a position as architect of South Africa's transformation. Through this narrative the company professes an affinity with the targets of its empowerment initiatives, binding them together in a collective energetic movement, which replaces inequality with unity in a shared goal.

The advertisement casts responsibility in a deeply personal and paternalistic register. The relationship between donor and recipient is described in terms of the individual ('we' and 'you') rather than the institutional, evoking connotations of parent and child—'we are *proud* of your achievements'. The language of personal friendship and affection between company and beneficiary is then broadened to encompass all of South Africa: 'we, too, are passionate supporters of our beautiful country'. Such emotionally charged language, and the appeal to a moral bond (rather than commercial relations) between recipient and company, jars with the ubiquitous rhetoric of social investment and human capital found in official company policy and reports. The emotional register is, of course, far more engaging. The title of the advertisement— 'We Have Come a Long Way'—suggests that this bond between sponsor and scholar is not only personal and moral, but a metaphor for the relationship between the company and the country. Yet despite the obvious appeal of this vision, the practice of empowerment through education in Rustenburg is a great deal more complex and indeed conflicted than this emancipatory ideal of mutual interdependence and development would suggest.

In order to comply with the Mining Charter, the company must 'aspire to a baseline of 40 percent HDSA (historically disadvantaged South African) participation in management within 5-years'[18] (Department of Minerals and Energy 2004a: 4.2). The corporate commitment to educational development thus focuses on enhancing human capital in communities surrounding Anglo Platinum operations (Anglo Platinum 2005b: 3). In order to do so, activities included: the provision and renovation of schools; support for maths, science and literacy training programmes targeted at 'empowering educators . . . (and) learners'; the provision of scholarships for vocational skills development; and the development of mine schools and early learning centres (ibid). The heavy focus on maths and science education highlights the dual function of the company's commitment to educational development. On the one hand it is represented as a key area of the company's socio-economic development work. On the other, the focus on technical schooling aims to identify, select and train a target group of black students to fill future positions in the mining industry. Accordingly, the recruitment ratio of 70:30 in favour of HDSA candidates stands as a 'guiding principle' for Anglo Platinum's investment in education. The mission 'to empower' thus fuses with the imperative to create a pool of future black employees at management level.

One of the programmes supported by Anglo Platinum is *Platinum Future*[19], a year-long residential academy between school and university funded jointly by seven mining companies. It provides intensive science and maths teaching with the aim of producing engineers, metallurgists, rock mechanics, geologists, surveyors and accountants to staff the mines. Each company selects students from their mining areas. At the end of the year, recruitment units at each of the companies compete in a kind of human auction to offer university scholarships to the best students. Those students are then tied to the company for three to five years after graduation.

The aim of the company's educational programmes was, as Grace put it, 'to select the brightest and the best at a young age and invest in excellence . . . to *change their mindsets*' so that they may 'visualise a different future path, become confident and empowered'. Brochures and company reports speak of 'providing life-changing experiences and opportunities which would otherwise have been beyond their reach' (Anglo Platinum 2003e: 6). At *Platinum Future* there is a focus on exposing participant students not only to technology, science and maths, but also to 'business principles and norms'. Similarly, the director of *LearnLife*[20] (an educational summer camp for high-school age students sponsored by Anglo Platinum), himself a former church minister turned 'social entrepreneur', described the programme's 'bottom line' thus:

> Upliftment and development, the feeling of togetherness and striving towards our dreams are of the utmost importance . . . Empowering people to empower themselves.

Grace was one of those responsible for selecting the targets of Anglo Platinum's educational empowerment. Her passion for her work emerged most strongly in the deep affection she expressed for the recipients she hand-picks for *Platinum Future* and other Anglo Platinum projects, whom she referred to as 'my kids':

> I love my *Platinum* kids. I don't have much understanding of teachers. Teachers are the bane of my life, but the children, and the chance to give them a future . . . that, I love.

At the annual cheese and wine party for sponsors and donors of *Platinum Future*, Grace left the mingling minor dignitaries, educators and donors to find her '*Platinum* kids' in the dormitories and classrooms of the programme. In the well-equipped classrooms, the walls were papered with technical diagrams of mines and mining, alongside posters of 'Anglo Platinum's values' or 'Xstrata Business Principles'. While the students funded by the different companies mix in class, their dormitories are separated according to sponsor— Grace's 'Anglo Girls' live together in the Anglo Platinum dorm, while the Xstrata students share their own dorm and so on. Once we located the right dorm, Grace's scholars rushed up to her, hugging her and giving her letters and pictures that they had drawn for her. 'She is our hero' one of them said

as they showed Grace how tidily they kept their rooms and the work they had
been doing. Grace asked if they were working hard for Anglo. She told me:

> I know them all so well, I picked them, so I've been with them through the
> whole process, they're my girls and they're brilliant. You wouldn't believe the
> poverty that some of them come from. I just want to see them succeed. All of
> them, but especially the girls. South Africa needs more girls like this, succeed-
> ing and moving up.

The relationship between company and scholar is thus enacted in terms of an
intimate personal attachment rather than an institutional arrangement. Just
as in the newspaper advertisement, Grace stressed the long-lasting nature of
the bond between them: 'I know them so well . . . I've been with them through
the whole process'.

The little notes and drawings that the scholars give Grace, while apparently
trifles, are significant. For, while they appear to be 'gratuitous gifts', disinterested from the politics of sustaining a relationship, these surprise presents
are, as Bourdieu tells us, crucial to keep 'friendship' going, as they 'neutralise the action of time and ensure the continuity of interpersonal relations'
(Bourdieu 1977: 7), in this case over many years of educational support. Thus,
Grace received these letters whenever she went to visit 'her *Platinum* kids' at
the academy, as signs of a personal relationship which appears separate from
the relationship between Anglo Platinum and their scholars. Yet, as an agent
of the company delivering social benefits, this distinction is problematic. Support for projects and the granting of bursaries is steeped in personal relations
of affection and gratitude which develop between the frontline CSR officers
and the beneficiaries of their projects. In this way, the relations of patronage
and the bonds of affection and control that these create, work to close the
space between the company, as donor, and the beneficiary or recipient.

The affection, warmth and protectiveness expressed by Grace, and returned
by her 18 year old protégées, acts as a powerful and potentially coercive bond:

> Last year, Xstrata (another mining company) poached *my* girls—I brought
> three of the best and brightest girls to *Platinum Future* and the Xstrata people
> went in early and offered them a scholarship for uni—and Xstrata didn't even
> sponsor the programme, they just steal the bright students we produce.

The possessive commitment, verging on ownership, to the talent she has dis-
covered and nurtured acts as a cohesive force imparting loyalty for Anglo to

a new generation of 'empowered' recipients as they come under the authority of its paternalistic responsibility. After all, the power of the gift, in contrast to the supposed neutrality of commercial transaction, has always been seen to rest on its ability to generate long and strong bonds between individuals.

Grace's comment exemplifies the twin forces of affection and ownership that define the kind of patron-client relations that the company's SED work generates. However, her anger at the way in which Xstrata 'poached [her] girls' also points to the rejection of reciprocity which such an act involves. Those who Grace picks for *Platinum Future* spend a year at the academy preparing for the rigours of university and a life as a mining professional. For many of them, this will not have been their first encounter with Anglo Platinum. Many will have attended *The Bridge*[21], the company's after-school maths and science programme in Rustenburg. Others might have been picked by Grace or one of her colleagues to receive a bursary to attend the *LearnLife* summer programme, or they might even have attended one of the mine's own primary schools. Thus their relationship to Anglo Platinum, and in some cases individual SED officers, can already have dated back a number of years. Grace makes clear her expectation that, at the end of the academy, the company will select the brightest among their scholars for an Anglo university bursary, extending the bond for another four years. Finally, reciprocity is expected in the form of three or more years service to the company after graduation. The delay is crucial. As Bourdieu points out: 'delay (in reciprocating the gift) is also a way of exacting from him the deferential conduct that is required as long as relations are not broken off' (Bourdieu 1977: 7). In the case of Xstrata poaching the Anglo girls, relations have been broken off. The long-lasting relationship between corporate sponsor and beneficiary has been severed, thus denying the expected reciprocity.

In the case of bursaries—323 of which were granted in 2005 and 657 in 2008 to the value of R50.9 million in 2008 (Anglo Platinum: 2008: 88)—the lines between gift and market relations are blurred. On the one hand, bursaries and scholarships represent a central vehicle of Anglo Platinum's empowerment mission. They offer the promise of both affirmative action and the meritocratic selection of beneficiaries amongst the target group and thus embody the central values of self-empowerment: to help those who are willing (and able) to help themselves. Official company policy refers to this as 'talent management' aiming 'to identify, develop and retain high-potential and high-performing individuals' (Anglo Platinum 2008: 88). Bursaries are awarded through a fair and meritocratic selection process, according to a straightforward bureaucratic procedure accompanied by a contract which binds the recipient to repay the educational support with a number of years service to the company.

Yet on the other hand, the apparent meritocratic rationalism of the bursary schemes clouds the dynamics of power and dependency which define corporate patronage—a kind of patronage that extends far beyond the individual relationship between the scholar and the corporate sponsor. As virtually the only supplier of bursaries to school children in Rustenburg hoping to go to university, and within a context of intense poverty, Anglo Platinum and its rival mining companies become, in effect, the main local providers of a ticket to higher education and a bright future in metallurgy, engineering or rock mechanics. Thus I argue that the company's investment in education, while offering the promise of empowerment to individuals, provides a mechanism whereby relations of authority and subordination may be both fortified and mystified through the synthesis of 'moral ties' and 'meritocratic symbolism' (Bourdieu 1984: 9).

The educational benefits offered by the company are not, however, available to everyone: not everyone is seen to be eligible for empowerment. There is an ongoing debate within Anglo Platinum's CSI unit as to whether educational investment should be directed towards school-support through public-private partnerships or towards learner-support by selecting the most 'promising' students to benefit directly from the company's subvention through bursary schemes and outside school programmes. The overt aim of the latter approach is to create a scientific and technical elite, with the hope that the benefits will, ultimately, trickle down to the rest of society[22]. Thus Elaine, one of Grace's colleagues in the SED unit, commented:

> It's become confusing, on the one hand we have the mines saying we must focus on maths and science to produce good company employees, and on the other there's the Mining Charter saying we must focus on community upliftment—so which is it?

Gill, who worked alongside Grace and Elaine, was unambiguous in her opinion that it should be the former:

> Some say we should be supplying education to the masses. I believe in giving it to a few good kids . . . I want to pick out a few with excellence and give them a future. We used to have these "Anglo adopted schools". The idea is, if you

target the educators you uplift the masses, you're not just helping a few, you reach more. But the results didn't show a big enough impact.

Just as in the case of 'empowerment through enterprise' then, the process of 'empowerment through education' represents an exclusionary process of identification, isolation and elevation of an elite group of beneficiaries, making the company the architect of a new class of empowered subjects:

> Look, selection is crucial—you can *uplift* anyone but for it to be to a meaningful level they must have potential . . . So I believe in going straight to the kids, not the school—cut out the middleman. We had an external review a while back and the report said, why the hell are you supporting government education? . . . If you just want to throw meaty bits over your shoulder to the wolves then your project has been successful—but if you want to add value to Anglo you have to go direct to learners. Don't go through teachers, don't go through schools or the department of education. Go direct to the learners . . . we're not in the business of taking bad students and making them better.

School, according to Gill, is simply a middleman. Grace agreed: 'I can take a good kid from a beleaguered school and give him what his teacher is not'.

This is precisely the aim of *LearnLife*, an extra-curricular summer programme for 'future leaders'. At the *LearnLife* summer camp Gill introduced me to Thabo, a 14 year old participant. Afterwards she remarked: 'he's so good—why isn't he doing maths and science? Then I could bring him in on one of the Anglo projects. He should do maths and science, he would be so good at Anglo, but he's doing history'. Through the practice of CSR, the enduring paternalism within the company is projected outside in their external relations with the so-called 'community' around the mines[23]. While Gill and her colleagues stressed that they are not in the business of 'grooming' people for the company, 'suitability for Anglo' was one of the qualities that inform their selection of beneficiaries. Recruiting 'the best and the brightest' involved not only selecting appropriate participants/targets for empowerment through education, but incorporating them into the 'Anglo value system' and inspiring in them a sense of loyalty, and I would argue, reciprocal obligation to the company. The company's investment in 'educational capital' thus serves as a mechanism for business to legitimately maintain and reproduce itself even within the context of national transformation. As Bourdieu points out, 'the controlled mobility of a limited category of individuals, carefully selected and modified by and for individual ascent, is not incompatible with the permanence of structures (of relations between classes)' (Bourdieu 1973: 71).

Competition between rival mining companies for ownership of this elite group of recipients is fierce, as each company strives to project itself as the best producers of empowerment and to incorporate the products of their empowerment projects into the company. Thus, Judy Steinberg, the director of *Platinum Future* explained:

> You've got a bunch of mining companies competing on the ground to give bursaries to the best students. And yes, there are companies that don't support us but come and poach the students and offer them bursaries for university. I'm only too happy for the students to be offered bursaries. But the companies don't like it—they might say 'hey you must give too if you want to take the best students'.

Grace explained that, in spite of the hot competition, Anglo Platinum had been able to get 'first dibs' on the best students in the Bojanala Platinum District (BPD):

> We know which are the best schools and then we run testing in the schools and this year we introduced psychometric testing so we can see if they'll be good in Anglo . . . When we started doing *Platinum Future*, I said, 'no way am I giving money to kids I haven't seen. I want to see the school records and be in the interviews so that I can pick the brightest and the best'. Because I'm personally involved I get first choice and the other mining houses pick up the ones we don't want.

Through their role as community donors, the company's education unit gains access to areas of information and governance which otherwise would be denied them and which can directly serve to further their commercial interests. In this case it is the school records and exam results of all students from all schools in the BPD, which roughly represents Anglo Platinum's target zone for its CSR interests. The fact that Anglo Platinum has access to this information highlights the extent of their influence over education in the area, where structures of governance and channels of accountability are weak. More importantly, by establishing themselves as a vehicle of 'empowerment', under the banner of the national government's BEE imperatives and the demands of the Mining Charter, the company can assert a common interest and common cause with local government, legitimising their intervention in educational development in the BPD, and crucially, the selection of who gets to benefit from such support.

The combination of affection and ownership encapsulated in Grace's reference above to 'my school children', extended beyond the personal relations between scholar and sponsor, to the institutional arrangements between the company and their target schools. These included various schools that Anglo Platinum had or continued to support with donations, either as a supplement to government funding, or in the case of pre-schools which receive no resources from government, as the sole source of funding alongside minimal school fees. Elaine explained the stress on sustainability. Yet even as she said it, the extent to which this commitment to self-sustainability translated into a personal capacity to relinquish control and ownership of the gift was thrown into doubt:

> We put in one third and they have to raise two thirds themselves. Then, they can ask us for assistance if they need it but we try not to encourage it because we want them to be sustainable . . . This is a very nice school, it's all equipped by the mines . . . that's the idea—that they do it for themselves and that we don't

Figure 6.1. Anglo Platinum supported pre-school, Rustenburg (pupils wear the company colours—red and blue). Author's photograph.

interfere too much—what are those kids doing in that sandbox over there—they'll break it! They shouldn't allow it, I'll have to speak to the teachers.

Later Elaine said: 'both Grace and I are very hands on. If we're giving money away we want to know exactly how it's being spent—we're both very in control of the projects we're doing'. Thus despite the commitment to autonomy and independence, and the rejection of a 'culture of hand-outs', these field visits served as a constant reminder of the provenance of the gift, affirming the authority of the company even in the same moment as it was being denied.

An 'Everlasting Gift'

If education becomes a gift, the promise of empowerment and sustainability becomes instead the currency of patronage, and potentially, control. The number of those who receive the bursaries and benefits provided by Anglo Platinum alone, are few. But, the aspiration to be an Anglo scholar, a *'Platinum* kid' or a participant in *LearnLife*—to be recognised and chosen as a suitable target for 'empowerment'—can be as powerful as the material benefit itself in its capacity to shape relations between the company and the community, and to establish the company's moral authority as the conveyor of social improvement; even for the majority who are never chosen. So, in a classroom of 25 students aged between 14 and 16 at Orange Grove High School (the recipient of significant subvention from the mining houses), all but two of the predominantly female class said that when they finished school they wanted to be a rock mechanic, metallurgist or chemical engineer (not perhaps the expected aspirations of teenage girls and boys in South Africa or elsewhere). The dissenting two wanted instead to be a mine doctor and a human resources manager.

Meanwhile, the promise, or just the possibility, of inclusion serves to elevate the company as a central agent of empowerment, securing for Anglo Platinum a dominant voice in the educational development of Rustenburg. Indeed, the power of social-giving to project the moral claims of the company onto the so-called 'community' of Rustenburg, allows the mining companies, and Anglo Platinum in particular, to exhibit and maintain an unrivalled position as the town's benefactors, developers and patrons. This was manifest in the communal ceremonies held to celebrate the corporate patrons of the town's educational establishments. Such ceremonies blur the lines between 'social investment' and gift-giving. Indeed, a high level of ritualisation and public drama often attend the giving of gifts; as Mary Douglas reminds us, there is usually 'nothing secret about them' (Douglas 1990: xviii). And, the twin targets of education and youth make particularly emotive subjects for such exhibitions.

For example, a grand ceremony was held to mark the opening of the senior school addition to Orange Grove School, substantially funded by a donation from Anglo Platinum. According to Anglo Platinum's *Let's Talk* magazine the ceremony, commemorated with a plaque memorialising the donors, was attended by 'distinguished guests and dignitaries representing the mining houses, the Department of Education, parents and educators of the school'. The event was highly ceremonious: 'three choirs entertained the crowd with beautiful songs such as "praise the lord" and "catch a falling star"'. The head-mistress thanked the donors for their 'belief attitude in making this dream come true', referring to it as an 'everlasting gift' (Anglo Platinum 2004: 5).

This "everlasting gift" is not free. It brings with it the moral ties and social bonds which typify patronage. Grace explained:

> Generally we don't do whole-school support anymore or what we used to call 'Anglo-adopted schools', because we can't guarantee results. But we *gave* to Orange Grove because they could guarantee *returns*.

Grace shifts between the language of giving, to that of 'investment' from which the company expects returns. On one level, such returns are expected in the generalized form of improved exam results as evidence of the positive impact of the company's investment in enhancing the quality of education. However, in giving to Orange Grove, Anglo Platinum implicitly invited (or received) another form of reciprocity, which emerged in the deep gratitude that the school's headmistress, Julia Brodie, expressed for the gift:

> They have been very good to us, Anglo. They have a very personal commit-ment to their projects . . . You musn't give preference to their children—but it's difficult, if you have one place, you give preference to your sponsor . . . we have a lot of *mining kids* at the school. In fact Verity Reid at Anglo, who really worked to make this happen, her daughter was head-girl and her husband went here years and years and years ago.

Brodie's account highlights, once again, the way in which corporate social in-vestment in the town's development is embedded within personal relations of giving, sealing the bond between donor and recipient. The donation served to secure much-coveted places for Anglo's 'mining kids' at the only English-speaking (as opposed to Afrikaans) high school in town[24].

While the company has no direct involvement in the day-to-day running of the school, the substantial donation serves to inspire the perception that the company—as much as local government, the school or parents—is responsible for educational benefits, development and change. As the company steps in to provide basic social functions, the rights and entitlements that might be expected from the state are transformed into gifts, leaving the recipients dependent on the goodwill and patronage of their corporate donors. For, as Muehlebach writes, 'the willingness to do good on the part of companies is not met with an accompanying social obligation; the duty of these good corporate citizens is not met with a corresponding right to citizenship' (Muehlebach 2009: 4). The moral authority accrued from their role as agents of educational empowerment not only co-opted support from recipients, but served to silence dissent, in large part owing to the enduring power of the gift to demand gratitude.

This was exemplified at the annual 'Grant-Making Ceremony' of the 'Rustenburg Community Foundation'. During her list of acknowledgements to the foundation's various donors, including a large donation from Impala Platinum for a rural school development, Adelle Farmer forgot to thank Anglo Platinum for a smaller donation to the foundation the previous year. The following day Adelle was informed by an employee of Anglo Platinum's CSI office that, having attended the ceremony, he was 'dismayed' that she had failed to acknowledge their contribution, alongside that of Impala's:

> Now I have to spend my time writing a letter to say how deeply sorry I am that I *forgot* to thank them for the R10,000. I'm so pissed off, but I have to do it since we fought to squeeze even that out of them and if I don't we'll never see another penny because they said we were an Impala initiative. You know Impala, which was at the time Gencor, gave us money to set up the foundation twelve years ago. They wanted us to put up a big billboard with their name on it. But we knew if we did then none of the other mines would touch us. So they put it up and we took it down. And still we're seen as an 'Impala Initiative'. They get petty about not putting their name on a board or verbal thanks at a ceremony, but they can't give 10,000 rand of technical support and hope to get the world's approval. But we must be grateful.

The passionate commitment to 'empowering people' which was common among CSR officers, was often accompanied by a rejection of claims of entitlement from those they sought to empower, as exemplified by Grace's comments:

People around the mines feel an *entitlement* over and above the level of pro-ductivity they are willing to put in. Even *my school children*—who we've been *giving* a 40,000 rand bursary, which is more than their parents will be able to *earn* in a life time and you know those are the kids who phone me the first night they're on the programme and tell me they don't like the food . . . They should be praising the mines not attacking them.

The recipients of the company's 40,000 rand bursaries are placed in a position of indebtedness in which they are expected to receive the bursary with grati-tude and not complain. The sense of reciprocity, or lack thereof, is implied as the CSR coordinator criticises people for expecting more than they can give back in terms of productivity. Crucially, the 'gift' is juxtaposed with 'entitle-ment', so asserting the dominance of the company as a paternalistic institution.

Grace implicitly contrasted this sense of entitlement with the work ethic of managers at the company:

Martin, my husband, would literally work 18 hours a day and every Satur-day and Sunday if there was maintenance and the people under him are now working like that. These guys work really, really hard to earn the money that CSI then *gives away*. You can appreciate where these guys are coming from— they're at the face and mining life is tough and they see SED giving the money away that he's earning, to some worthless guy who doesn't do anything while he's slogging away to pay his bond and car and pay for his kids to go to college.

The gift thus appears as the antithesis to entitlement, which is 'alienable', de-fined in terms of the impersonal rather than the personal. In contrast, own-ership of social responsibility or community investment projects around the mines tends to remain with the donor, the company. The gift (whether mate-rial good or social benefit) has been handed over to the recipient, yet a degree of control remains with the donor: 'while giving', the company is, at the same time, 'keeping' (Eyben 2003: 10).

The theory (or perhaps ideology) of the gift is, as Mary Douglas stated, 'a theory of human solidarity' (Douglas 1990: xiii). But the gift has both a light and a dark side[25]: on the one hand, personal commitment, passion and warmth; on the other, paternalism, patronage, control, and crucially, exclusion. In this respect, gift relations have a much greater capacity to 'make friends' and co-opt 'support' than the supposedly asocial realm of market transactions. In par-ticular, by providing benefits in the form of a gift for which the recipient can-not make a commensurable return, the donor commands a level of deference and compliance, confirming that domination is exercised as much through benevolence and the creation of 'consensus' as through coercion. Gifts wrapped up as corporate social investment or responsibility projects around mining operations thus contain intricate dynamics of power and morality. For as Sahlins warns us, 'generosity is a manifest imposition of debt, putting the recipient in a circumspect and responsive relation to the donor during all that period the gift is unrequited' (Sahlins 1972: 133). The latent power of the gift to oppress the recipient was poignantly encapsulated in Anna-Clare's words: 'they're giving it to us for free, so what can we do?'

The moral bonds associated with the 'gift' and the values of autonomy and market rationalism propounded by the discourse of 'economic empowerment' are conventionally seen as antithetical. Yet it appears that CSR invokes the former as its rationale while delivering the latter. The beneficiaries of the company's social investment thus become subject to conflicting demands: on the one hand to demonstrate their capacity for self-empowerment, on the other hand, to show gratitude and deference for the company's beneficence. While the targets of the company's 'empowerment work' are apparently converted to the emancipatory promise of business, uplifted through educational and training programmes, and transformed into ideal market players, they are simultaneously subjected to the coercive powers of the gift which serve to reassert the hierarchy of donor over recipient. CSR becomes, in the end, an instrument of social control and subjectification, as much as a conduit of empowerment. Thus, as the appeal to the concept of responsibility—and the agenda of care it implies—authenticates the role of Anglo Platinum as a dominant institution of governance in Rustenburg, CSR serves to empower the corporation rather than the supposed subjects of their empowerment initiatives.

The relationship between the company's CSR operatives and the beneficiaries they seek to empower embodies broader tensions surrounding Anglo American's relationship to the 'new South Africa', and more broadly, the position of big business in the post-apartheid state. The company asserts its role as a key player in the development of the nation through a narrative of transformation and responsibility. At the same time, the discourse of CSR serves to reject claims of entitlement and obligation. As such, while the company projects itself as a vehicle of empowerment through the market, CSR in fact serves to extend and revitalise (rather than constrain) the company's authority and the old social hierarchies of power and dependence through which it is exercised.

The result is a vision of successful social upliftment—of which the company is both agent and architect—to the exclusion of any who disrupt the picture and fall outside this moral economy of responsibility. The practices of CSR thus serve to exclude large sections of society while demarcating a select target zone of responsibility (the 'community') which is bound into the relations of corporate patronage and clientelism. So what happens to those who are outside these webs of corporate gifting; those who sit beyond the 'community' of beneficiaries? An underlying theme of this chapter has been 'community'. Not only does it provide a canvas onto which the company's claims to social improvement are projected, but in so doing the 'community' itself is constituted, and demarcated as a target group of recipients. The effect of this process is twofold. Firstly, as discussed above, those who become targets of the company's empowerment initiatives, through enterprise and education, become subject to relations of patronage, and are therefore brought into the paternalistic structures of corporate authority. Secondly, the practice of CSR creates geographies of inclusion, and exclusion, epitomised in the marginal and liminal position of the informal settlements, which disrupt the vision of social improvement as they fall outside the company's 'community' of social responsibility.

Thus I return, in the next chapter, to Edenvale, where the disjuncture between state provision and corporate responsibility that lies beneath the claims to partnership are brought into sharp focus. In Edenvale, as in Mayfair, Park Heights and Rustenburg's other informal settlements, those who are not considered to be members of the 'host community' (or in the rhetoric of CSR, 'legitimate stakeholders') have no claim or entitlement to the benefits or social goods provided through the mechanisms of corporate social investment. This unsettles the vision of corporate social investment and its claim to bring the margins and peripheries into the inclusive and emancipatory embrace of 'the market'.

7 Between the Company and the Community
The Limits of Responsibility?

Diwe

'I've come here today, to see what they have to offer', Diwe said to me; 'they don't come to us, so we must come to them'. Diwe, whose partner had been a temporary contractor at the Rustenburg Mine, had lived in Edenvale for the past three years and was attending Anglo Platinum's annual 'Community Participation Day' on 4 June 2005. 'At heart, I am a business woman' she said, before asking if I had any 'social enterprise', 'empowerment' or 'business projects' for which I could recruit her. Diwe appeared as the model of entrepreneurialism, the kind of convert the company strove to produce through its 'empowerment' work. In all but the material goods, she embodied the ideal type small entrepreneur imagined in the inclusive vision of a new corporate-driven development, bringing the opportunities of the market to empower the margins; extending the promise that in the new South Africa, 'everyone can be a businessman'. Like many others Diwe had embraced the entrepreneurial spirit that 'empowerment through enterprise' commands, in which freedom means freedom to do business alongside all others. She was one of many thousands who inhabit excluded margins such as Edenvale, hopeful entrepreneurs in search of opportunities. Here, in the 'borderland' (metaphorically and geographically speaking) between the mines and the formally recognized community, 'disadvantaged young people from post-revolutionary societies, from inner cities and from other terrors incognita . . . seek to make good on the promises of the free market' (Commaroff and Commaroff 2000: 308).

Thus, it was not only the tangible benefits that Diwe sought from the company, though of course these are much in demand, but also acknowledgement of her status as a potential participant in the company's CSR programmes; to be 'seen', as it were, as a suitable target for 'empowerment' which the company extended to the 'community', but which had up to this point seemed elusive. In quest of recognition as 'stakeholders', and the possible benefits this brings, there are many like Diwe who aspire to be selected as a potential small business contractor, or future Anglo bursary holder (see Chapter 6). As Deborah James has written of rural squatters, the prospect of success is 'tantalizing':

> The promise of accelerated social mobility . . . is a vivid one. Although people like Amos Mathibela with his entrepreneurial and leadership skills are outnumbered by the multitude of their real or prospective followers with fewer prospects of upward mobility, the promise is there: one to be realized (or thought to be achieved). (James 2011: 334).

Thus, the power of this 'new' South African dream to recruit followers to the ideology of empowerment through enterprise lies, as it does with the American dream, in the aspiration rather than the fulfilment of that illusory yet persistent promise.

Just as the systems of patronage generated by the practice of CSR create categories of 'beneficiaries' or 'recipients', so where there are beneficiaries there are also those who are excluded from the educational, medical or infrastructural advantages provided by CSR initiatives. The discursive construction of a 'community', demarcated through the practices of CSR as they are pitched at particular groups and target zones, is itself a moral project; one which is mediated through the technologies of social investment and the mechanisms of partnership and 'stakeholder engagement'. Here the discursive capacity of CSR works to define the territory under the company's purview, and to render the informal settlements as external to the company's social responsibility as they disrupt the picture of upliftment and empowerment it strives to portray. As I continue the analysis of the company's social investment in Rustenburg, these exclusionary processes are the main focus of this chapter.

As CSR around the mine generates webs of patronage and clientelism, CSR personnel saw themselves as empowerers of a hand-picked bunch of beneficiaries and expressed resentment at the expectation of handouts from others. For gifts are given, but should not be claimed. The corporate discourse of 'self-empowerment' thus implicitly rejects any claims of entitlement. As we saw in the previous chapter, Anglo Platinum's entrepreneurial development initiative, *The Business*, describes its goal as 'unleashing the unlimited socio-economic potential of disadvantaged job seekers surrounding the mine'. But aspiring participants must heed the warning on the front of the brochure, in a speech bubble next to the photograph of a newly empowered graduate of the programme: 'I used to expect the mine and the government to give me everything to make me happy. I can't believe how I now see life differently'. A profile of another success story of the company's empowerment initiatives has a similar message: 'since Bennet attended (*The Business*) he became so motivated he started finding opportunities for business everywhere! . . . He never stops, hence the nickname the "Duracell Bunny"'. The injunction to 'help oneself' and 'exploit the opportunities given' acts to reinforce the denial of obligation. Individuals who do not respond to the moral injunction to help themselves have, it seems, only themselves to blame:

> Everyone in Rustenburg is always looking to the mines for the town's failures, for their own failure, and for the solutions. Perhaps they should to start looking to themselves . . . because when the mines close, we'll all be gone (Refinery Manager, Anglo Platinum, Rustenburg).

Implicit within the construction of the ideal subject of empowerment—one who can 'help oneself'—is the rejection of those who cannot or do not follow this model: those who, as one CSR officer put it, 'squander the opportunities provided by the mine and sit waiting for handouts' (Gilbert Mogapi, Anglo Platinum, Rustenburg). Thus we find Victorian discourses of the 'deserving' and 'undeserving poor' re-animated and re-defined in the contemporary register of CSR: on the one hand the 'deserving' who have earned their status as beneficiaries by demonstrating their will and capacity for upliftment and conversion to the entrepreneurial spirit; and on the other the 'undeserving poor', who are rendered dependent and idle through social welfare. As Polanyi (2001) showed us, it was just such moral rendering of the corrosive effects of social welfare, and the edifying influence of the market which provided the legitimation for reforming the Poor Law in 1834[1].

The true subjects of empowerment are juxtaposed with the myriad 'false' claims on the company for 'endless supplies of cash' about which CSR officers often complained: 'we're not made of money, we're not a bottomless pit, but everyone thinks we are'. They saw it as their responsibility to sort the 'legitimate' subjects of empowerment (those who reject the role of 'beneficiary' and, as Anglo's empowerment arm, Anglo Zimele[2], put it, 'stand on their own two feet'), from those who try to 'take advantage of' or 'exploit' the company. The

inclusive vision of economic empowerment, whereby the goals of transformation and development are asserted to embrace all through the emancipatory
power of market opportunities, gives way to exclusive practices of patronage,
delivered by the company to those who, so we are told, 'can help themselves'
and do not 'think the mine owes them', as Grace put it. The celebration of a
new era of entrepreneurialism thus rebukes those who 'squander' or fail to
seize the opportunities of the market, facilitated through CSR.

When claims to compensation or entitlement were made on the company,
CSR officers dismissed these as illegitimate or driven by, as Gill (an SED coordinator at Rustenburg) put it, 'ulterior motives'. To illustrate this, let me
return to the June 4 public participation day, when a decision was made to
cancel the 'open discussion forum' that had been planned. Instead, the Recreation Club in Anglo Platinum's Waterval mining complex was filled with
stalls presenting what the company had to offer, or had done, in the various
areas of its CSR work. There was a stall for black economic empowerment
(BEE) procurement offering Cadbury's Top Deck chocolate bars (a layer of
white chocolate on a layer of dark chocolate) with a ribbon attached on which
was printed 'Add Value, Not a Face'. There was another for educational bursaries handing out application forms; a stall for HIV/AIDS prevention dis-
tributing awareness leaflets; and one for environmental management with
large technical diagrams of the new Acid Converting Plant, explaining how
the sulphur dioxide which it produced would be used as fertilizer. Above the
entrance table, posters listed the issues raised at the last open day (May 2004)
and the ways in which the company had responded to these, or was in the process of doing so. Nox, a CSI manager at Rustenburg Section, and her colleague
Grace, explained the company's decision to cancel the discussion forum so
as to avoid the 'fiasco' of a previous stakeholder event held earlier in the year,
which, according to Grace, had been 'invaded' by a group of people who 'came
only to make demands, and make trouble':

> Grace: If we have an open day, people come and say "oh our home has cracks
> in it because of the blasting in the mines", or "our children are sick because
> of the pollution". At the last meeting Nox was completely mobbed by people
> making these claims, weren't you?
>
> Nox: Yes, people were coming with all sorts of claims about what the mine
> had done to them. But you know, what people really want is jobs. There's such
> unemployment and they've come here from all over to find jobs and they are

expecting to find them at the mine . . . then they complain 'you give jobs to migrant workers from Guateng or Eastern Cape, but not to locals'. But they are not from Rustenburg themselves. Maybe they have been living here some years now, but they're migrants too!

Grace: You know I really felt for you—it was like going into the lions den. But you know, we say to them, 'ok, we'll bring a mine doctor to check your children', and of course he'll say it's not the mine making them sick. Look at my children, they live right on the mine and they aren't sick. Or we'll say 'ok we'll bring an engineer to your house to check the cracks'. But it's not the mine, it's the poor building and materials, no concrete, nothing. But what they want is jobs . . . They have all these expectations that the mine will just provide. These are people who are not happy with their lives because if you were happy with your life would you bother going to an Anglo meeting. And Nox has to tame them.

Since the event recounted by Nox and Grace, Anglo Platinum public participation meetings had been a little short on both drama and participation. The June 4 open day was the third in a series of 'stakeholder consultations' held by Anglo Platinum in Rustenburg between March and June that year. The first two events, both of which were held at 9am on consecutive Tuesday mornings in the Recreation Club, specifically concerned environmental pollution issues, with the aim of explaining to the public the reduction in emissions achieved by the new Acid Converting Plant. Highly technical presentations were made by the manager of the converting plant and an environmental consultant who had been contracted as a 'third party' to facilitate the meeting. It was attended by around fifteen to twenty people, including several management-level employees of the mines, a union representative and directors of Rustenburg EcoWatch, an environmental pressure group operating in the Rustenburg area, run by Karl and Neelius, two retired mining engineers who lived on small-holdings in the area outside Rustenburg, and who described the group's objective as 'to keep the mines clean' (Neelius). 'We're watching them' Karl said, 'we're monitoring the emissions . . . but mostly now they talk to us and listen to us because we speak the same language as them'[3]. The meetings remained highly technical. The only time 'social issues' entered the arena during the meeting was in a question from Karl: 'when are you going to do something about the informal settlements? We have some in Kroondal now and the ecological degradation that they are causing to the landscape is terrible, they have to be moved'. In response to this, the facilitator explained, 'we'll deal with social issues at the 4 June open day'.

Writing about stakeholder participation in England, Elizabeth Harrison describes how participants are expected to conform to an ideal of the 'good citizen', demonstrating their worthiness for social welfare initiatives. Conversely, those who refuse or fail to conform are perceived as 'subversive' as they 'disrupt or negate the intended processes or outcomes of public policy' (Barnes and Prior 2009, quoted in Harrison 2009). In the community participation processes at the Rustenburg mines, those who are seen to 'make demands' on the company risk being categorised as 'troublemakers', or worse. Earlier, Grace had referred to the presence of these apparently unwelcome guests at the stakeholder forum as an 'invasion'. By making 'claims' on the company—whether in relation to health, housing or jobs—they transgress the unwritten rules of engagement, disrupting the apparent efficacy of the company's community upliftment and empowerment agenda. For in doing so they are perceived to have given voice to an illegitimate sense of entitlement, rather than demonstrating that they are willing and able to be empowered 'to help themselves'.

Diwe went away empty-handed from the June 4 stakeholder event, except for a bunch of pamphlets, and the promise of feedback within three months to the list of questions and comments left on a clipboard at the entrance. The scheduled interactive question and answer session for the afternoon had been cancelled after the 'fiasco' of the last meeting, in its place, the clipboard on which 'local stakeholders' could sign up and leave comments or complaints. I asked Diwe what had gone before in the way of community projects led by any of the mining companies. She said a couple of years previously a mining company had initiated a recycling and waste collection project in the area of Edenvale in which she lived: 'one of the companies came, Impala I think maybe, and they said we could do a business with collecting waste, some recycling too. . . We made a business plan . . . but I don't know what happened, I never saw it again'. She added, 'I'm very interested in the BEE procurement, so I come to all the stakeholder workshops to find a project . . . but it's very difficult to start something in Edenvale'.

A Joint Responsibility

The dramatic expansion and urbanisation of the area within the Rustenburg Local Municipality (RLM) has created enormous developmental pressures, manifest most starkly in the rapid expansion of informal settlements which surround the various Rustenburg mining operations and which now account for an estimated 10–20 percent of the population of the RLM (Rustenburg Local Municipality 2005: 13). The RLM's 2005 Integrated Development Plan states that:

> This is a stark reality, in that the municipality now continues to see an influx of migrant and seasonal workers, *imported crime activities*, over burdening of existing resources, shrinking land availability, widening gap between 'haves' and 'have nots' (ibid: 4).

In most of Edenvale, as in the other informal settlements in the Rustenburg area, there is no access to basic services. Only a very small corner of Edenvale has access to water tanks and a sewage system. According to Prosper Masinga, a union shop steward at Anglo Platinum who lives in Edenvale:

> We have a mobile clinic which comes to the place I live in—one mobile clinic for 20,000 people and Anglo built sewage and supply water to the bit of the camp I live in, but that's the only one I know. That's it.

The clinic which comes once or twice monthly is provided by the Department of Health. According to Jerry Mosenyi, the company had plans to fund another such clinic at some point in the future. There are no schools in Edenvale, (the nearest school is over 3km away[4]), and only one tarred road which goes from the edge of the settlement to the Anglo Platinum mining compound.

The informal settlements have become categorised as a problem of their own, isolated from the list of core development issues identified in planning processes which commonly read as education, healthcare services, water provision, SME development, and informal settlements. In formal documentation, both Rustenburg Municipal Council and Anglo Platinum stress their commitment to working in public-private partnership to meet the urgent development challenges of these areas. According to the discourse of partnership, this is to be achieved through the 'Integrated Development Process'. In the Municipality of Rustenburg, as in all municipalities in South Africa, there is a sophisticated Integrated Development Plan (IDP), a strategy for multi-stakeholder partnership to which all parties claim to subscribe. CSR managers within the mining companies commonly referred to the IDP as 'the motherboard', 'template' or even, 'bible' guiding the company's SED activities and stated their commitment not only to working with local government, but also to being guided by them on CSR planning: 'we all really subscribe to it—you know it has become a bible to many of the people because these are the real needs of the community identified in here' (Jerry Mosenyi, CSI officer,

Rustenburg). Nox explained that needs assessment was made on the basis of dual and complimentary processes of stakeholder engagement: through the IDP and through the company's in-house systems:

> Well, you see it's a combination. First of all we have our own broad priorities— infrastructure, small business, education and HIV—although infrastructure is more for the new remote mines in Limpopo, not so much for Rustenburg anymore. Then we undertake needs assessment, first with reference to the Integrated Development Plan for the RLM, and secondly through our own stakeholder engagement as part of SEAT. So we hold 'community participation' meetings like this one next week on June 4th.

The national government requires that all municipalities in the country produce a comprehensive IDP every five years, and review the plan annually in consultation with all local stakeholders, from representatives of the corporate sector to local ward councillors. The IDP aims to provide a participatory mechanism for needs assessment and a forum for multi-stakeholder collaboration through which to respond to them. In Rustenburg, a central focus of the IDP is diversifying the economy away from a reliance on mining, by developing small and medium sized business and encouraging large non-mining industrial business to move to the area, together with a strategy for rural and agricultural development.

The support which Anglo Platinum provided to this collaborative pursuit of the IDP goals was not simply financial. Anglo Platinum personnel spoke of 'donating' the company's 'expertise' and 'technical know-how' in areas such as environmental management, urban planning and water delivery, in order to help 'build capacity' in local government. During the time I was in Rustenburg the company had seconded two technical advisors to the municipal offices for a period of two years. The first, an environmental manager was involved in designing the new environmental plan for the RLM. The second, a housing officer, had been seconded to the council's planning department, ostensibly to help deal with the acute shortage of housing in the area, and the rapid growth of informal settlements.

But, while the inhabitants of the informal settlements are often the subjects of formal discussions, they are rarely participants in the conversations. With the exception of a small area of Edenvale and Mayfair, another settlement which surrounds the Xstrata Chrome mining areas, the informal settlements remain outside the existing structures aimed at recruiting stakeholder participation such as the IDP. As the largest of the informal settlements with an estimated population of somewhere between 20,000 and 40,000, Edenvale has some level of formal recognition, but was only granted the formal status of a 'ward' of the Rustenburg municipality in 2005, and as such, is represented by elected Ward Counsellors who attend the annual IDP review. However, the formal discourse of the IDP continues to distinguish between 'formal stakeholders', defined as 'permanent residents' of the RLM, and 'informal stakeholders' (Rustenburg Local Municipality 2005: 25). In the 2005 IDP, the ward which represents Edenvale, was formally categorised as 'Edenvale Squatters' (ibid: 54). This classification explicitly emphasises not only the spatial liminality of the informal settlements, but imposes a temporal liminality on them. This distinction is replicated in documentation relating to Anglo Platinum's local SED activities, and in the discourse of the company's frontline SED officers, in which, informal settlers were commonly categorised, not only as informal stakeholders, but as illegal squatters or invaders.

As a result, social responsibility for the informal settlements was displaced between the IDP mechanisms of the Rustenburg Municipality and the 'community' of beneficiaries as it is constructed through the patronage and clientelism generated by CSI, so revealing the disjuncture between state provision and corporate responsibility. This tension was further compounded by the febrile relationship between the RLM, Anglo Platinum and the Royal Bafokeng Administration[5] (RBA)—which owns a significant amount of the land leased by the mining companies and has developmental (though not legal) jurisdiction over the territory under its domain[6]. Displaced within this institutional triad of authority, the informal settlements have become the subject of competing attempts to deny, rather than assert social responsibility. As Jeremy Brooke, ex-Community Affairs Manager for Anglo Platinum remarked: 'the informal settlements are just a disaster—not that I was *personally responsible* for that . . . but those are the areas that *no one wants to take responsibility for*'.

While Anglo Platinum's SED officers stressed that the IDP was their 'motherboard' or 'template' guiding the company's SED activities, a very different picture emerged from the annual IDP representative forum meeting at the Rustenburg Civic Centre in May 2005. The hall was packed with over 300 Ward Counsellors from each of Rustenburg's thirty-five wards and any other people who wanted to attend the open meeting. No representatives from any of the five mining companies were present. Odette Kambalame, the IDP manager in the RLM, told me:

They sit on the advisory panel of the IDP and meet to tell us their needs and plans, but when that meeting happens is up to them—sometimes it doesn't, or . . . instead most companies send a junior manager with no power to the meetings. They send the 'photocopy boy' who knows nothing and can't make any decisions. If they followed the IDP, as they say they do, they would come to us to ask, where is the need that we have identified through our community consultation process? But with them, people just manoeuvre their way in and then the mine just hands them the money. There is no identification of need. I have never seen them at an IDP representative forum.

At the IDP representative forum 'The Informal Settlements' was listed as an item on the agenda, a separate category in its own right. The Rustenburg Mayor opened the meeting, with a brief obituary for a ward counsellor, PJ Xhosa, who had died the previous Sunday. In his obituary the Mayor spoke of PJ Xhosa's work 'at the forefront of negotiating for those people in Edenvale to be relocated to a more formal township':

> The big problem in the squatter camp is that this is a big camp and there is no water there because the squatter camp land belongs to the mines and there was a view that mining would happen in that area.

After the plenary session was formally concluded with a roll-call of all the ward counsellors present, a prayer in Setswana and token budget approval, the assembly broke into eight separate working groups to address the priorities listed on the agenda: education, infrastructure, health, tourism, small-business, sports and leisure facilities, roads, and the 'Informal Settlements Commission'.

However, the Informal Settlements Commission discussion was constrained by the absence of a critical group of actors—the mining companies—making debate on the whole range of urgent issues listed (including water provision and sanitation) fruitless and resolution impossible. The first point for discussion was water. The issue of relocation which had been raised by the Mayor in his obituary of PJ Xhosa, was the subject of heated yet brief discussion ending in frustration:

> RP Nkosi, Ward Counsellor (Park Heights): I want to know how this consultation works, because they have never consulted with us. We did not have the consultation of the budget and it was not presented to the community.
>
> Facilitator (from the RLM council): It is very important when we report back that we can say consultation was done and on what day it was held.

RP Nkosi, Ward Counsellor (Park Heights): Ok, but now I see on the budget that in Protea Park Extension Four they are requesting a swimming pool. We have no toilets. They cannot have a swimming pool when we have no waste removal, no sewage system.

Celia Kabene, Ward Counsellor (Edenvale): It's premature to talk about waste removal now, we can't talk about waste removal when people don't even have water.

Gladys Mogwaza, Ward Counsellor (Edenvale): The people who don't have water to drink will come and take water from the swimming pool!

Facilitator: I don't want to talk about swimming pools, let's leave swimming pools where they are and move on.

Gladys Mogwaza, Ward Counsellor (Edenvale): We are not talking about a nice-to-have, we must focus on the priorities . . . When are they going to put the water in?

Facilitator: They cannot put in full water systems . . . because some of the informal settlements are going to be moved for the mine . . . So we've all agreed on water tanks in all the informal settlements. OK, water's done, let's move on to clinics.

Celia Kabene: I want to know the time-frame for people being moved because we have no water or sanitation but I don't have the information as to when we are being moved.

Facilitator: The RLM is working with the mining company. Their plans are to put in water and sanitation in the new place so that when people move there it is fully developed. Because people are going to be relocated, they obviously aren't going to pump in lots of money to the place which will be moved for the mine. So they'll first put in a few tanks of water. Now, let's move on, the tar road.

Soon after, the facilitator stopped the discussion and instructed us to return to the plenary. Celia Kabene never got an answer as to when the residents of her ward would be relocated. Indeed, speaking to both the planning office in the council and the company's SED office, no clear plans seem to have been made (or were told to me) either for the relocation of the informal settlement or for the sinking of new mine shafts in the area it currently occupied. In the meantime, neither the mine nor the local government were making moves to provide full water and sanitation systems to Edenvale.

Beyond the 'Community'

As spaces of exclusion from service provision, the liminality of the informal settlements reveals the fissure between CSR and state responsibility. They expose the failure of partnership, of which programmes such as Circle of Hope[7] and processes such as the IDP were intended to be shining examples. Local government officers responsible for the IDP represented this as a failure on the part of the mining companies to acknowledge their responsibility in both creating and providing for the informal settlements:

> They won't accept responsibility for the informal settlements. The mineworkers want to be with their wives. So their wives are coming to be with them and are living in the informal settlements. That is who is living in the informal settlements—it's the families of their employees (Odette Kambalame, IDP Manager, Rustenburg Local Municipality).

However, Anglo Platinum employees, from hostel managers to SED officers, stressed that the true obstacles to delivering development to the informal settlements were, on the one hand the incapacity of local government, and on the other, the RBA's prohibition on the formalisation of 'illegal settlements'. Thus, Nox Ndovulu, Anglo Platinum regional CSI coordinator, explained:

> I must tell you, you try and coordinate with local government to come up with a joint venture between the company and local government, but because of lack of capacity there are no decision-makers, people don't turn up to meetings, they're not committed.

Nox's assessment of the failure of local government officers to 'turn up to meetings' or take decisions, thus echoed almost completely Odette Kambalame's converse account of how the IDP process was undermined by the mining companies who either sent 'the photocopy boy' to meetings or were absent altogether.

At the same time, with regards to the RBA, any attempt at social investment in infrastructure or development more broadly, Anglo personnel explained, would be taken as an act of formalising a settlement of illegal squatters on Bafokeng land. Thus Kobus, a hostel manager, had remarked while pointing to the informal settlement outside the fences of Hostel A:

> You see the squatter camp over there. We'd like to do something for them, give them water or sanitation, but the Bafokeng Administration would accuse us of formalising an illegal settlement on their land. They are squatting ille-

gally on the land—it is Bafokeng tribal land . . . The mine is not allowed to give anything. So they get nothing from them and nothing from us.

Similarly, Daniel Enele (an Anglo Patinum SED officer) described his relationship with the 'squatters' of Robega, an informal settlement close to the Bafokeng Rasimone Mine (a joint venture between Anglo Platinum and Royal Bafokeng Holdings that falls within the territory of the RBA). Enele stressed their status as illegal land invaders:

> Fortunately I have only this Robeja in my territory unlike Jerry Mosenyi who is in charge of the areas around Waterval, he has many areas like this, many squatters in his area. Here, they played a very clever game. A few came in and then they advised many others to *invade* the land and fill it up with people and shacks because they know that the government couldn't tell them to leave. They are the only outsiders who live in Bafokeng territory.

At the same time, Enele's comments exemplified the conventional representation of informal settlements, not only as illegal land invaders, but as the common locus of crime, violence and social corruption:

> These ones in Robejo are not so bad as other squatter camps though, they are not so violent. At first, they were demanding and threatening, always demanding—they came to a meeting carrying guns. Now the chairman of the informal settlement and myself—we're the best of friends . . . When I needed to see him because they were squatting on the land where we want to sink a ventilation shaft, I go out of the office . . . I go to his place and I take a loaf of bread and I sit and have tea with him in his shack . . . People say, 'what are you doing going from the office to the shack?' But I go anyway.

This dual construction of the informal settlements as both illegal, and the source of illegality, was pervasive. During our discussion of the development challenges in the Bojanala Platinum District (which incorporates those areas under the jurisdiction of the RBA), the Bafokeng Queen Mother, SB Motlegi, explained:

> The major challenge is poverty and then poverty brings a lot of underlying things—you get prostitution and drug abuse. People are flocking to this area— with this free movement from one place to another you get all these things.

This resonated with the account given by Annie du Toit, a housing coordinator for Anglo Platinum Rustenburg. Despite commenting earlier that a large number of Anglo Platinum mineworkers were living in the informal settlements, she explicitly placed them outside the zone of the company's responsibility, while categorising them as the source of 'theft, noise and pollution':

> The informal settlements aren't really a problem for us. Unless they are adjacent to our housing suburbs—then there can be problems with theft, noise and pollution . . . It is a concern to think that people live in shacks—but that will be addressed by the IDP I'm sure.

Thus the failure to accept developmental responsibility for the informal settlements reveals the institutional fissures and fragmentation which lie beneath the claims to community partnership and tri-sector collaboration that are encapsulated in the commitment to 'integrated development' and the 2003 Memorandum of Understanding between the RLM and RBA[8]. Yet, as each party attempts to distance themselves from this responsibility, the tension between them serves to collectively reinforce the construction of the informal settlements as *outside* the welfare 'community', and mainstream society in general. While each party shifted the burden of responsibility to the other, all drew on a common discourse that sought to undermine the legitimate status of informal settlers as citizens, and therefore deny their claims to developmental benefits or social welfare whether provided by the mining companies, the local government or the RBA. Local government officers and company CSR personnel alike constantly emphasised that the informal settlements are 'very new, they are migrants', or, as Gilbert Mogapi put it, 'for most people in the squatter camps—this is not their permanent address'. Equally Carol Flynn, a CSR consultant hired by Anglo Platinum to carry out a socio-economic impact assessment in Rustenburg in 2004 commented: 'they're all migrants in the squatter camps, these aren't local guys and if the company puts infrastructure in, it'll be making them permanent and they don't want that'. Explaining her own frustration with the apparently intractable situation she added, 'the trick is to do something, but not too much'.

The persistent categorisation of their status as 'migrants' serves a dual purpose. Firstly, as the IDP statement exemplifies, it provides a narrative that serves both the RLM and the mining companies, according to which Rustenburg's 'social tensions' can be attributed to the moral and social degradation 'imported' by an 'influx of migrant(s)' (Rustenburg Local Municipality 2005:4). Thus the IDP lists one of the priorities for the RLM as 'rebuilding the moral fabric of society' (ibid: 53). Just as Chapter 5 showed how the informal settlements were viewed as a threat to the physical and moral integrity of the workplace, a source of corruption and contagion, within corporate paradigms of HIV management, so they are categorised as such within the broader development discourses that dominate discussions around planning and social improvement in Rustenburg. Secondly, this classification underpins the representation of the informal settlements as transitory, impermanent, and usually, illegal, and in so doing to reject claims to entitlement by casting their inhabitants—many of whom have lived in the area for a number of years—as, in effect, 'non-stakeholders'. Thus the disjuncture between the mechanisms of CSI and the IDP process serves constantly to reinforce the representation of the informal settlements as transient, to excise those who live in them from the institutional map of stakeholders, and by casting them as 'informal' or 'illegitimate' stakeholders, to deny any claims to entitlement. This reminds us how, as discussed in the previous chapter, corporate responsibility is conceptualised as something which is dispensed, or *given* voluntarily to projects or people selected by the company, thus eschewing claims to entitlement, particularly from those who fall outside the demarcated zone of social responsibility.

This brings us back to Diwe, who opened this chapter, striving to be recognized as a 'stakeholder', to be selected as a target of the company's empowerment initiatives. Over twenty years ago, Fred Cooper wrote that 'the city is inhabited by those still waiting to win as well as those who have won' (Cooper 1987: 181). This is even more true today than it was then, despite the emancipatory promise of the market, extended by the giants of corporate capitalism to aspiring entrepreneurs at the margins. If winners in contemporary capitalism are defined by their capacity to claim benefits from those with the power or resources to deliver them (in this case a mining company), then the odds are certainly stacked against Diwe and others like her who, presumed lacking in these marketable assets, skills or simply potential are further marginalised from the exclusionary processes of empowerment (Ong 2006). For the paradox of CSR lies in the fact that it expounds a doctrine of self-empowerment, demanding that beneficiaries demonstrate their will and capacity to 'help themselves' to a piece of the market, while at the same time, rejecting any form of 'claim-making' on the part of potential beneficiaries and corresponding obligation on the part of the company. Through the master narratives of economic empowerment and conversion to an entrepreneurial spirit, CSR appears, not only as an authenticating discourse for corporate capitalism, but an extension of supposedly market-based values. Yet steeped in the morality of gift-gifting rather than the supposedly autonomous relations of the market, in reality it serves to further entrench the social hierarchies and vast economic disparities which define life around the mines, between mine employee and unemployed, between stakeholder and squatter. The 'empowerment' delivered through CSR is highly selective, exclusive, and certainly elusive to those such as Diwe who sit beyond the 'community' of corporate social investment, but continue on in the hope of attaining empowerment through enterprise.

Conclusion: Market Myths and Moral Discourse

Corporate Capitalism and the
Pursuit of Moral Authority

Big Business doesn't really have the power most
people think it has, does it?

(Harry Oppenheimer, quoted in
the Johannesburg *Sunday Times*,
26th May 1963[1]).

This book began in the Regent's Park Marriott Hotel in London, and ended at the Anglo platinum mines in Rustenburg. It set out to examine the new regimes of authority that are generated in pursuit of corporate social responsibility, and to reveal the interplay of global agendas, national politics and local practices through which these regimes are constituted. In particular, my goal has been to show *how* the discourse of CSR—and its claims to moral purpose—serve to authenticate and extend the authority of corporations, not only over the economic but over the social and political order, as TNCs are elevated as both agents and architects of development. It has tracked the practice of CSR across multiple sites from the global headquarters of the Anglo American Corporation in London, to its headquarters, and those of its subsidiary Anglo Platinum, in Johannesburg, to the platinum mines of Rustenburg. At the same time, it has gone beyond the company itself, to the broader arenas in which CSR is performed through the mechanics of partnership and the appeal to a global collaboration between business and society.

The contribution of a multi-sited ethnography of CSR thus lies in the revelation of continuity across space, and time, as much as the discovery of localised difference (which is commonly assumed to be the business of anthropology). This ethnographic pursuit sheds light on the proselytising capacity of the CSR movement—simultaneously flexible and consistent—to extend its vision of development through business, and empowerment through 'the Market', and to find currency in the localities that it seeks to transform. The power of CSR lies then in its malleability, as a project that can be adapted to respond to the political economic imperatives of a particular national context, while retaining some fundamental elements. Not only does CSR offer corporations a new source of moral legitimacy, but it opens up new avenues of practice with which to confront dynamic social challenges as they emerge, from international development targets to the national goals of BEE in South Africa. Thus from plush London hotels to mine schools on South Africa's platinum belt, CSR takes on new clothes to respond to the particular imperatives of post-apartheid South Africa.

As such, CSR represents a discursive strategy and a set of practices with which particular companies negotiate, rather than supersede the state. Within the polarised academic literature on CSR, corporations appear either as supranational economic imperialists bypassing state regulation in ever more creative ways, or as global corporate citizens, stepping into the breach where the old artefacts of state power have failed to deliver development. Analysts have tended to emphasize both the novelty and the global dimensions of CSR as one of a number of transnational ethical regimes that 'escape state order' (Pálsson and Rabinow 2005: 93). But far from rendering the state obsolete, CSR provides a mechanism with which TNCs confront the tensions between the global political economy and state authority, as it serves to authenticate their power and influence on the government's development agenda. Here, we see the processes of CSR converge with and incorporate national processes of development, in this case, enabling the company to reposition itself at the forefront of the post-apartheid economy.

Just as the latest orthodoxy of international development champions a re-vitalised and 'remoralised' incarnation of market discourse as a vehicle of social improvement and inclusion for the marginalised, so in South Africa, CSR has become a crucial element in shaping and reinforcing a dominant national ideology that champions economic empowerment in place of social justice. This vision of development extends the promise of emancipation from the political, social and economic shackles of the past and present, through the empowering opportunities of 'the market' which, as Manzo puts it, has become 'the privileged subject around which all struggles for economic justice must orient themselves' (Manzo 1992: 253). The effect has been to establish business as a moral, and patriotic, duty in itself. By providing a moral narrative of commitment to national development, CSR banishes questions surrounding the inequitable distribution of wealth and resources in South Africa, and in particular, in the nation's mineral economy. The logic of business itself—and entry into the market—comes to stand for the values of freedom and empowerment which lie at the heart of South Africa's new national political agenda.

In this way a particular national rendering of CSR has gained currency in South Africa by appropriating, and indeed shaping, key components of national reconstruction— those of 'economic empowerment' and 'transformation'. This specifically South African ideology of 'patriotic capitalism', finds echoes elsewhere in the world where hyper-liberalisation has been embraced and authenticated within a narrative of nationalist development and patriotic corporate endeavour. Chopra describes a similarly 'patriotic' framing of neo-liberalism which serves to seal a pact between political and economic elites by crowning them collective collaborators in the nation's progress, through the boons of economic growth:

> The Indian state, in justifying its adoption of pro-globalization and pro-liberalization policies applauds the professional choices of this very class as positive contributions to the Indian nation! This newly formed elite group, which no doubt is substantially comprised of the older elite groups in addition to new entrants, and the Indian state thus appear to have embarked afresh on a shared history, one founded on a neoliberal view of the nation and the world (Chopra 2003: 440).

Chopra underlines the capacity of this vision of national development to colonise political debate and to narrow the terms of discussion surrounding liberalisation in India, promoting it to a sacred plane where it becomes 'beyond question' (ibid: 424). Just as in South Africa, the discourse of collaboration and partnership have been key components of this process, drawing together the new class of political and economic elites (which, as Chopra notes, incorporate the old) as collective guardians of the patriotic mission to embrace the global market.

As corporate South Africa proclaims its commitment to patriotic capitalism through the idiom of corporate citizenship, CSR has become a key mechanism with which the company negotiates the crucible of state-business relations and post-apartheid transformation on the one hand, and the imperatives of global diversification on the other, simultaneously projecting its status as global company and 'proudly South African'. CSR thus emerges as a source of immense moral and political power, extending well beyond the economic sphere; an authority that relies simultaneously on the projection of a novel global ethic and a (re)invention of a particular, nationally-rooted past. What appears as a paradox of old and new—a collision of the modern forms of global hi-tech business with the historical legacy of past industrial relations— is in fact the very source of power that CSR provides. Thus, the ethnography of corporate HIV care programmes, in Chapters 4 and 5, revealed how CSR represents a new mechanism of industrial discipline, which incorporates the discourse of contemporary global ethics and colonial corporate paternalism in equal measure.

The moral authority which the company accrues through CSR is achieved, not simply through a broad appeal to good corporate citizenship, but through the company's intervention in specific development challenges and national crises. This is exemplified most powerfully by the way in which Anglo has positioned itself in relation to the fight against HIV/AIDS. Yet the corporate response to the HIV pandemic is framed in two seemingly contradictory narratives. The company casts its HIV strategy in terms of a broad social, political and indeed moral project: 'taking a stand' against the failure of the state's response to the crisis. Yet at the same time, the language of 'enlightened self-interest' and the commitment to 'the business case' for CSR seeks to reaffirm a bottom line to such acts of corporate morality. This has the effect of conflating the imperatives of human care, with the pursuit of productive efficiency, emphasising the need to protect the interests of the company (its 'human capital') from the ravages of a threat, the cause of which is externalised beyond the domain of the company, and onto the failure of the state.

At the point of implementation, I argued, this tension translated into a disjuncture between the company's territorial zone of authority and the so-called 'community', challenging the appeal to community-public-private partnership (CPPP) as the basis of CSR. Thus while the corporate model of HIV management espouses an inclusive commitment to partnership and solidarity within the framework of a progressive global coalition to fight HIV, the practices it generates reconstitute the social authority of the company. CSR can thus be seen to inspire a commanding duty of care on the part of the corporation, while placing the 'beneficiary' in a position of dependence and subordination. In short, the beneficiaries of this ethical agenda, those commonly referred to as 'partners in development', come under the authority of the company as they become subject to its notions of responsibility and recipients of its paternalistic concerns.

As it circumscribes the lives of its workforce through a moral economy of trust and compliance, the corporate HIV wellness programme separates the workplace from the social world outside its borders. CSR serves to reinforce corporate command of space within the company's purview. Yet this spatial map of corporate responsibility, and corporate authority, is disrupted. The liminality of those who fall between the benefits provided through CSR and state welfare services, in particular those who live in the informal settlements, become a potent representation of the disconnection between corporate responsibility and state authority. The complex social realities around the mines confound these neat distinctions between direct and indirect responsibility (or between 'social responsibility' and 'social investment') territorialised within bounded zones of 'the mine' and 'the community' beyond its borders. Through the practices of 'community engagement' and social investment, the company identifies and constructs a 'community' of beneficiaries. In the end, this fantasy of 'community', refracted through the model of 'corporate-community engagement' laid down in the panoply of CSR tools, is imposed to the benefit of some, and the exclusion of many.

While this programme of corporate-driven development has undeniably delivered various tangible social benefits to recipients, it is the intangible prospect of empowerment through enterprise that has proved so alluring. On this promise of inclusion into the emancipatory project of 'the market', CSR has established itself as the development orthodoxy of the new millennium. But its mechanisms have served to entrench social positions and to enhance social inequalities, making the achievement of this goal unattainable for most. As an elite-sponsored programme of social improvement, the project of CSR brings new inequalities and new forms of exclusion even as it projects an inclusive vision of empowerment through the supposedly limitless opportunities of enterprise. For those such as Diwe, who experience CSR as exclusion rather than empowerment, corporate benevolence serves not only to deny them the patronage extended to beneficiaries, but to dismiss their credentials for membership on account of their apparent failure to 'help themselves'. Still, as Diwe showed us in Chapter 7, spurred on by the enticing yet elusive promise of the South African dream, the hope remains that 'in the new South Africa, everyone can be a businessman'.

The discourse of CSR is powerful, as is the ideal of 'self-sustainability' which it extends. The practices generated in pursuit of this mission strive to convert 'beneficiaries' to the values and virtues of the market, with the injunction to help yourself to a piece of the market and grab the opportunities that it offers. Not only does this vision reflect the BEE agenda of the post-apartheid state, it takes us back to the Regent's Park Marriott in London, echoing the pursuit of development through enterprise valorised as the latest orthodoxy of the global development industry. And, it takes us back to

Clem Sunter's 'rules of the game' model of 'winners' and 'losers' for all social, political and economic realities from trade liberalisation to the fight against HIV—an idiom which implicitly invokes classic representations of 'the market'. 'Winners' in this vision of individual maximisation are, as James Carrier puts it, 'autonomous, rational and calculating; losers are dependent, muddled and cannot defer gratification' (Carrier 1997: 28). Most importantly, Carrier points out, this ideal type 'market self' is supposed to be 'free of the immoralities of dependence on others' (ibid). This is the freedom that CSR has advocated in its pursuit of 'winners', suitable targets for empowerment[2].

Yet, while the promise of empowerment holds out this vision, and indeed injunction, to independence and autonomy, the practice of CSR is steeped in relations of patronage and clientelism. The coercive bonds of the gift, enacted through CSR, inspire deference and dependence rather than autonomy and empowerment. The moral bonds created by these forms of corporate largesse reinforce old social hierarchies. In bringing together that most persuasive combination of forces, benevolence and economic power, this moral economy of subvention and dependency represents a far stronger mechanism for recruiting loyalty than the supposed autonomy offered through the market model of empowerment which the company claims to extend to its 'partners'. Not only do gifts make 'friends' (and of course, 'slaves'[3], as Sahlins tells us), but the enduring moral bonds they create are much better at enlisting support, commanding allegiance and manufacturing consensus than the imagined cold rationality of the 'free market'. Gift-giving is fundamental to 'primitive exchange' Sahlins explains, as 'material flow underwrites or initiates social relations' (Sahlins 1972: 186). Within the realm of corporate capitalism, CSR performs an equally essential function in reverse: social bonds created through corporate benevolence are harnessed to underwrite material flow, alerting us, not only to the possibility, but the necessity of conjuring morality at the heart of big capitalist enterprise. Again we are reminded of the words of the Rustenburg community worker with which this book began: 'as long as we accept handouts from the mines, we'll be their slaves'. In the end, Sahlins warns, the 'economic relationship of giver-receiver' becomes the 'political relation of leader-follower', as philanthropic benevolence serves to secure 'the power residing with the chief from the wealth he has let fall to the people' (ibid: 133, 140).

Thus, the logic of the gift works through CSR to reassert asymmetrical relations of dependency, rather than the liberation of autonomy through enterprise. Beneficiaries are, therefore, caught between a didactic vision of

empowerment through the market—a symbolic construct which claims itself free of social ties, moralities and politics—and the coercive relations of
gift-giving, enacted through corporate practices of 'social upliftment'. The
contradiction is clear. The discourse of CSR espouses a vision of development through business, in line with the ideology of corporate capitalism. This
evangelical project is extended to targets, holding out a model of independence, self-help and entrepreneurialism through which beneficiaries—and
the communities in which they live—will be re-made as empowered, market-
oriented actors. But while it preaches the market values of individualism,
maximisation and enterprise, the practice of CSR delivers and relies upon a
moral economy of patronage and clientelism, the supposed antithesis to the
market doctrine espoused as the basis of corporate citizenship. The practices
and processes that constitute this moral economy of CSR, the central focus of
this book, connect multiple actors, management and mineworker, company
and beneficiary, in ways that are, I argue, integral to the reproduction and
expansion of corporate capitalism. At the same time, these bonds—the products of CSR—are both novel and strikingly reminiscent of colonial era corporate benevolence. CSR appears (and is widely seen) as a radical break from
the paternalism of Victorian and colonial forms of industrial philanthropy.
But, like its 'predecessor', CSR serves to reinforce capitalism by transforming
models of social development—and the identification of social needs—into
those amenable to the pursuit of corporate interests and authority.

Is the contemporary phenomenon of CSR then, little more than a pale
shadow of the largesse of Charlie Stott and his fellow mine managers, or the
grand philanthropic endeavours of 'Oppenheimer and Son' and the pantheon
of mining magnates and grand industrialists of the past? Does the intrusion
of this moral discourse into the supposedly modern world of market relations
signify, as Graeber (2001) suggests, an underlying repugnance within capitalism towards the harsh logic of the market, demanding redemption through
the morality of the gift? Does CSR offer then an antidote to the dehumanising
effects of global capitalism, unleashing a ritual purification within the profane
world of business[4], holding out hope of collective responsibility, reciprocal relations and mutual interdependence in place of individual maximisation?

In her ethnography of exchange in a Fijian village, Christina Toren describes the imperative to subject money earned in the market to ceremonial
forms of gift exchange in order that it should be 'divested of moral neutrality, (and) purified of any potentially threatening associations with the market'

(Toren 1989: 160). Like much classic economic anthropology[5], Toren's study revealed how market relations must take on the cloak or form of gift relations in order to preserve social structures ordered through giving. CSR, and its core doctrines of 'empowerment through enterprise' and 'enlightened self-interest', attempts to do the opposite: to reassert the primacy of impersonal market relations and expunge the profoundly moral dynamics which contradict the market orthodoxy of capitalism they sustain. Here, in striking contrast, the gift masquerades as impersonal market relations so denying the moral bonds and social relations of donor and recipient, control and subordination which the practice of CSR in reality generates. With CSR then, we find a dramatic reversal: rather than the market polluting the integrity of the gift economy, it is the gift which must be denied as it is seen to challenge the integrity of the 'market' construct.

Within the apparently depersonalised world of global corporate capitalism and amoral market rationality that it propounds, the moral force and social politics of giving prevail. The phenomenon of CSR thus confounds Mauss' representation of the gift as the antithesis to the amorality of the modern market economy and 'cold reasoning of businessman, banker or capitalist' (Mauss 1967: 73). And, it confounds the Anglo chairman's memorable description of the market as a natural force comparable with gravity that transcends human agency and social relations, as he told me:

> The market is like gravity—you can erect tall buildings and fly in an aeroplane, but one thing you can't do is dance around on a tightrope. There's nothing moral about gravity; but if you don't pay attention to it, it will grind you up.

The power of neoliberal ideology has widely been seen to rest on its capacity to claim the total abstraction of 'the market' (like gravity) from social relations and questions of morality, as Bourdieu puts it, 'severing the economy from social realities' (1998b). But the discourse of CSR, unsettles this interpretation, as it works to secure and extend corporate capitalism, by *incorporating* rather than *excluding* the social world from its project. Taken in by the power of the market discourse itself, we persist in thinking of neoliberal capitalism and moral economy as two separate, distinct and opposing rationalities. But the moral movement of CSR, and the social bonds it creates, sustains and furthers the interests of corporate capitalism. These moral relations are at work at the heart of neoliberalism; they are intrinsic to its working; they are a source of its power. And, I have argued here, they are central to its capacity to command consent, silence dissent and co-opt support to its project. CSR thus represents a powerful response to critiques of neoliberalism as a global economic project that precludes social realities and the imperatives of human welfare and governance. It does so by offering an apparent space *within* the structures of global capitalism for self-governance, self-discipline and collective social responsibility, driven by the powerful corporate actors who were once the targets of such criticism. For, the power of this movement lies in its capacity to colonise rather than alienate the very structures capable of obstructing the drive of corporate capitalism[6].

In this way claims to moral probity are entwined within economic imperatives, asserting that the interests of material accumulation can be pursued alongside those of moral well-being. The discourse of CSR enables corporations to accrue moral authority as agents of progress and development, while simultaneously asserting their commitment to a global economic order governed by the supposedly amoral, asocial and secular logic of 'the market'. In the end, the moral economy of CSR represents, not an opposition to the contemporary world of corporate capitalism, nor a limit to it, but the very mechanism through which corporate power is replenished, extended and fortified.

Notes

Preface and Acknowledgements

1. Marcus 1995.
2. Desjarlais 2003: 18.

Introduction

1. 'Timeo Danaos et dona ferentes' (*Virgil* Aeneid 2.49); 'I fear the Greeks even when they come bearing gifts' (author's translation).

2. Thus Barry writes: 'ethical problems have generally been reckoned to be external to the market. The potential ethical dilemmas business corporations might have to confront have been traditionally resolved elsewhere (by the political system) and have been translated into the form of legal regulations and taxation that impact on the conduct of business . . . but they are not reckoned to be the explicit concern of business' (Barry 2004: 196).

3. See for example, Benioff and Southwick's recent book *Compassionate Capitalism: How Corporations Can Make Doing Good Integral to Doing Well* (2009).

4. (SABC News, 19 March 2005). The Rustenburg Integrated Development Plan (2005) goes even further, claiming that Rustenburg is 'viewed as the fastest growing city in Africa' (Rustenburg Local Municipality 2005: 18). According to the town's mayor, 'we have about 6–8 percent growth per annum—that is far, far above the national average—the only city on the whole continent that is nearing 6 percent is Cairo' (Rustenburg Mayor 28 April 2005).

5. The informal settlements have been given fictitious names to ensure anonymity.

6. This was reflected in the *Political Declaration* of the World Summit: '[we will] actively promote corporate responsibility and . . . the full development and effective implementation of intergovernmental agreements and measures, international initiatives and public-private partnerships' (World Summit on Sustainable Development 2002).

7. As Bendell puts it, a movement from 'barricades to boardrooms' (Bendell, 2004: 1).

8. These have included the Mining, Minerals and Sustainable Development Programme (2002), and the Global Mining Initiative (GMI), both of which have been coordinated by the International Council of Mining and Metals (ICMM), the World Bank's Extractive Industries Review (EIR) and the Extractive Industries Transparency Initiative (EITI) coordinated by the Department for International Development (DFID), to name but a few.

9. See Kirsch 2009.

10. Anglo American's former chairman occupies leading positions on a number of international CSR initiatives such as the World Business Council for Sustainable Development (WBCSD), Business Action for Africa and the Global Business Coalition (GBC) on HIV/AIDS.

11. See for example Bendell 2004.

12. See for example Mitchell's study of the genealogy of corporate philanthropy and social responsibility in *The Generous Corporation* (Mitchell 1989); and Bell's study of the Carnegie corporation's inquiries into poverty in South Africa in the 1920s, 1930s and 1980s driven by what she describes as its founder's 'personal crusade "to better the world"' (Bell 2000: 484).

13. Until now, the study of CSR has remained the domain of business and management studies. Such studies have tended to take a managerial or technical approach to CSR, asking 'in which situations does it work well' and 'where not', or 'how can it be fixed?'; and offering 'lessons learned' for removing obstacles to 'successful implementation' (see for example Carroll's [1991] constantly invoked four part pyramid model of CSR; or Grayson and Hodges guide to 'corporate social opportunity' [2004]). For further examples of this managerial approach see also Wagner and Schaltegger 2006; Lynham et al 2006; McIntosh et al 2002; and Moser 2001.

14. This is exemplified in the title of a recent book by Wilson and Wilson (2006).

15. See for example Moody 2007, Doane 2005, Chandler 2003, Evans et al 2002 and Madeley 1999.

16. See for example Frynas 2005 and Pendleton 2004.

17. See for example Friedman 1970 and Henderson 2001, 2005. Friedman laid out his position on CSR in an article for the *New York Times Magazine* in 1970: 'there is one and only one social responsibility of business—to use its resources and engage in activities to increase its profits' (Friedman 1970).

18. See for example Fox 2004, Hopkins 2007, Marsden 2000 and Zadek 2001.

19. Sharp similarly highlights this tendency to read development discourse in general, and CSR in particular, as merely a superficial smokescreen or statement of motive and intent (Sharp 2006: 215).

20. See Chapter 4.

21. At the 2006 Annual General Shareholders Meeting, Anglo American's chairman reported that, amidst steadily rising commodity prices over the past few years, the price of platinum rose by 20 percent in 2006, copper rose by 51 percent and zinc rose by 70 percent as compared with the previous year (25 April, Institute of Electrical Engineers, London). In 2006, Anglo Platinum recorded an operating profit of $2,398 million—the highest in its history (Flood 2006).

22. Primary uses for the platinum mined by Anglo Platinum are in auto-catalysts for cars (50.6 percent), jewellery (24.8 percent), chemical and electrical (11 percent) and others, including medical applications, the glass and petroleum industries,and electronic components such as computer hard-drives, iPods and LCD flat screens (13.6 percent) (Anglo American 2007: 24).

23. See for example Ferguson's ethnographic account of the ongoing cycles of growth and decline on the Zambian copperbelt and the consequent periods of urban expansion and desolation of towns such as Luanshya and Kitwe (Ferguson 2006, 1999). See also Linda Waldman's study of the enduring legacies of decline, unemployment and ill-health in the abandoned former asbestos mining towns of the Northern Cape (Waldman 2005).

24. Thus Adam Smith's much cited phrase has become the mantra of free-market doctrine and the sanctity of 'self-interest': 'it is not from the benevolence of the butcher, the brewer, or the baker, that we expect our dinner, but from their regard to their own interest' (Smith 1991 [first published 1776]: 20).

25. This is not to say that we have moved from an amoral market logic to a moral one—even the most hardline free-market discourse was as evangelical in spreading its morality of individual maximisation, competition and self-interest (albeit while claiming to be anything but moral). But as Ferguson points out 'the morality of the market has long denied its own status as morality, presenting itself as mere technique' (Ferguson 2006: 80–81). Where previously the morality of market capitalism was denied by its most powerful actors, the visible morality of this new doctrine of corporate social responsibility is undeniable.

26. See also Garsten and Hernes 2009; Pitluck 2009; Shever 2008; and Welker 2009.

27. See Foster's ethnography of Coca Cola, *Coca-Globalization: Following Soft Drinks from New York to New Guinea* (2008).

28. See Ferguson's Foucauldian analysis of the 'apparatus' of development in Lesotho, *The Anti Politics Machine* (1994).

29. Anthropologists and sociologists have challenged this Manichean dichotomy between moral and market logics, contesting the discourse of a market free from moral norms and social relations, as the antithesis to EP Thompson's moral economy (Bloch and Parry 1989; Carrier 1997; Granovetter 1985; Keane 2008). Thus they have sought to reveal how the logics of capitalist exchange and accumulation are tightly bound up with social identities and moralities (see for example, Miller 1997; Gude-

man 2001; and Osella and Osella 2009), and how markets are themselves both 'moral-ized' and 'moralizing' (Fourcade and Healy 2007: 286). But the extent to which cor-porate capitalism, the very heart of the neoliberal project where we have been told by the conventional wisdom of our time to expect to find economic practice at its most amoral and asocial, is embedded in moral relations has remained relatively unexam-ined. Only recently have we begun to question this taken-for-granted binary between morality and economy on which so much of our own sense of capitalist modernity is premised (see for example Maurer 2008; Miyazaki 2003; and Robbins 2009).

30. For anthropological exploration of this classic binary of the collision between 'community' and 'market', see Gudeman's *Economy's Tension* (2008).

31. Due to the prominence of Anglo and its founding family, the Oppenheimers, in the economic, social and political life of the country, the company and the family have both been the subject of numerous biographies and histories. These include Jamieson 1990; Pallister et al 1987; Sampson 1987; Innes 1984; Epstein 1982; Jessup 1979; Hocking 1973; and Gregory 1962. These tend to fall into two camps, those such as Jamieson's and Hocking's which display a romanticised reverence for Anglo and the Oppenheimers; and those such as Innes' and Gregory's mammoth works in which the social and politi-cal are subordinated to microscopic detail of the company's financial dealings.

32. More recently ethnographers have revealed the enduring power of these la-bour regimes as workers, or former workers, negotiate the post-colonial and post-apartheid workplace (see Phakathi 2005; Bezuidenhout 2005; Barchiesi and Kenny 2002; and Moodie et al 1994).

33. Perhaps it is precisely the territoriality of mining and the ways in which it shapes the life-worlds of mineworkers and mining communities in diverse physical and social geographies that has fascinated ethnographers for so long (see for exam-ple Nash 1993; Taussig 1980; Harris 1989; Ballard and Banks 2003; Kirsch 2006; and Welker 2009).

34. Additionally, 41 percent come from the Americas, 11 percent from Europe and 13 percent from the rest of the world (including the company's expanding opera-tions in China) (Anglo American 2007: 6).

35. According to a 2003 study by the Chamber of Mines, the mining industry di-rectly contributed 7.5 percent of the total gross domestic product (GDP) (R66.8 billion) (Randera 2003). The total contribution including all secondary industries that rely on mining is far greater still, estimated to be around 40 percent (Fearnley 2005: 146).

36. The South African gold industry has been in steady decline since the 1980s. Owing to declining mineral grades and rising costs, combined with the slide in global gold prices, production levels had fallen to their lowest point since 1956 (this infor-mation was gathered from www.mbendi.co.za, a mining industry portal, and the Jo-hannesburg Stock Exchange's 'news room'—www.jse.co.za). According to Lester et al, in 1998 alone, around 64,000 jobs 'were shed in the gold-mining industry', and the effect of this on mining towns such as Welkom in the Free State where 100,000 mine

employees were laid off (Lester et al 2000: 34, 256), as well as on the areas from where migrant workers come, has turned booming urban centres into desolate ghost towns.

37. The Anglo Group has a 45 percent share in De Beers (which remains a privately owned company) and has been the largest single shareholder in De Beers since 1926 (Gregory 1962).

38. Anglo Platinum 2008: 19.

39. South Africa has an estimated 71 percent of the world's platinum reserves (United Nations 1980: 38). It also has the world's largest reserves of gold, manganese, chromium, vanadium and alumino-silicates (Lester et al 2000: 34). In 2006 77.6 percent of world platinum supply came from South Africa (Anglo American 2007: 25).

40. Today, Anglo Platinum is responsible for around 40 percent of newly mined (as opposed to recylced) platinum production globally (Anglo Platinum 2008: 19). In 2005, Anglo Platinum reported a total workforce in South Africa of 74,498, of which they describe 58 percent as 'own employees' and 41.7 percent as 'contract staff' (Anglo Platinum 2005a: 74). Contract staff are considered to be employees of the firm sub-contracted, and not of Anglo itself and are therefore not eligible for the housing, training or medical benefits given by the company to its 'own' employees.

41. Egoli, the informal name given to Johannesburg, comes from the Zulu eGoli, meaning 'place of gold'.

42. Rustenburg is not, and never has been a 'company town' in the conventional sense, unlike other thriving or former mining towns such as Welkom (once the booming centre of gold production, under the domain of Anglo American, now the most commonly invoked example of a post-mining ghost-town); Kleinzee, the diamond mining town built by De Beers (Carstens 2001); or Prieska in the Northern Cape, a former asbestos mining town, now impoverished, polluted and inhabited by former mineworkers seeking compensation for asbestosis (Waldman 2005). The town was not built by a single mining company from the ground up. Established in 1851, Rustenburg existed long before the discovery of the platinum reefs as the trading centre for expansive citrus and tobacco farming lands now almost entirely occupied by the various mining operations.

43. The complex relationship between the RBN and the Rustenburg Municipality is beyond the scope of this book, but has been well documented by Bozzoli (1991) and Manson and Mbenga (2003). The RBA has a quasi governmental role, recognised by Article 12 of the new South African constitution as a 'Traditional Authority'. Nevertheless it falls under the legislative jurisdiction of the RLM's local government authorities. A large area of the land on which the mining operations of Impala Platinum are located is owned by the RBN. The RBA not only receives substantial royalties from the companies (including Impala and Anglo Platinum) who mine platinum on RBN land, but, through their privately owned company Royal Bafokeng Holdings, they have engaged in joint ventures with them, including a 50 percent joint venture with Anglo Platinum in the Bafokeng Rasimone Mine and a 17 percent shareholding of all

Impala's platinum operations. As a result of the enormous revenues from platinum, the Bafokeng have colloquially become known as 'the richest tribe in Africa' (Manson and Mbenga 2003). The visible disparity of wealth and infrastructure development between the areas under the RBA (in particular the city of Phokeng) and other areas of the Rustenburg municipality, combined with the RBA's (unofficial) policy of providing educational bursaries, jobs and development support exclusively to 'citizens' of the RBN has created tensions between the two.

44. Unemployment rates for the Bojanala district municipality are 37 percent (Anglo Platinum 2008: 38).

45. See Sibongile Khumalo's article in the *Mail and Guardian*, 'World Cup Revs up Tourism in Rustenburg' (Khumalo 2009).

46. According to a number of long-term residents of Rustenburg, the platinum mine closed twice in 1957 and 1971.

Chapter 1

1. This quote was taken from comments by Sir Mark Moody-Stuart during an interview on BBC News on-line (Cronin 2006).

2. See for example Hopkins 2007; Marsden 2000; and Matten and Crane who argue that 'corporations enter the arena of citizenship at the point where traditional governmental actors fail to be the 'counterpart' of citizenship . . . reinvigorating (or replacing) the welfare state' (Matten and Crane 2003: 10–11). Clearly, this assessment of corporations as guarantors and 'administrators of our citizenship' (ibid: 17), glosses over the important differences between philanthropic endeavour, or even responsibility, underscored by a commitment to 'creative voluntarism', and the reciprocal bonds of duty and entitlement on which citizenship is traditionally seen to be premised.

3. See for example Barry 2004; Garsten and Jacobsson 2007; and Shamir 2008.

4. According to Jonathan Porritt, BAE recently launched a range of environmentally-friendly weapons including 'lead-free' bullets, rockets with reduced toxins and grenades that produce less smoke (Porritt 2006: 15).

5. See Crewe and Harrison (1998) and Stirrat and Henkel (1997).

6. The Commission's report commands business to 'focus their efforts on coordinated action to tackle poverty—working in partnership with each other, with donors, with national governments, and with civil society' (Commission for Africa 2005: 74).

7. This is exemplified in reports such as that from the NGO SustainAbility and the Skoll Foundation which offers 'entrepreneurial solutions to insoluble (social) problems' (SustainAbility et al 2007:1); or the WBCSD's guide which proposes 'business solutions in support of the Millennium Development Goals' (World Business Council for Sustainable Development 2005: 6).

8. Similar versions of this mantra have become ubiquitous in the rhetoric of CSR advocates and industry publications: the triple bottom-line of 'profits, people and the planet' (International Finance Corporation [IFC] 2004: x).

9. See note 2.

10. This recalls Kaysen's memorable description of (or prescription for) the corporation: 'the modern corporation is a soulful corporation' (Kaysen 1957: 14).

11. BHP Billiton and Rio Tinto are two of world's largest mining companies.

12. This was organised by Save the Narmada Movement in India and the Alternative Energy Project for Sustainability.

13. NGO and Trade Union Statement at the European Conference on Corporate Social Responsibility, Maastricht, 7–9 November 2004 (quoted in Blowfield 2005: 515).

14. See for example Zadek (2001); Warhurst (2005); and Covey and Brown (2001).

15. Another such attempt to ensure accountability in the reporting of corporate responsibility (as opposed to its social impact) is the Global Accountability Index, to which Walmart, Nestle, Exxon Mobil and Anglo American subscribed. The results assign percentage scores for each organisation's capabilities in various areas of accountability. Anglo American received 46 percent for their transparency capabilities, 56 percent for their participatory capabilities, 78 percent for their social and environmental impact evaluation capabilities and so on. However, Sonnenberg and Hamann note that despite the enthusiasm for case studies in corporate reporting, 'even in relatively uncontroversial areas such as corporate donations there is a general reluctance among companies to disclose . . . non-selective data. Instead the focus on selective, positive information and case studies persists (Sonnenberg and Hamann 2006: 316).

16. CSR reports are then auditted by an 'independent third party' hired by the company. This 'assurance' work, as it is called, is generally undertaken by global accountancy firms such as KPMG and PriceWaterhouseCoopers that have recently branched out into 'social and environmental auditing'. For example, Anglo American's social reporting is 'assured' by KPMG (Anglo American 2005a: 3). Their 2004 *Report to Society* was declared top sustainability report by the Association of Certified and Chartered Accountants, UK (Anglo American 2005b: 3).

17. Executive Committee—the most senior team managing the company

18. Sir Mark Moody-Stuart stepped down from the role of chairman in August 2009.

19. See for example, DFID's 2006 White Paper, *Making Governance Work for the Poor*.

20. Emerging out of the *Publish What You Pay* campaign which was led by a coalition of NGOs demanding corporate accountability, the EITI is a prime example of the capacity of CSR to incorporate and appropriate not only the language of anti-corporate campaigns, but their agendas. The stated aim of the EITI is to bring together extractive companies, host governments and development agencies to ensure accountability in the payment and expenditure of revenues from resource exploitation.

21. Http://www.panda.org/about_wwf/how_we_work/businesses/conservation_partner/index.cfm. Last accessed 10 February 2006.

22. Chatham House rules were not applied at this conference.

23. On another occasion, this was echoed by an associate director of BITC who commented: 'luckily in the UK there's been a shift from the *negative* end of NGO's putting pressure to the *positive* end of business opportunity which is what we try to build on'.

24. The best example of this is Christian Aid's report *Behind the Mask: The Real Face of CSR* (Pendleton 2004) which seeks to expose fraudulent claims to social investment made by British American Tobaco, Coca-Cola and Shell.

25. Such as *The Partnering Toolbook* (Tennyson 2004) and the *Brokering Guidebook* (Tennyson 2005), both produced by the International Business Leaders Forum (IBLF) Partnering Initiative. CSR has become a discipline in its own right quickly taken up by US and European business schools as a key component of MBA graduate programmes, research agendas and its own journal (*Journal of Corporate Citizenship*). One of the most famous—the International Centre for Corporate Social Responsibility at Nottingham University—was founded in 2002 with a £3.8 million endowment from British American Tobacco. Meanwhile, the University of Cambridge now offers a post-graduate certificate in 'Cross-sector Partnership '.

26. As Cooley and Ron argue, while many have taken the extension of market competition to NGOs as evidence of a 'robust global civil society' injected with the efficiency of the market, the competition for funding, tenders and short-term contracts in reality has the opposite effect. Such competitive pressures subvert agendas and create a 'fiscal uncertainty' that weakens, rather than strengthens civil society (Cooley and Ron 2002: 6). On the corporatisation of NGOs, see also Chapin 2004.

27. This contemporary play on the classic General Motors' slogan 'what's good for General Motors is good for America' has become something of a catchphrase among advocates of CSR.

Chapter 2

1. This comparison was made explicitly by the Minister of Mines, Dr AJR van Rhijn in the South African parliament in 1957: 'Almost all the countries in the world have their industrial kings and mining magnates . . . In the United States the names of Carnegie, Rockefeller and Ford are well known to every schoolchild . . . As Sir Ernest is a world figure it is perfectly natural that I should compare him with those ' (Hocking 1973: 330).

2. This model of the corporation as social organisation advocated by Theodore Houser emerged in the post war period (see also Kaysen 1957) and disappeared with the rise of free market capitalism in the 1980s.

3. This is concretely expressed in Ernest Oppenheimer's request for the company headquarters to look like something between a cathedral and a bank (Johannesburg City Council 1986: 130).

4. The key figures of the Oppenheimer dynasty are founder of Anglo, Ernest Oppenheimer, his son Harry who was chairman of Anglo and De Beers from 1957 to 1982 and 1984 respectively. Harry's son Nicholas is a non-executive director of Anglo and chairman of the De Beers Group; and Nicholas' son, Jonathan is Managing Director of De Beers Consolidated Mines.

5. Both Ernest Oppenheimer and Harry were elected members of parliament in 1924 and 1948 respectively (Pallister et al 1987: 49).

6. Social scientists have long been interested in the role of human values such as trust, loyalty and communalism within and between firms, where according to mainstream economics the amorality of market logics reign (see for example Dore 1983; Granovetter 1985; Gudeman 2001; Harriss 2003; Thrift 1998; Yanagisako 2002). With CSR discourse, we find a renewed focus on values such as trust, extended to a normative vision of the relationship between business and society much more generally.

7. An article in the *Mail and Guardian* called on Ernest Oppenheimer's grandson and great grandson, Nicholas and Jonathan Oppenheimer, to follow their paternal legacy and 'establish their place in the pantheon of philanthropists' (Jones 2005: 19).

8. Anglo HQ in Johannesburg.

9. Arguably, the overt mutual and personal hostility between white English-speaking business and the Afrikaner government, served to further legitimise the economic marriage of convenience between the two.

10. For example, Yudelman, who positions himself in neither the 'Marxist revisionist' nor the 'liberal' camp, nevertheless states that: 'In South Africa . . . the major mining houses have been locked into an inextricable embrace with the state since the first decade of the twentieth century' (1983: 6). This state-business 'symbiosis', he argues, was in large part due to the shared need of the government and the mining industry to subjugate and discipline labour to staff the mines (ibid: 3, 4).

11. O'Dowd published an earlier book (1991) which, like that of his Anglo colleague Bobby Godsell's (Godsell and Berger 1988) combined a liberal historical viewpoint with future-scanning.

12. In 2002 a case was brought under the US Alien Tort Claims Act by the Khulumani Support Group and the Apartheid Claims Task Force against Anglo American, De Beers and other TNCs seeking reparations for profits earned by the companies from the apartheid regime (this follows the successful case for compensation brought by Ed Fagan against German companies for profiting from the slave labour of Jews during the holocaust) (Fassin 2007: 183; Anglo American 2003a). The case is on-going, but on 8 April 2009, the federal district court issued a ruling in this case that restricted the claims in the case to those against Daimler, Ford, General Motors, IBM and Rheinmetall Group (Hamblett 2009).

13. For a more detailed discussion of the failure of 'experiments in settled labour' see Jeeves and Crush (1995) and Laburn-Peart (1995).

14. Since 1998 the Anglo American Chairman's Fund, along with the De Beers Fund, is managed by Tshikulu Social Investments, a non-profit company set up by Anglo, to which a number of other South African corporate clients have recently signed up. In 2006 the Chairman's Fund, together with the AngloGold Ashanti Fund, made contributions of R491 million to 5,012 community projects. That year, a second foundation was established at the Company's London headquarters, the Anglo American Group Foundation, which makes grants to international NGOs including Engineers without Borders and Care.

15. Lipton argues that the violent conflict between mineworkers' unions and management which preceded these reforms should be seen as a 'combative partnership' that was ultimately instrumental in effecting 'a retreat from apartheid without wrecking the economy' (Lipton 2000: 214). In contrast, Mamdani argues that it was precisely reforms such as the recognition of union rights that enabled the structures of economic power to remain intact even after the end of apartheid (Mamdani 1996).

16. The same quote appeared in a full-page Anglo American advertisement in the British newspaper *The Guardian* in September 2010: 'As our founder Sir Ernest Oppenheimer said, our purpose is to "create value for our shareholders, but to do so in such a way as to create a real and lasting contribution to the communities in which we operate"' (Anglo American 2010: 17).

17. On the 'African Renaissance movement', see Ferguson 2006: 112.

18. This allowed them to head off the possibility—which at that time looked like a probability—of mineral resource nationalisation as laid down in the ANC's original Freedom Charter, or as Cummings suggests, to endorse a plan to 'dismantle the structure of apartheid without Marxist revolution' (Cummings 1995: 15).

19. Nelson Mandela.

Chapter 3

This title is borrowed from the fourth volume of Paul Scott's Raj Quartet following the struggle for power and position in the transition to Indian Independence (Scott 1975).

1. Former CEO of AngloGold Ashanti.

2. For anthropological accounts of the supranational flow of global capitalism see also Kapferer 2005; Gille and Riain 2002; Tsing 2000.

3. In South Africa, 'transformation' has become a catch-all term synonymous with affirmative action.

4. Seekings and Nattrass (2006) argue that South Africa cannot be characterised as neoliberal due to the persistence of a strong state welfarism. Yet even social welfare is increasingly cast according to a discourse of market 'winners' or 'losers' (see Chapters 6 and 7). Despite apparent contradictions between the political discourse of redis-

tribution, notably around processes of land reform (James 2009), and the individualist ideology of the market, the two are increasingly inseparable.

5. John Saul writes of the betrayal of redistributive politics, as the post-apartheid state capitulated to the 'dictates of the global economy', the very antithesis of the socialist imperatives enshrined in ANC's 1955 Freedom Charter: 'for in the teeth of high expectations arising from the successful struggle against a malignant apartheid state, a very large percentage of the population—among them many of the most desperately poor in the world—are being sacrificed on the altar of the neo-liberal logic of global capitalism' (Saul 2001: 429). Economic restructuring has been the subject of much debate (see Kahn 1996; Nattrass 1994; Kaplinsky 1994; Sender 1994).

6. An article in the Johannesburg *Business Report* reported that the loss to mining companies over a two day period in July 2002 was R50 billion (£5 billion) of shareholder value (Smith 2004). Following the leak, the government issued a statement that the draft charter 'does not in any way represent official government policy' (*Business Report* 31 July 2002, quoted in Hamann 2004b: 192).

7. At the time of conducting this research (September 2004–July 2005) the international currency exchange rate fluctuated between 11 and 12 South African Rand to the UK Pound. However, during this time the Rand strengthened against the US Dollar from approximately 8R to 1US$, to 6R to the Dollar.

8. The ex-minister for minerals and energy, Lulu Xingwana publicly attacked 'rich, white cartels that are continuing even today to loot our diamonds, *taking them to London*, ... and [monopolising] the mining industry' (Michaels 2004).

9. Conversely, Fig argues that it is precisely pressure from a more 'ethically informed' shareholder and asset manager base in the UK that has driven the 'triple bottom line' approach in companies such as Anglo (Fig 2005: 611).

10. This was neatly encapsulated in an Anglo American advertisement entitled 'Mining our way: greater share value from greater shared values' in *The Guardian* newspaper (Anglo American 2010: 17).

11. As Kahn highlights, in certain areas of economic policy, in particular the restructuring of labour, elements of interventionism remain (1996: 1), ie. the Labour Relations Act, the Employment Equity Act No. 55 (1998) and new labour laws that seek to protect workers from increasing casualisation (Adler and Webster 2000). Nevertheless since the mid 1990s there has been a dramatic rise in sub-contracting across the economy (see Bezuidenhout and Kenny 1998; Crush et al 2001: 6; von Holdt 2005; Theron 2005; Mosoetsa 2005). As Campbell shows the casualisation of labour has created intense insecurity among the mining labour force, as companies '"contract out" functions previously carried out by in-house permanent employees' (Campbell 2003: 156). The rise of CSR, and the benefits it extends to (permanent) employees and the broader 'community' around the mines must be seen within this context of

sub-contracting, and the 'flexibility' and insecurity it generates for corporations and workers respectively.

12. Patriotic capitalism was the theme of the Annual South African Black Management Forum, November 18–20 1999, entitled *Patriotic Capitalism: The Dilemma of the New Millennium* (Business Day 1999; Sowetan 1999, quoted in Comaroff and Comaroff 2000: 304)

13. The BEE scorecard defines the term 'HDSA' as 'any person, category of persons or community, disadvantaged by unfair discrimination before the Constitution of the Republic of South Africa, 1993 (Act No 200 of 1993) came into operation' (DME 2004b: 2).

14. The disposal of assets as BEE deals has been seen to parallel the creation of an Afrikaner business class following the Nationalist accession to power in 1940s, and the formation of new Afrikaner companies such as Gencor, as part of the state's effort to shift control of industrial capital away from white English-speaking business interests (O'Meara 1983).

15. Such schemes respond to Article 4 of the Charter which stipulates that companies must 'establish targets for employment equity, particularly in the junior and senior management categories . . . The stakeholders aspire to a baseline of 40 percent HDSA participation in management within 5-years' (DME 2004a: 4.2).

16. In Anglo Platinum, according to a study conducted in 2006, 80 percent of senior management were white (of which 96.9 percent were men). Of the 20 percent of black senior managers, 87.5 percent were men (Benchmarks Foundation 2007: 31).

17. CEO of Anglo Platinum.

18. Meanwhile, the sense of a closeted world of privilege where personnel made brief forays into the wider world of Johannesburg, rather than a progressive institution reflective of post-apartheid South Africa, is not dispelled by the company's diversity-awareness drive, whereby Anglo Platinum offered staff at its corporate office in Johannesburg, the opportunity to go on an Anglo-organised tour of Soweto. 'Never been to Soweto in your life? Don't despair', leaflets in the foyer of Anglo Platinum's fifteen-storey glass HQ in Johannesburg stated, inviting employees on a company tour half a century after the Oppenheimer Tower was built in the township as a tribute to Ernest Oppenheimer (Thale 2002).

Chapter 4

1. By 2009, the rollout had been extended beyond the company's flagship workplace treatment programme in South Africa, to most of the Group's operations worldwide.

2. Responses among business have ranged from the provision of comprehensive 'wellness programmes' by TNCs such as Anglo, Daimler Chrysler and Old Mutual, to

small and medium-sized enterprises (SMEs) that cannot afford such large-scale provision, but have established workplace health insurance schemes for their employees.

3. In 1999 *Business Report* headlined with 'Nearly Half of Mine Workers Have HIV' (quoted in Fassin 2007: 310). Most other studies have been somewhat more conservative. Fearnley (2005) places national HIV prevalence at 22.8 percent compared with 25 percent across the mining industry. A 2005 study reported an estimated average 24 percent prevalence across all Anglo's South African operations (Knight 2005: 20). Another put it at 23 percent among the 145,000 employees of Anglo's South African operations (Brink 2005). A survey conducted by the Wits Health Consortium in 2002 put the best estimate for HIV prevalence at Anglo Platinum specifically at 24.6 percent (Anglo Platinum 2003a: 21; Stevens et al 2006), 4.5 percent above the national prevalence for adults, which, at the time, was estimated by UNAIDS to be 20.1 percent (Chirambo and Caesar 2003: 6). According to the Wits study 'the highest prevalence was in the lower-income grades and among contractors at prevalence levels of 24% and 22% respectively among those tested' (Stevens et al 2006: 138). Five years on, the Anglo Group estimated average prevalence across its Southern African operations as significantly lower, 18 percent of the workforce, around 50 percent of whom are now enrolled in the workplace programmes of the various subsidiaries (Anglo American 2008: 30).

4. Wilson writes 'there is no other country in the world whose urban industries . . . [h]ave employed such a large proportion of oscillating migrants for so long a period of time' (Wilson 2001: 105). The role of migrant labour in the political economy of South Africa has been at the forefront of public and academic debate for over half a century (see Crush and James 1995a; Davies and Head 1995; Lipton 1980; McCulloch 2009; Moodie 1994; and Murray 1980; Ramphele 1993; Williams et al 2002; Yudelman and Jeeves 1986).

5. While not categorized as an 'occupational illness' like tuberculosis or asbestosis, HIV is nevertheless, as Fassin states, 'a pathology closely related to the ways this workforce is employed' (Fassin 2007: 188). Yet, while 'legislation places responsibility for the surveillance, treatment, notification and compensation of TB-infected employees on the mine owners' (Anglo Platinum 2003a: 53), HIV is treated as an externality, despite 50 percent of TB cases among miners being associated with dual HIV infection (Guild et al 2001, cited in Anglo Platinum 2003a: 51).

6. See for example Cohen 2002; Connelly and Rosen 2006; Evian et al 2004; Lisk 2002; Matangi 2006; Rosen et al 2003.

7. A similar study based on AngloGold's mines found that providing ART to workers would add $4–6 (up to 2 percent) to the cost of producing an ounce of gold, in contrast to an extra $9 per ounce, if the company did nothing (d'Adesky 2003).

8. See for example Dickinson 2006.

9. Marks emphasises the hard edge of self-interest and exploitation beneath the claim of corporate benevolence. This she suggests is manifest in the company's moral

indignation at the government's failure to address the HIV crisis and their more pro-
fessive corporate response. Such claims to benevolence, she suggests, look very different when considered against the long historical view of the mining industry's interest
in the living labour capacity of its workforce, and more recently in light of the first
sign that the industry could be held to account for their occupational health record in
South Africa in the form of a legal victory for asbestosis and mesothelioma sufferers in
their case against another mining giant, Cape Industries (Marks 2006: 570).

10. These include the partnership between Merck and the Gates Foundation in
Botswana and the Bristol Myers Squibb Foundation's *Secure the Future* programme
which has pledged $100 million in cash and drug donations to the cause of combating
HIV in sub-Saharan Africa (Hartwig et al 2006: 141).

11. Anglo American 2007: 8.

12. The Global Business Coalition was set up in 1997 with initial grants from the
Bill and Melinda Gates Foundation, the United Nations Foundation and the Open
Society Institute. Since then, it has grown from its original 10 member companies (including Anglo American) to a coalition of over 200 TNCs. Its advisory board is made
up of 17 of the world's leading corporate chairmen.

13. See Chapter 2.

14. Fassin gives an account of an event in a similarly plush Johannesburg hotel
during which a presentation by the coordinator of AngloGold's workplace HIV programme combined economic calculation with the language of compassionate benevolence in a strikingly similar way (Fassin 2007: 182–183).

15. The apartheid regime attempted to maintain a constant flow of cheap labour
to staff the mines, while simultaneously restricting the movement of black South Africans into urban areas from the designated 'native reserves' through a series of laws,
such as the Black Urban Areas Consolidation Act 25 of 1945, the Native Laws Amend-
ment Act of 1957 and the Black Abolition of Passes and Co-ordination of Documents
Act of 1952 (Wolpe 1972). These made it all but impossible for black South Africans to
reside permanently and legally in urban areas until the Abolition of Influx Control Act
of 1986. Packard argues that the mining industry colluded with state apparatus, providing the essential legitimation for these exclusionary controls, ie that these controls
were necessary to contain outbreaks of tuberculosis at the mines (Packard 1989a: 300).

16. Pre-emptive HIV testing was outlawed in 2001.

17. Another study (this one not commissioned by the Chamber of Mines) conducted
at Carltonville on male mineworkers and sex workers in 'hotspots' around the mines
showed increasing rates of HIV infection. In 1998 around 50 percent of the women in
the 'hotspots' (reaching nearly 60 percent among women of 25 years of age) and 28.5
percent of male mineworkers studied were HIV positive (Williams et al 2000: 11, 44).

18. The rise in HIV has been accompanied by a massive rise in opportunistic infections such as TB, malaria and meningitis which are exacerbated by the close living

conditions of hostel life (Molapo 1995: 95). According to Packard and Coetzee, 'the overall incidence . . . of TB among black mineworkers . . . is estimated to be around 16 in every 1,000. This level has not been seen on the mines since the 1920's' (Packard and Coetzee 1995: 109). The level however varies across the industry: the rate of increase of tuberculosis in the gold industry is three times that at the platinum and coal mines (Guild et al 2001). Perhaps of even greater concern is the impact of HIV on an increasing level of multi-drug resistant tuberculosis among mineworkers (ibid: 112).

19. Deborah James refers to the 'simple as ABC' approach as a 'chant-like refrain from an earlier era of anti-AIDS measures' (2002: 179).

20. Since then, Anglo has a direct contract with GlaxoSmithKline to guarantee supply at a discounted rate. The cost of treatment has therefore dropped by 62 percent from US$1.70 a day to US$0.65 per day (Knight 2005: 28). The company's Health Economics Unit now estimates the cost of its wellness programme as R3,320 per participant/per year (Interview 2 June 2005).

21. See Robins 2004; Hodgson 2006; van Rijn 2006.

22. As Thornton argues, Mbeki's position cannot simply be described as one of 'denialism': its 'roots' run much deeper, its effect much more profound, as it rejects the medical dimensions of health and illness in favour of social and ideological factors (Thornton 2008: 171).

23. A recent report on 'Business as a Partner in Strengthening Public Health Systems in Developing Countries', from the Clinton Global Initiative, warns companies which fail in their social responsibility that 'they make a *moral mistake* of seeing profits but not people. But they also make the *management mistake* of investing where there is only short term return' (Nelson 2006: 1). Similarly the South African Chamber of Mines states, 'the mining industry has been proactive adopting an attitude of both caring employer as well as developing a business case against HIV/AIDS (Chamber of Mines of South Africa 2003: 58).

24. According to Anglo American's 2006 *Report to Society*, by the end of 2006, the average uptake of VCT across the business units was 63 percent—a significant increase from 2003 when it was less than 10 percent (Anglo American 2006a: 26). This figure does not however reveal the striking variation between business units such as Goedehoop and Rustenburg. The report also notes that of the 23,500 employees estimated to be HIV positive, 11,400 were in the Anglo wellness Programme, and 4,600 were receiving ART, concluding that 'we estimate that we have reached 65% of the HIV-Positive employees who are in need of treatment' (ibid: 28, 27).

25. As Francis Wilson memorably described hostel living (1972).

26. This resonates with Geeta Patel's ethnography of health insurance and sexuality in India, in which she asks, 'what happens when care of the self, the right to health and the right to life are detoured through risk?' (Patel 2006: 27).

27. The extent to which the flow of SED and CSR resources to the 'community' are controlled through narratives of booming or waning profits is discussed in Chapter 6.

28. In South Africa charge nurses carry the title 'sister'.

29. This accords with Mann's study of public health workers which showed the significance for policy making of a personal and collective desire to lay claim or 'to "own" the problem . . . by keeping the discourse at a medical and public health level' (Mann 1996: 6).

30. It is perhaps unsurprising that the lines along which the struggles over HIV policy are drawn within the company should, in some respects, reflect those of broader national struggles. As Schneider underlines, 'public debate on AIDS has been dominated by a series of responses and counter-responses in which actors have competed to set the agenda for AIDS in South Africa' (Schneider 2002: 145).

Chapter 5

1. In 2008, Anglo Platinum reported a drop in average HIV prevalence to 22 percent, while the number of those undergoing VCT and in the wellness programme has significantly increased. By December 2008, 45,008 full-time employees across Anglo Platinum (75 percent of the workforce) had undergone VCT, 5,043 employees were enrolled in the wellness programme and 2,314 of those were on ART (Anglo Platinum 2008: 84–85). Across the whole Anglo American Group, average prevalence at the Southern African operations in 2008 was estimated at 18 percent of the workforce, around 50 percent of whom are enrolled in workplace programmes of the various subsidiaries (Anglo American 2008: 30).

2. The way in which the subjectivity of miners was shaped by colonial regimes within mining compounds has been well documented by a number of anthropological and sociological studies conducted during the 1970s and re-examined more recently (see for example Burawoy 1974, Rex 1971, Bulmer 1975, Elder 2003, Gordon 1977, Badenhorst and Mathers 1997). In these studies the hostel, or labour compound, appears as a 'total institution' (Goffman 1961, quoted in Ramphele 1993: 30), in which oversight of virtually all areas of work and domestic life was seen to be crucial for maintaining a compliant labour force.

3. Jobs are graded according to the Paterson Scale—a system established specifically for the mining industry in the 1970s (Carstens 2001: 147). Anglo Platinum allocate housing according to this system (upper grades [UMOs—union men officials] being eligible for mine houses in suburban complexes, while lower grades [MDPs] are eligible either for the hostels or the 'living out allowance' of R811 per month). Unions continue to campaign against this system of allocation which they argue is inherently racist: 'housing should depend on affordability only. Not what level you are at, what race you are. But then of course they have to address the disparity of wages as well' (Bafana Hendricks, NUM, Johannesburg).

4. The Circle of Hope plan also makes reference to a second cohort of 'community peer educators' to be drawn from outside the 'workplace' (Anglo Platinum 2003b: 16).

5. In many ways this recalls Moodie's analysis of the bonds between mine management and black miners during the apartheid era as dependent on an 'implicit contract' which he describes as a 'moral economy' of obligation and accommodation on the part of managers, and consent on the part of workers (Moodie 1994: 76–118; 1986: 1).

6. See Deborah James' study of a peer education programme in Durban, South Africa (James 2002).

7. According to Anglo's 2006 *Report to Society* one third of those who have started ART have dropped out: 'About 7.6% have died, 10.5% were non-adherent to treatment and 8.4% left employment' (Anglo American 2006a: 27).

8. That is, put on medical leave.

9. The Strategic Business Plan states that employees will be provided with six months of ART after they have been dismissed (Anglo Platinum 2003c: 9). However, the medical staff and HIV coordinators at the Rustenburg operations stated they continue treatment for only three months.

10. An information pamphlet produced by the wellness programme states: 'ART must be taken continuously to suppress the virus'.

11. The 'shebeens' refer to bars outside the hostel.

12. One study found that 75 percent of hostel residents at the Anglo Platinum operations in South Africa came from outside the North West Province (Conflict Resolution Consortium [CRC] 2001).

13. 'Babyfoot' is the game known as foosball (or table soccer) in the United States.

14. Morvite is a pre-cooked sorghum powder fortified with vitamins and minerals. It aims to provide a significant contribution to recommended daily allowances for protein, vitamins and minerals.

15. See Chapter 6.

16. See Coleman 2007; Putney 2001; and Tranter 1998. Even within neoliberal capitalism we find similar corporate attempts to moralise employees through spiritual training, as Daromir Rudnyckyj (2009) reveals in his ethnography of Islamic training at the Krakatau Steel plants in Indonesia.

17. See Chapter 4.

18. In 2006 the Joint Civil Society Monitoring Forum, reported that 'political and managerial oversight as well as overall commitment to the ARV treatment plan vary from province to province', not only due to the variation in income and capacity of provincial governments, but due to the 'failure of systematic national management and oversight' by the government (Ndlovu and Daswa 2006: 2). While wealthier provinces such as Gauteng and the Western Cape (where the state roll-out began) are 'scaling up' much more rapidly, ARV progress in poorer provinces such as the Eastern Cape (the traditional 'labour sending' areas for the mining industry) is moving at a 'snail's pace' (ibid).

19. Campbell also noted a striking lack of union involvement in the HIV project in the mining community she studied: 'the mineworkers union played even less of a role in the project than the mining houses' (Campbell 2003: 155).

20. The position of contractors in the mining industry requires more sustained research, but was beyond the scope of this book (see Crush et al 2001; Webster and von Holdt 2005).

21. An Anglo Platinum survey conducted in 2003 recorded prevalence rates within the Rustenburg Local Municipality as: '22% of men in the community, 37% of women in the community, 29% of mine workers and 69% of sex workers' (Anglo Platinum 2003a: 26).

22. Masinga referred to the percentage of all mineworkers (including contractors) employed at all the mining companies in the Rustenburg area who are living in the informal settlements, and it is therefore much higher than the percentage of Anglo Platinum mineworkers living outside the hostels.

23. As has been a common criticism among scholars of CSR (see for example Hertz 2001; Frynas 2005; Jenkins 2004).

Chapter 6

1. Dickens 1958: 106.

2. Hocking 1973: 351

3. Bleskop is a township on the outskirts of Rustenburg next to the Turfontein mine shaft.

4. In his ethnography of a diamond mining town, Carstens writes, 'the most efficient administrative design for every company is a system in which paternalism, as the hegemonic ingredient of company power, can be extended to all employees in a manner that takes care of their basic needs, according to what is morally acceptable to company directors and materially acceptable to employees' (Carstens 2001: 4). This form of paternalistic, hegemonic control of the workforce has been the subject of a rich body of mine ethnography in Southern Africa (see for example Burawoy 1972; Gordon 1977; Moodie 1994).

5. Laidlaw (2000) argues however, that the 'free gift makes no friends', but is instead harmful to the recipient.

6. However, as I explore in Chapter 7, stakeholder meetings can have quite the opposite effect.

7. This resonates with Welker's study of CSR in an Indonesian mining town, where, she notes, 'corporate security begins in the community' (Welker 2009: 147).

8. See Chapter 3.

9. See Chapter 3 for a discussion of 'transformation' within the corporate levels of the company.

10. The name of this programme has been changed.

11. 'Anglo Platinum reports that in 2004-5 it supported the creation of 48 new business and provided training to 145 emerging entrepreneurs' (Anglo Platinum 2005a: 18).

12. Well-resourced NGO's are funded almost exclusively by 'local businesses, churches, Impala Platinum, Anglo American Chairman's Fund, Anglo Platinum, PSG and Sun City' (Anglo Platinum 2003c: 16).

13. According to James, 'after 1994, donors began to give funds to the government rather than directly to NGOs. This has forced NGOs to bid for money, often pitting them against rival NGOs'. This can have the effect of '[blunting] the advocacy role' and '[enforcing] a compliance with government policy' (James 2002: 174). In this case, the compliance is not with government policy, but with corporate strategy.

14. This challenges the claim made by Bernstein and Berger in *Business and Democracy: Cohabitation or Contradiction?*: 'business activity demands, requires and in turn creates a 'thickening web' of institutions, organisations, self-regulating mechanisms and professionals that comprise important components of civil society outside the state' (2000: 6).

15. Elias is an SED advisor at Anglo Platinum.

16. A phrase first coined by Lipton three decades ago in her study of labour at the Anglo Mines (Lipton 1980: 193).

17. *The Star* reported that: 'South Africa's 2010 World Cup bid struck gold . . . yesterday when Anglo American . . . pledged R15-million towards this country's campaign to host the showpiece of the beautiful game' (Mark 2003: 24).

18. For a discussion of the stipulations of the Mining Charter, see Chapter 3.

19. The name of the programme has been changed.

20. The name of the programme has been changed.

21. The name of the programme has been changed.

22. An external evaluation of the Amplats School Development Programme conducted in 1999, made the case for a broader systemic approach instead of direct learner-support: 'the problem with this approach is that it is much less narrowly focused on specific kinds of pupil achievement than the first, and must deal with the problems of variable teacher quality . . . It, consequently, takes longer to achieve a lower level of impact on specific pupils. Its great benefit is that, if applied systematically to a succession of schools, it will result in a more generalized improvement in school quality. If Amplats is less concerned about its own HR development plans, and about the development of a quality HR base for the Province in general, we recommend that this option be retained' (Anglo Platinum 1999: 6).

23. See Chapter 2 for an account of paternalism within the company and its self-construction as a 'family club'.

24. Despite the demise of apartheid and change in local government, Afrikaans has prevailed as the dominant language in most of Rustenburg's public schools (as

well as in daily public discourse in shops and restaurants in the predominantly 'white' areas of town). This has placed great pressure on the few English-speaking public schools, not only among black Rustenburgers, but among the influx of English-speaking white Rustenburgers since the platinum boom.

    25. See Eyben 2003.

Chapter 7

    1. 'Never previously in all modern history has a more ruthless act of social reform been perpetrated; it crushed multitudes of lives while merely pretending to provide a criterion of genuine destitution in the workhouse test' (Polanyi 2001: 82).

    2. Zimele means 'to stand on one's own two feet'.

    3. As Kirsch has shown, the marginalisation of particular groups is accentuated further by their exclusion from the supposedly participatory processes of environmental planning and community consultation around the Ok Tedi Mines in Papua New Guinea (Kirsch 2001).

    4. Furthermore, the majority of schools within a 5km radius of Edenvale are either Afrikaans or Setswana medium schools. The great pressure on English-language schools in Rustenburg further restricts access to education for residents of the settlements, the majority of whom come from outside the North West Province and are not Setswana speakers.

    5. See Introduction, note 44.

    6. On 12 January 2003 a Memorandum of Understanding (MOU) between the RLM and RBA was signed by the Rustenburg Mayor and Kgosi (King Leruo Loltlegi of the Royal Bafokeng Nation [RBN]), and witnessed by President Mbeki. The MOU represents an effort to harmonise the legal authority of the Rustenburg District Council with the 'traditional authority' of the RBN as recognised by Chapter 12 of the Constitution of South Africa, and as landowner of the Bafokeng area (Memorandum of Understanding 2003: 1.4). However it also states that 'in terms of the current legislative framework, the Bojanala Platinum District Municipality exercises jurisdiction over the area . . . of Rustenburg Local Municipality (RLM) which includes areas of Royal Bafokeng Nation' (1.2). Thus while the MOU acknowledges the 'institutional independence' of each party (2.4), it commands that they 'consensually commit themselves to co-operate with each other on all matters of mutual interest and . . . develop mechanisms through which to practice and achieve such co-operation' (2.6). In particular, the MOU emphasised the imperative to collaborate in 'social programmes that aim to promote and uplift the lives of people' (4.1.1.4). Target areas for cooperation include 'infrastructure, health, economic development, tourism, arts and culture'. This is to be achieved primarily by monthly meetings between Kgosi and the Corporate Executive of the RBN, and the Executive Mayor of Rustenburg and the Municipal Managers (4.1.3).

7. See Chapter 5.

8. See note 6, this chapter.

Conclusion

1. Lanning and Mueller 1979: 3.

2. A century ago, Georg Simmel had captured both the allure and the danger of this model of the modern market player who is 'free' because, 'he is free to take up business relations and co-operation wherever he likes' (Simmel 1978 [1900]: 343). The cost of this freedom from social ties and dependencies, Simmel warned, was the destruction of community (Keane 2008).

3. '"Gifts make slaves," the Eskimo say, "as whips make dogs"' (Sahlins 1972: 133).

4. See for example, Garsten and Hernes 2009 who make an argument along these lines.

5. See for example Bloch and Parry 1989; Richards 1996; Harris 1989.

6. See Bourdieu's essay *Acts of Resistance against the Tyranny of the Market*, for the argument that neoliberalism works by excluding all structures that can impede 'the logic of the pure market' (1998a: 96).

References

Achbar, Mark, and Jennifer Abbot. 2003. The Corporation. Los Angeles: Big Picture Media Corporation.

Adler, Glenn, and Eddie Webster. 2000. Introduction: Consolidating Democracy in a Liberalising World—Trade Unions and Democratisation in South Africa. In *Trade Unions and Democratisation in South Africa, 1985–1997*, edited by G. Adler and E. Webster. New York: St Martin's Press.

Andreasson, Stefan. 2006. The ANC and its Critics: "Predatory Liberalism", Black Economic Empowerment and Intra-Alliance Tensions in Post-Apartheid South Africa. *Democratization* 13 (2):303–322.

Anglo American. 1997. Submission to the Truth and Reconciliation Commission. Johannesburg: Anglo American Corporation of South Africa Ltd.

———. 2002. Good Citizenship: Our Business Principles. London: Anglo American PLC.

———. 2003a. Anglo American Strongly Rejects Efforts to Claim Apartheid Reparations. Johannesburg: Anglo American Corporation of South Africa Ltd.

———. 2003b. Economic Assessment Toolbox (SEAT) Overview. London: Anglo American PLC.

———. 2004a. Report to Society 2004: Creating Enduring Value. London: Anglo American PLC.

———. 2004b. Anglo American PLC Group HIV/AIDS Policy. Johannesburg: Anglo American Corporation of South Africa Ltd.

———. 2005a. Report to Society: A Climate of Change. 2005. London: Anglo American PLC.

———. 2005b. Anglo's "Sustainability" Award. *Anglo World*, 23, May, 7.

———. 2005c. Update—Transformation and Black Economic Empowerment. Johannesburg: Anglo American PLC.

————. 2005d. We Have Come a Long Way. Anglo American Advertisement. *Mail and Guardian*, 30 July, 11.

————. 2006a. Report to Society 2006: A Climate of Change. London: Anglo American PLC.

————. 2006b. Update—Transformation and Black Economic Empowerment. Johannesburg: Anglo American Corporation of South Africa Ltd.

————. 2007. Anglo American Fact Book 2006/7. London: Anglo American PLC.

————. 2008. Report to Society 2008: Making a Difference. London: Anglo American PLC.

————. 2010. Real Mining. Real People. Real Difference. *The Guardian*, 30 September, 17.

Anglo Platinum. 1999. Evaluation of the Amplats School Development Programme. Johannesburg: Anglo Platinum Ltd.

————. 2003a. Circle of Hope Community Project Strategic Business Plan. Johannesburg: Anglo Platinum Ltd.

————. 2003b. Circle of Hope Community Project Case Study 26 October. Johannesburg: Anglo Platinum Ltd.

————. 2003c. Anglo Platinum's Community-Based HIV/AIDS Care and Support Strategic Plan. Johannesburg: Anglo Platinum Ltd.

————. 2003d. Circle of Hope Community Project Activity Analysis Report 13 November. Johannesburg: Anglo Platinum Ltd.

————. 2003e. Schools Project Case Study: Edumap. Johannesburg: Anglo Platinum Ltd.

————. 2004. Best in the Northwest! *Let's Talk Magazine*, 3, 4–5.

————. 2005a. Annual Report 2005. Annual Report 2005, Volume 2: Sustainable Development Report. Johannesburg: Anglo Platinum Ltd.

————. 2005b. SED Mission, Objectives and Strategy. Johannesburg: Anglo Platinum Ltd.

————. 2005c. Know Your Status! *Our Voice!*, July, 14.

————. 2005d. Employee Discloses Health Status! *Our Voice!*, August, 14.

————. 2008. Annual Report 2008. Annual Report 2008, Volume 2: Sustainable Development Report. Johannesburg: Anglo Platinum Ltd.

Badenhorst, Cecile, and Charles Mathers. 1997. Tribal Recreation and Recreating Tribalism: Culture, Leisure and Social Control on South Africa's Gold Mines 1940–1950. *Journal of Southern African Studies* 23 (3):473–489.

Bakan, Joel. 2004. *The Corporation. The Pathological Pursuit of Profit and Power*. London: Free Press.

Baker, Mallen. 2007. NGOs and Business—Spot the Difference–Makers. *Ethical Corporation* (February):5.

Ballard, Chris, and Glenn Banks. 2003. Resources Wars: The Anthropology of Mining. *Annual Review of Anthropology* 32:287–313.

Barchiesi, Franco, and Bridget Kenny. 2002. From Workshop to Wasteland: De-industrialization and Fragmentation of the Black Working Class on the East Rand (South Africa), 1990–1999. *Internationaal Instituut voor Sociale Geschiedenis* 47:35–63.

Barry, Andrew. 2004. Ethical Capitalism. In *Global Governmentality: Governing International Spaces*, edited by W. Larner and W. Walters. Oxford: Routledge.

Beckmann, Sabine, Rai, Benjamin O. Alli, Claire Mulanga, Marie Lavollay, Myriam Vuckovic, and Franklyn Lisk. 2005. HIV/AIDS Workplace Programmes and Public-Private Partnership (PPP) through Co-Investment—Extension of Treatment and Care into the Community. International Labour Organisation, GTX, Stellenbosch University and the Global Fund to Fight AIDS, Tuberculosis and Malaria.

Bell, Morag. 2000. American Philanthropy, the Carnegie Corporation and Poverty in South Africa. *Journal of Southern African Studies* 26 (3):481–503.

Bell, Trevor, and Greg Farrell. 1997. The Minerals-Energy Complex and South African Industrialisation. *Development Southern Africa* 14 (4):591–613.

Benchmarks Foundation. 2007. *The Policy Gap. A Review of the Corporate Social Responsibility Programmes of the Platinum Mining Industry in the North West Province* [cited 30 July 2007]. Available from http://www.benchmarks.org/downloads/070625_platinum_research_summary.pdf.

Bendell, Jem. 2003. Waking up to Risk—Corporate Responses to HIV/AIDS in the Workplace. *Technology, Business and Society Programme Paper.* Geneva: UNRISD and UNAIDS.

———. 2004. Boardrooms and Barricades. A Contemporary History of the Corproate Accountability Movement. *Technology, Business and Society Programme Paper.* Geneva: UNRISD.

Benioff, Marc, and Karen Southwick. 2009. *Compassionate Capitalism: How Corporations Can Make Doing Good Integral To Doing Well.* Franklin Lakes, NJ: Career Press.

Berlan, Amanda. 2008. Making or Marketing a Difference? An Anthropological Examination of the Marketing of Fair Trade Cocoa from Ghana. *Research in Economic Anthropology* 28:171–194.

Bernstein, Ann. 1999. *Submission to the Truth Commission.* Cape Town: Juta.

Bernstein, Ann, and Peter Berger, eds. 2000. *Business and Democracy: Cohabitation or Contradiction?* Vol. 10, *Development and Democracy.* Johannesburg: Centre for Development and Enterprise.

Bezuidenhout, Andries. 2005. Postcolonial Workplace Regimes in the Engineering Industry of South Africa. In *Beyond the Apartheid Workplace: Studies in Transition*, edited by E. Webster and K. Von Holdt. Scottsville, SA: University of KwaZulu-Natal Press.

Bezuidenhout, Andries, and Bridget Kenny. 1998. Subcontracting in the Mining Industry. *Innes Labour Brief* 10 (1):30–36.

Biehl, João. 2007. *Will to Live: Aids Therapies and the Politics of Survival.* Princeton, NJ: Princeton University Press.

Blim, Michael. 2005. The Moral Significance of Petty Capitalism. In *Petty Capitalists and Globalization: Flexibility, Entrepreneurship and Economic Development,* edited by A. Smart and J. Smart. Albany: State University of New York Press.

Bloch, Maurice, and Jonathan Parry. 1989. Introduction: Money and the Morality of Exchange. In *Money and the Morality of Exchange,* edited by M. Bloch and J. Parry. Cambridge: Cambridge University Press.

Blowfield, Michael. 2005. Corporate Social Responsibility: Reinventing the Meaning of Development. *International Affairs* 81 (3):515–524.

Bond, Patrick. 2000. *Elite Transition: From Apartheid to Neoliberalism in South Africa.* Scottsville, SA: University of Natal Press.

Bourdieu, Pierre. 1973. Cultural Reproduction and Social Reproduction. In *Knowledge, Education and Social Change,* edited by R. Brown. London: Tavistock.

———. 1977. *An Outline of a Theory of Practice.* Translated by R. Nice. Cambridge: Cambridge University Press.

———. 1984. *Distinction: A Social Critique of the Judgement of Taste.* Translated by R. Nice. Cambridge, MA: Harvard University Press.

———. 1998a. *Acts of Resistance against the Tyranny of the Market.* Translated by R. Nice. New York: The New Press.

———. 1998b. The Essence of Neoliberalism [cited 29 December 2007]. Available from http://mondediplo.com/1998/12/08bourdieu.

———. 2000. Making the Economic Habitus: Algerian Workers Revisted. *Ethnography* 1 (1):17–41.

Bozzoli, Belinda, with Mmantho Nkotsoe. 1991. *The Women of Phokeng: Consciousness, Life Strategy and Migrancy in South Africa 1900–1983.* Portsmouth: Heineman Educational Books Inc.

Bream, Rebecca. 2006. Gold Fever Spurs Frenzy of Mining Acquisitions. *Financial Times,* 31 August 2006, 31.

Bream, Rebecca, and Alec Russell. 2007. Upheaval at Anglo American as Patricians Leave the Stage. *Financial Times,* 10 August 2007, 9.

Brink, Brian. 2005. An Interim Appraisal of the Anglo American AIDS Treatment Programme. *Second South African AIDS Conference.* Durban.

Brink, Brian, and L. Clausen. 1987. The Acquired Immune Deficiency Syndrome. *Journal of the Mine Medical Officers' Association of South Africa* 63:10–17.

Brown, Katherine. 2009. Economics and Morality: Introduction. In *Economics and Morality: Anthropological Approaches,* edited by K. Brown and B. L. Milgram. Lanham, MD: Altamira Press.

Bulmer, Martin. 1975. Sociological Models of Mining Communities. *The Sociological Review* 23:61–92.

Bundy, Colin. 1988. *The Rise and Fall of the South African Peasantry*. Cape Town: David Philip.

Burawoy, Michael. 1974. Another Look at the Mineworker. *African Social Research* 14:239–287.

———. 1974. *Constraint and Manipulation in Industrial Conflict*. Lusaka: University of Zambia.

Burawoy, Michael, and Katherine Verdery. 1998. *Uncertain Transition: Ethnographies of Change in the Post-Socialist World*. Lanham, MD: Rowman and Littlefield.

Business Day. 1999. Patriotic Capitalism: The Dilemma of the New Millennium. *Business Day*, 22 November.

———. 2002. Taming the Hurricane. *Business Day*, 12 September, 2.

Business in the Community. 2006. Reports to Business in the Community's PerCent Standard 2006 and the London Benchmarking Group. *The Guardian*, 6 November, 4.

Cameron, David. 2006. Speech delivered at the Business in the Community Annual Conference. London, 9 May.

Campbell, Catherine. 1997. Migrancy, Masculine Identities and Aids: The Psychosocial Context of HIV Transmission on the South African Gold Mine. *Social Science and Medicine* 45 (2):273–281.

———. 2003. *'Letting Them Die': Why Aids Prevention Programmes Fail*. Bloomington: Indiana University Press.

Carmody, Padraig. 2002. Between Globalisation and (Post) Apartheid: the Political Economy of Restructuring in South Africa'. *Journal of Southern African Studies* 28 (2):255–275.

Carr, William J P. 1959. Raising the Standard of South Africa's Urban Natives. *Optima* 9 (4):219–232.

Carrier, James. 1997. Introduction. In *Meanings of the Market: The Free Market in Western Culture*, edited by J. Carrier. Oxford: Berg.

———. 2008. Think Locally, Act Globally: The Political Economy of Ethical Consumption. *Research in Economic Anthropology* 28:31–53.

Carroll, Archie. 1991. The Pyramid of Corporate Social Responsibility: The Moral Management of Organizational Stakeholders. *Business Horizons* 34:39–48.

Carstens, Peter. 2001. *In the Company of Diamonds: De Beers, Kleinzee, and the Control of a Town*. Athens: Ohio University Press.

Cefkin, Melissa, ed. 2009. *Ethnography and the Corproate Encounter. Reflections on Research in and On Corporations*. Oxford: Berghan.

Chamber of Mines of South Africa. 2003. The Voice of Mining. Johannesburg: Chamber of Mines of South Africa.

Chandler, Geoffery. 2003. The Curse of CSR. *New Academy Review* 2 (1):3–9.

Chapin, Mac. 2004. A Challenge to Conservationists. *World Watch* November/ December:17–31.

Chirambo, Kondwani, and Mary Caesar. 2003. *Aids and Governance in Southern Africa: Emerging Theories and Perspectives. A Report on the IDASA/UNDP Regional Governance and AIDS Forum.* Cape Town: Institute for Democracy in South Africa.

Chopra, Rohit. 2003. Neoliberalism as Doxa: Bourdieu's Theory of the State and the Contemporary Indian Discourse on Globalization and Liberalization. *Cultural Studies* 17 (3/4):419–444.

Clark, Nancy. 1993. The Limits of Industrialisation Under Apartheid. In *Apartheid's Genesis 1935–1962,* edited by P. Bonner, P. Delius and D. Posel. Johannesburg: Ravan Press and Witwatersrand.

Cohen, Desmond. 2002. Human Capital and the HIV Epidemic in Sub-Saharan Africa. In *ILO Programme on HIV/AIDS and the World of Work Working Paper* Geneva: ILO.

Coleman, Simon. 2007. Of Metaphors and Muscles: Protestant 'Play' in the Disciplining of the Self. In *The Discipline of Leisure: Embodying Cultures of 'Recreation',* edited by T. Kohn and S. Coleman. Oxford: Berghahn.

Comaroff, John, and Jean Comaroff. 2000. Millennial Capitalism: First Thoughts on a Second Coming. *Public Culture* 12 (2):291–344.

Commission for Africa. 2005. Our Common Interest: Report of the Commission for Africa. London: Commission for Africa.

Conflict Resolution Consortium. 2001. Rustenburg/Anglo Platinum Stabilisation Project Report. Rustenburg: Conflict Resolution Consortium.

Connelly, Patrick, and Sydney Rosen. 2006. Treatment for HIV/AIDS at South Africa's Largest Employers: Myth and Reality. *South African Medical Journal* 96 (2):128–133.

Cooley, Alexander, and James Ron. 2002. The NGO Scramble: Organizational Insecurity and the Political Economy of Transnational Action. *International Security* 27 (1):5–39.

Cooper, Frederick. 1987. *On the African Waterfront: Urban Disorder and Transformation of Work in Colonial Mombassa.* New Haven, CT: Yale University Press.

Covey, Jane, and David Brown. 2001. *Critical Cooperations: An Alternative Form of Civil Society-Business Engagement.* Boston, MA: Institute for Development Research.

Crewe, Emma, and Elizabeth Harrison. 1998. *Whose Development? An Ethnography of Aid.* London and New York: Zed Books.

Crisp, Jeff. 1983. Productivity and Protest. Scientific Management in the Ghanaian Gold Mines, 1947–1956. In *Struggle for the City: Migrant Labour, Capital, and the State in Urban Africa,* edited by F. Cooper. Beverly Hills, London and New Delhi: Sage Publications.

Cronin, Jon. 2006. *Let Business Lift Africa Out of Poverty* 2006 [cited 4 July 2006]. Available from http://news.bbc.co.uk/1/hi/business/5099990.stm.

Cruikshank, Barbara. 1999. *The Will to Empower: Democratic Citizens and Other Subjects.* Ithaca, NY: Cornell University Press.

Crush, Jonathan. 1992. Power and Surveillance on the South African Gold Mines. *Journal of Southern Africa Studies* 18 (4):825–844.

Crush, Jonathan, and Wilmot James , eds. 1995a. *Crossing Boundaries—Mine Migrancy in a Democratic South Africa.* Cape Town: The Institute for Democracy in South Africa.

———. 1995b. Introduction. In *Crossing Boundaries—Mine Migrancy in a Democratic South Africa*, edited by J. Crush and W. James. Cape Town: Institute for Democracy in South Africa.

Crush, Jonathan, Alan Jeeves, and David Yudelman. 1991. *South Africa's Labor Empire: A History of Black Migrancy to the Gold Mines.* San Fransisco, Boulder and Oxford: Westview Press.

Crush, Jonathan, Theresa Ulicki, Teke Tseane, and Elizabeth Jansen van Veuren. 2001. Undermining Labour: The Rise of Sub-contracting in South African Gold Mines. *Journal of Southern African Studies* 27 (1):5–31.

Crush, Jonathan, Brian Williams, Eleanor Gouws, and Mark Lurie. 2005. Migration and HIV/AIDS in South Africa. *Development Southern Africa* 22 (3):291–318.

Cullinan, Kerry. 2005. *Health Minister Promotes Nutritional Alternative to ARV Roll-out* [cited 12 May 2007]. Available from www.health-e.org.za/news/article.php?uid=20031252.

Cummings, Richard. 1995. A Diamond Is Forever: Mandela Triumphs, Buthelezi and de Klerk Survive, and ANC on the U.S. Payroll. *Journal of Intelligence and Counterintelligence* 7 (Summer):21–35.

D'Adesky, Anne-Christine. 2003. *Global AIDS—The Private Sector Starts to Take Notice* [cited 5 May 2007. Available from www.aegis.com/pubs/amfar/2003/AM030704.html.

Dale, Michael Otto. 1997. South Africa: Development of a New Mineral Policy. *Resources Policy* 23 (1/2):15–26.

Dansereau, Suzanne. 2005. Win-Win or New Imperialism? Public-Private Partnerships in Africa Mining. *Review of African Political Economy* 32 (103):47–62.

Davies, Robert, and Judith Head. 1995. The Future of Mine Migrancy in the Context of Broader Trends in Migration in Southern Africa. *Journal of Southern African Studies* 21 (3):439–450.

De Neve, Geert. 2008. Global Garment Chains, Local Labour Activism: New Challenges to Trade Union and NGO Activism in the Tiruppur Garment Cluster, South India. *Research in Economic Anthropology* 28:213–241.

Department for International Development (DFID). 2003. DFID and Corporate Social Responsibility. London: DFID.

————. 2006. Making Governance Work for the Poor. London: DFID.

————. 2009. Prosperity for All: Making Markets Work. London: DFID.

Department of Minerals and Energy SA. 2004a. Broad-based Socio-Economic Empowerment Charter for the South African Mining Industry [cited 10 October 2006]. Available from http://www.dme.gov.za/minerals/min_miningcharter.stm.

————. 2004b. Scorecard for the Broad Based Socio-Economic Empowerment Charter for the South African Mining Industry [cited 3 July 2007]. Available from http://www.dme.gov.za/minerals/pdf/scorecard.pdf.

————. 2008. Presidential Mine Health and Safety Audit.

Desjarlais, Robert. 2003. Sensory Biographies: Lives and Deaths Among Nepal's Yolmo Buddhists. Berkeley: University of California Press.

Dezalay, Yves, and Bryant Garth. 1996. Dealing in Virtue: International Commercial Arbitration and the Construction of a Transnational Legal Order. Chicago, IL: Chicago University Press.

Dickens, Charles. 1958, first published 1854. Hard Times. New York and Toronto: Rinehart and Company Inc. Original edition, 1854.

Dickinson, David. 2004. Corporate South Africa's Response to HIV/AIDS: Why so Slow? Journal of South African Studies 30 (3):627–649.

————. 2006. Smokescreen or Opening a Can of Worms? Workplace HIV/AIDS Peer Education and Social Protection in South Africa. African Studies 65 (2):321–342.

Doane, Deborah. 2005. The Myth of CSR. Stanford Social Innovation Review (Fall 2005):23–29.

Dolan, Catherine. 2007. Market Affections: Moral Encounters with Kenyan Fairtrade Flowers. Ethnos 72 (2):239–261.

————. 2008. Arbitrating Risk through Moral Values: The Case of Kenyan Fairtrade. Research in Economic Anthropology Special Issue on Hidden Hands in the Market: Ethnographies of Fair Trade, Ethical Consumption and Corporate Social Responsibility 28:271–297.

————. 2009. Virtue at the Checkout Till: Salvation Economics in Kenyan Flower Fields. In Economics and Morality: Anthropological Approaches, edited by K. Brown and B. L. Milgram. Lanham, MD: Altamira Press.

Dore, Ronald. 1983. Goodwill and the Spirit of Market Capitalism. British Journal of Sociology 34:459–482.

Dorsey, Michael. 2005. Conservation, Collusion and Capital. Anthropology News 46 (7):45–46.

Douglas, Mary. 1990. Foreward: No Free Gifts. In The Gift, by M. Mauss. London: Routledge.

Dunn, Elizabeth. 2005. Standards and Person-Making in East Central Europe. In *Global Assemblages. Technology, Politics and Ethics as Anthropological Problems*, edited by S. Collier and A. Ong. Oxford: Blackwell Publishing.

Ecks, Stefan. 2008. Global Pharmaceutical Markets and Corproate Citizenship: The Case of Novartis' Anti-Cancer Drug Glivec. *Biosocieties* 3:165–181.

Economist. 2004. Business: Two-faced Capitalism; Corporate Social Responsibility. *Economist*, 24 January, 59.

Elder, Glen. 2003. *Hostels, Sexuality and the Apartheid Legacy: Malevolent Geographies*. Athens: Ohio University Press.

Elkington, John. 1998. The "Triple Bottom Line" for Twenty-First-Century Business. In *Companies in a World of Conflict*, edited by J. Mitchell. London: Royal Institute of International Affairs.

Epstein, Edward Jay. 1982. *The Diamond Invention*. London: Hutchinson and Co.

Evans, Geoff, James Goodman, and Nina Lansbury, eds. 2002. *Moving Mountains: Communities Confront Mining and Globalisation*. London and New York: Zed Books.

Evian, Clive, Matthew Fox, William MacLeod, Sarah Jane Slotow, and Sydney Rosen. 2004. Prevalence of HIV in Workforces in Southern Africa, 2000–2001. *South African Medical Journal* 94 (2):125–130.

Eyben, Rosalind. 2003. Who Owns the Gift? Donor-Recipient Relations and the National Elections in Bolivia. Paper delivered at *EIDOS Workshop on 'Order and Disjuncture: the Organisation of Aid and Development*. School of Oriental and African Studies, London, 26–28 September.

Farmer, Paul. 1997. Social Scientists and the New Tuberculosis. *Social Science and Medicine* 44 (3):347–358.

Fassin, Didier. 2007. *When Bodies Remember. Experience and Politics of AIDS in South Africa*. Berkeley: University of California Press.

Fearnley, Carina. 2005. HIV and AIDS Risk Management at Rustenburg Section, Anglo Platinum. *Applied Earth Science: Transactions of the Institute of Mining and Metallurgy* 114 (Section B):B146–B153.

Fedderke, Johannes, and Farah Pirouz. 2002. The Role of Mining in the South African Economy. *South African Journal of Economic and Management Studies* 5 (1):1–28.

Ferguson, James. 1994 first published 1990. *The Anti-Politics Machine: 'Development', Depoliticisation and Bureaucratic Power in Lesotho*. Minneapolis: University of Minnesota Press.

———. 1999. *Expectations of Modernity. Myths and Meanings of Urban Life on the Zambian Copperbelt*. Berkeley: University of California Press.

———. 2005. *Global Shadows. Africa in the Neoliberal World Order*. Durham, NC: Duke University Press.

———. 2006. Seeing Like an Oil Company: Space, Security and Global Capital in Neoliberal Africa. *American Anthropologist* 107 (3):377–382.

Fig, David. 2005. Manufacturing Amnesia: Corporate Social Responsibility in South
Africa. *International Affairs* 81 (3):599–617.

Fine, Ben, and Zavareh Rustomjee. 1996. *The Political Economy of South Africa: From
Minerals-Energy Complex to Industrialisation*. London: Hurst and Company.

Fischer, Edward. 2009. Capitalsim in Context. Seeing Beyond the "Free" Market. *Anthropology News* (October):10–12.

Flood, Chris. 2006. Platinum Market Set for Record Year. *Financial Times On Line*, 14
November. Available from http://www.ft.com/cms/s/8c868090-73e5-11db-8dd7-
0000779e2340.html.

Foster, Robert J. 2008. *Coca-Globalization: Following Soft Drinks from New York to
New Guinea*. Basingstoke: Palgrave Macmillan.

Foucault, Michel. 1972. *The Archaeology of Knowledge*. Translated by A. M. S. Smith.
London: Tavistock.

———. 1990 first published 1978. *The History of Sexuality Volume 1*. Translated by R.
Hurley. Harmondsworth: Penguin.

Fourcade, Marion, and Kieran Healy. 2007. Moral Views of Market Society. *Annual
Review of Sociology* 33:285–311.

Fox, Tom. 2004. Corporate Social Responsibility and Development: In Quest of an
Agenda. *Development Southern Africa* 47 (3):29–36.

Frankel, Glenn. 1999. *Rivonia's Children*. London: Weidenfeld & Nicolson.

Friedman, Milton. 1970. *The Social Responsibility of Business Is to Increase Profits*
[cited 4 January 2007]. Available from http://www.colorado.edu/studentgroups/
liberarians/issues/friedman-soc-resp-business.html.

Froud, Julie, Sukhdev Johal, Adam Leaver, and Karel Williams. 2006. *Financialization
and Strategy: Narratives and Numbers*. London and New York: Routledge.

Frynas, Jedrzej. 2005. The False Developmental Promise of Corporate Social Responsibility: Evidence from Multinational Oil Companies. *International Affairs* 81
(3):581–598.

Garsten, Christina, and Tor Hernes. 2009. Beyond CSR: Dilemmas and Paradoxes of
Ethical Conduct in Transnational Organization. In *Economics and Morality: An-
thropological Approaches*, edited by K. Browne and B. L. Miligram. Lanham, MD:
Altamira Press.

Garsten, Christina, and Kerstin Jacobsson. 2007. Corporate Globalisation, Civil Society and Post-Political Regulation—Whither Democracy? *Development Dialogue*
49 (October):143–157.

Gaskell, Elizabeth. 1973 first published 1854–1855. *North and South*. Oxford: Oxford
University Press.

George, Gavin. 2006. Workplace ART Programmes: Why Do Companies Invest in Them and Are They Working? *African Journal of AIDS Research* 5 (2):179–188.

Gille, Zsuzsa, and Sean O Riain. 2002. Global Ethnography. *Annual Review of Sociology* 28:271–295.

Godsell, Bobby, and Peter Berger, eds. 1988. *A Future South Africa: Visions, Strategies and Realities*. Cape Town: Tafelburg Publishers.

Gordon, Colin. 1991. Government Rationality: An Introduction. In *The Foucault Effect: Studies in Governmentality*, edited by G. Burchell, C. Gordon and P. Miller. Chicago, IL: Chicago University Press.

Gordon, Robert J. 1977. *Mines, Masters and Migrants: Life in a Namibian Compound*. Johannesburg: Ravan Press.

Graeber, David. 2001. *Toward and Anthropological Theory of Value: The False Coin of Our Own Dreams*. New York: Palgrave.

Granovetter, Mark. 1985. Economic Action and Social Structure: The Problem of Embeddedness. *American Journal of Sociology* 91:481–510.

Grayson, David, and Adrian Hodges. 2004. *Corporate Social Opportunity*. Sheffield: Greenleaf Publishing.

Gregory, Theodor Emanuel. 1962. *Ernest Oppenheimer and the Economic Development of South Africa*. Cape Town, London and New York: Oxford University Press.

Grillo, Ralph. 1973. *African Railwaymen: Solidarity and Opposition in an East African Labour Force*. Cambridge: Cambridge University Press.

Gudeman, Stephen. 2001. *The Anthropology of Economy*. Oxford: Blackwell Publishing.

———. 2008. *Economy's Tension: The Dialectics of Community and Market*. Oxford and New York: Berghahn Books.

Guild, R., R. I. Ehrlich, J. R. Johnston, and M. H. Ross. 2001. *SIMRAC Handbook of Occupational Health and Practice in the South African Mining Industry*. Johannesburg: Safety of Mines Advisory Committee.

Habib, Adam, and Rupert Taylor. 1999. Anti-Apartheid NGOs in Transition. *Voluntas* 10 (1):73–82.

Hamblett, Marc. 2009. Judges Narrows in Apartheid Torts Case Against Apartheid Companies. *New York Law Journal* (9 April).

Hamann, Ralph. 2004a. Corporate Social Responsibility, Partnerships, and Institutional Change: The Case of Mining Companies in South Africa. *Natural Resources Forum* 28 (4):278–290.

———. 2004b. Corporate Social Responsibility in Mining in South Africa. Phd Thesis, University of East Anglia, UK.

Harper, Richard. 2000. The Social Organization of the IMF's Mission Work: An Examination of International Auditing. In *Audit Cultures*, edited by M. Strathern. London: Routledge.

Harris, Olivia. 1989. The Earth and the State: The Sources and Meanings of Money in Northern Potosí, Bolivia. In *Money and the Morality of Exchange*, edited by J. Parry and M. Bloch. Cambridge: Cambridge University Press.

Harrison, Elizabeth. 2009. Performing Partnership: Invited Participation and Old People's Forums. Unpublished paper.

Harriss, John. 2003. "Widening the Radius of Trust": Ethnographic Explorations of Trust and Indian Business. *Journal of the Royal Anthropological Institute* 9 (4):755–773.

Hartwig, Kari, Alana Rosenberg, and Michael Merson. 2006. Corporate Citizenship in Africa: Lessons from Bristol-Myers Squibb Company's Secure the Future. In *Corporate Citizenship in Africa*, edited by W. Visser, M. McIntosh and C. Middleton. Sheffield Greenleaf Publishing.

Henderson, David. 2001. *False Notions of Corporate Social Responsibility*. London: Institute of Economic Affairs.

———. 2005. The Role of Business in the World Today. *Journal of Corporate Citizenship* 17:30–32.

Hertz, Noreena. 2001. *The Silent Takeover*. London: Heinemann.

Herzfeld, Michael. 2000. Uncanny Success. Some Closing Remarks. In *Elites: Choice, Leadership and Succession*, edited by J. d. Pina-Cabral and A. P. d. Lima. Oxford: Berg.

Ho, Karen. 2009. *Liquidated. An Ethnography of Wall Street*. Durham, NC: Duke University Press.

Hocking, Anthony. 1973. *Oppenheimer and Son*. Johannesburg: McGraw-Hill.

Hodgson, Ian. 2006. *Dazed and Confused: The Reality of AIDS Treatment in South Africa* [cited 15 July 2006]. Available from www.opendemocracy.net/globalization-hiv/southafrica_3170.jsp.

Holbrooke, Richard, and Mark Moody-Stuart. 2006. Business Has Vital Role to Play in Fighting Aids. *Financial Times*, 22 May.

Hopkins, Michael. 2007. *Corporate Social Responsibility and International Development: Is Business the Solution?* London: Earthscan.

Houser, Theodore V. 1957. *Big Business and Human Values*. New York: McGraw-Hill.

Hutchinson, Sharon. 1992. The Cattle of Money and the Cattle of Girls Among the Nuer, 1830–1883. *American Ethnologist* 19 (2):294–316.

Innes, Duncan. 1984. *Anglo American and the Rise of Modern South Africa*. New York: Monthly Review Press.

———. 1992. Empowerment in the Workplace. In *Power and Profit. Politics, Labour and Business in South Africa*, edited by D. Innes, M. Kentridge and H. Perold. Cape Town: Oxford University Press.

International Finance Corporation. 2004. *HIV/AIDS in the Mining Sector*. Ottawa: Golder Associates Ltd.

James, Deborah. 2002. "To Take the Information Down to the People": Life Skills and HIV/AIDS Peer Educators in the Durban Area. *African Studies* 61 (1):169–191.

———. 2011. The Return of the Broker: Consensus, Hierarchy and Choice in South African Land Reform. *Journal of the Royal Anthropological Society* 17 (2):318–338.

Jamieson, Bill. 1990. *Goldstrike! The Oppenheimer Empire in Crisis.* London: Hutchinson Business Books.

Jeeves, Alan, and Jonathon Crush. 1995. The Failure of Stabilisation Experiments on South African Gold Mines. In *Crossing Boundaries—Mine Migrancy in a Democratic South Africa*, edited by J. Crush and W. James. Cape Town: The Institute for Democracy in South Africa.

Jenkins, Heledd. 2004. Corporate Social Responsibility and the Mining Industry: Conflicts and Constructs. *Corporate Social Responsibility and Environmental Management* 11 (1):23–34.

Jessup, Ernest. 1979. *Ernest Oppenheimer: A Study in Power.* London: Rex and Collings.

Jochelson, Karen, Manyaola Mothibeli, and Jean-Patrick Leger. 1991. Human Immunodeficiency Virus and Migrant Labour in South Africa. *International Journal of Health Services* 21 (1):157–173.

Johannesburg City Council. 1986. *Johannesburg—One Hundred Years.* Johannesburg: Chris van Rensburg Publications Ltd.

Johnson, R W. 1998. Colonialism Returns to South Africa. *New Statesman*, 21.

Jones, Jim. 2005. Getting More than Giving. *Mail and Guardian*, 24 March, 16.

Kahn, Brian. 1996. *Exchange Control Liberalisation in South Africa.* Cape Town: Institute for Democracy in South South Africa.

Kapelus, Paul. 2002. Mining, Corporate Social Responsibility and the "Community": The Case of Rio Tinto, Richard's Bay Minerals and the Mbonambi. *Journal of Business Ethics* 39:275–296.

Kapferer, Bruce. 2005. New Formations of Power, the Oligarchic-Corporate State, and Anthropological Ideological Discourse. *Anthropological Theory* 5 (3):285–299.

Kaplinsky, Raphael. 1994. "Economic Restructuring in South Africa: The Debate Continues": A Response. *Journal of South African Studies* 20 (4):533–537.

Kaysen, Carl. 1957. The Social Significance of the Modern Corporation. *American Economic Review* 47 (2):311–319.

Keane, Webb. 2008. Market, Materiality and Moral Metalanguage. *Anthropological Theory* 8:27–42.

Khumalo, Sibongile. 2009. World Cup Revs up Tourism in Rustenburg. *Mail and Guardian*, 24 June.

Kirsch, Stuart. 2001. Changing Views of Place and Time Along the Ok Tedi. In *Mining and Indigenous Lifeworlds in Australia and Papua New Guinea*, edited by A. Rumsey and J. Weiner. Adelaide, Australia: Crawford House.

———. 2006. *Reverse Anthropology: Indigenous Analysis of Social and Environmental Relations in New Guinea*. Palo Alto, CA: Stanford University Press.

———. 2009. Sustainable Mining. *Dialectical Anthropology* 34 (1):87–93.

Klein, Naomi. 2000. *No Logo*. London: Harper Collins.

Knight, Lindsay. 2005. Access to Treatment in the Private-Sector Workplace: The Provision of Antiretroviral Therapy by Three Companies in South Africa. Geneva: UNAIDS.

Laburn-Peart, Catherine. 1995. Housing as a Locus of Power. In *Crossing Boundaries—Mine Migrancy in a Democratic South Africa*, edited by J. Crush and W. James. Cape Town: The Institute for Democracy in South Africa.

Laidlaw, James. 2000. A Free Gift Makes No Friends. *Journal of the Royal Anthropological Institute* 6 (4):617–634.

Lamont, James, and Kevin Morrison. 2004. Anglo American Looks Far Afield. *Financial Times*, 6 September, 14.

Lanning, Greg, and Marti Mueller. 1979. *Africa Undermined. Mining Companies and the Underdevelopment of Africa*. Harmondsworth: Penguin Books Ltd.

Lester, Alan, Etienne Louis Nel, and Tony Binns. 2000. *South Africa: Past, Present and Future: Gold at the End of the Rainbow?* Edinburgh: Pearson Education Ltd.

Lipton, Merle. 1980. Men of Two Worlds: Migrant Labour in South Africa. *Optima [Special Issue]* 29 (2/3):71–201.

———. 1985. *Capitalism and Apartheid—South Africa 1910–1984*. Aldershot: Gower.

———. 1988. Sanctions and South Africa. Dynamics of Economic Isolation. In *Special Report No. 1119*. London: The Economist Intelligence Unit.

———. 2000. White Liberals, "the Left" and the New Africanist Elite in South Africa. *International Affairs* 76 (1):209–219.

———. 2007. *'Liberals, Marxists and Nationalists'. Competing Interpretations of South African History*. Basingstoke: Palgrave Macmillan.

Lisk, Franklyn. 2002. Labour Markets and Employment Implications of HIV/AIDSs. In *ILO Programme on HIV/AIDS and the World of Work Working Paper* Geneva: ILO.

Litvin, Daniel. 2003. *Empires of Profit: Commerce, Conquest and Corporate Responsibility*. London: Texere.

Lovett, G. O. 1955. The Racial Gulf in South Africa. *Optima* 5 (1):15–20.

Loxton, Lynda. 2004. Experts React to Mbeki's Swipe at Anglo Chief. *The Star*, 13 September, 2.

Luetchford, Peter. 2008. *Fair Trade and A Global Commodity: Coffee in Costa Rica*. London: Pluto Press.

Lynham, Susan, Robert Taylor, Larry Dooley, and Vassi Naidoo. 2006. Corporate Leadership for Economic, Social and Political Change: Lessons from South Africa. In *Corporate Citizenship in Africa*, edited by W. Visser, M. McIntosh and C. Middleton. Sheffield: Greenleaf Publishing.

Mabe, Thabo. 2005. State of the City Address to the Official Opening of Council. Rustenburg Civic Centre, SA.

Macalister, Terry. 2005. "I am an African". Interview: Nicky Oppenheimer, Chairman of De Beers. *Guardian*, 2 July, 21.

Madeley, John. 1999. *Big Business, Poor Peoples: The Impact of Transnational Corporations on the World's Poor.* London and New York: Zed Books.

Magubane, Bernard. 1979. *The Political Economy of Race and Class in South Africa.* New York: Monthly Review Press.

Makgetla, Neva Seidman. 2004. The Post-Apartheid Economy. *Review of African Political Economy* 31 (100):263–281.

Mamdani, Mahmood. 1996. *Citizen and Subject. Contemporary Africa and the Legacy of Late Colonialism.* Princeton, NJ: Princeton University Press.

Mann, Jonathon. 1996. Human Rights and AIDS: The Future of the Pandemic. In *AIDS Education: Interventions in Multicultural Societies*, edited by I. Schenker, G. Sabar-Friedman and F. Sy. New York: Plenum.

Mann, Michael. 1992. The Rise of Corproate Social Responsibility in South Africa. In *Power and Profit. Politics, Labour and Business in South Africa*, edited by D. Innes, M. Kentridge and H. Perold. Cape Town: Oxford University Press.

Manson, Andrew, and Bernard Mbenga. 2003. 'The Richest Tribe in Africa': Platinum-Mining and the Bafokeng in South Africa's North West Province, 1965–1999. *Journal of Southern African Studies* 29 (1):25–47.

Manzo, Kathryn. 1992. *Domination, Resistance and Social Change in South Africa: The Local Effects of Global Power.* London: Praeger.

Marcus, George E. 1995. Ethnography in/of the World System: The Emergence of Multi-Sited Ethnography. *Annual Reviews in Anthropology* 24:95–117.

Mark, Jonty. 2003. A Golden Boost. *The Star*, 4 October, 28.

Marks, Shula. 2006. The Silent Scourge? Silicosis, Respiratory Disease and Gold Mining in South Africa. *Journal of Ethnic and Migration Studies* 32 (4):569–589.

Marks, Shula, and Stanley Trapido. 1987. *The Politics of Race, Class and Nationalism in Twentieth Centruy South Africa.* Harlow, UK: Longman.

Marsden, Chris. 2000. The New Corporate Citizenship of Big Business: Part of the Solution to Sustainability. *Business and Society Review* 105 (1):9–25.

Martin, Emily. 1997. Managing Americans: Policy and Changes in the Meanings of Work and Self. In *Anthropology of Policy*, edited by C. Shore and S. Wright. London and New York: Routledge.

Matangi, Caroline N. 2006. Skills Under Threat: the Case of HIV/AIDS in the Mining Industry in Zimbabwe. *Journal of International Development* 18 (5):599–628.

Matten, Dirk, and Andrew Crane. 2003. Corporate Citizenship: Towards an Extended Theoretical Conceptualization'. *ICCSR Research Paper Series.* Nottingham: ICCSR, University of Nottingham.

Maurer, Bill. 2008. Re-socializing Finance? Or Dressing in Mufti? Calculating Alternatives for Cultural Economies. *Journal of Cultural Economy* 1 (1):65–78.

———. 2009. Afterword: Moral Economies, Economic Moralities: Consider the Possibilities! In *Economics and Morality: Anthropological Approaches*, edited by K. Browne and B. L. Miligram. Lanham, MD: Altamira Press.

Mauss, Marcel. 1967 first published 1925. *The Gift*. Translated by I. Cunnison. London: Cohen and West Ltd.

Mbeki, Thabo. 2004. Guilt of the Masters. *This Day*, 13 September, 3.

McCulloch, Jock. 2009. Counting the Cost: Gold Mining and Occupational Disease in Contemporary South Africa. *African Affairs* 108 (431):221–240.

McDonald, Leighton. 2004. HIV/AIDS Treatment for Employees—Do We Wait for Government's Programme? *AIDS Analysis Africa On-line* 15 (2):1–10.

McIntosh, Malcolm, Ruth Thomas, Deborah Leipziger, and Gill Coleman. 2002. *Living Corporate Citizenship: Strategic Routes to Socially Responsible Business*. London: Prentice Hall.

Memorandum of Understanding (MOU). 2003. Memorandum of Understanding between the Royal Bafokeng Nation, the Bojanala Platinum District Municipality (BPDM) and the Rustenburg Local Municipality. Rustenburg, SA.

Michaels, Jeremy. 2004. Cartels are Stealing our Nation's Wealth. *Cape Times*, 15 September, 12.

Miller, Daniel. 1997. *Capitalism—An Ethnographic Approach*. Oxford: Berg.

Mining, Minerals and Sustainable Development. 2002. *Breaking New Ground: Final Report of the Mining, Minerals and Sustainable Development Project*. London: Earthscan.

Mines and Communities. 2001. *The London Declaration*. Available from http://www .minesandcoes.org/Charter/londondec.htm.

Mistry, Neeraj, and Ben Plumley. 2002. HIV/AIDS Workplace Protocols and Practices for Businesses in Resources Poor Settings. Global Business Coalition on HIV/AIDS (GBC).

Mitchell, James Clyde. 1956. *The Kalela Dance*. Manchester: Manchester University Press.

Mitchell, Neil J. 1989. *The Generous Corporation: A Political Analysis of Power*. New Haven, CT: Yale University Press.

Mitchell, Timothy. 2002. *Rule of Experts*. Berkeley: University of California Press.

Miyazaki, Hirokazu. 2003. The Temporalities of the Market. *American Anthropologist* 105 (2):255–265.

Molapo, Matsheliso Palesa. 1995. Job Stress, Health and Perceptions of Migrant Mineworkers. In *Crossing Boundaries—Mine Migrancy in a Democratic South Africa*, edited by J. Crush and W. James. Cape Town: The Institute for Democracy in South Africa.

Moll, Terence. 1991. Did the Apartheid Economy Fail? *Journal of Southern African Studies* 17 (4):654–677.

Moodie, Dunbar. 1986. The Moral Economy of the Black Miners' Strike of 1946. *Journa l of Southern African Studies* 13 (1):1–35.

Moodie, Dunbar, with Vivienne Ndatshe. 1994. *Going for Gold: Men, Mines and Migration*. Johannesburg: Witwatersrand University Press.

Moody-Stuart, Mark. 2006. Business and NGOs in Sustainable Development—Endless Wars or Common Cause? *Optima* 52 (1):22–37.

Moody, Roger. 2007. *Rocks and Hard Places: The Globalization of Mining*. London and New York: Zed Books.

Moore, Henrietta. 2004. Global Anxieties. Concept-Metaphors and Pre-Theoretical Commitments in Anthropology. *Anthropological Theory* 4 (1):71–88.

Moser, Titus. 2001. MNCs and Sustainable Business Practice: The Case of the Colombian and Peruvian Petroleum Industries. *World Development* 29 (2):291–309.

Mosoetsa, Sarah. 2005. The Consequences of South Africa's Economic Transition: The Remnants of the Footwear Industry. In *Beyond the Apartheid Workplace, Studies in Transition*, edited by E. Webster and K. von Holdt. Scottsville, South Africa: University of KwaZulu-Natal Press.

Motau, S. 1985. South Africa's Troubled Townships. *Optima* 33 (4):90–99.

Msomi, S'Thembisi. 2004. Mbeki Lashes Out at Anglo CEO. *Sunday Times (South Africa)*, 12 Septmber.

Muehlebach, Andrea. 2009. The Moral Neoliberal: Thoughts of Corporate Social Responsibility. Unpublished paper delivered at the Canadian Anthropology Society and American Ethnological Society Meeting, Vancouver, 13–16 May.

Munusamy, Ranjeni. 2004. Anglo, State Push to Mend Rift. *This Day*, 13 September, 4.

Murray, Colin. 1980. Migrant Labour and Changing Family Structure in the Rural Periphery of South Africa. *Journal of Southern African Studies* 6 (2):139–156.

Murray, Georgina. 2000. Black Empowerment in South Africa: "Patriotic Capitalism" or a Corporate Blackwash. *Critical Sociology* 26 (3):183–204.

Nafus, Dawn, and Ken Anderson. 2009. Writing on the Walls: The Materiality of Social Memory in Corporate Research. In *Ethnography and the Corproate Encounter. Reflections on Research In and On Corporations*, edited by M. Cefkin. Oxford: Berghahn.

Nash, June. 1993 first published in 1979. *We Eat the Mines and the Mines Eat Us*. New York: Columbia University Press.

Nattrass, Jill. 1988. *The South African Economy: its Growth and Change*. Cape Town: Oxford University Press.

Nattrass, Nicoli. 1994. Economic Restructuring in South Africa: The Debate Continues. *Journal of Southern African Studies* 20 (4):517–543.

———. 1999. The Truth and Reconciliation Commission on Business and Apartheid: A Critical Evaluation. *African Affairs* 98 (392):373–391.

Ndlovu, Nhlanhla, and Rabelani Daswa. 2006. Monitoring Aids Treatment Rollout in South Africa: Lessons from the Joint Civil Society Monitoring Forum. *Budget Brief* 161.

Nelson, Jane. 1998. *Building Competitiveness and Communities. How World Class Companies Are Creating Shareholder Value and Societal Value.* London: The Prince of Wales Business Leaders Forum and The United Nations Development Programme.

———. 2006. Business as a Partner in Strengthening Public Health Systems in Developing Countries—An Agenda for Action. edited by C. G. Initiative: The International Business Leaders Forum and Harvard University. London.

Nguyen, Vinh-Kim. 2005. Antiretroviral Globalism, Biopolitics, and Therapeutic Citizenship. In *Global Assemblages—Technology, Politics and Ethics as Anthropological Problems*, edited by A. Ong and S. Collier. Oxford: Blackwell Publishing.

Nkala, T. 2004. Where Actually Lies Allegiance of These Multinationals? *The Star*, 20 September, 22.

Noseweek. 2004. When Barry Left Sally. *Noseweek*, 8–12.

O'Dowd, M C. 1970. The Achievements of Japan. *Optima* 20 (4):142–154.

———. 1991. *Understanding South Africa.* London: British-South African Policy Studies Trust.

Oke, S. 1987. *The Strike in Retrospect: The Lure of the Low Road.* Johannesburg: Mathison and Hollidge.

O'Meara, Dan. 1983. *Volkskapitalisme: Class, Capital and Ideology in the Development of Afrikaner Nationalism.* Cambridge: Cambridge University Press.

———. 1996. *Forty Lost Years: The Apartheid State and the Politics of the National Party 1948–1994.* Athens: Ohio University Press.

Ong, Aihwa. 2006. *Neoliberalism as Exception. Mutations in Sovereignty and Citizenship.* Durham, NC: Duke University Press.

Oppenheimer, Harry. 1973. Anglo American Corporation Annual Statement to Shareholders. Johannesburg.

Oppenheimer, Nicholas. 1980. Investment in South Africa Today and Tomorrow. In *Financial Mail Conference 'Investment in 1980'.* Johannesburg.

Optima. 1978. Practical Social Responsibility. *Optima* 27 (4):117–127.

Osella, Filippo, and Caroline Osella. 2009. Business and Community Between India and the Gulf: Muslim Entrepreneurs in Kerala, India. *Journal of the Royal Anthropological Institute* 15 (1):202–221.

Packard, Randall. 1989a. *White Plague, Black Labour: Tuberculosis and the Political Economy of Health and Disease in South Africa.* Pietermaritzburg, South Africa: University of Natal Press.

———. 1989b. The "Healthy Reserve" and the "Dressed Native": Discourses on Black Health and the Language of Legitimation in South Africa. *American Ethnologist* 16 (4):686–703.

Packard, Randall, and David Coetzee. 1995. White Plague, Black Labour Revisted. In *Crossing Boundaries—Mine Migrancy in a Democratic South Africa*, edited by J. Crush and W. James. Cape Town: The Institute for Democracy in South Africa.

Pallister, David, Sarah Stewart, and Ian Lepper. 1987. *South Africa Inc: The Oppenheimer Empire*. Johannesburg: Media House Publications in association with Lowry Publishers.

Palsetia, Jesse. 2005. Merchant Charity and Public Identity Formation in Colonial India: The Case of Jamsetjee Jejeebhoy. *Journal of Asian and African Studies* 40 (3):197–217.

Pálsson, Gisli, and Paul Rabinow. 2005. The Iceland Controversy: Reflections on the Transnational Market of Civic Virtue. In *Global Assemblages—Technology, Politics and Ethics as Anthropological Problems*, edited by A. Ong and S. Collier. Oxford: Blackwell Publishing.

Parry, Jonathan. 1986. The Gift, the Indian Gift and the "Indian Gift". *Man* 21 (3):453–473.

Patel, Geeta. 2006. Risky Subjects: Insurance, Sexuality and Capital. *Social Text* 89 (24):26–65.

Paton, Alan. 1948. *Cry, the Beloved Country*. Middlesex, UK: Penguin Books Ltd.

Pendleton, Andrew. 2004. *Behind The Mask: The Real face of CSR* [cited 11 May 2006]. Available from http://www/christian-aid.org.uk/indepth/0401csr/csr_behindthe mask.pdf.

Petryna, Adriana, Andrew Lakoff, and Arthur Kleinman, eds. 2006. *Global Pharmaceuticals: Ethics, Markets, Practices*. Durham, NC: Duke University Press.

Phakathi, Timothy Sizwe. 2005. Self-Directed Work Teams in a Post-Apartheid Gold Mine: Perspectives from the Rockface. In *Beyond the Apartheid Workplace, Studies in Transition*, edited by E. Webster and K. von Holdt. Scottsville, South Africa: University of KwaZulu-Natal Press.

Phaswana, Fred. 2006. Africa—Taking Control of its Destiny. *Optima* 52 (1):60–72.

Pitluck, Aaron. 2009. Moral Behavious in Stock Markets: Islamic Finance and Socailly Responsible Investment. In *Economics and Morality: Anthropological Approaches*, edited by K. Browne and B. L. Milgram. Lanham, MD: Altamira Press.

Plan Associates. 2001. Greater Rustenburg Informal Housing Strategy. Rustenburg: Complied for the Housing Strategy Forum.

Polanyi, Karl. 2001 first published in 1944. *The Great Transformation*. Boston: Beacon Press.

Porritt, Jonathon. 2006. Sustainability Is Central to Survival. *Guardian*, 6 November, 15.

Porter, Theodore. 1995. *Trust in Numbers: The Pursuit of Objectivity in Science and Public Life*. Princeton, NJ: Princeton University Press.

Power, Michael. 1997. *The Audit Society—Rituals of Verification*. Oxford: Oxford University Press.

Prahalad, Coimbatore Krishnarao. 2006. *The Fortune at the Bottom of the Pyramid. Eradicating Poverty Through Profits*. Upper Saddle River, NJ: Wharton School Publishing.

Putney, Clifford. 2001. *Muscular Christianity: Manhood and Sports in Protestant America, 1880–1920*. Cambridge, MA: Harvard University Press.

Rajak, Dinah. 2006. The Gift of CSR: Power and the Pursuit of Responsibility in the Mining Industry. In *Corporate Citizenship in Africa: Lessons from the Past; Paths to the Future*, edited by W. Visser, M. McIntosh and C. Middleton. Sheffield: Greenleaf Publishing.

———. 2008. "Uplift and Empower": The Market, Morality and Corporate Responsibility on South Africa's Platinum Belt. *Research in Economic Anthropology* 28:297–324.

———. 2009. "I am the Conscience of the Company": Responsibility and the Gift in a Transnational Mining Corporation. In *Economics and Morality: Anthropological Approaches*, edited by K. Browne and B. L. Miligram. Lanham, MD: Altamira Press.

———. 2010. "HIV/AIDS is Our Business": The Moral Economy of Treatment in a Transnational Mining Company. *Journal of the Royal Anthropological Institute* 16 (3):551–571.

———. 2011. Theatres of Virtue: Collaboration, Consensus and the Social Life of Corporate Social Responsibility. *Focaal* 60 (2011):9–20.

Ramphele, Mamphela. 1993. *A Bed Called Home: Life in the Migrant Labour Hostels of Cape Town*. Athens: Ohio University Press.

———. 2005. Citizenship is Stewardship. *Business Day*, 15 September, 18.

Randera, Faizel. 2003. The Mining Industry and HIV/AIDS. *Chamber of Mines of South Africa for the 'Tripartite HIV/AIDS Summit*. Johannesburg.

Reader, John. 1997. *Africa: Biography of a Continent*. London: Penguin.

Reed, John. 2005. Making up for Perverse Policies. *Financial Times*, 14 September, 12.

Reichardt, Markus. 2007. Water Resources—Miners vs the Hippos. *Ethical Corporation*, (May):16.

Relly, Gavin. 1981. Reform and Reaction in South Africa. *Address to the South Africa Club*. London, 8 October.

———. 1982. Forward. In *Social Responsibility in South Africa—The Work of the Anglo American and De Beers Chairman's Fund*. Supplement to *Optima* 31 (1):iii–iv.

———. 1985. Address on the Occasion of the Graduation Ceremony of the University of Cape Town, 28 June.

Rex, John. 1971. The Compound, Reserve and Urban Location—the Essential Institutions of Southern African Labour Exploitation. *SA Labour Bulletin* 1 (4):7–17.

Reynolds Whyte, Susan, Michael A. Whyte, Lotte Mienert, and Betty Kyaddondo. 2006. Treating AIDS: Dilemmas of Unequal Access in Uganda. In *Global Phar-*

maceuticals: Ethics, Markets, Practices, edited by A. Petryna, A. Lakoff, and A. Kleinman. Durham, NC: Duke University Press.

Richards, Paul. 1996. Chimpanzees, Diamonds and War: The Discourses of Global Environmental Change and Local Violence on the Liberia-Sierra Leone Border. In *The Future of Anthropological Knowledge*, edited by H. Moore. London: Routledge.

Robbins, David. 2001. Anglo American's Corporate Social Investment in South Africa. Johannesburg: Anglo American Corporation of South Africa Ltd.

Robbins, Joel. 2009. Rethinking Gifts and Commodities: Reciprocity, Recognition, and the Morality of Exchange. In *Economics and Morality: Anthropological Approaches*, edited by K. Brown and B. L. Milgram. Lanham, MD: Altamira Press.

Robins, Steven. 2004. "Long Live Zacki, Long Live": Aids Activism, Science and Citizenship after Apartheid. *Journal of Southern African Studies* 30 (3):651–672.

Rofel, Lisa. 1999. Rethinking Modernity: Space and Factory Discipline in China. In *Culture, Power, Place: Explorations in Critical Anthropology*, edited by A. Gupta and J. Ferguson. Durham, NC: Duke University Press.

Rosaldo, Renato. 1989. Imperialist Nostalgia. *Representations* 26:107–122.

Rosen, Sydney, Jonathon Simon, William MacLeod, Matthew Fox, and Donald Thea. 2003. AIDS Is Your Business. *Harvard Business Review* 81 (1):5–11.

Rosen, Sydney, and Jeffrey Vincent. 2004. The Cost of HIV/AIDS to Businesses in Africa. *AIDS* 18 (317–324).

Rudnyckyj, Daromir. 2009. Spiritual Economies: Islam and Neoliberalism in Contemporary Indonesia. *Cultural Anthropology* 24 (1):104–141.

Russel-Walling, Edward. 2006. Improving our Impacts—Anglo's Socio-Economic Assessment Toolbox (SEAT). *Optima* 52 (1):50–59.

Rustenburg Herald. 2005a. BRPM Millionaires (again). *Rustenburg Herald*, 4 January, 2.

———. 2005b. Major Empowerment Deal. *Rustenburg Herald*, 11 January, 7.

———. 2005c. Mega Mining for CANSA. *Rustenburg Herald*, 15 April, 3.

Rustenburg Local Municipality. 2005. Draft Integrated Development Plan 2005/2006. Rustenburg: Rustenburg Local Municipality.

Sahlins, Marshall. 1972. *Stone Age Economics*. London: Tavistock Publications.

Sampson, Anthony. 1987. *Black and Gold: Tycoons, Revolutionaries and Apartheid*. London: Hodder and Stoughton.

Sampson, Steven. 2005. Integrity Warriors: Global Morality and the Anti-Corruption Movement in the Balkans. In *Corruption: Anthropological Perspectives*, edited by D. Haller and C. Shore. London: Pluto Press.

Sanders, Todd, and Harry West. 2003. Power Revealed and Concealed in the New World Order. In *Transparency and Conspiracy. Ethnographies of Suspicion in the New World Order*, edited by T. Sanders and H. West. Durham and London: Duke University Press.

Satre, Lowell. 2005. *Chocolate on Trial: Slavery, Politics and the Ethics of Business.* Athens: Ohio University Press.

Saul, John S. 2001. Cry for the Beloved Country: The Post-Apartheid Denouement. *Review of African Political Economy* 28 (89):429–460.

Saunders, Christopher C. 1988. *The Making of the South African Past: Major Historians on Race and Class.* New York: Barnes and Noble Inc.

Sawyer, Suzanna. 2004. *Crude Chronicles: Indigenous Politics, Multinational Oil and Neoliberalism in Ecuador.* Durham, NC: Duke University Press.

Schneider, Helen. 2002. On the Fault-line: The Politics of AIDS Policy in Contemporary South Africa. *African Studies* 61 (1):145–167.

Schoepf, Brooke. 2001. International AIDS Research in Anthropology: Taking a Critical Perspective on the Crisis. *Annual Review of Anthropology* 30:335–361.

Scott, James. 1985. *Weapons of the Weak. Everyday Forms of Peasant Resistance.* New Haven, CT: Yale University Press.

———. 1998. *Seeing Like a State.* New Haven and London: Yale University Press.

Scott, Paul. 1975. *A Division of the Spoils.* London: Heineman.

Seekings, Jeremy, and Nicoli Nattrass. 2006. *Class, Race and Inequality in South Africa.* New Haven, CT: Yale University Press.

Seidel, Gill, and Laurent Vidal. 1997. The Implications of "Medical", "Gender and Development" and "Culturalist" Discourses for HIV/AIDS Policy in Africa. In *The Anthropology of Policy*, edited by S. Wright and C. Shore. London and New York: Routledge.

Sender, John. 1994. Economic Restructuring in South Africa: Reactionary Rhetoric Prevails. *Journal of Southern Africa Studies* 20 (4):539–543.

Shamir, Ronen. 2004. The De-Radicalization of Corporate Social Responsibility. *Critical Sociology* 30:669–689.

———. 2008. The Age of Responsibilization: On Market-Embedded Morality. *Economy and Society* 37 (1):1–19.

Sharp, John. 2006. Corporate Social Responsibility and Development: An Anthropological Perspective. *Development Southern Africa* 23 (2):213–222.

Shever, Elana. 2008. Neoliberal Associations: Property, Company and Family in the Argentine Oil Fields. *American Ethnologist* 35 (4):701–716.

Shore, Cris. 2002. Introduction: Towards an Anthropolology of Elites. In *Elite Cultures. Anthropological Cultures*, edited by C. Shore and S. Nugent. London and New York: Routledge.

Sillitoe, Paul, and Robin Wilson. 2003. Playing on the Pacific Ring of Fire: Negotiation and Knowledge in Mining in Papua New Guinea. In *Negotiating Local Knowledge: Power and Identity in Development*, edited by J. Pottier, A. Bicker and P. Sillitoe. London: Pluto Press.

Simmel, Georg. 1978 first published in 1900. *Philosophy of Money.* London: Routledge and Kegan Paul.

Smart, Alan, and Josephine Smart. 2005. Introduction. In *Petty Capitalists and Globalization: Flexibility, Entrepreneurship, and Economic Development*, edited by A. Smart and J. Smart. Albany: State University of New York Press.

Smith, Adam. 1991 first published 1776. *The Wealth of Nations*. Buffalo, NY: Prometheus Books.

Smith, David. 2009. Anglo American Sheds 15,000 Jobs as Profits Are Hit by Falling Metals Prices. *Guardian*, 31 July.

Smith, Nicky. 2004. Mining Charter Stifles Spending on Exploration. *Business Report*, 9 September.

Sonnenberg, Dan, and Ralph Hamman. 2006. The JSE Socially Responsible Investment Index and the State of Sustainability Reporting in South Africa. *Development Southern Africa* 23 (2):305–320.

Sparshott, Jeffrey. 2009. Anglo American to Slash Jobs. *Wall Street Journal* [online], 21 February.

Stevens, W., A. Apostolellis, G. Napier, L. Scott, and G. Gresak. 2006. HIV/AIDS Prevalence Testing—Merits, Methodology and Outcomes of a Survey Conducted at a Large Mining Organisation in South Africa. *South African Medical Journal* 96 (2):134–139.

Stirrat, Roderick L., and Heiko Henkel. 1997. The Development Gift: The Problem of Reciprocity in the NGO World. *Annals of the American Academy of Political and Social Science* 554:66–80.

Stirrat, Roderick L, and Dinah Rajak. 2007. *Parochial Cosmopolitanism and the Power of Nostalgia: Some Manifestations of Development Practice, Monograph Series on Alternate Discourses on Development*. Colombo: Colombo Institute for the Advanced Study of Society and Culture.

Stone, Oliver. 1987. Wall Street. Hollywood: 20th Century Fox.

Sumartojo, Esther. 1993. When Tuberculosis Treatment Fails: A Social Behavioral Account of Patient Adherence. *American Review of Respiratory Disease* 147:1311–1320.

Sunter, Clem. 1987. *The World and South Africa in the 1990's*. Cape Town: Human and Rousseau Tafelburg.

———. 2004. Foreword. In *HIV/AIDS in the Mining Sector*. Ottawa: Golder Associates Ltd.

SustainAbility, Skoll Foundation, Allianz, and DuPont. 2007. *Enterprising Solutions to Insoluble Problems*. London: SustainAbility [cited 24 July 2007]. Available from http://www.sustainability.com/compass/register.asp?type=download&articleid=250.

Taussig, Michael. 1980. *The Devil and Commodity Fetishism in South America*. Chapel Hill: University of North Carolina Press.

Tennyson, Ros. 2004. *The Partnering Toolbook*. London: International Business Leaders Forum.

———. 2005. *The Brokering Guidebook: Navigating Effective Sustainable Development Partnerships*. London: International Business Leaders Forum, The Partnership Initiative.

Thale, Thmoas. 2002. *A Soweto Park Brings the Past Alive* [cited 20 September 2006. Available from http://www.joburg.org.za/aug_2002/park.stm.

Theron, Jan. 2005. Employment Is Not What It Used to Be: The Nature and Impact of Work Restructuring in South Africa. In *Beyond the Apartheid Workplace, Studies in Transition*, edited by E. Webster and K. von Holdt. Scottsville, South Africa: University of KwaZulu-Natal Press.

Thompson, Edward P. 1993 first published 1991. *Customs in Common*. New York: The New Press.

Thornton, Robert. 2008. *Unimagined Community. Sex, Networks, and AIDS in Uganda and South Africa*. Berkeley: University of California Press.

Thrift, Nigel. 1998. Virtual Capitalism: The Globalisation of Reflexive Business Knowledge. In *Virtualism. A New Political Economy*, edited by J. Carrier and D. Miller. London and New York: Berg.

Torchia, Andrew. 1988. The Business of Business: An Analysis of the Political Behaviour of the South African Manufacturing Sector Under the Nationalists. *Journal of Southern Africa Studies* 14 (3):421–455.

Toren, Cristina. 1989. Drinking Cash: The Purification of Money Through Ceremonial Exchange in Fiji. In *Money and the Morality of Exchange*, edited by J. Parry and M. Bloch. Cambridge: Cambridge University Press.

Trahar, Tony. 2006. Creating Value for South Africa. In *Media and Analysts Lunch*. Johannesburg.

Tranter, Neil. 1998. *Sport, Economy and Society in Britain 1750–1914*. Cambridge: Cambridge University Press.

Trapido, A., P. Nokuzola, B. Williams, N. White, A. Soloman, R. Goode, C. Macheke, A. Davies, and C. Panter. 1998. Prevalence of Occupational Lung Disease in a American Journal of Industrial Medicine Random Sample of Former Mineworkers, Libode District, Eastern Cape Province, South Africa. *American Journal of Industrial Medicine* 34 (4):305–313.

Truth and Reconciliation Commission of South Africa. 1998. Truth and Reconciliation Commission of South Africa Report Volume 4. Cape Town: Juta.

———. 2003. *Truth and Reconciliation Commission of South Africa Report*. Cape Town: Juta.

Tsing, Anna. 2000. The Global Situation. *Cultural Anthropology* 15 (3):327–360.

UNAIDS. 2008. Epidemiological Factsheet on HIV and Aids. Geneva: Joint United Nations Programme on HIV and AIDS.

United Nations. 1980. The Activities of Transnational Corporations in the Industrial, Mining and Military Sectors of Southern Africa. New York: United Nations Centre on Transnational Corporations, UN.

United Nations Development Programme (UNDP). 2005. The Poor Needs Business to Invest in Their Future. *Financial Times Business and Development Supplement*, 14 September, 5.

van Blommestein, Johannes 1971. The Ernest Oppenheimer Hospital. In *Doctors of the Mines*, edited by A. P. Cartwright. Cape Town: Purnell.

van Rijn, Kiran 2006. The Politics of Uncertainty: The Aids Debate, Thabo Mbeki and the South African Government. *Social History of Medicine* 19 (3):521–538.

von Holdt, Karl. 2005. Political Transition and the Changing Workplace Order in a South African Steelworks. In *Beyond the Apartheid Workplace, Studies in Transition*, edited by E. Webster and K. von Holdt. Scottsville, South Africa: University of KwaZulu-Natal Press.

Vidal, John, and Michael White. 2002. UK to Take Big Firms to Earth Summit. *Guardian*, 12 August.

Visser, Wayne, and Clem Sunter. 2002. *Beyond Reasonable Greed: Why Sustainable Business is Much Better!* Cape Town: Human and Rousseau Tafelburg.

Waddell, Steve. 2004. NGO Strategies to Engage Business: Trends, Critical Issues and Next Steps. Oxfam America, Civicus and Global Action Network.

Wagner, Marcus, and Stefan Schaltegger. 2006. *Managing the Business Case for Sustainability: The Integration of Social, Environemntal and Economic Performance*. Sheffield: Greenleaf Publishing.

Waldman, Linda. 2005. When Social Movements Bypass the Poor: Asbestos Pollution, International Litigation and Griqua Cultural Identity. In *IDS Working Paper*. Brighton: Institute of Development Studies.

Warhurst, Alyson. 2005. Future Roles of Business in Society: The Expanding Boundaries of Corporate Responsibility and a Compelling Case for Partnership. *Futures* 37:151–168.

Webster, Eddie, and Sakhela Buhlungu. 2004. Between Marginalisation and Revitalisation? The State of Trade Unionism in South Africa. *Review of African Political Economy* 100:229–245.

Webster, Edward, and Karl von Holdt, eds. 2005. *Beyond the Apartheid Workplace, Studies in Transition*. Scottsville, South Africa: University of KwaZulu-Natal Press.

Welker, Marina. 2009. "Corporate Security Begins in the Community": Mining, the Corporate Responsibility Industry and Environmental Advocacy in Indonesia. *Cultural Anthropology* 24 (1):142–179.

Wickstead, Myles. 2005. Building a Strong and Prosperous Africa—the Role of Business. *Optima* 51 (2):4–8.

Williams, Brian, Denise Gilgen, Catherine Campbell, Dirk Taljaard, and Catherine MacPhail. 2000. *The Natural History of HIV/AIDS in South Africa: A Biomedical and Social Survey in Carletonville*. Johannesburg: Council for Scientific and Industrial Research.

Williams, Brian, Eleanor Gouws, Mark Lurie, and Jonathon Crush. 2002. *Spaces of Vulneraibility: Migration and HIV/AIDS in South Africa, Migration Policy Series No. 24*. Kingston (Ontario) and Cape Town: SAMP.

Wilson, Craig, and Peter Wilson. 2006. *Make Poverty Business. Increase Profits and Reduce Risks by Engaging with the Poor*. Sheffield: Greenleaf Publishing.

Wilson, Francis. 1972. *Labour in the South African Gold Mines, 1911–1969*. Cambridge: Cambridge University Press.

———. 2001. Minerals and Migrants: How the Mining Industry Has Shaped South Africa. *Daedalus* 130 (1):99–121.

Wilson, Godfrey, and Monica Wilson. 1945. *The Analysis of Social Change*. Cambridge: Cambridge University Press.

Wolfe, Tom. 1990. *The Bonfire of the Vanities*. London: Picador.

Wolpe, Harold. 1972. Capitalism and Cheap Labour Power in South Africa. *Economy and Society* 1 (4):425–456.

World Bank. 2004. Striking a Better Balance—The World Bank and Extractive Industries: The Final Report of the Extractive Industries Review [cited 13 November 2009]. Available from http://siteresources.worldbank.org/INTOGMC/Resources/finaleirmanagementresponseexecsum.pdf.

World Business Council for Sustainable Development (WBSCD). 2005. *Business for Development: Business Solutions in Support of the Millennium Development Goals*. Geneva: Atar Roto Presses SA.

World Summit on Sustainable Development (WSSD). 2002. *The Political Declaration* [cited 14 October 2005]. Available from www.johannesburgsummit.org/html/documents/summit_docs.html.

Yanagisako, Sylvia Junko. 2002. *Producing Culture and Capital: Family Firms in Italy*. Princeton, NJ: Princeton University Press.

Yudelman, David. 1983. *The Emergence of Modern South Africa: State, Capital, and the Incorporation of Organized Labour on the South African Gold Fields 1902–1939*. London: Greenwood Press.

Yudelman, David, and Alan Jeeves. 1986. New Labour Frontiers for Old: Black Migrants to the South African Gold Mines, 1920–1985. *Journal of Southern African Studies* 13 (1):101–124.

Zadek, Simon. 2001. *The Civil Corporation: The New Economy of Corporate Citizenship*. London: Earthscan.

Zadek, Simon, Peter Raynard, Cristina Oliveira, Edna do Nascimento, and Rafael Tello. 2005. *Responsible Competitiveness: Reshaping Global Markets through Responsible Business Practices*. London: Institute for Social and Ethical Accountability.

Zapiro. 2002. A Gift from the Corporate World! Cartoon. *Mail and Guardian*, 15 August.

Zwennis, Vivienne. 2003. The Ultimate Entrepreneur? *Lebone*, October, 16.

Index

Note: Page numbers in italic type indicate illustrations.